The English Civil Wars
in the Literary Imagination

Edited by
Claude J. Summers
and
Ted-Larry Pebworth

University of Missouri Press

Columbia and London

Copyright © 1999 by
The Curators of the University of Missouri
University of Missouri Press, Columbia, Missouri 65201
Printed and bound in the United States of America
All rights reserved
5   4   3   2   1   03   02   01   00   99

Library of Congress Cataloging-in-Publication Data

The English civil wars in the literary imagination / edited by Claude
   J. Summers and Ted-Larry Pebworth.
      p.   cm.
   Includes index.
   ISBN 0-8262-1220-4 (cl. : alk. paper)
   1. English literature—Early modern, 1500–1700—History and
criticism.   2. Politics and literature—Great Britain—History—17th
century.   3. Great Britain—History—Civil War, 1642–1649—
Literature and the war.   4. Literature and history—Great Britain—
History—17th century.   I. Summers, Claude J.   II. Pebworth, Ted-
Larry.
   PR438.P65E54   1999
   820.9'358—dc21   99-27376
                                                                      CIP

⊗™ This paper meets the requirements of the
American National Standard for Permanence of Paper
for Printed Library Materials, Z39.48, 1984.

Text design: Elizabeth K. Young
Jacket design: Susan Ferber
Typesetter: Bookcomp, Inc.
Printer and binder: Thomson-Shore, Inc.
Typefaces: Palatino, Formata

For
John W. and Katherine Presley

Contents

Acknowledgments

This book and the scholarly meeting from which it originated have profited from the great effort, wide learning, and scholarly generosity of the conference steering committee: Diana Treviño Benet, Achsah Guibbory, Robert B. Hinman, Judith Scherer Herz, John R. Roberts, and Michael C. Schoenfeldt, who all helped referee the submissions to the conference and offered valuable suggestions for revision. Their contributions have been extensive, and we join the authors of the essays in expressing gratitude for their insights and devotion. It is also our pleasant duty to acknowledge the support of the following administrators at the University of Michigan–Dearborn: Emily L. Spinelli, Chair, Department of Humanities; John W. Presley, Dean, College of Arts, Sciences, and Letters; and Robert L. Simpson, Provost and Vice Chancellor for Academic Affairs.

The English Civil Wars
in the Literary Imagination

Claude J. Summers and
Ted-Larry Pebworth

Introduction

The English civil wars, which cul-
minated in the execution of a king, the dismantling of the Established
Church, the inauguration of a commonwealth, and the assumption of
rule by a lord protector, unsurprisingly loom large in seventeenth-century
history and literature. For many people who lived through the wars and
the religio-political struggles that preceded and followed them, the period
was experienced as one of profound change and disequilibrium. The
phrase most frequently used to describe the brave new world of the civil
wars and their aftermath, "the world turned upside down," gives some
indication of the way the internecine conflict affected almost everyone,
though of course how particular groups reacted to the sea changes of
their society varied dramatically. For some, a world turned upside down
might be greeted exultantly as affording the possibility of redressing social
grievances or realizing millenarian dreams, while for others, it might
signify only the imposition of new forms of tyranny, and for still others,
perhaps in fact the majority, the feeling of disorientation might be the
result of what they saw as a deeply bewildering and unsettling breakdown
of authority of all kinds. Although historians continue to debate whether
the English civil wars constituted a genuine revolution or a more limited
constitutional crisis or rebellion, there can be no doubt that the momentous
events of midcentury deeply affected England's shifting and increasingly
diverse literary culture, even as the varied literature of the time helped
shape the events that transformed the nation.

This volume is a contribution toward understanding more precisely
the English civil wars' manifold and sometimes oblique presence in the
literature of the period. The historically informed essays of this collection
are interested not only in the representation of the civil wars, but also
more generally in the ways in which the civil wars are anticipated and
refigured and refracted in the century's literary imagination. As Nigel
Smith has noted, not only did the conflict influence the revolutions in

1

genre and form that characterize the literature of the mid–seventeenth century, but literature itself was at the very epicenter of the constitutional crisis. "Never before in English history had written and printed literature played such a predominant role in public affairs, and never before had it been felt by contemporaries to be of such importance."[1]

Not surprisingly, the tumultuous controversies of the midcentury yielded an extraordinary and unprecedented volume of propagandistic and explicitly political writing; but the religio-political crisis is evident as well even in those works that may at first glance seem utterly apolitical. Indeed, indirection and disguise were themselves frequent strategies of political representation in the era, as when Herrick disguises his bitter lament at the transformation of the Established Church by the Parliamentarians, "The Widdowes teares: or, Dirge of Dorcas," as merely an idiosyncratic celebration of the biblical widow Tabitha. Or when in *"Good Friday:* Rex Tragicus, *or Christ going to his Crosse"* he pointedly stages Christ's death as a king's execution, offering a prophetic warning of the fate that threatened Charles I and attempting to translate a dreaded disaster into a miraculous triumph. But the English civil wars and their associated conflicts are felt in all kinds of discourse, including love lyrics and religious meditations as well as topical or politically explicit works. The celebrations of rural retirement, the retreat to private spheres of emotion, and the adoption of stoic attitudes in the face of defeat or disappointment are themselves responses to the turbulent political climate, as of course are also the frequent bemoanings of the age's decline, especially by the Caroline poets, most of whom were Royalist in sympathy. Although, as M. Thomas Hester has noted, many Royalist writers attempted to link the puritan "war against poetry" with the Parliamentarian assault against the monarchy,[2] the conflict actually yielded some vital works of art by writers of all political persuasions and enabled a much wider range of voices than ever before to be heard. Not only do the wars constitute the most pervasive context in which to locate the vast bulk of mid-seventeenth-century literature, but their effects on and in literature were enduring. They continued to haunt the literary imagination long after the restoration of the monarchy in 1660.

The burden of these essays is to increase our understanding and appreciation of the various ways in which the seventeenth-century literary

1. Nigel Smith, *Literature and Revolution in England, 1640–1660* (New Haven: Yale University Press, 1994), 1.
2. See Hester's introduction to volume 126 of *The Dictionary of Literary Biography: Seventeenth-Century British Nondramatic Poets,* 2d ser. (Detroit: Gale Research, 1993), xii–xiii.

imagination responded to what was an inescapable and sometimes all too tangible reality. The original, abbreviated versions of the essays were presented at the twelfth biennial Renaissance conference at the University of Michigan–Dearborn, October 11–12, 1996.[3] The final versions printed here have benefited from the stimulating exchanges and responses afforded by the conference, and they intersect, reinforce, and challenge each other in significant and interesting ways. But the essays were written independently and without consultation among the authors. No topics or approaches were assigned and none were proscribed. All the essays are historically grounded and critically based, but they vary widely in their historical perspectives and critical techniques and presuppositions and in their scope and focus. The only criterion for selection is that each essay contribute to our fuller understanding of the presence of the English civil wars in the seventeenth-century literary imagination.

While the volume reflects a wide range of perspectives on the English civil wars, it is unified by recurrent concerns that transcend ideological boundaries. The balance of the collection is tilted somewhat toward Royalists, yet what is most striking about the volume as a whole is the repeated emphasis on an unexpected irenicism in partisans of both sides of the conflict. Of the fifteen essays in the book, six are on Royalist literary

3. Selected papers from the previous Dearborn conferences have also been published: those from the 1974 conference as *"Trust to Good Verses": Herrick Tercentenary Essays*, ed. Roger B. Rollin and J. Max Patrick (Pittsburgh: University of Pittsburgh Press, 1978); those from the 1976 conference on seventeenth-century prose as a special issue of *Studies in the Literary Imagination* (10.2 [1977]), ed. William A. Sessions and James S. Tillman; those from the 1978 conference as *"Too Rich to Clothe the Sunne": Essays on George Herbert*, ed. Claude J. Summers and Ted-Larry Pebworth (Pittsburgh: University of Pittsburgh Press, 1980); those from the 1980 conference as *Classic and Cavalier: Essays on Jonson and the Sons of Ben*, ed. Claude J. Summers and Ted-Larry Pebworth (Pittsburgh: University of Pittsburgh Press, 1982); those from the 1982 conference as *The Eagle and the Dove: Reassessing John Donne*, ed. Claude J. Summers and Ted-Larry Pebworth (Columbia: University of Missouri Press, 1986); those from the 1984 conference as *"Bright Shootes of Everlastingnesse": The Seventeenth-Century Religious Lyric*, ed. Claude J. Summers and Ted-Larry Pebworth (Columbia: University of Missouri Press, 1987); those from the 1986 conference as *"The Muses Common-Weale": Poetry and Politics in the Seventeenth Century*, ed. Claude J. Summers and Ted-Larry Pebworth (Columbia: University of Missouri Press, 1988); those from the 1988 conference as *On the Celebrated and Neglected Poems of Andrew Marvell*, ed. Claude J. Summers and Ted-Larry Pebworth (Columbia: University of Missouri Press, 1992); those from the 1990 conference as *Renaissance Discourses of Desire*, ed. Claude J. Summers and Ted-Larry Pebworth (Columbia: University of Missouri Press, 1993); those from the 1992 conference as *The Wit of Seventeenth-Century Poetry*, ed. Claude J. Summers and Ted-Larry Pebworth (Columbia: University of Missouri Press, 1995); and those from the 1994 conference as *Representing Women in Renaissance England*, ed. Claude J. Summers and Ted-Larry Pebworth (Columbia: University of Missouri Press, 1997).

figures (Fane, Herrick, Cleveland, Lovelace, Vaughan, and Cooper); six are on figures traditionally associated with the Parliamentarian side of the civil wars (Milton, Winstanley, Marvell, Overton, and Philips); two consider both Royalist and Parliamentarian writers; and the remaining essay explores how Royalist writers of the Restoration refashioned a puritan literary trope. What is neglected in the volume is the radicalism associated with the civil wars, and particularly with puritanism. But the omission of essays on writers as interesting and significant as the Leveller John Lilburne, for example, reflects the volume's bias toward canonical literature, rather than any bias against radicalism. Moreover, the contributors tend to evince less interest in explicitly polemical works than in texts that problematize the political. In any case, the collection is unified by its preoccupation with "moderate" voices and its recurrent concern with the ambiguities and complexities of literary response.

As Graham Roebuck illustrates in his account of the entry of the term *cavalier* into English and its naturalization during the civil wars, one response to the crises of midcentury was the proliferation of a new political lexicon. Concentrating on the peculiar history of *cavalier* but also considering its twin term *roundhead*, Roebuck demonstrates how the competing pamphleteers in the propaganda wars constructed ideologically loaded language to advance their cause and unfavorably characterize their opponents. Yet, as in the case of *cavalier* itself, no victory in the pamphlet wars could be taken for granted. Although it was created by Parliamentarians as a term of abuse, its meaning was ultimately transformed by Royalists into an epithet with favorable connotations.

The reactions to the political and military convulsions of the period by Mildmay Fane, second Earl of Westmorland, and Robert Herrick, his pensioner, are the subjects of the next two essays. Fane and Herrick both experienced the civil wars firsthand, as attentive observers if not active participants. Tom Cain examines Fane's manuscript verse, as well as his printed volume *Otia Sacra*, and traces the fluctuating responses of one of the period's most highly placed and privileged individuals to the evolving political climate of his age. In Cain's reading of his poetry and life, Fane emerges as a fascinating figure, conservative but thoughtful and essentially irenic, whose political allegiances and commitments were complicated rather than simple. Addressing timeless yet suddenly urgent questions of retirement and engagement, as well as more directly political topics, Fane's poetry wrestles with crucial questions of loyalty and accommodation.

Reading Herrick's *Hesperides* as a civil war document, M. Thomas Hester argues that while the poet strives to defend the embattled Caroline culture he also in effect confirms the puritan critique of that culture. Hence, *Hesperides* "provides both a picture of the threat that, in Herrick's term, the Puritans' deadly 'precis[ion]' . . . presented to the Caroline court and an emblem of the moral/aesthetic fissure of that court, which contributed to and made nearly inevitable the (un)timely cultural *'trans-shifting'* of the English civil war." Stressing the collection's satiric and elegiac modes, Hester finds Herrick's voice ultimately one of despair. The masque of *Hesperides,* he concludes, is finally a masque of death.

The ambivalences of other Royalists are explored in the essays by Daniel Jaeckle, Erna Kelly, and Alan Rudrum. Jaeckle focuses on one of John Cleveland's most ambitious poems, "The Kings Disguise," which was prompted by Charles I's daring escape from Oxford in 1646 in the disguise of a servant. The work is pivotal in Cleveland's career, for it marks his move from parroting a Royalist party line to examining a politically and morally dubious action of the king himself. Turning finally from witty history to typology as a means of making sense of his cause's imminent defeat, the poet expresses the complex emotions of a man both devoted to and disappointed in his king.

Coping with defeat is also the subject of Erna Kelly's essay. Examining Richard Lovelace's poems that address insects and other small creatures, she explains how a Royalist partisan was able to progress from anxiety and the cavalier coping skills of stoic retreat and immersion in pleasure that characterize many of his poems to works that view the political arena more dispassionately. In the emblematic poems addressed to small creatures such as the puritan heron and the turncoat fly, Lovelace is even able to express admiration and sympathy for his enemies. "Dissimilar enough from him to allow an unanxious assessment yet similar enough in the difficulties they faced to evoke empathy, the subjects of these poems enlarged Lovelace's understanding of England's civil wars, enabling him to make a private or separate peace."

Reminding us that the Scots, Irish, and Welsh were also participants in the civil wars, and that we might more accurately speak of the British rather than of the English civil wars, Alan Rudrum considers the response of Henry Vaughan and his circle in Breconshire to the Parliamentarian triumph. The Welsh Royalist gentry had the options of resistance, collaboration, or silence. While *Silex Scintillans* is clearly the work of an "ultra" Royalist and Laudian Anglican who refused to compromise or collaborate with the Parliamentarian conquerors, Vaughan was, however, capable of respecting those who chose to respond differently, as evidenced by his elegy "To the Pious Memory of C[harles] W[albeoffe]," which appears in *Thalia Rediviva.* This complex poem mourns a kinsman who served as a magistrate under the Commonwealth. Moreover, even in *Silex Scintillans* one can discern an irenic quality in works like "L'Envoy," which manages to be both highly partisan yet also conciliatory in its longing for peace.

The desire for peace is a hallmark of Sir John Denham's *Coopers Hill* as well. The topographical poem is the work of a man who attempted to avert the civil wars by espousing a *via media* that embraced principles of both Parliamentarianism and Royalism. Concentrating on the revised version of the poem, written during the Interregnum, Jay Russell Curlin explores how in his revisions Denham evokes the fresh memory of war's chaos to illustrate the dangers of immoderation. "Even after the dust of the war had long settled and the monarch for whom he had fought had found peace only in the grave, this defeated royalist," Curlin writes, "could speak of the evils of arbitrary power—and indicate how the victors had imitated the very abuses they had sought to reform."

Examining works in both manuscript and print, Elizabeth Clarke argues that women writers of the seventeenth century used the "private" discourse of the religious lyric to express some of the most radical literary comment on the civil wars. Writers as diverse politically and socially as Anna Cromwell Williams, Jane Cavendish, An Collins, and the poet Eliza use the tropes of spiritual inspiration and submission as strategies to enable and empower their voices. Since the conventions of the religious lyric ungendered the traditionally female stance of dependence, the genre was particularly congenial to women; moreover, the sense of equality before God assumed in the religious lyric may even have encouraged women to publish their religious verse. Clarke observes that when women writers rhetorically play "the submission card," it indicates female agency rather than male exploitation.

Probably the shrewdest and most subtle political poet of the civil war era, Andrew Marvell reveals his own ambivalences about his age's turbulent politics in many of his works, including his great country-house poem, "Upon Appleton House," dedicated to Lord Fairfax, the Parliamentarian general who retired in protest of the regicide. In a reading emphasizing the poem's inversions and parodies, and its subversion of genre, Hugh Jenkins examines the role of the "tawny mowers" in the fields of the estate, whom he identifies with the Levellers and other radicals who came to prominence in the civil wars. Jenkins argues that the poem's dominant subtext is the threat to property and property rights posed by such radicals and demonstrates how Marvell incorporates the Levellers as a parodic and ultimately destabilizing element in the poem. He concludes that "Perhaps more so than any other major poem of the period, 'Upon Appleton House' . . . captures the full impact of the radical forces so briefly liberated by the breakdown of traditional authorities during the Civil War period."

Andrew Shifflett brings to the fore Colonel Robert Overton, "an exemplary if now little-known man who dwelt for a time upon superlatives before falling on days more evil than any Milton knew." A respected soldier who was praised extravagantly by Milton, Overton was an independent who was imprisoned by both Cromwell and Charles II. Politically a "classical republican," Overton is particularly interesting for his literary tastes, associations, and practice. Shifflett examines in detail three topics that are fascinating in their own right, but which are also emblematic of the role of literature in the civil war era: the proving of his participation in a plot against the Protectorate by adducing a "copy of verses" found in his possession; his eloquent though unsuccessful appeal to Cromwell by citing an episode in Tacitus's *Annals*; and his transcription and adaptation of poems by Donne, Herbert, and other poets during his imprisonment after the Restoration.

The work of Katherine Philips, the most widely respected woman poet of the period, is also affected by the English civil wars. She was both the wife of a Commonwealth official and the devoted friend of many Royalists. In his essay, Robert Evans explores how Philips's pre-Restoration poetry responds to the complex period in which she lived. Evans argues that her poems on friendship and her verse essays are enriched when read in historical context, while her more explicitly political poems exhibit not only poetic skill but also nuanced political insight. Evans finds that her works document in interesting ways the psychological impact of the English civil wars on a thoughtful person, while her personal circumstances help reveal the contradictions and divisions of the era.

Jonathan Rogers considers how Royalist poets of the Restoration both discredited and appropriated the puritan apocalyptic rhetoric of the civil wars and Interregnum. Examining the complicated relationship between the Augustan and apocalyptic rhetorical modes in the 1660s, Rogers illustrates how poets like Abraham Cowley and John Dryden turned the radicals' language against them by portraying Restoration England as a type of the New Jerusalem. The Royalists represented the Restoration of Charles II "as the apocalyptic deliverance they had longed for during the tribulation that was the English civil wars and the Puritan ascendancy."

The final essays in the volume are all concerned with John Milton. M. L. Donnelly examines the chronology of Milton's expressed attitudes toward military virtue and suggests that the poet abandoned his youthful enthusiasm for the epic tradition's glorification of warfare at a particular moment, soon after he observed the failures of discipline and the graft and corruption of the first civil war. He came to the belief expressed in various ways in all his later works, including *Paradise Lost, Paradise Regained,* and *Samson Agonistes,* that military prowess and accomplishments were inferior skills that could not by themselves secure permanent good for humankind. Milton's rejection of the heroic celebration of warfare was, thus, the result of lived experience rather than of literary influence.

Diane Purkiss also evokes the actual experience of warfare in her essay on "The English Civil War and Male Identity." Drawing both on "realistic" narratives of the civil wars and on psychoanalytic theory, Purkiss examines Milton's representation of war in *Paradise Lost* as at least in part a response to pressures from within the poet's own masculine identity. Demonstrating how war and masculinity intersect but also trouble each other, she credits Milton with recognizing that the "masculinity of militarism is too complex, too contradictory, and too prone to excess to form a useful metaphor for Christian heroism, or to assuage the potent terrors that such militarism itself arouses."

Challenging recent "revisionist" interpretations of *Samson Agonistes,* Catherine Gimelli Martin reasserts the relevance of Milton's civil war treatises and republican principles to his tragedy. In order to understand the ethical aspect of Samson's agon in seventeenth-century terms, we must, Martin argues, return to its complex political source: the closely intertwined questions of individual, civic, and religious liberty to which Milton devoted his life, and which brought him into diametric opposition to Hobbes. *Samson Agonistes* in effect dramatizes the conflicting interpretations by Milton and Hobbes of such fundamental issues as human rights, covenants, natural and positive law, and right reason.

In their varied approaches and distinct conclusions, these essays add considerably to our understanding of the presence of the English civil wars in the seventeenth-century literary imagination. The essays illuminate important texts in which the civil wars are at either the forefront or in the background, and they elucidate significant literary figures while also calling attention to recurrent themes. Focusing on writers as major as Milton, Marvell, Herrick, and Vaughan, and as heretofore unappreciated as Fane, Overton, and the poet Eliza, they document both characteristic and highly individual responses to a turbulent and violent history.

Graham Roebuck

Cavalier

How did the name *cavalier* come to be applied to one of the contesting sides of the English civil wars, and how did it become a fixture in the literature of the period? Linked to *Roundhead*, it creates the phrase that, for the popular imagination, delineates the nature of the war, capturing its basic social antagonisms. "Cavaliers and Roundheads" seems to work just like the shorthand labels of other epic struggles, such as "Greeks and Trojans," "North and South," "Cowboys and Indians." Yet unlike these, "Cavaliers and Roundheads" reveals nothing of the geographical, confessional, ideological, or racial dispositions of the contest, and nothing of the constitutional dimension proclaimed by such pairings as "Royalist and Parliamentarian," "Monarchist and Republican" or "Confederacy and Union." There is a hint of absurdity about *Roundhead* and (although less obviously) about *cavalier*, which was exploited by the polemicists of the 1640s, that possibly anticipates the enmity in Lilliput between Big-Endians and those who break their eggs at the smaller end.

In order to trace the entry of *cavalier* into English, its naturalization, its political and polemical career in the civil wars, and its subsequent neutralizing, it is useful to survey briefly the current historical and literary debate. Almost as many "paper-bullets" fly now as when Clarendon used the phrase to characterize the declarations, protestations, manifestos, and pamphlets pouring from the 1640s presses. Those "paper skirmishes" were, he wrote, preludes of "sharper actions."[1] He had no doubt that the ephemeral, name-calling journalism of the time, with its propensity for

---

I am grateful for Professor M. Thomas Hester's insightful and helpful criticism of an earlier draft of this essay.

1. The first phrase is used by Clarendon (then Edward Hyde), in January 1643 in his satirical forgery, *A Speech made by Alderman Garroway, at a Common-Hall . . . wjth A Letter from a Scholler in Oxfordshire, to his Vnkle a Merchant in Broad-street. . . .* (1643); *Wing* G 281. The attribution is made and the pamphlet discussed (item 67B) in Graham Roebuck, *Clarendon and Cultural Continuity* (New York: Garland, 1981). Clarendon recalled this trope when composing his *History.* See Clarendon, *The History of the*

polarizing opinion, pointed in the direction of war—a war few or none wished for. Hence he rejected the view (discussed below) that a mass, spontaneous, popular eruption of antiauthoritarian sentiment was the cause of the conflict. Scholarly opinion, however, remains divided.

James Holstun, editor of *Pamphlet Wars: Prose in the English Revolution*, employs military terms to examine the present state of academic controversy:

> The period from 1640 to 1660 has always been one of the most contested eras of English social and literary history and, if anything, it now looms larger than ever—despite and even because of revisionist attacks on the very idea of an English Revolution, and an emerging counterattack.

For Holstun, the "revolutionary" doctrine is orthodox; interpretations analogous to Clarendon's, revisionist. He sees several other paradoxes as well. New historicism, far from sharpening the focus on seventeenth-century political discourse, has instead elided the English Revolution from the picture. And although it is a period hotly contested, there is a strange "critical neglect" of its literature. Is this a plot "concocted by formalist Tory editors"? Not wholly, Holstun concludes (although without retracting the charge), for even Christopher Hill himself has trouble writing about literature and the Revolution because for him " 'literature' includes almost exclusively works printed before 1642 and after 1660." Holstun, therefore, calling for a reconsideration of "literature," complains of the neglect of prose (especially pamphlets): "writers of revolutionary-era prose (Milton always excepted) continue to languish in the shadows of Sidney, Spenser, Shakespeare, Donne, Jonson, Herbert and Marvell."[2]

Scholars of an opposing political stamp—they say "civil war," not "revolution"—voice a similar complaint. Here is Timothy Raylor in his *Cavaliers, Clubs, and Literary Culture* complaining that "while the period leading up to and following the English Civil War has always fascinated historians, the literature of the period has generally been dismissed by critics as too timebound and partisan to be worthy of serious attention." One of two notable exceptions he cites is Christopher Hill. At this point, however, Raylor's analysis takes a quite contrary line to Holstun's. Raylor describes "the sophisticated appreciation we now have of the ideological complexities of those traditionally labeled 'Puritans'" and contrasts it with our ignorance of "cavalier culture"—a *"terra incognita."* Here, then,

---

Rebellion and Civil Wars in England, ed. W. Dunn Macray, 6 vols. (Oxford: Clarendon Press, 1988), 2:13, 206, 69.

    2. James Holstun, ed., *Pamphlet Wars: Prose in the English Revolution* (London: Frank Cass, 1992), 2–5, 11 n. 7.

are other writers of the period languishing in shadows, in this case, outside what Raylor terms the "charmed circle of the court."[3]

This essay is written in the hope of letting some light into both shadows, rather than adjudicating the argument over "revolution" versus "rebellion." The argument has, after all, continuously raged since the civil wars, in which time the meanings of key words have changed. In essence the modern argument replays the original debate. The main lines were set by Thomas May's *History of the Long Parliament* (1647) and Clarendon's *History of the Rebellion* (begun in 1646). One sees irresistible forces of change gathering to a violent and justified head; the other sees the contrivances of individual agents who, from a great variety of motives, create a constitutional crisis and rebellion.[4]

Recent scholarship seeking to account for the emergence of new political labels and political terms in the 1640s does so with an awareness of the extraordinary slipperiness of names and labels in the seventeenth century. The conservative-minded historian J. P. Kenyon notes that "for want of anything better we have to go on using such terms, and other terms which would almost certainly have been meaningless to contemporaries." A solution to the problem, it has been suggested, is to recover contemporary definitions of terms, the connotations and denotations of seventeenth-century language.[5]

3. Timothy Raylor, *Cavaliers, Clubs, and Literary Culture: Sir John Mennes, James Smith, and the Order of the Fancy* (Newark: University of Delaware Press, 1994), 19.

4. Nigel Smith, *Literature and Revolution in England, 1640–1660* (New Haven: Yale University Press, 1994), sets out to compare May and Clarendon: "May controls and directs spite as if he were Juvenal; Clarendon pretends to be Thucydides, taking the reader into a world of passions which only simulate disinterestedness" (346). How passions can simulate disinterestedness is left unexplained as Smith presses his case: "We know for whom May writes and why he does so. We know his history is propaganda. Clarendon's *History* is not, in its original incarnation, published propaganda (its first readers were royalist exiles), but it is the work of a sophisticatedly committed man, and the text confesses prejudice indirectly and in a way which has yet to be properly understood" (346). Clarendon's offense, sophisticated commitment, is further unmasked by Smith's assertion that when Clarendon puts "words into the mouth of the King," which actually *are* his words . . . his *History* becomes, in consequence, more committed and less discriminating" (349). What Smith's analysis contributes to the debate on civil war historiography or to understanding Clarendon is unclear.

See also Elizabeth Skerpan, *The Rhetoric of Politics in the English Revolution, 1642–1660* (Columbia: University of Missouri Press, 1992). She finds that rhetorical expectations stacked the cards against the revolutionaries.

5. Quoted in Thomas Healy and Jonathan Sawday, introduction to *Literature and the English Civil War*, ed. Healy and Sawday (Cambridge: Cambridge University Press, 1990), 6.

Most notable of these problematic terms is *revolution* itself. In "The Word 'Revolution' in Seventeenth-Century England," Hill argues that when the need to name the phenomenon of decisive, "one-directional political change occurred, the word dropped its earlier sense of circularity, and its primary reference to astronomy and astrology, and so assumed its modern meaning." New needs brought forth new words, such as those identified by Thomas Fuller in his *Church History of Britain* (1655), which Hill cites: "malignant," "plunder," and "fanatic." Hill's recommendation, therefore, which seems to echo J. P. Kenyon—at the other end of the political spectrum—is for

> serious linguistic study of the new words which appeared in the seventeenth century, and of old words whose meaning shifted. Such a study would tell us a great deal about the social changes which took place then, and might even help us date them.[6]

Scholars, for the most part, agree with him on the value of trying to establish the historical context of the political lexicon of the 1640s as a more attractive project than the anachronistic application of terms foreign to the times. There is division of opinion, however, on the question of how such terms arise. On the one hand—a view generally sympathetic to the "revolution" school—is the account of change without identifiable agents, a sort of "tide in the affairs of men"; a synchronism of politically engaged minds. For instance, Hill's account of the changes to denotations of key seventeenth-century terms does not tell *who* the agents of change were. Indeed, it is necessary to his view that change comes about by inevitable process. Hill's formula is that "men came to speak of 'revolutions and changes' to distinguish political revolutions . . . from traditional circular revolutions."[7] On the other hand, allowing more weight to the view that the events of the 1640s owed much to individual agents who—from a multiplicity of motives—created a constitutional crisis leading to war, one sometimes finds that new terms, strutting and fretting their hour upon the bloody stage of war, have left a paper trail behind them.

6. In *For Veronica Wedgwood These: Studies in Seventeenth-Century History*, ed. Richard Ollard and Pamela Tudor-Craig (London: Collins, 1986), 149–51.

Annabel Patterson's essay "The Very Name of the Game: Theories of Order and Disorder" in *Literature and the English Civil War*, however, detects a new "logical positivism abroad in historiography" that requires use of only the right words. This development is a reaction against the "loss of belief in objective historical knowledge" and the destabilizing effect of postmodernism. She objects to "English Civil War" because its seeming neutrality excludes other interpretations, "specifically those of definitive social change or ideological confrontation" (22).

7. Hill, "The Word 'Revolution' in Seventeenth-Century England," 140–41. *Synchronism*, according to the *OED*, arrived in print in 1588 in the context of scriptural exegesis.

The astrologer William Lilly provides the first coherent account in print of the appearance of the twin terms *Roundhead* and *Cavalier* in his 1651 publication *Monarchy Or No Monarchy in England,* a convenient prognostication, to which is appended his history of the civil war. Recalling London street life in the winter of 1641–1642, Lilly reports that Roundheads, hair cut short and modest in apparel but not in language, devised the opprobrious sobriquet *Cavalier* to identify their enemies:

> The Courtiers againe wearing long Haire and locks, and always Sworded, at last were called by these men [Roundheads] Cavaliers; and so after this broken language had been used a while, all that adhered unto the Parlament were termed Round-heads, all that tooke part or appeared for his Majestie Cavaliers, few of the vulgar knowing the sence of the word Cavalier; how ever the present hatred of the Citizens were such unto Gentlemen especially Courtiers, that few durst come into the City, or if they did, they were sure to receive affronts and be abused.[8]

Notwithstanding the doubts of some scholars, and some contemporaries, about Lilly's reliability,[9] his recollection is remarkably durable. Here is an agency of naming: "these men," and here is a distinct setting: "the City"; and the term "Citizens." This newly charged term, in the ensuing pamphlet warfare, reveals republican affinities. It begins to displace "subjects" as a description of political status in Parliamentarian publications. Lilly's stereotype of the cavalier is often elaborated, in woodcuts as well as texts—hair, the wide-brimmed feathered hats, high riding boots, sword, and spurs.[10] This vivid image persists, although recently Thomas Corns's

---

8. London: Humphrey Blunden, 107; *Wing* L 2228. Cited in the *OED* entry for *cavalier.* Following p. 74 is his history: *Severall Observations upon the Life and Death of Charles late King of England.*

9. Fellow astrologer John Booker blames Lilly for "writing to please his friends and to keep in with the times (as he formerly did to his owne dishonour) and not according to the rules of Art, by which he could not well erre." Recorded by Pepys, *Diary,* October 24, 1660, in *The Diary of Samuel Pepys,* ed. Robert Latham and William Matthews, 11 vols. (London: Bell and Hyman, 1970–1983). Bernard Capp, *English Almanacs 1500–1800: Astrology and the Popular Press* (Ithaca: Cornell University Press, 1979), takes a judicious approach, describing the charge of time-serving as "not wholly conclusive" (58), adding that he was "the most abused as well as the most celebrated astrologer of the seventeenth century [and he] deserves a closer scrutiny" (57). After the Restoration, Lilly experienced a "growing revulsion towards the cavalier politics of 'feathers and Damn blades'" (58).

Long before the Restoration he earned royalist enmity. *Mercurius Elencticus* of November 12–19, 1647, edited by George Wharton, describes him as "that Jugling Wizard *William Lilly;* the States Figure-Flinger Generall; a fellow made up of nothing but Mischiefe, Tautologies and Barbarisme." Quoted by Joad Raymond in *Making the News: An Anthology of the Newsbooks of Revolutionary England, 1641–1660,* ed. Raymond (New York: St. Martin's Press, 1993), 138.

10. A particularly good example is *An Exact Description Of a Roundhead and a Long-Head Shag-Poll: Taken our* [sic] *of the purest Antiquities and Records* (London: George

informative recontextualizing of the pamphlet war shows that "the officer corps of each side favoured long hair," that Puritan rank and file wore short hair at the start of the war, and there was little distinction in dress between the sides.[11]

It is especially interesting that few of the vulgar knew the sense of the word *cavalier*, but Lilly should not be doubted. It was an exotic word—a "hard word" according to seventeenth-century usage—deliberately selected to do propaganda work for which previous candidates for the job had failed. (These were usually biblical, such as the names of the enemies of Israel.) The label had to be brief, pithy, and picturesque, to rival *Roundhead*, which had taken hold earlier and had spread rapidly to the provinces, uniting popular sentiment against enthusiast reforms.

Roundhead has a specific moment of birth. Clarendon reports that insolent petitioners provoked some officers guarding the court to "strike some of the most pragmatical of the crew." Blood was spilled. Rushworth also reports it in *Historical Collections,* 1659, where he names the coiner: David Hide, a guard who threatened to cut "roundhead throats" on December 27, 1641. His and Clarendon's dates agree. It has recently been shown that Rushworth worked from his immense collection of contemporary pamphlets (later dispersed) and newsbooks when compiling his history. His annotation of a newssheet of December 1641 identifies the otherwise anonymous gentleman. The 1692 edition of his history provides further information about Hide, who is described as "a Reformado in the late army against the Scots, and now appointed to go in some command into Ireland." He is credited with the "first miniting" (i.e. "minting") of that term for those "Dogs that bawled against Bishops," as he called them.[12]

Tomlinson, 1642), *Wing* E 3638. This must have been published sometime after the middle of March 1642 [n.s.] when the king removed to York, for the woodcut has representations of London in one corner—a gibbet just outside the walls—and York in another. Beneath the woodcut is the quatrain,

> This Man of haire whom you see marching heere,
>   Is that brave Ruffian Mounseire Cavilier.
> But let him not make so much hast for hee,
>   Must be drawn back, and stayd by Gregore.

Gregory Roundhead in sober attire, short haired, clean-shaven, holds a halter attached to his enemy's neck.

11. Thomas Corns, *Uncloistered Virtue: English Political Literature, 1640–1660* (Oxford: Clarendon Press, 1992), 5.

12. See Frances Henderson, "Posterity to Judge—John Rushworth and His 'Historical Collections,'" *Bodleian Library Record* 15 (April 1996): 252–53; Clarendon, *History,* 1:456; *OED* entry for *roundhead,* def. 1.

The speed at which *Roundhead* spread in the countryside is illustrated by an excerpt from a 1642 letter of Lady Brilliana Harley, who was later to conduct the heroic defense of her home, Brampton Bryan: "at Ludlow they set up a maypole, and a thing like a head upon it, and so they did at Croft, and gathered a great many about it and shot at it in derision of Roundheads." Pro-Parliament, Lady Brilliana recounts her apprehension at an "insolent" Royalist insurrection in the countryside, knowing she would be safer in London. Her later letters also use the word *cavalier*.[13]

If any of the vulgar were sufficiently curious to consult the dictionaries of the time about the new term *cavalier*, they would have received little enlightenment. The term is, of course, imported from the Romance languages, with the principal sense of "horseman." The relevant dictionaries are cited in the appendix to this essay. Two significant definitions need comment here: i) Florio's 1611 addition of "a knight of the drawen sword, that an excellent whoremonger or notable wencher" and "a poore beggerly knight that hath nothing but his sword and cloake"; and ii) Bullokar's 1656 addition, pointing up the term as a reproachful nickname. Bullokar provides a sober and judicious summary account and a keen sense of the shift from neutrality to opprobrium. However, it looks as if Florio's additions of secondary meanings worked suggestively on the imaginations of those seekers for new terms in which to combine the vanity and luxuriance ("silk-worm"), ready violence, sexual depravity, and fallen fortunes leading to rashness of action and even desperation that the 1640s Roundheads needed to impute to their enemies. These are the key elements in the initial civil war application of the term. Other derogatory aspersions easily cohered, as propaganda requirements dictated. It became *the* word at the center of a galaxy of abusive terminology.

I suspend the account a moment to note how short-lived was this propaganda coup. The word is nearly innocuous now. *Cavalier* is, for instance, the brand name of a motor car. People of cavalier manners are almost admired despite their high-handedness. The word evokes a dashing, witty, free-spiritedness. Even while this term was being reconstructed to bear its political and propagandistic weight, it revealed innate resilience that carries over into the designation "Cavalier Poetry," where aesthetic considerations totally eclipse implications of barbarism, although without

13. Quoted in Jacqueline Eales, *Puritans and Roundheads: The Harleys of Brampton Bryan and the Outbreak of the Civil War* (Cambridge: Cambridge University Press, 1990), 143–44, 172.

eliding the sexual and adventurous suggestions. This general sense was available, at least to some, in the 1630s when Suckling wrote a letter (published in 1646) evoking the "lady-killing" sense of *cavalier*. He refers to a sexual encounter: "Curiosity would be as vain, as if a Cuckold should enquire whether a Cavalier pulld off his Spurs first or not."[14] Raylor's study, earlier cited, uses the word *cavalier* in its title, takes the sense of the word as synonymous with wit, and, in some measure, with Royalist courtly buffoonery. He describes the function of this kind of cavalier wit in the exiled court.

That such counterdefinitions of *cavalier* should occur is no surprise, since those who, historically, were castigated chose either to deflect it and wittily defuse it, or to accept it as an unjust label. It *is* surprising, however, that in the Interregnum a dictionary compiled by Milton's nephew, Edward Phillips, and published just two years after Bullokar's summary definition of the word as a "nick-name," should give such a nonrevolutionary account as this: "Cavalier, a brave man, a Knight, or Gentle-man, serving on Hors-back from the Italian Cavallo." After the Restoration, in private conversation at least, Puritans could still draw on the bitter connotations. Pepys records a diatribe against the debauchery of the restored clergy and the returned discontented cavaliers who "go with their belts and swords, swearing and cursing and stealing—running into people's houses, by force oftentimes, to carry away something." But, by the time that Defoe wrote *Memoirs of a Cavalier*, the term is innocent of the burden of guilt with which the 1640s Roundheads saddled it.[15]

Lilly's dating of *Cavalier* is corroborated, as is his dating of *Roundhead*, by Clarendon, writing in 1646 (*The History of the Rebellion* was not printed until 1702–1704):

> the two terms of '*Roundhead*' and '*Cavalier*' grew to be received in discourse, and were afterwards continued, for the most succinct distinction of affections

14. Suckling, *Fragmenta Avrea* (London: Humphrey Moseley, 1646), 61; *Wing* S 6126. Published as a nostalgic lament for one of the most glittering figures in the charmed circle of the court—wholly dispersed by 1646. On modern uses of the term, see the introduction to *Cavalier Poets: Selected Poems*, ed. Thomas Clayton (Oxford: Oxford University Press, 1978), xv, where Clayton surveys *OED* senses of *cavalier*, choosing adjectival uses tending to the general sense of free and easy, careless of manner.

15. Pepys, *Diary*, November 9, 1663, ed. Latham and Matthews, 4:374. Defoe, *Memoirs Of A Cavalier* (London, [1720]). Appearing at first anonymously, this work was subsequently given other titles and putative authors as attempts were made to attribute it to real historical figures who might have experienceed the events described. Defoe uses the term *cavalier* many times, but nowhere does he supply it with a string of epithets in the manner of the civil war pamphleteers.

throughout the quarrel: they who were looked upon as servants of the King being then called *'Cavaliers,'* and the other of the rabble contemned and despised under the names of *'Roundheads.'*[16]

There is no mistaking Clarendon's allegiance, and, although he does not here attribute the origins of the words to specific agents, or discuss their deployment, as he was the author of most Royalist pamphlets in the "paper skirmishes" of the first civil war, he well understood their history.

Of course, *cavalier* is, as Thomas Corns and others demonstrate, in Annabel Patterson's phrase, "ideologically loaded," along with "malignants" and others in the topical lexicon. Corns reveals a dimension of its political construction, but argues that the propaganda stereotype bore little relationship to the reality of the case. For instance, the charges of ungodliness seem unfounded when we learn that Royalist forces had more chaplains, regularly prayed, and that there was no marked inequality in the barbarity of either side. If anything, the New Model Army is more blameworthy, he concludes. This is not a view Pepys would subscribe to: He reports with approval Mr. Blackborne's talk of how the Puritan soldiers settled back into productive occupations following cessation of hostilities, whereas cavaliers continued their rapacious ways. This he attributes to the differences in temper between the two armies. The "spirits of the old Parliament-soldier[s] are so quiet and contented with God's providence, that the King is safer from any evil meant by them, a thousand times more then from his own discontented Cavalier[s]."[17] For Pepys and the like-minded, the old sense still has force in 1663.

The typical characteristics in the construction of *cavalier* begin appearing in Parliament's publications from June 1642.[18] Two instances can serve to demonstrate the pattern. *Propositions and Orders,* dated June 10, is a publication that authorizes the raising of an army to defend the king and both houses of Parliament (the fiction that the King has been taken over by desperate malignants was maintained in Parliament's papers). Many people are said to be

16. Clarendon, *History,* 1:456.

17. Corns, *Uncloistered Virtue,* 3–10; Patterson, "The Very Name of the Game," in *Literature and the English Civil War,* ed. Healy and Sawday, 29; Pepys, *Diary,* November 9, 1663.

18. An earlier instance is *The Right Honorable the Lord Kimbolton his Speech in Parliament, On Tuesday the third of January 1641. concerning the Articles of High Treason. . . .* (London: F. C. and T. B., 1642); *Wing* M 396. This is not an authentic speech, but is a Parliamentarian penman's swift and indignant response to Charles's attempt to arrest the five Commons members and Lord Kimbolton—in effect a royal coup d'état, and the very action Parliament needed to crystalize its case. A copy in the British Library (101.a.11) is endorsed "3 Jan. 1642."

baffled and injured by severall sorts of malignant men who are about the King, some whereof, under the names of Caviliers, without having respect to the Lawes of the Land, or any feare either of God or man are ready to commit all manner of outrage and violence, which must needs tend to the dissolution of this Government, the destroying of our Religion, Lawes, liberty and propriety.[19]

The full title includes reference to "Horse-men" who will be maintained by this levy. Clearly its authors did not think the dictionary equivalent *cavaliers* appropriate in *that* context. *New Propositions* of June 11 complains of

those armed Cavaleers at York committing several outrages already on his Maiesties Subiects, giving out severall words against the Parliament, both dangerous and scandalous, in a free declaration of their intents, what they intend to put in Act, if they once gaine strength by their supposed Forraigne supplies.[20]

Here the element of foreignness is added to the compound. The stage is set for the pamphleteers to embellish outrage and violence, and the rapine of England by foreign, godless papists.[21]

Royalist response was deliberately low-keyed rhetorically, although strongly argued. Hence the following, almost glancing, remark about *cavalier* in a document from York dated June 17, 1642: "For the language and behaviour of the Cavaliers (a word by what mistake soever it seemes much in disfavour) there hath not been the least complaint here."[22] More than a year later the Royalist newsbook *Mercurius Rusticus* extracts some profit from the label:

As the Rebells in their march towards *Glocester* passed through *Chiping Norton* in the County of *Oxford:* a woman of that Towne (whose zeal to the King and the Iustice of his cause could not containe it selfe though in the mid'st of his mortall Enimies) said in the hearing of some of the Rebells, *God blesse the Cavaliers:* (so are all good and faithfull Subjects called by the Rebells). This expression of the poore womans affection to the King and his loyall Subjects in

19. *Propositions and Orders by the Lords and Commons now Assembled in Parliament, for bringing in of Money or Plate, to Maintaine Horse, Horse-men, and Armes for the preservation of the Publicke Peace, and for the Defence of the King and both Houses of Parliament* (London: Edward Husbands and I. F., 1642); *Wing* E 2202. The *OED* citation is from a later version.
20. *New Propositions. Propounded by The Earle of Pembrooke. The Earle of Northumberland. The Earle of Essex. And the Earle of Holland. To the Lord Major, Aldermen, and Common Councell of the City in the Guild Hall* (London: T. Fawcet, 1642); *Wing* P 1121.
21. It is, of course, true that the queen, who escaped to France before the king removed to York, was actively assembling war matériel. The Parliament publications and the pamphleteers found in the queen's actions an inexhaustible fund of outrage. See, for example, Clarendon, *History*, 2:6.
22. *His Majesties Answer to the Petition of the Lords and Commons in Parliament assembled: Presented to his Majestie at York, June 17. 1642* (London: Barker and Bill, 1642); *Wing* C 1237. This adroit riposte is the work of Clarendon.

so innocent a prayer, so highly insensed the Rebells, that to punish so hainous a Crime, presently they tyed her to the taile of one of their Carts, and stripping her to the middle, for two miles march whipped her in so cruell a manner with their Cart-whips that her body in many places was cut so deep. As if she had been lanced with Knives.

The author even takes a leaf from his opponents' book, citing Scripture, and calling on the Lord to avenge this blood.[23] It seems that Royalists saw that *Cavalier* was, in itself, not to be the unqualified public-relations success Parliamentarian pamphleteers hoped for. They failed to make the term opprobrious. Of greater force was the charge of closet papism.

When the pamphleteers took center stage, after the first round of exchanges between Parliament and king, constitutional wrangles faded into the background, and the lurid literary imagination took over. As Patrick Collinson points out in *The Puritan Character*, the penchant for dichotomizing, which has sometimes been seen as an identifying property of Puritanism, is also an essential element in early modern thought. Binary oppositions of great ferocity occur in this literature, which went to school on the Scriptures. He also observes how conscious seventeenth-century politicians were of the power inherent in naming political opponents. The name *Puritan* is a case in point. By 1641 it was a commonplace that the opponents of the godly had worked "their masterpiece" with the label "Puritan."[24]

An anti-Royalist pamphlet of July 1642 names ten types of persons who mislead the King: papists; rash noblemen; well-born gentlemen of decayed estates; a sottish, drunken multitude; delinquents; cavaliers; debtors; giddy gentlemen; preachers; and discontented and ambitious lawyers.[25] The claims that this is the report of an eyewitness and that it is a letter from the country—both claims are false—become staples of the pamphlet wars. Parliamentary propagandists were at this stage well aware of their weakness in the more conservative countryside, where allegiances often went along with family alliances, and where many people held themselves aloof from both factions. The success of Royalist

23. Quoted in Raymond, ed., *Making the News*, 137–38.
24. Patrick Collinson, *The Puritan Character: Polemics and Polarities in Early Seventeenth-Century English Culture* (Los Angeles: William Andrews Clark Memorial Library, University of California, 1989). See particularly 13–14.
25. *Sundry Observations of severall Passages and Proceedings in the North, there taken by a Subject well-affected to the Protestant Religion, His Majesties Royall Honour and Greatnesse, and the Peace and Safety of this Kingdom; Sent unto a faithfull and intimate Friend of his in London* (London: F. C., 1642); *Wing* S 6179.

pamphleteers led to a fearful paradox: they won just sufficient support for the king's cause to enable him to make war—quite the opposite result to that intended, which was to achieve accommodation. Sir Philip Warwick, while admiring the wit and elegance of Clarendon's pamphlets in the king's name, which so well answered Parliament's arguments, feared that the contest was not to be settled by argument, and that the wit would "beget a Frowardness in men." "Our good Pen will harm Us," he concluded.[26]

Perhaps the best result the Parliamentary propagandists could hope for was rather to confirm the resolve of the committed and the godly (some of whom had a tendency to eschew politics) than to win over new adherents. Reinforcement of political attachment by means of invective against the enemy leads to an almost ludic sense in these pamphlets.[27] They are often scurrilous, unconstrained, and delighting in the pleasures of verbal abuse. (This is also true of many Royalist papers.) But they may also have played a role in deepening the actual ferocity of the war.

The authors of these pamphlets, who were also the instigators of Parliament's religious postures, were the Puritan London clergy. It is well known that the cry "To your tents, O Israel" rallied the crowds and apprentices of London in their demonstrations against prelacy.[28] One of the most notable of the clergy is John Goodwin, whose pamphlet *Anti-Cavalierism* virtually institutionalizes the term and also takes the armed struggle a crucial step from a reluctantly fought quarrel ostensibly about constitutional issues (many on both sides hoped it would be settled in one battle) to a kind of *Kulturkampf*, or holy war. He answers his question, "who is the anti-Christ?" like this (it is worth noting the mixture of common and learned words):

> I meane that Colluvies, that heape, that gathering together of the scum, and drosse, and garbage of the Land, that most accursed confederacy, made up of Gebal, and Ammon, and Amaleck, Philistims with the Inhabitants of Tyre, of Jesuits, and Papists, and Atheists, of stigmaticall and infamous persons in all kindes, with that bloody and butcherly Generation, commonly knowne by the name of Cavaliers.[29]

26. *Memoires of the reigne of King Charles I. With a Continuation to the Happy Restauration of King Charles II* (London: R. Chiswell, 1701).

27. See Collinson, *The Puritan Character*, 24.

28. See Clarendon, *History,* 1:486.

29. In the full title Goodwin pulls out all the stops: *Anti-Cavalierisme, or, Truth Pleading as well the Necessity, as the Lawfulness of this present vvarre, for the suppressing of that Butcherly brood of Cavaliering Incendiaries, who are now hammering England, to make an Ireland of it: wherein all the materiall Objections against the lawfulnesse of this undertaking are fully cleered and answered, and all men that either love God, themselves, or good men, exhorted*

The learned Puritan London clergy, who wrote these vituperations and controlled much of the propaganda output, were men like William Bridge, a frequent preacher to Parliament, who probably coined "Cavalierism"; John Jackson, who preached to volunteer soldiers; and Oxford-educated George Lawrence and Christopher Love, who cowrote *The Debauched Cavalleer,* published several days before the battle of Edgehill in 1642. They were all strong-willed men of intense biblical and theological learning. Lawrence and Love's pamphlet alternates almost comically malicious recitals of gossip and rumor about Cavaliers whoring, raping, and drinking with lengthy displays of etymology. Here is the last paragraph of five devoted to the word *cavalier:*

> The name it selfe, we confesse, is honourable, and is equivalent with our *Miles, Armiger, Armigerans, vel Equus auratus,* which is a Knight, a Souldier, or a golden horseman. But these unworthy miscreants have made the very name a reproach, as the *Anti-christian Prelates,* the name of *Bishop,* which in Saint *Pauls* time was worthy of *double honour,* but by reason of their tyrannical usurpation, is (as old *father Latimer* expresseth it) worthy of a more than a *double* (even) a *Treble reproach.*[30]

Some of these preachers were eventually disciplined by the side whose propaganda they had shaped. Love, for instance, was executed for plotting against the Commonwealth.

Goodwin, a Cambridge man—a greater proportion of the preachers were from that university—survived the Restoration to die of the plague in 1665. He was denounced by Thomas Edwards in *Gangraena*—almost a badge of honor for such sectaries—and described by Edmund Calamy as "a man by himself, was against every man and had every man against him." He wrote against divine right, against Edwards (of course), against Presbyterians, against Baptists, against the Fifth Monarchy men, against Parliament, and in favor of radical, democratic republicanism. This latter work was burned by the hangmen at the Restoration.[31] These men were almost invariably theocrats, yet at first they allied with the cause of

---

to contribute all manner of assistance hereunto. Whereunto is added the bloody intentions of Romish Cavalieres against the City of London above other places, demonstrated by five Arguments. By Jo: Goodwin (London: Henry Overton, 1642) 2; Wing G 1146.

30. *The Debauched Cavalleer* (London: Henry Overton, 1642) 3; *Wing L 656.* The rest of the title of this pamphlet reflects the typical style of the preachers, and their brand of learning: *Or the English Midianite. Wherein are compared by way of Parallel, the Carriage, or rather Miscarriage of the Cavaleers, in the present reigne of our King Charles, with the Midianites of old. Setting forth their Diabolicall, and Hyperdiabolicall Blasphemies, Execrations, Rebellions, Cruelties, Rapes, and Robberies.*

31. The Calamy quotation is cited by Wilfred W. Biggs in his pamphlet, *John Goodwin* (London: Independent Press, [1961]), to whose sketch of Goodwin's career I am indebted, and *DNB* 8:146.

moderate constitutional reform and the progressivism that became the Whig myth of history.

Thomas Corns shows how in *Eikonoklastes* Milton revives the work of these men: He reaches "into the furthest recesses of the shared political memory of English Puritanism, dragging up the royalist stereotypes with which, in the early 1640s, the parliamentarian propagandists began." Milton especially evokes the fiercest of the Cavaliers, the German Prince Rupert, "the oldest target of Puritan character assassination."[32]

When citizens of London began using *cavalier* as the historians and Lilly testify, they did so having heard the preachers many times beforehand construe it in their pulpits. Why did these propagandists, creating what were to become Royalist stereotypes, choose a word that seems to have been obscure in 1640? A possible answer is that the word fell back into obscurity after a flurry of activity when it first entered English in the late decades of Elizabeth's reign, and that these men encountered it in their reading, always in association with things morally repugnant to them.

When it comes to stereotypes, no doubt the London stage, silenced by Parliament and preachers during the war, played its memorial part. It is worth noting the noble prologue to act 3 of *Henry V* (1599) in which Chorus asks who would not follow these "choice-drawn cavaliers" to France, only to have the honor of war undercut by the Boy recalling what these "swashers" were really like in their protective habitat, the London alehouse. All were, and are, thieves. Bardolph is "white-livered and red faced"; Pistol has a "killing tongue and a quiet sword"; Nym, a drunkard, "scorns to say his prayers, lest 'a should be thought a coward." But his few best words are matched with as few good deeds (3.1.27–54).[33]

An examination of Parliament's propaganda following Rupert's entry into the war reveals a new burst of energy and a new focus that united many of the earlier strands. Notable among these is the reiteration of the charge of "butchery" and bloodthirstiness. In the language of Puritan pamphlets *butcher* usually signifies *bishop*, which name, as Lawrence and Love remark, is worthy of reproach. It perhaps originated in the Marprelate tracts. Also noteworthy is the naturalization of the word *plunder* from German at this time, which thereafter sticks to him and the

---

32. Corns, *Uncloistered Virtue*, 289.

33. Among Shakespeare's uses of *cavalier*—including variant forms—is this in *Pericles*: the miraculous Marina, who could make a puritan of the devil, works such an effect on Boult's brothel by her virtue that he "must ravish her, or sh'll disfurnish us of all our cavalleria and make our own swearers priests" (4.1.11).

other Royalist soldiers. So potent and useful a word, *plunder* could not long be confined to this context, as Claude J. Summers shows in his discussion of Herrick's poem in *Noble Numbers*, "To God, in time of plundering." Ironically, here it refers not to Royalist outrages but to the ejection from their livings of Laudian priests. Herrick "alludes to the Committee of Plundered Ministers, the agency empowered by Parliament" to enforce the ejections.[34]

Are the 1640s the oldest "shared political memory" of English Puritanism at the time of *Eikonoklastes*, as Corns suggests? Perhaps a better candidate is the Marprelate controversy on which the sectarian clergy were weaned. Indeed, in the same study, Corns portrays Milton as freeing himself from the "skittish frenzy of the Marprelate tradition" even as he sometimes uses its tone.[35] Learned and committed men, the London preachers read the work of the participants in the Marprelate pamphlet war—their enemy's work as well as the Puritan side of the contest. These pamphlets are a high-water mark of invective.

Thomas Nashe's reputation as a victorious controversialist drew future contenders to study his mocking tone. It was thought that Nashe wrote all the replies to Martin until modern scholarship revised the account. Izaak Walton, composing his *Life of Hooker* in the turmoil of the civil wars, writes about how the Marprelate tracts

> were grown into high esteem with the Common people, till Tom Nash appeared against them all, who was a man of a sharp wit, and the master of a scoffing, Satyrical merry Pen, which he imployed to discover the absurdities of those blind malitious sensless Pamphlets, and Sermons as sensless as they . . . so that his merry Wit made such a discovery of their Absurdities as (which is strange) he put a greater stop to these malitious Pamphlets, than a much wiser man had been able.[36]

As late as the 1670s Clarendon recalls that the spirit of Martin Marprelate was revived in the civil war pamphlets:

> Thom. Nashe was as well known an Author in those days, as Martin, who with Pamphlets of the same kind, and size, with the same pert Bufoonry, and

34. Claude J. Summers, "Herrick, Vaughan, and the Poetry of Anglican Survivalism," in *New Perspectives on the Seventeenth-Century English Religious Lyric*, ed. John R. Roberts (Columbia: University of Missouri Press, 1994), 57. The *OED* gives as the source of the word *plunder* a Dutch word for "household things," but the German verb *plündern* is more likely.

35. Corns, *Uncloistered Virtue*, 41, 204.

36. *The Life of Mr. Rich. Hooker, The Author of those Learned Books of the Laws of Ecclesiastical Polity* (London: Rich. Marriott, 1665), 88–89; *Wing* W 670.

with more salt and cleanliness, rendered that libellous, and seditious crew so contemptible, ridiculous, and odious, that in short time they vanished, and were no more heard of.[37]

Thomas Nashe, himself as learned as the Puritans, could seldom resist a new word. His enemy, Richard Lichfield, registers the point with his splendid invective sobriquet for Nashe: "that right glossomachicall Thomas," and again, "pantophainoudendeconticall Puppie." In this case, the new word is *caualiero*—"cavalier" in its pre-naturalization form. In one "Pasquill" pamphlet, the cavalier is set up as a patriot who breaks his staff upon Martin's face. In another, Pasquill is identified as the "renowned Caualiero" recently returned from foreign parts to scourge the Martinist "scabbe that is bredde in England." In a third, he predicts that the bishops whom he has come to defend shall see him "prick it and praunce it like a Caualiero that hath learned to manage Armes."[38] This, then, is the cavalier as heroic champion.

Yet the cavalier is by no means always an heroic champion in Nashe's writing. In *The Unfortunate Traveller*, Jack Wilton uses the term with familiar assurance in the following splendid passage when Jack is about to play his mischievous prank on "Monsieur Capitano." Jack tells him

> Perhaps (quoth I) you may haue some fewe greasie Caualiers that will seeke to disswade you from it, and they will not sticke to stand on their three halfe penny honour, swearing and staring that a man were better be a hangman than an Intelligencer . . . [but such] beggarly contemners of wit are huge burly bond Butchers like Aiax, good for nothing but to strike right downe blowes on a wedge with a cleauing beetle, or stand hammering all day vpon barres of yron.[39]

It is surely more than coincidence that Goodwin's *Anti-Cavalierism* speaks of "that Butcherly brood of Cavaliering incendiaries who are now hammering England." In *Christs Teares Over Ierusalem* (1593), which Puritan clergy must have carefully studied, Nashe places *cavalier* in another rich and suggestive context. It is a passage amplifying "vaine glory" and describes a degenerate cavalier:

---

37. *Animadversions Upon a Book Intituled, Fanaticism Fanatically Imputed to the Catholic Church, by Dr. Stillingfleet, And the Imputation Refuted and Retorted by S.C.* (London: R. Royston, 1673), 2–4; *Wing* C 4414.

38. [Richard Lichfield], *The Trimming of Thomas Nashe Gentleman* (London: Philip Scarlet, 1597) B2v; *STC* 12906. *The First parte of Pasquils Apologie* (1590) in R. B. McKerrow, ed., *The Works of Thomas Nashe*, 6 vols. (1904–1910; reprint, Oxford: Basil Blackwell, 1966), 1:136. *A Countercuffe* (1589), McKerrow, 1:51; *The returne of the renowned Caualiero Pasquill* (1590), 1:69. In *The returne*, 102, is another instance of "caualiero" as an honorable, knightly figure.

39. *The Vnfortunate Traveller*, in *Works of Nashe*, ed. McKerrow, 5:220.

Hee that taketh a glory to weare a huge head of hayre like Absalom. He that taketh a glory in the glystring of his apparraile and his perfumes, and thinks euery one that sees him or smels to him, should be in loue with him. Hee that taketh a glory to bring an othe out with a grace, to tell of hys cosonages, his surfettings, his drunkennes and whoredomes. Hee that (to be counted a Caualeir, & a resolute braue man) cares not what mischiefe he doe, whom he quarrels with, kils or stabbes.

Such was Pausanias that kild Phillip of Macedon, onlie for fame or vaine-glory.[40]

Here, in the works of Nashe, actual and attributed, where *cavalier* is used with such rich ambivalence, is probably the prime source for the political construction of the term *cavalier* by the godly preachers of the 1640s, arising from their study of the enemy's triumph in the previous great paper skirmish. They achieved some success with it, as we have seen, even if the enemy had the last laugh once again.

Appendix

Selected Dictionaries

William Thomas. *Principal Rvles of the Italian Grammer, with a dictionary for the better vnderstanding of Boccace, Petrarcha, and Dante.* London, 1550. *STC* 24020: cavalier = horseman, adding that "cavaliere" can mean "sylke worme."

Richard Percyvall. *Bibliotheca Hispanica.* London, 1591, 1599, 1623.

Riders Dictionarie, Corrected and Augmented. London, 1640. *STC* 19619: all editions give the sense of "horseman."

John Florio. *A Worlde of Wordes.* London, 1598. *STC* 11098: adds to the "horseman" definition that "Cavagliere" = "silke worme," lobster, and military fortification.

———. *Queen Anna's New World of Words or Dictionarie of the Italian and English Tongues.* London, 1611. *STC* 11099: adds that "cauagliére di scúdo" = "a poore beggerly knight that hath nothing but his sword and cloake." "Cauagliére della spáda guináta" = "a knight of the drawen sword, that an excellent whoremonger or notable wencher."

John Bullokar. *An English Expositor; Teaching the Interpretation of the hardest words in our Language.* London, 1656. *Wing* B 5430: This edition, augmented by "W. S.," gives: "Cavallier. A horseman, or one that serveth in the warrs on horseback; but of late become a nick-name, or term, by way of reproach, by some given and cast upon such as by siding

---

40. London: Iames Roberts, 1593, 54v; *STC* 18366; in *Works of Nashe*, ed. McKerrow, 2:108–9.

and taking part with the King, have been suspected and censured, of disaffection to the Parliament." Editions of 1616, 1621, and 1641 have no entry for the word.

Henry Cockerham. *The English Dictionarie: or, an Interpreter of hard English Words*. London, 1647. *Wing* C 4865: no entry; likewise, the 1623 edition; *STC* 5461a: no entry.

Thomas Blount. *Glossographia: or, a Dictionary Interpreting all such Hard Words whether Hebrew, Greek, Latin, Italian, Spanish, French, Teutonic, Belgick, British or Saxon; as are now used in our refined English Tongue*. London, 1656. *Wing* B 3334: "a Knight or Gentlemen, serving on horseback, a man of arms."

Edward Phillips. *The New World of English Words: or, a General Dictionary*. London, 1658. *Wing* P 2068: "Cavalier, a brave man, a Knight, or Gentleman, serving on Hors-back from the Italian Cavallo."

Tom Cain

"A Sad Intestine Warr"

Mildmay Fane and the Poetry of Civil Strife

In 1648, shortly before the execution of Charles I, Mildmay Fane, second earl of Westmorland, had a slim collection of his poems printed at his own expense, to be circulated privately under the title of *Otia Sacra*. It was not unusual for a peer to write verses or even plays (as Fane also did in the 1640s), but it was unprecedented to publish them, even in this restricted form. Fane's radical decision, in which he was encouraged by his friend and at this date pensioner, Robert Herrick, was almost certainly prompted by his enforced retirement from the world of political action at the very outset of the civil war. Fane had been one of the first active Royalist peers to be captured, and after his release in 1644 he had remained publicly disengaged from the conflict. His book must have been sent out to friends late in 1648—perhaps even later. It offered a semipublic justification for Fane's retirement, as well as a peaceful gesture of resistance to a new order in which he had no obvious place. But Fane also left a much larger body of more private, hitherto largely unpublished verse and prose, in which he is more open about his political attitudes, and which covers a longer period than *Otia Sacra*—covers in fact his whole writing life, from 1621, when he was 19, to 1665, a few months before his death.[1]

1. The poems of Fulke Greville, Lord Brooke, and of Edward, Lord Herbert of Cherbury, were published posthumously. Fane's account books suggest the date of publication of *Otia Sacra* and give details of payments to Herrick: entries "for the book" run from February 21, 1648, to February 1649, but large payments cease on July 21, 1648. They total £130. The title was thus probably conceived (and the two title pages engraved by Marshall) before the beginning of the second civil war, but the book may not have been ready for distribution until August 1648 or later. Payments to Herrick begin in November 1647 and continue until August 1660. See Northamptonshire Records Office, MS. Westmorland (A) Misc. vol. 7.

The political developments of the 1640s and 1650s in England gave a fresh impetus to the well-rehearsed classical and humanist debate between *otium* and *negotium*. Even before the oath of "engagement" to the authority of the new government was demanded of men like Fane in October 1649, the question of what duty was owed to the de facto power had presented itself in obvious ways. Increasingly, as both sides failed—in the view of such moderates as Fane—to make the compromises needed for lasting peace, retirement from public life became once more a defensible alternative to the call of public duty, as it had become for Montaigne in the midst of the French civil wars. Fane was one of the first English writers to confront this issue anew. In the next few years he was to be followed into such retirement, and into poetic celebration of it, by many men, among them his brother-in-law, the Lord General Fairfax, and with him Andrew Marvell, tutor to Fairfax's daughter. Throughout the 1650s a growing number of writers—Waller, Vaughan, Cowley, Walton, and Fane's friends Cotton and Benlowes prominent among them—found that the theme of pastoral retirement offered a means of articulating their political predicament. Political philosophers were also taking up the issue in a necessarily more explicit way. Hobbes, who was working on *Leviathan* in the late 1640s, was, as Quentin Skinner and others have shown, only one of a group of English theorists who were forced by the events of the 1640s to confront the questions of the rights of conquest, and of obligation to the de facto power. Fane was interested in political philosophy: he translated part of a treatise on *The Art of well governing a people* by Fulvius Pacianus in the 1650s, and knew (or knew of) *Leviathan* soon after it was published. He would have found much of *Leviathan* congenial, not just because it dealt so cogently with the problems of loyalty and obligation that he had experienced, but because he shared a strong temperamental attachment to peace and order. Hobbes was later to claim that his arguments had "framed the minds of a thousand gentlemen to a conscientious obedience to present government, which otherwise would have wavered in that point." Fane had already made such a decision once when he subscribed to the Covenant in 1644, but Hobbes's defense of those who had taken the Covenant and the Oath of Engagement, and thus saved their estates, and accepted the de facto power, must have been welcome, and may have helped reconcile Fane to the greater accommodation demanded after the king's execution.[2]

2. For the theme of retirement in poetry at this time, see James Loxley, *Royalism and Poetry in the English Civil Wars* (London: Macmillan, 1997), 192–241, and Annabel Patterson, *Pastoral and Ideology* (Oxford: Oxford University Press, 1988), especially 160–63.

The question of engagement, then, both in the sense of *negotium*, engagement with public affairs, and in the sense of allegiance that it carried in and after 1649, provides the context in which much of Fane's manuscript poetry was written, and in which *Otia Sacra* was published. The latter's contents seem at first surprisingly apolitical for a book published in 1648, the first part a Herbertian "offering with my Lord," followed by a short secular collection making few explicit references to the war. In fact the war is present throughout: Sometimes it is explicit, as in the intrusion into the devotional poems "To Prince Charles, in Aprill, 1648. Upon the hopes of his Return" (86), placed significantly between two Easter poems, or in references to the "Fury . . . Rage / Or Madness" of the age ("A Carroll," 29). More often it is implicit, as in the emphasis on the lessons of humiliation, patience, and repentance; in the recurrent theme of man's first (and lasting) disobedience; in the frequent recourse to imagery of battle, defeat, and imprisonment; in imagery of clouds, storm, and the prospect of fair weather to come; and, not least, in the celebration of retirement and the praise of the country life for which *Otia Sacra* is best known.[3]

The seemingly innocent title itself offers one of the most significant references to contemporary affairs, drawing attention to, and obliquely justifying, Fane's enforced withdrawal from the first civil war, and his detachment from the second one of May to August 1648. In the context of those months the title was fraught with meaning. In a general way *otia* (the plural of "peace" or "leisure") invokes all of the old humanist debate, from Petrarch to Milton, but the primary reference is undoubtedly to Virgil's *First Eclogue,* itself a poem about withdrawal from civil war, from which Fane takes the line used on his first title page, "Deus nobis haec Otia fecit" ("God made this peace for us"). Even if it was conceived during the period of uneasy peace in 1647 and early 1648, when army, Parliament, Scots, and defeated Royalists all watched each other with deep and mutual suspicion,

---

Both offer a corrective to the simpler view taken by Maren-Sofie Røstvig, *The Happy Man* (Oslo: Akademisk Forlag; Oxford: Basil Blackwell, 1954), and often followed by later scholars. For the political debate, see especially Quentin Skinner, "Conquest and Consent: Thomas Hobbes and the Engagement Controversy," in *The Interregnum: The Quest for Settlement, 1646–1660,* ed. G. E. Aylmer (London: Macmillan, 1972), 79–98. The translation of Pacianus "by M[ildmay] W[estmorland] 165[-]" is British Library MS. Add. 34,251. Hobbes, *Leviathan,* ed. C. B. Macpherson (Harmondsworth: Penguin Books, 1981), 719–20 (subsequently cited in the text), and *Six Lessons to the Professors of the Mathematics* in *The English Works of Thomas Hobbes,* ed. E. W. Molesworth (London: John Bohn, 1839–1845), 7:335–36. For Fane's knowledge of *Leviathan,* see his poem to Cleveland in Harvard fMS. Eng. 645, 107.

3. For the intrusion of the poem to Prince Charles, and an argument for *Otia Sacra* as part of a Cavalier "poetics of activism," see Loxley, *Royalism and Poetry,* 223–28.

this Virgilian reference would have seemed disingenuous if taken at face value. But *nobis* does not refer to the wider commonwealth. Virgil's *otium* was a private, pastoral peace found by Tityrus in the midst of civil strife from which he had been helped by "a god" to withdraw to his farm. *Otium,* moreover, had been used by Horace, Cicero, and others to mean "peace," not just in this sense of a blessed and leisurely tranquility, but as the opposite of war, while an *otiosus* was not just a man at leisure, but a noncombatant, a "civilian." Fane's use of it thus points to his inactivity as an honorable, God-given disengagement (but hence, in Hobbes's terms, an acceptance of the de facto power).[4]

Sacra is similarly suggestive, raising questions of motive only to scotch them. Its primary meaning is simply "holy," a usage that, in Fane's providential view, confirms the idea that his retirement is, like that of Tityrus, given by God. Ovid had also used *sacra* (as he had *otia*), to signify "poems," "things sacred" to the Muses, as Fane's were to God.[5] *Sacra*, however, was also commonly used to mean "cursed" or "execrable," as, again, by Fane's favorite Latin poet, Horace. Having thus noted the possibility of *otia sacra* meaning "fruits of a disgraceful retirement," though, Fane's elite audience might have recalled Horace's most powerful use of *sacer* in *Satires* 2.3.179–81, where the "cursed" man is one who is tempted not by retirement, but by its worldly opposite, glory: it is the man who turns his back on *otium* to take office who is *intestabilis* and *sacer*. Fane's *sacra* thus becomes, like *otia,* both challenging and self-justificatory about his retirement.

The suggestion that retirement needs justification is confronted again in the modified use of the *First Eclogue* for the title page of the secular part of *Otia Sacra*. Here, Virgil's "lentus in umbra" ("at ease in the shade") is taken from the end of line 4 of the *Eclogue,* significantly altered, and added to line 2, "sylvestrem tenui musam meditaris avena" ("you practice the woodland muse on a slender pipe"), so that the title page reads "*tutus* in Umbra / Sylvestram tenui Musam meditatus avena." The substitution of *tutus* ("safe") for *lentus* (which could also mean "lazy") is not countenanced by any variants of Virgil's text. It is deliberately challenging. Rather than avoiding the accusation that he has opted for safety in place of duty, loyalty, or glory, Fane is again asserting, in part through the contents of his collection, and in part by annexing the *First Eclogue* and with it the whole pastoral tradition of irenic retirement, that

4. See, for example, Horace *Odes* 2.16.5: "otium bello furiosa Thrace [rogat]"; cf. *Odes* 4.15.18. Cicero, *Epistulae ad Familiares* 9.6.3: "crudeliter enim otiosis minabantur." For a survey of the humanist debate, see Brian Vickers, "Leisure and Idleness in the Renaissance: The Ambivalence of Otium," *Renaissance Studies* 4 (1990): 1–37, 107–54.
5. See *Tristia* 4.10.19, "caelestia sacra"; and 2.224, "otia nostra."

his choice is an honorable one, divinely sanctioned and of impeccable classical pedigree.[6]

Fane is safe, but not at lazy ease in his retirement. It seems likely that in 1648 he saw himself in the predicament that Hobbes was about to describe, in which the defeat of the old order, which can no longer offer the protection that has been its side of the contract, leaves "the Commonwealth DISSOLVED, and every man at liberty to protecte himselfe by such courses as his own discretion shall suggest unto him" (*Leviathan*, 375). For Hobbes, this leaves the way open to honorable submission to the conquering power, which *can* offer protection. Fane had accepted this in 1644 when he took the Covenant, and considered doing so again a decade later when he conditionally welcomed Cromwell's appointment as Protector; but in 1648 the uncertainty of the situation, and his own divided loyalties, would have made this second step far less clear. The power to which he had submitted when he subscribed to the Covenant, and thus had "his life and corporall Libertie given him, on condition to be Subject to the Victor" (*Leviathan*, 273), had still been that of *king* and Parliament. The ascendancy of the army had changed that by 1648, but it left a contractual void in which retirement to the petty principality of Apethorpe, there patiently to await events, must have seemed the right way to "protecte himselfe." Thus it is that the theme of "Blest Privacie, Happy Retreat" ("My Countrey Audit," 8), should combine in *Otia Sacra* with religious meditation on the need to accept humiliation, on human disobedience and its consequences, hopeful glances at the exiled Prince Charles, and the exploration, as the title of one poem puts it, of "How to ride out a Storm" (161) until Fane could again serve king and Parliament. This emphasis on *otium* as a temporary but honorable solution is spelled out in "To my Gracious God" (121), which addresses the question of his leisure directly, as if anticipating charges of what Horace calls *inertia*:

> Retir'd into a Calm of Leisure, Led
> By Providence thus: grant me busied
> Here after for My King and Countreys good,
> The Church and State where I took Livelihood:
> That in my Calling I may never falter,
> But hew wood and draw water for thine Altar.

Herrick's poem encouraging publication supports the view that the production of *Otia Sacra* was in part a way of justifying what could have

---

6. The implications of the substitution are also discussed by Patterson (*Pastoral and Ideology*, 162), relating it to a long "process of interpretation" of the *Eclogues*.

seemed like ignoble, head-down *otium*, by giving Fane a new role as author. Writing, and still more publishing, was a form of *negotium*, of engagement with issues both immediate and immutable. "To the right Honourable Mildmay, Earle of Westmorland" opens with an emphasis on Fane's dual status as peer and poet:

> You are a Lord, an earle, nay more, a Man,
> Who writes sweet Numbers well as any can:
> If so, why then are not These Verses hurld,
> Like *Sybels* Leaves, throughout the ample world?

In the ascending hierarchy of the first line, it is the "Man, / Who writes sweet Numbers" who takes precedence, while in the closing lines of the poem Horace, champion of retirement for both Fane and Herrick, is invoked to warn of the dangers of a withdrawal that is not *seen* to be virtuous:

> *Vertue conceal'd* (with *Horace* you'l confesse)
> *Differs not much from drowzie slothfulnesse.*

In Horace's *Ode* 4.9, it is the lack of a poet to praise them that has con-demned heroes to the long night of oblivion: in Fane's case the great man can rescue himself from the charge of *inertia* ("drowzie slothfulnesse"), the worst kind of *otium*, by his own verse.

Herrick's poem implies that he knew Fane's work in manuscript. Five volumes of "These Verses" survive, and they contained by the late 1640s much more than the 130 or so poems selected for *Otia Sacra*. Fane's extant English verse in manuscript constitutes a corpus of over 560 poems, varying in length from two-line epigrams to satires or meditations of over two hundred lines, and, very unusually, emblem poems with emblems drawn by the author. Only 90 were published in *Otia Sacra*, together with another 40 English poems from another manuscript book (or books) now lost. In considering Fane's view of the war and its aftermath, therefore, we must add to those published in 1648 more than 470 English poems (plus about 300 in Latin), many of them more forthright than those in *Otia Sacra*, and, since they are often dated, showing significant shifts in attitude dictated by the state of affairs during the war and in the new Commonwealth. One book, in the Houghton Library at Harvard (fMS. Eng. 645, hereafter "Harvard MS"), contains dated poems covering the period 1637–1657. Another three books, long thought lost, are still in the possession of a branch of Fane's family, at Fulbeck Hall, Lincolnshire, originally the home of Mildmay's brother Francis. Of these, the two largest contain, with the Harvard MS, the bulk of the extant poetry: a handsome 12 × 16″ volume (hereafter *"Poems, 1623–1650"*) contains dated poems from those years, together with Fane's Latin *Vita Authoris*, while a second, slightly smaller (7.5 × 11.5″) volume (hereafter *"Poems, 1649–1665"*) collects poems from the last sixteen years of Fane's life. All three of these Fulbeck manuscripts, and a large proportion of the Harvard MS, are entirely in Fane's hand, and almost exclusively devoted to his own work. A fifth manuscript book, containing political prose of great interest together with sixteen more poems by Fane, is in the Westmorland Collection at Northamptonshire Records Office (MS. Westmorland (A) 6.vi.1, hereafter "Northamptonshire MS"). This is largely devoted to the 1640s, but, unlike the other books, also contains work in different hands and by other writers.[7]

Most readers of *Otia Sacra* would recognize a certain generosity in Herrick's judgment that Fane "writes sweet numbers well as any can." Nevertheless, this much larger body of unpublished poetry demands more attention from "the ample world" than *Otia Sacra* has received. It charts the reactions to a period of turmoil unparalleled in England of a conservative but cultivated, thoughtful, and irenic man placed by birth close to the center of political events, but driven by them, and by temperament, towards the periphery. The fact that many of the poems were private, never intended for wide circulation (if for any circulation at all) is itself important.[8] Taken together with his plays and the prose of

7. For the Harvard MS, see the articles by Eleanor Withington, "The 'Fugitive Poetry' of Mildmay Fane," *Harvard Library Bulletin* 9 (1955): 61–78, and "Mildmay Fane's Political Satire," *Harvard Library Bulletin* 11 (1957): 40–64. The Fulbeck MSS have been briefly treated by Gerald W. Morton, *A Biography of Mildmay Fane, Second Earl of Westmorland (1601–1666): The Unknown Cavalier* (Lewiston: Edwin Mellen Press, 1990), 69–96, 117–28; and T. G. S. Cain, "Robert Herrick, Mildmay Fane, and Sir Simeon Steward," *English Literary Renaissance* 15 (1985): 312–17 (largely dealing with the earliest manuscript, a small book covering the period 1621–1635). For the Northamptonshire MS, see T. G. S. Cain, "Herrick's 'Christmas Carol': A New Poem, and Its Implications for Patronage," forthcoming in *English Literary Renaissance* 29 (1999). I am very grateful to Mary Fry for her hospitality and patience in allowing me access to the Fulbeck manuscripts; to Tom Wayman, Claire Chambers, and James Reeson for their assistance; and to the Earl of Westmorland and Trustees of the Apethorpe Settlement (MSS) for permission to quote from manuscripts in the Westmorland collection at Northamptonshire Records Office.

8. There is little evidence for the circulation of Fane's manuscript poetry. I have found only one copy of a poem sent to a friend (probably Sir Edward Harley or the Earl of Clare), a short Latin poem of 1662, on the arrival of Queen Katherine, now in the Portland Collection, Nottingham University Library (PwV 217). There is no evidence that the manuscript books were lent, though such was not unusual: see

the Northamptonshire MS, the manuscripts offer a unique opportunity to follow the fluctuating responses elicited by the rapidly changing situation. At times, moreover, Fane's struggle to find rhetorical strategies to come to terms with the overturning of the socio-political world of which he was one of the most privileged inheritors, and with the nature of his obligations to the new order, inspires a poetry more engaged and engaging than the rather guarded, tepid verse of *Otia Sacra*.

The poetry is the more interesting because Fane was never a straight-forward Royalist. The manuscripts, and the external evidence, suggest that his commitment to monarchic government was complicated by an equally strong belief in the role of Parliament and (as he firmly told the king in 1643) "the knowne Lawes of the land (noe Arbittrary ones)." It was complicated too by suspicion of Laudian innovations; by mistrust of the king's advisers; by local friendships; by family ties; by financial interests; and, increasingly, by a strong desire for national peace and reconciliation. Because the poems reflect these factors over a number of years, and be-cause the external evidence is fragmentary and conflicting, it is more than usually possible for the literary or political historian to inscribe Fane in his or her own image. The most plausible view of him is as a moderate Puritan loyalist, critical of Charles's Personal Rule, committed to parliamentary government and the English Common Law, and dragged unhappily into conflict on the side of a monarch whom he regarded as easily misled. This version would emphasize his education at the Puritan Emmanuel College (a family concern, founded by his great-grandfather Sir Walter Mildmay, whose magnificent tomb at Apethorpe by Maximilian Colt must have served as a constant reminder of the source of his first name and the family's wealth), his hostility to Strafford, his memorandum of 1643 to the king urging his return to London to make peace, and his continuing friendship with such Parliamentarian activists as Sir Robert Harley and Sir William Armyne, the first of whom lent him money to help pay his fine for delinquency.[9] He can, with almost equal plausibility, be seen as a conservative, Anglican Royalist, captured while fighting for Charles, highly critical of Cromwell and Fairfax, distraught at the king's execution, and shown in his later verse to be waiting, and perhaps working, for the restoration of the monarchy. The truth is that he was at different times between the 1630s and 1660s all of these, and that part of the unique

---

Harold Love, *Scribal Publication in Seventeenth-Century England* (Oxford: Clarendon Press, 1993), 70–72.

9. Harley lent Fane £200 "borrowed to pay my fine in part": MS. Westmorland (A) Misc. vol. 7 (August 1644).

interest of his manuscript poetry is the way in which it charts his changes of attitude. Early on, his loyalty was far from precluding criticism of king and councilors, while later his hostility to the rebels did not shut off the possibility of accepting defeat and compromise for the sake of a peaceful commonwealth. Selective quotation could confirm one of a whole range of positions, but these manuscripts show him not as a time server, but as a man responding to rapidly changing political events. The journeys of Fane's brother-in-law Fairfax, or of his neighbor at Longthorpe, Oliver St. John, show how complex are personal political loyalties in this period. Another brother-in-law, John Holles, earl of Clare, is probably the closest to Fane in his attitudes. Lucy Hutchinson says dismissively that he was "very often of both parties, and, I think, never advantaged either." Clare did indeed change sides like a tennis ball, but Clarendon saw him as "a man of honour and of courage," guided by his conscience through a rapidly changing political landscape.[10]

Although Charles stood in 1635 as godfather to his eldest son, Fane was critical of the way the king conducted government during the 1630s. He was not a regular courtier, though his house at Apethorpe was visited more than once by the king, as it had been by his father (James had been introduced to Francis Villiers there, and his statue still stood, in Fane's time, in the courtyard). Fane had reservations about ship money, reservations that can hardly have been assuaged when he and his mother were fined the huge sum of £19,000 under the revived forest laws. Documented contact with the court in the late 1630s is all critical: the dowager countess wrote to Secretary Windebank in 1639 arguing wisely against any military action against the Scots, who knew "how uncertainly a war will be maintained which is to be maintained out of prerogative, imposition, and voluntary contributions." In 1640 Mildmay himself wrote to his cousin Sir Harry Vane the elder, Secretary of State and still at this time one of the king's trusted inner circle, complaining at his treatment by Charles in the matter of the gift of a disputed clerical living. He warns that Charles's refusal "to be informed is of dangerous consequence" and concludes angrily:

> My house has ever been obedient without dispute to his Majesty's commands and unwilling to contend with him; yet when we have any request to him, we

10. For Clare, see *Memoirs of the Life of Colonel Hutchinson Written by His Widow Lucy*, Everyman ed. (London: J. M. Dent, n.d.), 93; Clarendon, *History of the Rebellion and Civil War in England*, ed. W. Dunn Macray, 6 vols. (Oxford: Clarendon Press, 1888) 3:183 [7:187 in Clarendon's original division]. Clare was a trustee of Fane's will in 1665; like many of his contemporaries, he was a "passionate moderate," the oxymoron Donald Friedman uses to describe Fane; see *Otia Sacra* (Delmar, N.Y.: Scholars' Facsimiles and Reprints, 1975), vii.

find no more favour than his absolute opposers do. God send that way of his to work him no inconvenience.[11]

In 1640, this was the language of not-so-discreet threat rather than Cavalier loyalty, and it fits well with his attitude to Strafford's attainder, which he saw as a punishment for the latter's advice exactly a year earlier that the king should dissolve the Short Parliament, the calling of which to end the Personal Rule Fane had greatly welcomed.[12] His play *Candy Restored* celebrated in 1640 the brief hopes of a new partnership between king, Lords, and Commons. For him, as for many political Englishmen, the two houses, of both of which he had been a member, were the proper councilors of the king, through whom only he could make laws or raise taxes. Later, under house arrest in London, Fane wrote of how Parliament had been forced to take extra powers that would normally have been illegal so that

> one man by the seducement of a few evil Counsailers may not work his own ruine and withall become the overthrow of what is committed to his charge . . . to witt a Kingedome frutefull in more truly loyall & faithfull harts to administer advice to him for his own & Peoples good, & those too now by his own authorety (as at first they were convend) soe sitting still in Parlement for his Honor the good & preservation of both.
>
> For a King as God's substitute & answerable to Him for the good protection & safety of the People committed to his charge ought by the Counsaile (of such of those people as on behalf of the rest were soe by Himselfe & the Law of the land caused to meet) to be directed for the Welfare of all; & neither to encline to the seducement of His own privat will & affections which may as he is a man entitle Him to failings, nor yet to Those Dalila respects may deminish together with His own the strength & happiness of his Dominions.[13]

Fairfax could easily have subscribed to this. Though written late in 1643, it demonstrates that Fane's choice of sides in 1642 was not a foregone conclusion. He may in fact have been an unwilling participant from the very outset of the troubles: though he eventually obeyed the summons to join the king at York in 1639 for the first Scots campaign, he at first replied that he was ill. In 1640 he again apologized, this time due to the

11. For the fine, see Phillip A. J. Pettit, *The Royal Forests of Northamptonshire* (Gateshead: Northamptonshire Record Society, vol. 23, 1968), 87–88. This was one of the largest of all sums levied under this blatantly opportunist imposition, though it was commuted to a much smaller fine; see Pettit, *Royal Forests*, 92, and MS W (A) 4.7.3. For the countess's letter, see *Calendar of State Papers, Domestic Series of the Reign of Charles I*, ed. William Douglas Hamilton et al. (London: Longman & Co., 1873) [hereafter *CSPD*] May 6, 1639, 123–24. For Fane's letter, see *CSPD, 1639–1640*, 597, March 30, 1640.

12. See Fane, *Vita Authoris*, in *Poems, 1623–1650*, 6, and the Latin "Elogium Strafordianum" (ibid., 99).

13. Passage headed "Query" in Northamptonshire MS (ff. not numbered).

death of his mother, but he was in York by September, with his wife. In February 1642, as a representative of the House of Lords, he delivered the important "Propositions concerning the Adventure for Ireland" to Charles at Canterbury, and reported the king's consent on February 24, "almost the last joint act of King and Parliament." As war came closer, he signaled his choice of sides on April 5 by asking for his dissent to be recorded before a motion was put that the Commons's Declaration of Grievances and Remedies (a forerunner of the Nineteen Propositions) be supported by the Lords. He left London in late April and was not to sit in the Lords again until May 1660. Fane joined the king at York for the third time in four years in May. His conflicting allegiances are symbolically attested by the fact that the countess, again accompanying him, stayed with her sister, Lady Fairfax. "My lady Westmoreland," wrote Fairfax, "will be at Appleton to-morrow at night and stay two nights there. Her chief intention of coming was to see her sister, and for that time it will be not much chargeable." This visit took place just over a week after Fairfax had forced on the angry king (who tried to ride him down) the petition from the Yorkshire gentry urging reconciliation with Parliament.[14]

Fane's war was, perhaps to his relief, short. He began it as a commissioner of array in Northamptonshire, a strongly Parliamentarian county. He then accepted

> the charge of a commander of cavalry. . . . Thereafter, so that he might all the less blame the varied fortunes of war, he was captured by a party of the enemy rejoicing in the name of dragoons and in number about thirty before the battle had its successful outcome, and was hauled off to the Parliament which was left and consigned to the security of the Tower.[15]

14. See *CSPD 1638–1639*, 467, February 15, 1639; *Historical Manuscripts Commission* [hereafter *HMC*], *Report on the Manuscripts of The Duke of Buccleuch and Queensbury* (London: HMSO, 1899), 1:279; *HMC, Fourth Report, Appendix*, 295; *Lords Journals*, 4:607b–608a and 700a; C. V. Wedgwood, *The King's War* (London: Collins, 1958), 71; *HMC, Buccleuch*, 1:302; Clarendon, *History*, 2:186 [originally 5:346]; and Fairfax letter from York, June 13, 1642, in *Memorials of the Civil War . . . Forming the Concluding Volumes of the Fairfax Correspondence*, ed. Robert Bell (London: Richard Bentley, 1849), 1:14.

15. "Equitum Centurionis Curam accipit. . . . Posteaquam ut varias Belli Fortunas minus argueret ab Inimicorum Parte draconum nomine gaudente & numero triginte circiter antequam secunde praeliatum fuisset interceptus est & ad illud Parle[men]ti quod relictum erat ductus Turris securitati traditur & Custodiae." Fane, *Vita Authoris*, in *Poems, 1623–1650*, 8. Morton translates the crucial passage as "before their second battle," which is certainly wrong (*Biography of Mildmay Fane*, 36). Clifford Leech is also wrong in saying Fane was imprisoned earlier as a commissioner of array; see *Mildmay Fane's Raguaillo D'Oceano 1640 and Candy Restored 1641*, in Clifford Leech, ed., *Materials for the Study of the Old English Drama* (Louvain, 1938), 15:14. See also Anthony Fletcher, *The Outbreak of the English Civil War* (London: Edward Arnold, 1981), 362, 379, 381.

The first "successful" battle of the war was at Edgehill, on October 23, 1642, claimed as a Royalist victory; but a Parliamentary newsletter states that "the Earle of *Westmerland* is taken at Northampton," twenty-six miles from Edgehill, the news reaching the writer on October 27.[16] Since Fane was taken before a parliamentary committee on October 26 and committed to the Tower the next day, it is likely that his capture was somehow associated with Edgehill, but whether he was intercepted on his way there or back, was operating independently in Northamptonshire, or had become detached from the rest of the Royalist cavalry (who all pursued the enemy away from the field of battle) is not clear.

A long poem dated March 1643 describes Fane guiding a party of citizens around the Tower, where the inmates "Neither heard nor tride . . . linger out a life as if they dide" (*Poems, 1623–1650*, 85–88). While he was in the Tower, his brother Anthony was killed fighting for Parliament, an event that must have made Fane all the more anxious for peace. Despite their opposition, Anthony made Mildmay trustee of the £7,000 he left, £600 of which went to Mildmay himself.[17] It may have helped to pay the fine of £2,000, levied before he was released "upon his Honour unto the . . . Earl of *Manchester,* that he will be a true Prisoner in his [Fane's] House at *St. Bartholomew's.*" There he remained for almost a year, his estates in Kent, Northamptonshire, and elsewhere sequestrated. In November 1643 he wrote a letter and six-page memorandum "from my prison" (his London house) to the king, urging him to return to London and treat with the Parliament. There is wishful—as well as phallic—thinking in the proposition that when Charles returns "Then will both houses swell againe into their first proportion of worthy Members . . . with Reverence to your Majesty's Authoritye." The copy in the Northamptonshire MS is committed to religious reform in particular, and it has a powerful sting in its tail. Not only does Fane remind Charles that Parliament's "Endeavours att first [were] bent onely towards a through Reformation both in Church and state (for there is Nothing here below of that perfection as not to need amendment)," but he adds a defense of Parliament and a forceful reminder of the king's dilemma:

> Soe as the king of kings hath committed these Scepters to your Majestys Charge, soe hath this your kingdome att this tyme impos'd a speciall trust on these your Subjects called together by your Majesty to sitt in *Parliament* and to discharge their dutyes faithfully on its behalfe, By seeking meanes of redresse from

---

16. *Speciall Newes from the Army at Warwick since the Fight* (London: Henry Overton, October 29, 1642), A3r (Thomason Tracts, E124.33).

17. Public Record Office, *Wills Proved in the Prerogative Court of Canterbury,* 131, Cambell.

all such Grievances as it hath groaned under, and findeing wayes whereby to procure its securitye for the future. All which must have Influence from your Royall selfe, Therefore allthough the Noysome vapours of Malignancye rais'd from either partyes Mierye Factionists, have foulded thicke Cloudes of diffidence, and distrust, still shaddow those here from your presence, To which Clime and Horizon you can appeare noe other than sett whilst att this distance—Vouchsafe I beseech you to disperse togeather with such Cloudes of malevolency all difficultyes by entertaining this into your thoughts[:] Warres a Canker devouring kingdomes and people and those destroyed where sitts the king?

Though Charles may sometimes have considered this last point, he can rarely have had it put to him quite so directly by those around him at Oxford.

Fane's petition for the release of his estates is more predictably informed by a similar shift towards the Parliament: God having "discovered to him the danger Church and State were in" he recognizes that "he was formerly seduced. Is now resolved to sacrifice life and fortunes to the real service of King and Parliament, for which he was born. To this end begs to take the Covenant, and be restored to his liberty, and to such part of his fortune as to their wisdom seems fit." In February 1643 he took the Covenant, drafted by the Scottish Presbyterian Alexander Henderson, to whom Fane refers with respect in the Harvard MS (19–20).[18] On Lady Day 1644 (March 25, the old New Year's Day) he wrote "My Far-well to the Court" (*Poems, 1623–1650*, 98; *Otia Sacra*, 160), a politically significant title, couched in terms that are substantially similar to the words of his petition, but which assert political independence, and action rather than *otium*, in a much more forthright way:

> I will strive first in my self to be
> Soe much my Owne, as not to flatter thee
> And then my Cuntries, for whose wellfare still
> My native thoughts, prompt to impress my will
> & that, drawes Action forth wherby to showe
> To whom, & what, & when, & wher I owe
> Not as this Nod, or beck, or winke or glance
> Would dictate & imply to follow chance
> Fortune or Favours ever-turning-wheel
> But to be firme & constant, backt with steel

18. For a summary of the petition, see *Journals of the House of Commons* (London: House of Commons, 1803), 3:401. Fane refers to "this Busnes of more wayght" in an affectionate poem written to Sir William Armyne while Armyne was in Scotland negotiating the English acceptance of the Covenant (*An Ode sent into Scotland for a Frend by sea* 9:br [November]-3-1643, *Poems, 1623–1650*).

And resolutions for to guive the True
God what is his, & Cesar tribute due.

The sentiments of "My Far-well to the Court," and the essentially private, meditative prose passages in the Northamptonshire MS, suggest that this was not a wholly opportunistic change. According to his *Vita*, Fane was "easily brought to change his mind" when he considered both "the harvest of desolation and ruin in which so much horrible slaughter" had taken place, and the king's duplicity and reliance on a "secret" council. During these years his sympathies are not far from those of Parliamentarian peers like Manchester, or of such moderates as Simonds D'Ewes, another friend. "Chloris Complaint" (*Poems, 1623–1650*, 38; *Otia Sacra*, 129), dated in the manuscript July 25, 1644, echoes both the weariness with war and the resolve to serve king and Parliament, having previously "rov'd astray." Date and pseudonym suggest the speaker is Henrietta Maria, who had fled to France on July 14, but again there is wishful thinking in the sentiments expressed, which are much closer to Fane's own than to any she ever contemplated:[19]

> all our Passion's Hate
>> And wher a Mischief may befall
> All Dispositian's turnd to Prodigall
>> Nor is ther for Compassion
> Left any roome (now 'ts out of fashion).

> Befrend me wind, Ile trye the wave
> Though some ther be must sink, yet some 't may save
>> My Calender yet markes out Spring
> Dis-gust may shake; not blast the Blossoming
>> And therfore though I rov'd astray
> 'Tis reconciling Truth points now the way
>> In which I would be thought as farr
> From Variation as the Fixed'st starr
>> But with a Constant shining thence
> Serve King & Cuntry by my Influence.

These winds and waves are not only those that took the queen into exile, but those of the compromise that Fane has just made with a new order that may yet bring peace and compassion, and preserve the spring of his new partial freedom. Most important, echoing the petition, it is the wind

19. Patterson, *Pastoral and Ideology*, 162–63, is thus more reasonable than Loxley allows (*Royalism and Poetry*, 239) in assuming that the speaker is Fane, but the dates are suggestive, and the name was often used as a pseudonym for the queen.

that will help him steer by "reconciling Truth" towards "the real service of King and Parliament, for which he was born."

Fane's tactics eventually worked. He retained enough support in both houses for the Committee for Tendering the Covenant to report that as "he has dealt freely, they should deal freely and nobly with him. As he has suffered much by soldiers, has many children, and was one of the first Lords that took the Covenant, they recommend that he should enjoy three-quarters of his estates, and pay the remainder to the Parliament's use during pleasure of both Houses." This latter may have been further commuted to a fine of £1,000. It was a small sum to retain his estates, and (despite its huge cost in modern terms) no greater a burden than had been imposed on him in the years of the Personal Rule. From August 1644 until 1660 he was free to run his estates, to hunt and fish, to write his poetry of enforced retirement, and to stage private performances of his plays and entertainments. Until the Restoration he held no political office and lived largely on his estates at Apethorpe and Mereworth. He did not live quite so simple a life as Virgil envisaged for Tityrus: apart from Herrick, he supported (or was supported by) a household that in 1650 was still a small court, consisting of his large family, regular visitors, and fifty-nine servants, ranging from Henry Arney, his steward, and Foster, his chaplain, to the "foule wench." He and the countess each had a gentleman usher; there was a "gent of my chamber," a "gent of the horses," a barber, falconer, clerk of the Kitchen, and so on. Servants' wages came to over £200 per year, and about the same was spent on wine, while there were twenty-six horses in the stables. Occasionally he paid one or more trumpeters. Fane estimated his household expenses, excluding wages, at £2,468 a year. This was a special kind of rural retirement, financed with difficulty by his estates, and leavened by regular visits to his "great house" in London and occasional fishing trips "by sea in my vessel."[20]

Not all the poetry of these years deals explicitly with the civil wars: Fane's Puritan Anglicanism and his classical (and Herrickian) commitment to retirement and friendship are prominent themes in the unpublished manuscripts as much as in *Otia Sacra*. The war is never far away, however: these peaceful themes are, after all, familiar Cavalier strategies when, as Herrick puts it, "The bad season makes the poet sad." Fane's

20. MS Westmorland (A) Misc. vol. 15, f. 80r, and Misc. vol. 7 (March 1648/9). Lawrence Stone notes that he had in 1650 "contracted to pay his sister £5,000 and his six daughters £5,000 each, making £35,000 in all charged on an estate of about £5,500 a year" (*The Crisis of the Aristocracy, 1558–1641* [Oxford: Clarendon Press, 1965], 213).

use of them, in fact, is often explicitly as a response to the civil war, as in
the last verse of "Friendship's Salamander" (Harvard MS, 128), a poem
written "Whilst all the world is on a flame":

> Then though the thundring Canons roar
> The Trumpetts sound & Coulers fly,
> I am stil wher I was before,
> Much more in love with amity
> Whose Trophy I would raise as soon
> As others horse doe & Dragoon.

This, addressed to the earl of Exeter, a neighbor at Burghley, is typical both
in its irenic tone and in the explicitness with which the Horatian theme is
related to the contemporary turmoil. Fane had, we should recall, actually
raised a troop of horse; he had been captured by a troop of dragoons; and
he had probably heard the cannons roar at Edgehill, where five thousand
men were said to have been killed. The choice between stoical amity
and the burning world beyond it was a very real one.

Similarly self-aware as his response to rebellion, war, defeat, and the
prospect of peace and possibly restoration is Fane's recurrent paired
imagery of tempest and haven, captivity and deliverance, dark night and
bright sun. This too is often explicitly political, as in the opening verse of
"Post Tenebras Lux: Apres La Pluis Le Beau Temps":

> After a Dark & Dismall night
> The Sun arising in his Might
> So disipates Those Clouds of Tears
>   For His Decease
> As Clarefies again our Spheres
>   With hopes of Peace
> After a sad Intestine warr
>   Restoring His Succeeding Star.

The rising sun, it rapidly becomes clear, is Charles II; the clouds, the tears
shed for his father (the "deceased" sun); the "Dark & Dismall night," the
sequence of his overthrow and death, as the next verse confirms:

> It was no slight Dew or small Raine
> Showrd for the loss of Soveraign
> But a whol Cataract to destroy
>   At once our Joy
> And sinke our Barkes, til now at last
>   The Tempest past

> We may enioy again faier weather
> When Clouds pack all away together.[21]

In the light of such poems as this, it is not difficult to locate the political resonances of the images of storm and darkness, and sunlight and good weather when they occur, as they do with great frequency, in less politically overt contexts.

The longest of Fane's poems is, however, more plainly and directly political. "The Times Steerage" (*Poems, 1623–1650*, 32–35) is dated July 1643, written at roughly the same time as the first clear Royalist victories of the war at Adwalton Moor and Roundway Down. Fane, under house arrest in London, does not see military victory as a solution. As in "Chloris Complaint," he uses the image of a ship driven by the wind, emphasizing the providential character of the war (and betraying his own sense of helplessness). This wind, however, drives the ships in different directions, both of which he damns:

> Like Ships by the same wind favour'd, yet can stear
> A severall Course; soe now the Cavallier
> And the Bowle-Noddled-Crue pretend They fight
> Both that Religion & the lawes have right
> For Liberty tis doubtless thats their own
> Wherby all Property & safety's gon.

The idea raised at about the same time in the Northamptonshire MS of the king as liable to "seducement of His own privat will & affections" by "evil Counsailers" because he is merely a man also recurs:

> Our Gratious King
> Good in Himself, but ther's an other thing
> He is a Man, may not's affections cleav
> To be seduc't. Had not an Adam Eve?

But, though the opening lines suggest an even-handed rejection of both sides, and though Fane's analysis admits that Charles and his advisers have made mistakes, the greatest blame falls on those in Parliament who plot to limit the king's power and "bring new customs in / To Church and State." They have forced the king to leave London, and betrayed their role as loyal advisers. The king has left

21. *Poems, 1649–1665*, 92.

> Cause they left t'express
> The Counslers parts, and with commanding pride
> Petitions humbly not to be denide
> . . . .
> Who in their regencies admit noe peers
> But like Dictators that perpetuall are
> Sole moderators grow, of peace and war,
> A large prerogative. . . .

As in Fane's letter to the king, it is the extremists on each side who are responsible. The moderate Fane invokes a chillingly prophetic image as he refuses to accept the choice that they are forcing between Parliament and king:

> They know there is no question now to bring
> To censure, but who are you for? the King
> Or Parlement? As if a body & head
> Could severd be yet not the party dead.

His belief in the role of Parliament does not mean, however, that he accepts the argument for limited contractual monarchy, that

> the King is set
> But over them as Chevalier du guet
> He was at first but trusted from & for
> The Commonwealth as His Superior.

Nevertheless, this increasingly loyalist version of events still has significant moments of criticism of Charles, notably in identifying ship money as the origin of the confrontation:

> Wher sticks the Reformation? God began
> With His Vicegerent & our soueraign
> Moord all his Ship-mony to the latch, noe more
> It seemd t'oppress the subiect sore.

Fane finishes, as he had started, on a balanced note that admits Charles's earlier failures even as he invokes his goodness as the country's best hope. The "amendment" that is needed to save England must come from the king as well as his opponents:

> But the King in, & of Himself's soe good
> He will by them, & all be understood
> To have his thoughts bent forward, not reflect

> On By-past faults either in state or sect
> And that amendment may from all ensue
> Intends wherin He faild to Rule anew.

For all its bitter attacks on those who "seek t'have all things left at Liberty," this is in the end the poem of a peacemaker, whose counsel (especially the admission of earlier failures) would not have been welcomed at Oxford much more readily than at Westminster.

Fane is not usually as lengthy or explicit as this: his more usual strategy is to allegorize or mythologize the upheavals around him. Christian or classical myth is used to help understand the extraordinary changes he witnesses by placing them in historical or ontological perspective, in the great sweep of providential order. Biblical or classical types of fratricide, martyrdom, rebellion, or captivity provide antecedents that teach the lessons of acceptance and patience. Charles himself is transformed, by his defeat and imprisonment, from the weak Adam seduced by his advisers or his own frailties to a type of the persecuted Christ even before his execution makes the parallel a more complete one.

The execution of the king was clearly a decisive event in shaping Fane's attitude to the new regime. The version of the *Vita Authoris* in *Poems, 1623– 1650* sees it as the murder of a priest-king by the profane, and breaks off just after recording it:

> Who in telling, in writing, or in contemplating such things can refrain from tears? Yet it is so, and we saw our King so very devout, holy and peace-loving cut down with the blow of an axe, by the impious and utterly profane soldiers, Alas! our huge grief now imposes silence on our thoughts as well as on our pens and words. Let it suffice that wickedness so great be recorded in heaven to the end it may be punished.[22]

This is of a piece with the conclusion that the defeated Royalists must learn to be patient, to make their accommodation with the new order and await Providence. But silence was not the only response: Fane's recourse was to the pen, words filling the huge cultural void left by the execution. Shape was given to the events of 1649 by his Christian ontology. The people, not the king, are now the fallen Adam. Rebellion and rejection of the king echoed Adam's rebellion and rejection of the Father, the original cause of death, and was thus itself a form of parricide. "Man's first disobedience"

22. "Quis talia fando, scribendo, vel contemplando, temperet a lachrimis. Dum ita se res habet & Occisum securis ictu ab impiis & omnimodo profanis Militibus Regem nostrum tam Pium Sanctum & Pacificum vidimus (proh) Dolor Ingens nunc tam Cogitationibus quam pennis verbisque silentium imponit. Caelis nempe tanta sufficiat (puniendi causa) recordari scelera." *Poems, 1623–1650*, 8. The version of the *Vita* in British Library MS. Add. 34,220 is extended up to the Restoration.

is a recurrent motif in the poetry, an explanation of the turmoil even
before the final act of parricide, the ultimate negation of the King-Father,
made the breakdown of order complete. The punishment for Original
Sin was its reenactment now in the state: the concomitant disorder, war,
and death were (in a familiar paradox) themselves caused by the sin
that they were punishing. Thus the "sad intestine war" comes to seem
a terrible providential event for which no single group is responsible,
though its progress is helped along by "fomentors" on both sides. In a
number of religious poems, the account of the Fall and Redemption, and
the accompanying imagery of day and night, darkness and light, describe
the larger providential scheme, the fall of the English state, and the hope
of its salvation through the son, Charles II.

It is therefore no surprise to find Fane suggesting in the poems of the
1650s that just as mankind could only be saved by the death of Christ,
England could only have been redeemed by the death of the innocent
king. This version of history-with-hindsight is summarized in a verse,
probably written in the late 1650s, from "Preces & Lachrimae Sanctorum
Oblationes":

> Once This a Glorious Kingdom when a King
>   Endude with Vertues All Times mought admire
> Governd the Scepter & such Peace did bring
>   To Church & State as None could more desire
>   But too Good for such people Heavns decreed
>   As iust reward for Their sinns He should bleed.[23]

This Christ-King is a far cry from the one who, in the prose "Query"
of nearly two decades earlier had to be prevented from working "his
owne ruine" and that of his people. The identification is so pervasive in
Fane's later work that the dead king is always present in those many
post-1649 poems, especially those written for Christmas or Easter, when
the dead Christ is the explicit subject. In an annual series of carols, the
identification is only strengthened by the refusal of a sinful, parricidal
regime to countenance the celebration of the Nativity (his enthusiasm for
which is part of the evidence that Fane was more conservative Anglican
than Presbyterian). In "On Good Friday—1659," which is ostensibly a
straightforward religious lyric, "the Reconciling Day / That with the
Father the Sonn made our Peace" invokes the royal as well as the divine
pairing of father and son, with the anticipated coming of Charles II

---

23. *Poems, 1649–1665*, 32. Judging by adjacent poems in the manuscript, it dates
from 1658–1661.

reconciling the guilty people of England to their martyred king and father. A simple line from a pre-1649 poem, "The Father did redeem us by the Son" becomes, in this context, poignantly prophetic.

In a more confusing use of classical myth, Charles I becomes in one poem the murdered Remus, in another his killer, Romulus. As Remus he is the victim of a deeply unnatural murder, a type of Abel more than of Christ, destroyed in a fratricidal frenzy that has seized the whole country:

> Are we more fell than Beasts? doth Power
> And Force incite us to devower
> Each Other? is not Fury blind
> To Cause us t' rush on our owne kind?
> Or is our Sin soe great; noe Fate
> 'Save This may serve to Expiate
> Bereft at Once of speach & sence
> What may be read or guathered thence
> But that for Remus bloud once spilt
> Posterety should feel the Guilt.

This, from a poem addressed "To the People of England—June-5–1659" (*Poems, 1649–1665*, 95), is typical in its mixture of distressed questioning of the sources of "popular fury" and the proffered answer, that the continuing strife is an atonement for the fratricidal murder that is also patricidal, since Remus was, like Charles, the father of his country.[24]

If this presents a classical version of Original Sin, a poem that comes soon after it in the manuscript, "Le Monde Renversé" (99), offers Charles as Romulus, in his role as *pater patriae* rather than killer of his brother. The patience that has been a recurrent theme since *Otia Sacra* is now strongly tinged with optimism that the son will come to claim his inheritance, that, as he puts it here:

> There flowes a mercy from the Horescope
> May bring home Those who yet Abroad Distrest
> Will make the Conquest Glorious and us blest.
>
> . . . .
>
> Our Romulus is lost: our Rome noe more
> The Giddy Storme Us root & branch up tore

24. A Latin poem of 1652 attacks the "Paricidas Anglicanos" (Harvard MS, 122), while in *Poems, 1649–1665*, a post-Restoration poem calls a regicide "the Father-killing-Traytor" (83). Clarendon too speaks of the execution as "parricide" (*History*, 4:492 [originally 11:244]). René Girard observes "The act of regicide is the exact equivalent, vis-à-vis the polis, of the act of patricide vis-à-vis the family." *Violence and the Sacred* (Baltimore: Johns Hopkins University Press, 1977), 74.

Fortune's as Wind's inconstant & may blowe
That uppermost again that now lies lowe
   Wherfore let none despair: This Loss may bring
   Our Hopes to Ank'rage; & that send a King.

The motif of the coming of the new king, of course, invokes another powerful Christian parallel, with Charles II's anticipated arrival to ransom his people, to judge the wicked and to reward the patient and loyal, if not always meek, assuming obvious millenarian significance. Ironically, Marvell, whom Fane may well have known through Fairfax, if not earlier, had hailed Cromwell in similar terms in the *First Anniversary,* while Dryden, from a neighboring Northamptonshire family of lesser (and Parliamentarian) gentry, was to make Charles II the millenarian "Prince of Peace" in 1660 in *Astraea Redux.*

If the two Charleses are associated by Fane with Christ, Abel, or Remus, Cromwell should be, but never quite is, Satanic. Fane does mythologize him as Haman, on the grounds that he should be hanged, not crowned. When Cromwell avoids Haman's fate and dies in bed, he becomes Goliath in an epigram "Nec Sicca morte Tyranni":

In Peace, at home, in bed to die
Cannot found Guilt of Tyranny
'Cause not imbude in Blood but drye
   Yet mark what follows (Truth being started)
   This man of Garth Golia Farted
   Beshit his bed & soe departed
   Leaving a Savour behind him &c.[25]

This is one of a group of poems that greet Cromwell's death with unseemly glee. It may be that Fane resisted giving Cromwell or Fairfax more heroic mythic status as Lucifer, Cain, or Romulus. Despite this, a number of poems do treat both men with much more respect. Fairfax, satirized in 1653 as "Prince Tomaso ali: Black Tom" in the opening poem in the Harvard MS, had in 1645 been addressed with unironical respect in a poem "Upon Sir Tho: Fayer-Fax whose vertues make Him shine a bright star in our Horizon" (Northamptonshire MS). After comparing him favorably with Alexander and Caesar, Fane hails his brother-in-law as "He [who] Ill-humors doth repell / Clowdes-& Night-chasing-Light: whose splendid Ray / Is the Faier-Blazon of Our hopefull Day." In a poem of June 1648 it

25. *Poems, 1649–1665,* 101.

is "noe dishonour now nor sham at all" for the Royalists of Kent "To take a Route from the Lord Generall" (Harvard MS, 29).

Soon after he had moved to satirical rejection of Black Tom in October 1653, Fane was willing in a poem dated January 1653 (i.e. 1654; Harvard MS, 132) to come to conditional terms with the newly installed Protector, for the very Hobbesian reason that he was now the only man capable of restoring peace:

> Brave Captain though thine honor gaind increase
>   By war let all concluded be in peace.
>   T'is commendable after Pallas spear
>   Had brandisht been Her Olive branch to wear
>   For, being Protector & anoynted thence,
>   All suppling lenatives He should dispence
>   Unto the People; make the sword to bend
>   Into a sickle, th'Helmet to defend
>   Hive-like the laboring Bee; if this He'l doe
>   I'le say He shall be my Protector too.

The distraught reaction to the king's death has given way to a desire for peace and healing that is, at this stage, stronger than his hopes of restoring the monarchy. But the two need not be in conflict: the Hobbesian contract is conditional on the Leviathan delivering peace, and there is nothing contradictory in thus provisionally accepting the Protector while awaiting the peaceful return of the king, especially if such acceptance is sustained by an un-Hobbesian belief in Divine Providence.[26] As in so many of the poems, the primary interest is in the "suppling Lenatives" of peace, and the poem can plausibly be read as the work of a man who has been considering chapter 17 of *Leviathan* and is here subscribing in verse to that Covenant by which he accepts Cromwell as holder of the "Common Power" under whose protection his subjects "by their owne industrie, and by the fruites of the Earth, . . . may nourish themselves and live contentedly" (227).

"An Epigram upon His Highnes entertainment in the Citty translated" (Harvard MS, 133) goes further. It recognizes Cromwell as "This other Cesar," and displays a surprising willingness to engage with concepts

26. Some saw Cromwell's assumption of quasi-royal power as leading to the restoration of monarchy, and Fane may have been one of those "very many" royalists whom Clarendon criticized for believing "that the making Cromwell king for the present was the best expedient for the restoration of his majesty." *History,* 6:21 [originally 15:32].

of democracy and destiny, and a new order in which the conqueror will
frame new laws out of chaos:

> He who soe many Crowns despisd, seeks you
> The harts of men, nothing of stage or shew
> He brings his own bayes, broaken scepters yeild
> That Liberty He guave might take the feild
>> Now are yea first made Cittizens, time past
>> Were servants unto Kings; learn this at last
>> To yeild to th'reigne of those whose power who skans
>> Shall find them but your fellow Cittizens
> The Conquring souldier's deaf but yet He knows
> How to change armes int'Lawes & making showes
> And thence puts on the Gowne, soe what of late
> A Chaos lay a new world will Create.

Though a translation, this was not written under compulsion. It has
Roman republican as well as Hobbesian overtones, but Fane may have
been most influenced by the conciliatory strategy adopted in the period
immediately following Cromwell's installation as Lord Protector, when a
marked effort was made at rapprochement with "that part of the political
nation which might be open to persuasion that the preservation of the
traditional social order was high on the priorities of the new regime."[27]

It is not clear how long Fane entertained such hopes of Cromwell.
Certainly, the majority of poems that mention him are hostile, and it may
be that Fane gradually concluded that the Protector was not able to deliver
his side of the contract by bringing genuine peace closer. Cromwell's
angry opposition to the marriage of Fane's niece Mary Fairfax to the duke
of Buckingham in 1657 may not have helped, but a more likely motive
is suggested by an anguished poem of 1658, "Upon taking up Severall
Persons of Honer & quallety by the Maior & souldiery & securing them
at Northampton the 14th of Aprill—1658" (*Poems, 1649–1665*, 107), which
laments the arrest of a number of Royalist friends and neighbors, among
them the rich Catholic Lord Brudenell. These were among the first of a
series of arrests of Royalists that year, and Fane increasingly vested his
hopes, and probably what political and social influence he retained, in
the restoration of Charles II. Some of that influence resulted in action,
in a return to *negotium* at least by proxy. His second marriage, in 1638,
to Mary Vere, daughter of a Protestant champion, had brought him not
only Fairfax and Clare as brothers-in-law, but Horatio Townshend as a
stepson and the Presbyterian Harleys as cousins. All played important

27. Ivan Roots, "Cromwell's Ordinances," in *Interregnum*, ed. Alymer, 147.

roles in the Restoration. The Harleys "were in constant consultation with the court-in-exile just before the Restoration"; Clare was involved in an offer of restoration in 1659; and it was Townshend who gave his uncle Fairfax the letter from Charles that persuaded him to reassemble his old troops and begin negotiations with Monk. Earlier, Townshend, though a member of Richard Cromwell's Council of State, had attempted to seize Kings Lynn for Charles, an event Fane celebrates in verse in "Aug: 3: 1659: Upon a Rumor of a Generall rising" (*Poems, 1649–1665*, 94).[28]

Townshend was only about seven when he became Fane's stepson, so that it is reasonable to assume that he grew up under his influence. Although Fane's deliberate emphasis on retirement, patience, and reconciliation cannot have been entirely to Townshend's taste, it is likely that they were in close political sympathy in the late 1650s, when the Sealed Knot was at its most active, and Fane's poems of these years grow increasingly optimistic about developments. He remained, however, a peacemaker, a loyalist in his own terms rather than a seeker for revenge; a fitting place to end this survey of his changing attitudes is his moving prayer for peace and reconciliation dated from Townshend's house at Raynham, Norfolk, in June 1659 (*Poems, 1649–1665*, 31). Again, the emphasis is on patient waiting on Providence: "Lord in whose hand it is," this poem opens,

> To make a Metamorphosis
>   And whose sole will creates
> A change in Kingdoms, Powers, & States
>   Smile on This sinfull Land.

The change in question here is the now-imminent restoration of the monarchy, which can only come about if God will "Cancel the guilt of all our crimes / Let not the Conquering sword / Prevail, but sunshine of thy word." Sun and light, harmony and blessings, are all dependent on the return of Charles II, whose anticipated reign of peace and justice is inescapably reminiscent of the millennium. But if this is a prayer for the Restoration, it is for the restoration through Charles, as the new Leviathan, of social harmony, a harmony in which "All Tunes may agree," in which "Peace & Truth" are one, and in which "the Guilt of *all* our Crimes," not just those of erring Royalists, is canceled.

---

28. For the Harleys, see Newton E. Key, "Comprehension and the Breakdown of Consensus in Restoration Herefordshire," in *The Politics of Religion in Restoration England*, ed. Tim Harris, Paul Seaward, and Mark Goldie (Oxford: Basil Blackwell, 1990), 193. For Clare, see *The Letter-Book of John Viscount Mordaunt, 1658–60*, ed. Mary Coate (Camden Society, 3d ser. 69, 1945), 95.

M. Thomas Hester

Herrick's Masque of Death

Alas! What boots it with uncessant care
To tend the homely slighted Shepherds trade,
And strictly meditate the thankles Muse,
Were it not better don as others use
To sport with *Amaryllis* in the shade,
Or with the tangles of *Neaera's* hair?
. . . .
And when they list, their lean and flashy songs
Grate on their scrannel Pipes of wretch'd straw.
. . . .
Fame is the spur that the clear spirit doth raise
(That last infirmity of Noble mind)
To scorn delights, and live laborious dayes;
. . . .
Fame is no plant that grows on mortal soil.
—John Milton, *Lycidas*

Central to the apologiae in which the Royalists and the Puritan Parliamentarians justify the "providence" of their vision of English civilization is the ancient idea that the health of an individual, a nation, or a race is indicated by the quality of its art and learning. After all, as Sir Philip Sidney had confirmed in his seminal English humanist apologia, "Poesy, . . . of all human learning the most

---

Quotations of John Milton's poetry are from the edition of Merritt Y. Hughes, *John Milton* (New York: Odyssey Press, 1937); quotations of his prose are from the edition of J. Max Patrick, *The Prose of John Milton* (Garden City, N.Y.: Anchor Books, 1967). Quotations of the poetry of Robert Herrick are from the edition of J. Max Patrick, *The Complete Poetry of Robert Herrick* (Garden City, N.Y.: Anchor Books, 1963); citations of *Hesperides* and *His Noble Numbers* will be identified parenthetically in my text as *H* and as *NN*, followed by the poem number in the Patrick edition. The following first few pages reproduce some material on Herrick's collection that was part of my much longer essay on the second generation of British seventeenth-century poets, the introduction to volume 126 of *The Dictionary of Literary Biography: Seventeenth-Century British Nondramatic Poets*, 2d ser. (Detroit: Gale Research, 1993).

ancient, . . . always hath been the light-giver to ignorance."[1] According to the Puritan platform, the Royalist, prelatic, and poetic spokesmen of the Caroline cause are merely "Blind mouths [whose] lean and flashy songs / Grate on their scrannel Pipes of wretch'd straw" while they "sport with *Amaryllis* in the shade, / Or with the tangles of *Neaera's* hair" (*Lycidas* ll. 119, 123–24, 68–69). Archbishop Laud, Milton charged, would "mould a modern Bishop into a primitive" compounded of the "Falshood and Neglect" that threatened to dominate English civilization in the shape of "those sencelesse *Ceremonies* which wee onely retaine as a dangerous earnest of sliding back to *Rome*"; and the songs and masques that these Caroline "Libertines" use to "defend their . . . Heathen, . . . prelatical Sparta" are merely the "new-vomited Paganisme of sensuall Idolatry" (*Of Reformation,* 53, 44, 45; *The Reason of Church Government,* 112, 113; *Of Reformation,* 42). To the Puritan party, the Caroline culture is a deadly enervating obsession with "Epicurean" "carnall and sensuall delite" (and disorder) that would "turne [the English] Kingdome of Grace into a Kingdome of Pleasure, pride and ease," "a mere carnall and temporall, yea profane and heathenish Kingdom" of "voluptuous and salacious goates." George Wither's characterization of the court poets of the "wanton" Charles and his Catholic queen represents well the Puritan appraisal of the Caroline apologists:

> For wicked ends [they]
> Have the *Castalian Spring* defil'd with gall;
> And chang'd by witchcraft, most Satyricall,
> The bayes of *Helicon,* and myrtles mild,
> To pricking hauthornes, and to hollyes wild.

Reviving the tropes and charges that the earlier generation of Sidneyan poets such as Spenser had hurled at the "superstitious paganism" of Continental and residual English Catholicism, the Puritan apologists warned that these same forces of uncreation, operating now at the cultural heart of the nation, threatened to metamorphose England's sacred mount of poetic truth into a wanton garden of delights and disorder; as P. W. Thomas phrases it, while the Caroline "Court behaved as though the Golden Age had arrived through the miraculous intercession of the divine Stuart, [to the Puritan] godly it looked a thoroughly carnal kingdom, more like

---

1. For a fuller treatment of this concept in classical and Renaissance poetic apologiae, see M. Thomas Hester, *Kinde Pitty and Brave Scorn: John Donne's Satyres* (Durham: Duke University Press, 1982), chapter 2. Sidney's *Defence* is quoted from *A Defence of Poetry,* ed. Jan Van Dorsten (Oxford: Oxford University Press, 1966), 18, 48.

Babylon than the New Jerusalem: . . . the pollution of the high seriousness and moral earnestness of the mainstream of English humanism, . . . [the] breakdown of a national culture."[2]

To the Royalist spokesmen of the Caroline party, on the other hand, such terms of abuse merely showed the Puritan party to be a reincarnation of Sidney's *mysomousoi*—those "zealous Ignorants," "men that profess . . . to destroy Wit and Learning," who have brought about

> the thick darkness of these verseless times,
> These antigenious times, this boystrous age,
> Where there dwells nought of Poetry but rage:
>
> . . . .
> . . . these more barbarous dayes our times,
> When what was meant for ruine, but refines.

The Puritan party has made these

> . . . Times which make it Treason to be witty,
> Times where Great Parts do walk abroad by stealth,
> And Great Witts live in *Plato's* Common-wealth.[3]

Parliament is not just (in Marchemont Nedham's quip) "thirty fools and twenty knaves," but a "Monster [that] doth rule thee," said Alexander Brome—a monster led by such anti-Creators as Pym and Hampden, whose "wretch'd . . . *Spirit* [has] mov'd o'r the goodly frame / O' the *British world*, and . . . taught *Confusion* [and] Chaos," said Abraham Cowley, so that now, Brome urged, "the Christian Religion / Must seek a

2. David Calderwood, *Altar of Damascus* (1621), 156; John Bastwick, *An Answer of John Bastwick* (1637), 19; William Prynne, *Lord Bishops, None of the Lords Bishops* (1640), 8, 10, 18: as cited in Achsah Guibbory, *Ceremony and Community from Herbert to Milton: Literature, Religion, and Cultural Conflict in Seventeenth-Century England* (Cambridge: Cambridge University Press, 1998); Wither, *The Great Assizes Holden in Parnassus,* quoted in C. V. Wedgwood, *Poetry and Politics under the Stuarts* (Cambridge: Cambridge University Press, 1960), 73; Thomas, "Two Cultures? Court and Country under Charles I," in *Seventeenth-Century England: A Changing Culture,* ed. W. R. Owen (Totowa, N.J.: Barnes and Noble, 1981), 276.

3. Sir John Denham, "A Speech against Peace at the Close Committee," *The Poetical Works of Sir John Denham,* ed. Theodore Howard Banks (New Haven: Yale University Press, 1928), 125, also quoted in Wedgwood, 87; David Lloyd, *Memoires* (1668)—a description of Sidney Godolphin, quoted by Graham Roebuck in his essay on Godolphin in *Seventeenth-Century British Nondramatic Poets,* 2d ser., ed. Hester, 132; Alexander Brome, "To *Colonel* Lovelace *on his* Poems," *Poems,* ed. Roman R. Dubinski (Toronto: University of Toronto Press, 1982), 1:289. Jasper Mayne, "To the Deceased Author of these Poems," in William Cartwright, *Comedies, Tragi-Comedies, With other Poems* (London, 1651), B6.

new Region."[4] In these terms, then, "Great *Strafford*," the king's advisor, had to die, said Denham, because "He's not too guilty, but too wise to live" when "Eloquence" succumbs to "Rage," and when, in the terms of Owen Felltham, "CHARLES the First," that is, "CHRIST the second," succumbs to "Judas" Cromwell and "Pontius Pilate" Bradshaw.[5] The Caroline church-court, in other words, is not just a "political" structure, but a divine form framed by Providence to thwart threats to Christian civilization.

The following pages review Robert Herrick's *Hesperides* from the dual perspective of this civil war lexicon—in order to suggest some ways in which Herrick's collection strives (or, more accurately, strains) to defend the cultural poetic of Caroline civilization, and to point out some ways in which the collection, especially its second half, supports the Puritan critique of that faltering, embattled ethos. Viewed as a representative civil war document, *Hesperides* provides both a picture of the threat that, in Herrick's term, the Puritans' deadly "precis[ion]" (*H* 83) presented to the Caroline court and an emblem of the moral/aesthetic fissure of that court, which contributed to and made nearly inevitable the (un)timely cultural *"trans-shifting"* of the English civil war.

Whether one explains the Caroline ethos and its Stuart hagiography as an extension of the "cult of Elizabeth" that had previously proven such a successful appropriation of the residue of Roman Catholic Mariology; as the sum result of the Jacobean-Stuart propounding of the strictest readings of a hierarchical theory of the divine rights of kings; or even as the aghast response to the grasp of the reins of power by what they saw as the forces of republican factionalism, classless appetite, and religious fanaticism at its most rapacious; there remains a considerable strain in the Caroline ethos that resulted in the world turned upside down. And it is not merely a strain resulting from threat of the Puritan Parliamentarians, but a strain deriving from the commitment of religious imagery and the energies of spiritual devotion to the "service" of a "policy" and "art" of a court that was increasingly unresponsive to and—in its extravagant

---

4. Brome, *"Upon the Cavaleers departing out of* London," *Poems* 1:95; Cowley, "The Civil War," *The Collected Works of Abraham Cowley,* ed. Thomas O. Calhoun et al., (Newark: University of Delaware Press, 1989), 1:124; Brome, *Poems,* 1:95.

5. Denham, "On the Earl of Strafford's Tryal and Death," *Poetical Works,* 153–54; also quoted in Wedgwood, *Poetry and Politics,* 65 (John Cleveland sounds the same note on "Wise and Valiant" Strafford, "Who was harried hence / 'Twixt Treason and Conscience": *The Poems of John Cleveland,* ed. Brian Morris and Eleanor Withington [Oxford: Clarendon Press, 1967], 66); Felltham, "An Epitaph to the Eternal Memory of Charles I . . . ," *The Poems of Owen Felltham,* ed. Ted-Larry Pebworth and Claude J. Summers (University Park, Pa.: Seventeenth-Century News, 1973), 65–66.

isolationism and narrowing elitism—increasingly alienated from its time and its traditions. In many ways, as articulated by the court poets at least, such language intimates a desperate attempt to return to the "paradise" of Elizabethan harmony. But neither James nor Charles was able to inspire the confidence and devotion that had helped Elizabeth shape England into a confident, international state proud of its traditions and image. James's offensive divine-right theory, which lacked basis in English custom and any appeal to the increasingly restless gentry and commercial classes, was muted by the muddling moderation of his policies and the endless befuddlement of the "Spanish Match." And the subsequent effort of Charles to make the divine-right theory into a reality on the Gallic model was simply a recipe for disaster, especially when the increasing religious nonconformity was met by the crypto-Catholic rigors of Laud. And as rapid disintegration set in, Charles and his court retreated deeper into the remote indulgences and privileges of their own insulated royal "stage" and increasingly refused to confront in a timely fashion the national and international changes the world was undergoing as they framed an aesthetic that was increasingly distant from the Christian humanist—and English Protestant—traditions from which the Tudors had drawn their strength.

To sense what often seems like a near desperation to figure the insulated Caroline court as heir to the internationally successful Elizabethan project, one needs only turn to the deification of his father, which Charles I commissioned Rubens to portray in bold allegorical hyperbole on the ceiling of the Banqueting Hall; or to recall the steady allegorical hyperbole that dominated the "stage" of that hall in the form of the masques, plays, and poetic contests such as Carew's *Coelum Britannicum;* or the poet laureate Davenant's extravagant *Salmacida Spolia* with its figuration of Charles as "Philogenes or Lover of his People" and his French Catholic Queen Henrietta Maria as Pallas's divine gift to the meritorious monarch. The masques and plays of the court enabled a myth of innocence amidst a world at ideological and actual war, often blurring the borders of theater and reality, furtively skirting and often invading the borders of blasphemy in order to devise a sort of stylized insulation against the "noise" threatening their garden. One wonders if the entire Caroline pageant might best be seen as an elaborate, very stylish and stylized dance of death boldly enacted by an aristocratic troupe too intelligent to believe with confidence in its ultimate viability. As Graham Parry phrases it, many people in the period did respond to "the mysterious divinity of kingship as feelingly as other men did to the reality of religious power in their lives"; indeed, the cult of the king often seemed to serve as a substitute for religion.[6] However, in this case one cannot help but notice that it is often a bit too much; and not just because the Caroline poets' attempts to endorse the "Court of love" put them in the uncomfortable position of applying all the lyrical and allegorical machinery of English Protestant poetics to a French courtly model being revived by a Catholic devotee. There is more, in fact, than merely a trace of tension at the heart of the Caroline aesthetic. It is more often a note of disillusionment, as overheard, for example, in Carew's inability to find a successor to Donne's "monarchy of wit"—a note that often becomes a sort of disenchantment that at times approaches nostalgia but that yet endorses finally a disengagement with the Caroline cultural project. *Hesperides* "rehearses" (*H* 371) this conflicted note.

Published in 1648, *Hesperides* is poised at the very precipice into which the Caroline establishment was falling—one year after Herrick had been deprived of his ecclesiastical living at Dean Prior, three years after the beheading of Archbishop Laud, and less than one year before the "divine" Charles I would be legally executed after the defeat of the political, religious, and social forces with which Herrick identified. In some ways, in fact, Herrick's poetic collection might be profitably read as an affirmation of the king's warning that "in [his] Fall and Ruine you see your own."[7] Indeed, as Ann Baynes Coiro has pointed out,

6. Parry, *The Seventeenth Century: The Intellectual and Cultural Context of English Literature, 1603–1700* (London: Longman, 1989), 38. Parry's second chapter, "The Iconography of Charles I, 1625–1649," offers an especially helpful appraisal of the theatricality of Charles and his court, and of how the Caroline court, "excessively distracted by sophisticated game-playing," was simply "insufficiently aware of its dangerous isolation, and indifferent to the growing bitterness in the world outside" (35). The strained view of Charles I as a misunderstood "lover" of the people continued after his death, in the *Eikon Basilike* published a few days after his death, for example, which presents a revealing subtitle: *the Portraiture of his Sacred Majestie in his Solitudes and Sufferings.* From the first days of his reign, the Latin anagram of the king's name (*Charolus Stuartus=Christus Salvator*) set the tone and terms of what became after his death an elaborate "cult of Charles the Martyr," to which Milton, of course, responded immediately, firmly, and fully in his *Eikonoklastes* (Parry, *Seventeenth Century*, 39–40). On the change of the crown from a "universalistic and suprapersonal" symbol during the reign of Elizabeth to "the badge of an embattled party [adept at] paying tribute to God in the person of Caesar" (119–20) during the reign of Charles I, see Malcolm MacKenzie Ross, *Poetry and Dogma: The Transfiguration of Eucharistic Symbols in Seventeenth-Century English Poetry* (New Brunswick: Rutgers University Press, 1954); on the ways in which "political verse . . . comes of age" (3) during this period, see Ruth Nevo, *The Dial of Virtue: A Study of Poems on Affairs of State in the Seventeenth Century* (Princeton: Princeton University Press, 1963), especially chapters 1 and 2.

7. Tanner MS 57, fol. 427v, cited in Robert Ashton, *The English Civil War: Conservatism and Revolution, 1603–1649* (London: Weidenfeld and Nicolson, 1978), 347.

Hesperides is, in many ways, a memorial volume, [and one of the] strongest identifying characteristics of [Herrick's] persona . . . is his obsession with death. . . .
It may be argued that in Herrick's epigram book, death is the major structuring
device.[8]

Opening with a prefatory poem on "The Most Illustrious, and Most
Hopefull Prince, Charles, Prince of Wales"—whose birth, as Patrick has
noted, had been followed immediately by the appearance of Hesperus,
the evening star, in the midday sky, but whose *"Light* [of] *Expansion"*
had certainly been dimmed by 1648—and closing with the poet's own
defiant epitaph, framed "to withstand the blow / Of overthrow, / . . . Tho
Kingdoms fal" (*H* 1129), *Hesperides* might well be framed overall to affirm
what King Charles I would predict. But, at the same time, however much
Herrick (as Jonathan Post phrases it) "wished to belong fully, not just
politically, to the *ancien regime*,"[9] it is the entire problem of *identity* with
the royalist cultural theater that seems most troubled and troubling in
this conflicted or, to use Herrick's own term, inherently "torne Booke"
(*H* 960). One source of this conflict stems from Herrick's distance from
his overriding desire to be a Caroline courtier and an active member of
the poetic coterie. Poised at the very precipice into which the Caroline
establishment was to fall, it is not surprising that *Hesperides* seems framed
above all to transform the artifacts and objects of that world into delicate
poetic rituals that might survive their author's disappointments and
their age's revolution. While ranging from an enduring nostalgia for a
world of "Elizabethan" charm to a sort of ostentatious display of the
vulgarity he saw overwhelming his world, *Hesperides,* in its mixture of
pagan and Christian customs, might well be seen as a sort of lyrical (and
elegiac) companion to the masque, relegated to Dean Prior, determined
to maintain the world of "one continued festival" (Carew's terms) before
the crudely "precise" *mysomousoi* took over.[10]

8. Coiro, *Robert Herrick's "Hesperides" and the Epigram Book Tradition* (Baltimore:
Johns Hopkins University Press, 1988), 210–11.
9. Patrick, *Complete Poetry of Robert Herrick,* 9 n. 1; Post, "Robert Herrick: A Minority
Report," *George Herbert Journal* 14 (fall 1990–spring 1991): 1.
10. On the ceremonial in *Hesperides,* see A. Leigh DeNeef, *"This Poetick Liturgie":
Robert Herrick's Ceremonial Mode* (Durham: Duke University Press, 1974), and Robert
H. Deming, *Ceremony and Art: Robert Herrick's Poetry* (The Hague: Mouton, 1974); on its
"Elizabethan" character, see Leon Mandel's *Robert Herrick: The Last Elizabethan* (Chi-
cago: Argus Press, 1927). On Herrick as a Stuart poet, see especially Claude Summers,
"Herrick's Political Poetry: The Strategies of His Art," in *"Trust to Good Verses": Herrick
Tercentenary Essays,* ed. Roger B. Rollin and J. Max Patrick (Pittsburgh: University of
Pittsburgh Press, 1978), 171–83; Summers, "Herrick's Political Counterplots," *Studies
in English Literature, 1500–1900* 25 (1985): 165–82; and Achsah Guibbory, "The Temple
of *Hesperides* and the Anglican-Puritan Controversy," in *"The Muses Common-Weale":*

One source of the conflict at the heart of the collection stems from Herrick's distance from his overriding desire to be a Caroline courtier and an active member of that poetic coterie. In spite of all his efforts in poems such as "A Country Life" (*H* 662), "The Wake" (*H* 761), and "The Hock Cart" (*H* 140) to consecrate the Stuart program of "pastoralized" nationalism, Herrick most wanted to be a courtier (Cavalier) poet fashioning his "Poetick Liturgie" (*H* 510) within the literary metropolis of London, at those "lyric feasts / Made at the *Sun,* / The *Dog,* and the triple *Tunne*" (*H* 911). The "*rude* River in Devon," however, knows only a "people . . . churlish as the seas; / And rude (almost) as rudest Salvages" (*H* 86), he bemoans. His "Mirth" has been "turn'd to mourning" by his "banishment / Into the loathed West" (*H* 371) and its "loathed Country-life" (*H* 456), for "Devon-shire" and its "warty incivility" (*H* 86)—unlike London, "blest place of [his] Nativitie" (*H* 713)—are "dull" and "loath'd so much" (*H* 51).

As in his dedication of the volume to Prince Charles and his many encomia throughout to King Charles as the "brave Prince of Cavaliers" and "best of Kings" (*H* 37) whose misfortunes in war "makes the Poet sad" (*H* 612), Herrick can manage a fulsome praise for the "Sweet Country life" as lived by Endymion Porter—but that poem remains unfinished. His efforts to present "His content in the Country" as the classical *vita bona* is strained—he "blesse[s his] Fortunes" only when he sees "Our own beloved privacy" (*H* 552); his attempt to figure "His Grange, or private wealth" as a pastoral paradise is qualified by the concluding description of his "rural privacie" as merely "*some* ease / Where . . . *slight* things do *lightly* please" (*H* 324); and that poem is undercut by his riddle poem, "The Grange," which suggests that only a brown mouse could be "well contented in this private Grange" (*H* 410). His splendid song in praise of the ritualistic worship of the harvest hock cart at the estate of Mildmay Fane is almost totally overturned by the somber reminder at its conclusion that the celebration of the "Sons of Summer, by whose toile, / We are Lords of Wine and Oile," is actually only a "pleasure [that] is like raine, / Not sent ye for to drowne your paine, / But for to make it springe againe" (*H* 140). The warmest praise for "this dull *Devon-shire*," in fact, is restricted to his "confession" that "I ne'r invented such / Ennobled numbers for the Presse, / Then where I loath'd so much" (*H* 51).

Poetry and Politics in the Seventeenth Century, ed. Claude J. Summers and Ted-Larry Pebworth (Columbia: University of Missouri Press, 1988), 135–47. Carew is quoted in Parry, *Seventeenth Century,* 35.

Herrick, that is, is compelled to find "delight" in "disorder," within the world of his own "discontent." Exiled (like Ovid) from the Caroline "Roman" court, he nevertheless attempts to support the *ethos* and aesthetic of that lost world by composing a sort of Caroline mannerist verse that aims to transform the "Garden" of poetic kinds into Laudian ceremonies of poetic ritual that will somehow transcend or, at the very least, offer a rebuff to the forces of *"Times trans-shifting"* that have relegated him to the country where he must be "content" and that now threaten—in the shape of a Puritan antipoetry that is "too precise in every part"—to leave all of England "lost in an endlesse night."[11] As he informed his readers in the first poem of *Hesperides*, his mission as a courtly epic poet of English civilization—and scourge of Puritan precisianism—is to sing

> of *Brooks*, of *Blossoms*, *Birds*, and *Bowers;*
> Of *April*, *May*, of *June*, and *July-flowers*.
> I sing of *May-poles*, *Hock-carts*, *Wassails*, *Wakes*,
> Of *Bride-grooms*, *Brides*, and of their *Bridal-cakes*,
> I write of *Youth*, of *Love*, and have Accesse
> By these, to sing of cleanly-*Wantonnesse*.

He will "sing (and ever shall) / Of *Heaven*," he asserts. But like his qualified portrait of his pastoral "content" in Devon, his "songs" eventually become (as Coiro points out) epigrams and epitaphs about *"Times trans-shifting."* And more and more he does not "sing" but has to "write," to "write of *Hell*," until his book becomes largely a sort of lyrical anatomy of the world of the Stuarts in which "delight," "content," and "The holy incantation of a verse" are but moments recollected in *un*tranquility that he strives to save from the harvest of all-powerful Time through the delicate patterns and euphonies of neoclassical poetic ritual.

Indeed, as the concluding poems of *Hesperides* show, it is ultimately not a cultural revival that the poet invokes in his celebrations of native traditions and customs such as the Maypole games;[12] rather, it is an attempt to "trust to Good Verses [that] only will aspire, / When Pyramids, as men, / Are lost in funeral fire," to capture in those "numbers sweet

11. On the "mannerism" of Herrick, see especially Louis Martz, "The Masques of Mannerism: Herrick and Marvel," in *From Renaissance to Baroque: Essays on Literature and Art* (Columbia: University of Missouri Press, 1991), 149–73; and Louis Martz, *The Wit of Love: Donne, Carew, Crashaw, Marvell* (Notre Dame: University of Notre Dame Press, 1969).

12. See Leah Marcus, *The Politics of Mirth: Jonson, Herrick, Milton, Marvell, and the Defense of the Old Holiday Pastimes* (Chicago: University of Chicago Press, 1986), especially 140–68.

[that] / With endless life are crowned" (*H* 201) those wild "civilities" that are on the verge of being erased by the troops of "Zelot." It is perhaps an indication of his desperate fear that the country will not sufficiently oppose the Puritan onslaught that his Corinna never manages to "get up" and participate in the national holiday despite seventy lines of warning that they may "die / Before we know our liberty" (*H* 178). Just as he sought in the classicism of the Jonsonian model of civic poetry a form to withstand the winds of change and dislocation, so Herrick's carpe diem poems, which dominate the first half of the collection, especially those focusing attention on English habit and custom, seem framed as attempts to resist the tide of change and disorder he must have seen all around him in the last two decades of the Caroline reign.

Indeed, their sheer defiance, exuberance, and number in the first half of *Hesperides* seem to offer a compelling alternative to those forces that would allow no more "erring Laces, . . . Cuffe neglectful, . . . tempestuous petticote, [or] carelesse shooe-string"—and certainly no "delight" growing out of any "Sweet disorder" or "Wantonnesse" (*H* 83). It is a largely ebullient voice that mocks the rigor of the Puritan program with an array of Ovidian carpe diem songs of the type popular at the Caroline court Herrick wished to join. But even those poems that directly challenge the directives of those fastidious warriors against poetry, especially those that frame the celebration of those ancient "pagan" rites such as the Maypole to be "Devotion," recall in many ways Richard Corbett's touching "Farewell" to those "fairies . . . of the old profession" who "now, alas, . . . are all dead, / Or gone beyond the seas, / Or further for religion fled" ("A Proper New Ballad, Intituled the Fairies' Farewell, or God-a-Mercy Will"). In fact, as shown by several readers (in the seminal work of Roger Rollin, for instance), Herrick does seem to turn his volume into a program of "secular religion,"[13] especially the first half of *Hesperides*, which he packs with the very ceremonies, rituals, church furniture, ecclesiastical clothing, books of worship, and social and civic attitudes and stances "of the old profession" to which the Puritans most vigorously objected. But, once again, those poems seldom emphasize the doctrinal content of the rituals; the religious materials "serve purposes of an ordering that is more artistic than religious," more aesthetic or political than spiritual.[14] In *Hesperides*

13. Rollin, *Robert Herrick*, rev. ed. (New York: Twayne Publishers, 1992).
14. William Oram, "Herrick's Use of Sacred Materials," in *"Trust to Good Verses,"* 211. Death in *Hesperides,* Oram points out, is often "ceremonialized—wrapped, so to speak, in a covering of ordered language," and without any Christian stress on the afterlife, so that "the divine meditation is secularized." Guibbory warns us, however, not to deny the religious emphasis of the collection and shows ways in which Herrick's collection,

"Father Ben" Jonson's Penshurst (or Herbert's *The Temple* in "The pillar of Fame") becomes Herrick's "Fairie Temple" of "mixt Religion, . . . Part Pagan, part Papisticall," where the secular priest of poetry "lowly to the Altar bows, . . . Hid in a cloud of Frankincense" (*H* 223).

In other words, the *"Sacred Grove"* Herrick promised to his queen (*H* 265), the *"great Realme of Poetry"* he promised his king (*H* 264)—even the "Poetick Liturgie" that he promised *"Mistresse* Penelope Wheeler" would transform her into "a Saint" (*H* 510)—still share the limitations endemic to the Caroline aesthetic it sought to "Canoniz[e]" (*H* 510). A bit like the theater of the court and its mannerist poets with their nearly exclusive focus of attention on the command of the styles they assumed, Herrick's plentiful generic "Garden" of epigrammatic pastoral verse yet falls short of the vigor of a Herbert, a Jonson, or a Crashaw.[15] It remains a delicately balanced "song" about the end of a way of life—a way of life whose essential artifice and "play" was not to sustain it in the face of the *"trans-shifting"* forces that confronted it. It in no way belittles the achievement of *Hesperides,* that is, to suggest that Herrick's collection remains only as convincing as (although certainly more artistically enduring than) the court aesthetic it strove to support: Herrick's poetic "pillar of Fame" strives to ensure that "Poetry perpetuates the poet" (*H* 794) even as it conveys a vivid swan song about the aesthetic it strove to "resurrect."

The inevitable limitation and insufficiency of its attempt to provide an "eternall . . . Repullulation" (*H* 794) of the court and himself through a poetic "liturgy" gradually and relentlessly become clear in the second

---

"appearing the year after he was ousted from his parish by the Puritans, reaffirms and re-presents a Laudian ideal of worship, which he could no longer publicly perform, . . . [thus offering] a daring, imaginative declaration of religious as well as political and poetical allegiance" (Guibbory, "Temple of *Hesperides*," 147).

The extent of Herrick's "high Church" or crypto-Catholic position is more fully evinced in *His Noble Numbers,* which responds in counterpoint to the despair of *Hesperides,* which, as Graham Roebuck has pointed out to me, starts with epigrams and swells to an anthem. Summers ("Tears for Herrick's Church," *George Herbert Journal* 14 [fall 1990–spring 1991]: 51–71) presents a convincing analysis of "The Widdowes teares" as "a moving meditation on the death of Anglicanism"—and as a sort of elegiac microcosm of *"Noble Numbers* as a whole" (66)—and extends his argument in "Herrick, Vaughan, and the Poetry of Anglican Survivalism," in *New Perspectives on the Seventeenth-Century Religious Lyric,* ed. John R. Roberts (Columbia: University of Missouri Press, 1994), 46–74. I would add that the emphasis on authority and individual free will in those poems moves Herrick's "defiant Laudianism" to the circumference of its Roman Catholic inclinations.

15. See, for example, R. V. Young, "Style and Structure in Jonson's Epigrams," *Criticism* 17 (1975): 201–22; and "Jonson, Crashaw, and the Development of the English Epigram," *Genre* 12 (1979): 137–52.

half of the collection. Just as the light and delightful opening octave of the initial "Argument of his Book" (*H* 1) is countered by the emergence and finality of *"Time"* and by the cold acknowledgment that one must also *"write* of hell," so the volume overall—framed by poems celebrating the power of poetry, punctuated at its precise numerical middle by the poem on the poet's "losse of his Finger" (*H* 565)[16]—falls in its concluding poems to a series of noisy, ugly, and often bitter and obscene epigrams on the inevitability of decay and death, and the eventuality of the *"Hell"* of *"Times trans-shifting"* through every sphere of the fragile Caroline world.

In the mordant, "drooping" (*H* 1013) second half of *Hesperides*, as "the voice of the 'Roman citizen' " in exile gradually comes to dominate and as the epigram "gradually replace[s] the . . . ceremonial lyric" as the dominant genre, the "singer of country festivals and pretty girls [assumes] the futile role [of] a voice of sense in a senseless time."[17] Indeed, as A. B. Chambers points out, "extreme brevity becomes increasingly the norm towards the end of *Hesperides*, often in the form of harsh distichs that ruthlessly satirize and contemptuously minimize their subject matter. . . . [C]elebration is collapsing inward on hollowness, and even fame's sturdy pillar [eventually], for all its poetic reality, appears to have been built on shifting sand. . . . [T]he nightmarish vision is of minuscule particles, some of them momentarily but surrealistically beautiful, swirling their way through a centerless void." And as this "rapidly trans-shifting world" grows more unstable and the "abundant plenitude"[18] of the first half of the collection is more severely compressed by the gravity of mortality, so the meaning of the title of *Hesperides* changes. A poetic collection aptly identified with the delightful garden of golden fruits (and with the *"inexhausted* Fire" of hope in the future of Prince Charles) gradually becomes a poetic land of the daughters of Night at the western extremity of civilization—Hesiod's land of Hesperus, the evening sun, where "the Bodies light is declining" (*H* 576), to be "lost in an endlesse night" (*H* 952), a land of fading light at the precipice of the chaos that England was

16. First noticed by A. B. Chambers, *Transfigured Rites in Seventeenth-Century English Poetry* (Columbia: University of Missouri Press, 1992), 257.

17. Coiro, *Robert Herrick's "Hesperides,"* 208, 210. Summers ("Counterplots") and Post ("Minority Report") correctly focus attention, not on the poet's return to London "to die," but on the sense of *exile* of the poet's experiences: "Herrick's anxiety is different from that of the refugee's, for his fear is that the once familiar has become strange. . . . [T]he poet who worries elsewhere about being abandoned by the daffodils and damsels now [*H* 713] worries about being abandoned by his mother country" (Post, 11).

18. Chambers, *Transfigured Rites*, 257, 254.

becoming through "the engulfing of tradition in disorder and change"[19]—
the land of death and the dying where "good dayes" are gone forever
(*H* 570), and "All things are subject to Fate" (*H* 575). Those "golden apples"
Hercules carried from the classical garden, as figures for those delightfully
balanced lyrics that dominated the first half of *Hesperides*, turn out in the
preponderant epigrams and last rites of the second half to be mere figures
for the knowledge of fallen man's mortal "Putrefaction" (*H* 432). It is not
insignificant that Herrick's penultimate poems on the body of his "Booke"
figure the collection as an "*Absyrtus*-like" corpse (*H* 960), "bound[ed]" by
night (*H* 1019), denied its "lot" by men (*H* 1123), and inclined to suffer
"the Muses *Martyrdom*" (*H* 1128).

After submitting that his remaining fingers "but stand / Expecting
when to fall," Herrick's "Roman" poet spends the majority of these remaining poems "Upon the troublesome times" (*H* 596), recounting the
victories of "*Times trans-shifting*" over him, his acquaintances, his party,
and his "lost" court. After his finger he loses his "good dayes" (*H* 570),
his pipe (*H* 573), his poetic mentor (*H* 575), the affection of Lucia (*H* 599),
his health (*H* 617), "Good Luck" (*H* 621), "All . . . but [his] wit" (*H* 830),
Dean Prior (*H* 652), his inspiration (*H* 714), and his hair (*H* 852). Blanch
also loses her hair (*H* 571); the world is losing its light (*H* 576); Urles loses
the use of his feet and hands (*H* 577); and Franck's eyes are going (*H* 578),
as is the fragrance of the rose (*H* 686) and of nearly everyone's breath.
(Halitosis seems the sign of national and personal decline and imminent
death.) The combmaker loses his teeth (*H* 595); the poet is wracked with
headaches (*H* 591); the "golden age" of Charles and his music is declining
(*H* 612); Silvia loses a pearl from her bracelet (*H* 705); Franck loses two
teeth (*H* 728); Trugger is lame (*H* 882); and the war is lost (*H* 1102). The
poet's dog dies (*H* 967); the death of Julia and other "saints" is foreseen
(*H* 584); Jonson's death is recalled three times (*H* 575, 910, 911); Prue's
dusty demise is foreseen (*H* 782); and three other maids (one Irish) die
(*H* 838, 848, 593), as do Master Arthur Bartly (*H* 663), Mary Stone (*H* 764),
Hench's wife (*H* 842), Henry Lawes's brother (*H* 907), Lucia (*H* 814),
another virgin (*H* 912), Lady Crew (*H* 978), a baby (*H* 640), and a priest
(*H* 644). Anthea is quite ill (*H* 1054), and her poet-lover writes a score of
poems on his own imminent death, the loss of "majestie" and the king
(*H* 971), his "torne Booke" (*H* 960), his ragged vestments (*H* 970), and
his need of crutches (*H* 913) as this "Wearied Pilgrim" (*H* 1088) "droops"
towards death (*H* 1099), "lost in an endlesse night" (*H* 952), "lost and

19. Alastair Fowler, *A History of English Literature* (Cambridge: Harvard University Press, 1987), 105.

alone" (*H* 954). The final poems of farewell (*H* 1124–30) to his "*Absyrtus-like*" poetic corpse conclude with an emblem of his own tombstone and epitaph (*H* 1129, 1130). Such a turn was always there in Herrick's unfolding poetic anatomy, of course; the first half of the collection does record the death of at least twelve humans and one sparrow; and we should not forget that the first reference in the collection to Julia was a plea for the "Roses" to "Droop, droop no more" and to celebrate his beloved's "*Recovery*" (*H* 9), the third recalled a fall she had taken (*H* 27), the next her absence (*H* 35), the next her inevitable loss (*H* 39), the next, save one, to her as executor of the "dead" poet's last will (*H* 59); it was not until poem 67, on the possible effect of her voice on the "Damn'd," that Julia was not seen shadowed by loss and death.[20] Nevertheless, it is not until the second half that we always hear "Putrefaction" hurrying near—or, in terms of the title, that "Hesperides" reverts to its origin as the land of the dying and the dead, as a classically pagan figure for the loss and death facing Herrick, the Caroline court and church, and the light of civilization as they saw it.

Hesperides is a "glittering" song about the essential "liquefaction" of the fallen world, which does manage at its supreme moments to transform the particles of *concordia discors* into "*Pyramides*" (*H* 201, 211) of "Fame" that enroll the precious fragility of mortal being. "For old *Religions* sake" the poet will offer "Candles, . . . a new Altar," and the words of "Saint *Ben*" in his poetic "*Psalter*" (*H* 604); he performs "Funerall Rites [for] the Rose" (*H* 686), "*Ceremonies* for Candlemasse Eve" (*H* 893), "for Candlemasse day" (*H* 892), and "for Christmas" (*H* 784), mingling the "Churching" of Julia with the plea for Corinna to join the ancient "May-pole" celebrations, inviting them to go "to the *Altar of perfumes* . . . i'th'Temple" (*H* 445) of his "Poetick Liturgie" where he strives to enshrine "*eternall Images*" (*H* 496). But inevitably, as he laments his being unable to "leave this loathed Country-life, and then / Grow up to be a Roman *Citizen*" and to spend his "mites of Time" where "Cities shall . . . love thee" (*H* 456), the strain of doubt about this alternative vision leads Herrick to apply the ceremonial rudiments of a Laudian form of devotion merely to the creation of "Good Verses." After that final onslaught of brutal epigrams on disease, death, and disaster—punctuated by forlorn warnings about "Warre" (*H* 1102), "A King [who is] No King" (*H* 1103), "Plots not still

---

20. And, as Rollin suggests, the curious death of the poet's father moves mysteriously but continuously throughout the collection: "a preoccupation with the paternal is a significant dimension of the identity theme of Herrick's persona" ("Sweet Numbers and Sour Readers: Trends and Perspectives in Herrick Criticism," in "*Trust to Good Verses*," 7).

Prosperous" (*H* 1104), and "Distrust" (*H* 1121)—the collection concludes with a series of poems (*H* 1123–30) that reverts to establishing what is essentially a personal, secular immortality of poetic fame. This final view contrasts with that evoked humorously earlier in the collection, where the "young" poet joked that *"No lust theres like to Poetry"* (*H* 336) and assured himself, in one of his eight poems entitled "Upon himself," that

> Thou shalt not All die; for while Love's fire shines
> Upon his Altar, man shall read thy lines;
> And learn'd Musicians shall to honour Herricks
> Fame and his Name, both set, and sing his Lyricks. (*H* 366)

Given the Caroline lexicon of cultural apology, the significant term here is "learn'd." Indeed, early in *Hesperides,* in addition to the learned musicians, the poet invokes his "learn'd Diocesan" (*H* 168); the "learn'd [Magi who] brought *Incense, Myrrhe,* and *Gold*" (*H* 213A); the "learnt . . . Train" of the hospitable Sir Lewis Pemberton's country house (*H* 377); and the Earl of Dorset, who is "learnt i'th'Muses" (*H* 506)—even the apparition of his Venus-like mistress calls him to join the "Dancing [of] the learned Round" (*H* 575). But "learning" in the second half of the collection appears only once—as the "learned" physiologists of declining physical "health" (*H* 683). The "good precepts [of] Learning" (*H* 505), exemplified perhaps in the "Wisdome, Learning, Wit, or Worth" of Master J. Warr (*H* 134), nearly disappear from the world of the second half of the collection. Traces of Jonson's *"True-wit"* are still visible in Sir John Mynts (*H* 526), Endymion Porter (*H* 626), Denham's *Coopers Hill* (*H* 673), and Charles Cotton (*H* 947), but like "wisdom"—which appears in the second half only once, as the *"Distrust"* that *"doubt*[s] *a faithful friend"* (*H* 1121)—"wit," "the great over-plus" of bygone days with "Ben" at "the *Sun,* / The *Dog,* and the triple *Tunne,*" is a scarce "Tallent" that when once spent "the world sho'd have no more" (*H* 911). Thus, like the mythological masques and Christic iconography of the Stuart court, as he searches for an "Art above Nature" (*H* 560) that can move him beyond the grasp of a country and an "art" that are "too precise" (*H* 83), Herrick may still fancy that the king can "cure the Evill" and that a national faith in the mysterious powers of Charles, his "Adored *Cesar*" (*H* 161), can vanquish "The bad season [that] makes the Poet sad" (*H* 612); but, as the penultimate poem of *Hesperides* asserts emblematically, it is finally only to the "Pillar" of secular poetry that he turns in response to his (representatively Caroline) disenchantment with the world's *"trans-shifting."*

One might profitably compare Herrick's anatomy of his dying world with Donne's 1611 *Anatomy of the World* and its prophetic vision of the imminent loss and "witty ruin" of "All just supply, and all Relation: / Prince, Subject, Father, Sonne"—even "art, and correspondence too" (ll. 99, 214–15, 396). Donne concluded that

> Verse hath a middle nature: heaven keepes soules,
> The grave keeps bodies, verse the fame enroules. (ll. 473–74)

In a similar vein, at the conclusion of his own anatomy of the "ruin" Donne predicted, Herrick strives to assert that even "tho Kingdoms fall" and even when "all wit in utter darkness did and . . . will sit," the "Pillar" of his own verse "never shall / Decline or waste" (*H* 1129):

> *The pillar of Fame.*
> Fames pillar here, at last, we set,
> Out-during, *Marble, Brasse,* or *Jet,*
> Charm'd and enchanted so,
> As to withstand the blow
> Of   overthrow:
> Or   Outrages
> Of storms orebear
> What we up-rear
> Tho Kingdoms fal,
> This   pillar   never   shall
> Decline or waste at all;
> But stand for ever by his owne
> Firme and well fixt foundation.

Herrick's "fixt foundation," however, finally comprises his application of a ubiquitous *contemptus mundi* indictment by which "all" does "decline and waste" before the rude harvest of Time's ravenous maw. Donne sought to "enroule" the "fame" of what he calls "a glimmering light, / A faint weak love of vertue and of good"—to "reherse" or inscribe in his song (as Graham Roebuck has shown) the exemplary Elizabeth Drury as an emanation, channel, or vestige of the "incomprehensible" *Idea* of female "vertue" that is most worthy of man's "memory" and that might encourage his "Progress" beyond the "emprison[ment]" of the "strict grave" of this "cinder" of world, the "practice" of which might "Create a new world."[21] Donne then justifies his own "boldly invad[ing]" the "great

21. Roebuck, " 'Glimmering Lights': Anne, Elizabeth, and the Poet's Practice," in *John Donne's "Desire of More": The Subject of Anne More Donne in His Poetry,*

Office" of poetic prophecy—especially in times when "all" is "call[ed] in doubt"—by reference to a "Song" that is beyond man's "engraving." But Herrick, in the penultimate and final poems of his anatomy of civil-war England, offers a disturbing (and depressing) figure for the unalterable limits that Herrick—or "Time"—places on his own voice and culture. As a sort of "signature" (in the root, "Roman" sense of *firma*) of Herrick and the Caroline culture, in its final admissions that its Muse is indeed "wanton" and that his sole remaining hope is for a literary "fame," this conclusion suggests that the "obsession with death" of this collection produces finally only a pagan (or an erotic) embrace of death in its striving for the (momentary) delight of earthly "fame."[22]

"The pillar of Fame," Rollin points out, is at once "a hieroglyphic poem, an emblem of *Hesperides,* the poet's grave marker, and a ritual pronouncement upon the setting up of that marker. The pronouncement's theme is, appropriately enough (given Herrick's affinity for Horace), a variation upon one of that Roman poet's more stately lines." But however "Charm'd and enchanted," the fact remains that over half of the lines of the poem refer to agents of limitation and decline. As "an emblem of [the classical or 'pagan' character of] *Hesperides,*" it is telling, also, that this penultimate poem is spoken not by the poet but by a choric, Horatian "we"—what Coiro calls "a new, plural voice"—and that this "grave marker" is to be engraved with the last line of the last poem of the collection, which is borrowed from Ovid, as Coiro points out, and Martial. This elision or "trans-shifting" of the poet's voice serves but as an instance of his final Stoic "withdrawal" like a true *"Roman* Citizen" (*H* 456).[23] As coda for the catalog of universal cultural death in which "Kingdoms [and their spokesmen] fal," the elision of the poet's voice in his tombstone and epitaph does "stand for," according to Rollin, the inevitability of Puritan "overthrow" as

---

ed. M. Thomas Hester (Newark: University of Delaware Press, 1996), 172–82. See also Edward W. Tayler, *Donne's Idea of a Woman: Structure and Meaning in "The Anniversaries"* (New York: Columbia University Press, 1991). Donne is cited from *The Complete Poetry of John Donne,* ed. John T. Shawcross (Garden City, N.J.: Anchor Books, 1967).

22. Achsah Guibbory, "'No Lust Theres Like to Poetry': Herrick's Passion for Poetry," in *"Trust to Good Verses,"* 79–88, points out how "for Herrick, poetry is the product of a heat which is almost sexual, and his poems . . . capable of arousing a delightful excitement that is similar to sexual passion" (79). But then, once again, in the twilight of *Hesperides,* poems such as *"The Vision"* (*H* 1017), in which "wilde and wanton" Herrick dreams of receiving the laurel crown from *"Anacreon's* head," might just as readily figure forth a warning about the limits of poetry and Anacreon's fame (he is "reeling like to fall") as much as the likelihood of Herrick's poetic immortality.

23. Rollin, *Robert Herrick,* 197; Coiro, *Robert Herrick's "Hesperides,"* 215, 216. See George Parfitt, *English Poetry of the Seventeenth Century,* Longman Literature in English Series (London: Longman, 1985), 28–29.

much as it "makes [any] claim for immortality without qualification." Like a true poetic Stoic, that is, Herrick kills his voice before the *mysomousoi* can. (Such an understanding of the conclusion of the collection would heed Rollin's suggestion that we attend to the role of absent fathers in the collection, especially when we recall that in 1592 Herrick's own father left a written monument—his will—and then silenced himself.) The withdrawal, self-destruction, and reversion of the poet's voice—in which the Muses "crown" (*H* 1123, 1127) the dead poet in metaphors literally borrowed from classical poetry—concludes Herrick's collection with just the right defiantly Stoic gesture. It is the final attempt to imitate that classical creed of self-sufficiency and indifference to externals that had made Neostoicism an appealing "refuge from religious persecution [and] political impotence" during the late Renaissance.[24] Perhaps, that is, the last poems evince what Milton called "that last Infirmity of Noble Mind"—although the Puritan poet would suggest that textual suicide and "Jocund" poems, even as products of a "chaste" life (*H* 1130), would constitute more a "scrannel" than a "well fixt foundation" for immortality, and that, after all, the poet who sang the "Funerall Rites of the Rose" (*H* 686) and the death of all Nature's "Daffadills" (*H* 316) should recall that "Fame is no plant that grows on mortal soil."

Thus, *Hesperides,* despite or perhaps most fully in its strained attempt to embody the Sidneyan neoclassical tradition of the English High Renaissance within which both Cavaliers and Puritans drew their apologiae, actually fits in an uncomfortably "precise" manner the Puritan apologists' reading of the "wanton" Caroline culture as the reversion to a "ceremonial" Roman (and Roman Catholic) paganism. Herrick's attenuated, tentative, contradictory acts of praise and ceremony are, indeed, the ultimate acts of reversion—in the root sense of the word as a *turning back*—to a pagan poetic. And that, as the Puritans saw and the Parliamentarians foretold, was the same as the atavistic "foundation" of the Stuart court's ceremonial "masque."

The poetic Herrick of 1648, then, is finally a voice of despair. As a satirist he offers an attack on the failures of his times—even of his beloved Stuart court. But he found no viable or clearly articulated moral alternative to the foolishness, degradation, ineptitude, indifference, and ill manners he obscenely castigates—unless one accepts the claims of the opening and closing clusters of his poems, where he argues for the "Firme . . . foundation" of his own poems, as if the act of poetic invention itself

---

24. Rollin, *Robert Herrick,* 195. Isabel Rivers, *Classical and Christian Ideas in English Renaissance Poetry* (London: George Allen and Unwin, 1979), 49.

would be enough to offset the moral and literal demise of the Stuart world by the *mysomousoi* of the Parliamentarian "precision." In a way he may never have meant it, that is, his "wild civility" remains "wild" and (as he submits in the *consolatio* to *Hesperides, His Noble Numbers*) his "Wit wanton" (*NN* 1)—at least in terms of the criteria and pedagogical project of the English neoclassical tradition to which he repeatedly asserts his allegiance, that tradition that had affirmed nothing more than poetry as the best teacher and civilizer because of the patterns or examples worthy of imitation figured forth in its "fore-conceits." Herrick found no such "Idea," no "glimmering light" worthy of imitation beyond the erection of his own pillar of fame as a "Jocund" poetic "wanton." It may be significant, then, that "Zelot" appears as poem number 666; but it is definitely significant that—just before the final eight poems that serve as the poet's last will and testament in *Hesperides*—Herrick's last poem on the state of England is the ugly, nightmarish "The Hagg" (*H* 1122), which transforms song into an obscene epigram about the threatening, fearsome, "farting . . . stink" of the Uncreating Word that slouches towards London, making even "night afraid of the sounding."[25] Thus, even as Herrick erases his own presence in the last two poems of the collection, the masque of *Hesperides* remains a masque of death. It would canonize his poet "Father Ben," but it never itself attains Jonson's moral earnestness nor an exemplary alternative to the world of decay and death it "smells" all around it.

The poet of *Hesperides* is indeed "sad."

25. Coiro sees "The Hagg" as "a fitting conclusion to the body of *Hesperides*, where the 'sweet' of love poetry, the 'salt' of correction, and the 'gall' of mockery maintain an uneasy and dynamic tension. Here at the end, however, they come together in a final dark song of ugliness" (*Robert Herrick's "Hesperides,"* 214). With Alan Gilbert ("Robert Herrick on Death," *MLQ* 5 [1944]: 61–68), I would urge that the poem also accords with the theme of the doom of Judgment Day in *Hesperides,* and that it thus prepares the reader in some ways for *His Noble Numbers,* that "lengthy palinode that supplements what comes before it and also [attempts to] contravene it" (Chambers, *Transfigured Rites,* 257–58) as it moves from its initial "Confession" of his "wanton Wit" (*NN* 1) and "His Prayer for Absolution" for his "unbaptized Rhimes [and] wild unhallowed Times" (*NN* 2) to its concluding meditation on Christ's "Sepulcher" (*NN* 271) and untitled epigram on the eternal Circle of the divine Alpha and Omega (*NN* 272).

Daniel Jaeckle

From Witty History to Typology

John Cleveland's
"The Kings Disguise"

At three in the morning on April 27, 1646, Charles I fled from Oxford. It was a difficult moment for the king. At Naseby in the previous year the New Model Army had defeated the Royalist forces, and now Fairfax's legions were moving to surround the king's stronghold at Oxford. Fearing his capture and desperate for a new strategy, Charles cut his hair, trimmed his beard, put on the clothing of a servant, and left town disguised as an attendant of one of his royal chaplains, Michael Hudson, and his friend John Ashburnham.[1] After wandering a mazy path for eight days, Charles arrived in Southwell on May 5. There he surrendered to the Scots in hopes that he could negotiate a peace with them and so begin the road back to real power. Unfortunately from the king's point of view, the Scots were unwilling to accept his terms, just as he was unwilling to accept theirs. So seven months after he entered their camp, they traded Charles for the money that Parliament owed them and returned to their native soil. In effect, then, the day that the king arrived among the Scots he became as much their prisoner as their guest.

Serving as judge advocate in Newark and thus in a good position to observe the immediate aftermath of Charles's escapade firsthand, John Cleveland was attracted to this historical moment as worthy of his poetic

---

1. Ashburnham briefly describes some of the circumstances surrounding the journey in *A Narrative by John Ashburnham of his Attendance on King Charles the First from Oxford to the Scottish Army and from Hampton-Court to the Isle of Wight* (London: Payne and Foss, 1830), 2:58–87. In addition, a number of letters survive to document the confusion in the days after Charles left Oxford. See, for example, the letter from Colonel George Payne to Major-General Brown dated April 29, 1646, in *Memorials of the Great Civil War in England from 1646 to 1652*, ed. Henry Cary (London: Henry Colburn, 1842), 1:12–13.

skills. For the monarch of England to take on the appearance of a servant was just the kind of perplexing event capable of evoking the paradoxical wit that Cleveland was fond of displaying. Shortly after the event itself he penned "The Kings Disguise," one of his most complex poems. This complexity follows from the fact that Cleveland found himself in the position of mustering his powers of invention not to satirize enemies of the crown or to praise its friends, as was his wont, but to examine a politically and morally dubious action of the king himself. As several of the poem's critics have noted, in the process he revealed his growing concern as the Royalists faced defeat.[2] At the same time, however, he also discovered the limits of his usual way of interpreting history in terms of witty and partisan characterizations of friends or foes: unsatisfied with the initial results of his effort, he ultimately turned to a troubled typological reading to define his complex attitude toward the king. This essay traces the twists and turns of the poem as Cleveland moves from witty history to Christian typology in order to come to terms with the king's disguise.

I

The poem's first verse paragraph of ninety lines is vintage Cleveland in that, just as he did in earlier poems like "The Mixed Assembly" and "Smectymnuus, or the Club-Divines," so too here he writes as if a witty display will serve to characterize a historical event. He strings together one strained image after another in his usual epigrammatic and appositive style. The following couplets suggest the speed and imaginative range typical of his earlier occasional poetry:

2. On Cleveland's role as judge advocate at Newark, see *The Poems of John Cleveland,* ed. Brian Morris and Eleanor Withington (Oxford: Clarendon Press, 1967), xvii; and S. V. Gapp, "Notes on John Cleveland," *PMLA* 46 (1931): 1079–80. Cleveland was in the garrison when Charles ordered it to surrender to the Scots in early May. According to Morris and Withington, *Poems of John Cleveland,* 86, a version of "The Kings Disguise" was published by January 21, 1647, but it was probably written shortly after the time of Charles's appearance at Southwell. Lee A. Jacobus, *John Cleveland* (Boston: Twayne, 1975), 75, suggests that the poem expresses Cleveland's "total dismay at the failure of his cause and at the denigration of the king." But there is also a not-so-veiled indictment of the king himself, at least in the opening paragraph. Donald Bruce, "An Oxford Garrison of Poets in 1642," *Contemporary Review* 261 (1992): 255, may go too far when he claims that Cleveland was "wholly sceptical about the king" and that the first few lines reveal open indignation. Perhaps closest to the mark is A. D. Cousins, "The Cavalier World and John Cleveland," *Studies in Philology* 78 (1981): 83, when he argues that "The Kings Disguise" concludes a series of poems that express "a growing bitterness and sense of outrage" that "blow away the amused contempt of the earlier works." For another helpful reading, see James Loxley, *Royalism and Poetry in the English Civil Wars: The Drawn Sword* (New York: St. Martin's Press, 1997), 138–47.

> This Privie-chamber of thy shape would be
> But the Close mourner to thy Royaltie.
> Then breake the circle of thy Tailors spell,
> A Pearle within a rugged Oysters shell.
> Heaven, which the Minster of thy Person owns,
> Will fine thee for Dilapidations.[3]

The rapid movement of images—a privy chamber, a mourner, a tailor's magical circle, a pearl in an oyster shell, and fines for dilapidations—illustrates the kind of verbal wit that made Cleveland famous in his own day. The end-stopped couplets, the strained rhymes, and the use of such a long and technical word as "Dilapidations" are also distinctive of his poetic style. To keep a reader's patience from flagging as he fashions his string of conceits, Cleveland has an array of tactics, not the least of which is this extended negative comparison:

> It is no subtile filme of tiffany ayre,
> No Cob-web vizard, such as Ladies weare,
> When they are veyl'd on purpose to be seene,
> Doubling their lustre by their vanquisht Skreene:
> No, the false scabberd of a Prince is tough
> And three-pil'd darknesse, like the smoaky slough
> Of an imprisoned flame. (ll. 51–57)

This jump to a lengthy antithetical construction slows the cascade of comparisons so that readers may catch their breaths before returning to another sequence of nearly independent couplets. Finally, after Cleveland expands the list of analogies as far as he dares, the paragraph closes triumphantly with a simile of mystery:

> As Temples use to have their Porches wrought
> With Sphynxes, creatures of an antick draught,
> And puzling Pourtraitures, to shew that there
> Riddles inhabited, the like is here. (ll. 87–90)

But if in typical Clevelandesque fashion the first verse paragraph delights in creating a host of metaphors for the mysterious disjunction between Charles's outward appearance and his inner royalty, nevertheless in this imaginative outpouring Cleveland is not completely comfortable. On the contrary, in the opening lines he has difficulty finding a tone that does not condemn the king's action:

3. *Poems of John Cleveland*, ed. Morris and Withington, 6. Further quotations of the poem are from this edition and are cited by line numbers in the text.

AND why so coffin'd in this vile disguise,
Which who but sees blasphemes thee with his eyes?
My twins of light within their pent-house shrinke,
And hold it their Allegeance to winke.
Oh for a State-distinction to arraigne
Charles of high Treason 'gainst my Soveraigne. (ll. 1–6)

Cleveland is disappointed, even angry with his king for doing precisely what his foes wished to do themselves, namely, cover his royalty, as if in a first step toward stripping him of his power altogether. This treasonous act, or what would be treasonous if there existed a legal distinction so defining it, has left Charles's supporters without a center, for by hiding his majesty in the coffin of a servant's clothing the king has disappeared from view. The initial question of "why" haunts the long opening section of the poem. Even though it is never again directly raised, the implication throughout is that the disguise is a disgraceful mistake. Thus, after referring to the sacrilege of Charles's attire, Cleveland adds, "By which th'art halfe depos'd" (l. 35). If the king goes halfway toward deposing himself, it is only a matter of time before his enemies complete the job. According to Cleveland then, whatever the king's intentions, he is damaging his cause and distressing his forces.

Yet the opening passage is more complicated than the poet's initial questioning and only half-veiled criticisms may suggest. A large number of the conceits in the first part of the poem depend on the distinction between the king's exterior servility and his hidden majesty, as these three couplets indicate:

Angell of light, and darknesse too, I doubt,
Inspir'd within, and yet posses'd without.
Majestick twilight in the state of grace,
Yet with an excommunicated face.
Charles and his Maske are of a different mint,
A Psalme of mercy in a miscreant print. (ll. 39–44)

Although Cleveland may be puzzled and dismayed by the king's donning of the disguise, he does not abandon his Royalist beliefs by suggesting that Charles has forfeited his right to rule. If the mask is a form of spiritual darkness covering the king, beneath it Charles is still an angel of light and a psalm of mercy. In this passage and indeed throughout the first verse paragraph, Cleveland shows himself to be deeply conflicted, it is true, but not completely without hope that Charles may yet emerge from beneath his disguise to shine once more.

Moreover, by implication Cleveland blames this moment of crisis as much on the rebel Parliament and its forces as on the king himself. In forming his conceits, for example, he alludes to the purification of Cambridge by "*Manchesters* Elves," to the "self-denying Ordinance," and to "the *Warwick*-Castle-Vote." In addition, no less than seven couplets are dedicated to the "*Hue* and *Cry*" after the King, a scandalous article that appeared in *Mercurius Britanicus* in the summer of 1645.[4] Once Cleveland gets started against this target, he returns to his habitual practice of attacking a clear foe, a practice common in his earlier occasional poems. Yet even in this satiric passage, the poet complicates matters by beginning with a tie between Charles and his enemies: "A Libell is his dresse, a garb uncouth, / Such as the *Hue* and *Cry* once purg'd at mouth" (ll. 71–72). The opposition may have much to answer for, but then so does Charles, to the extent that he follows their lead by muffling his majesty in the dark skin of his disguise.

The first and by far the longest section of the poem, then, mixes typical Cleveland wit, serious questioning of the king's action, and criticism of the forces that have placed Charles in his current position. If Cleveland had called it quits after these first ninety lines, roughly his standard length for an occasional poem,[5] "The Kings Disguise" would have been one of his better poetic performances, signaling his serious concern for the state of the nation in his characteristically conceited manner, and doing so with a depth of emotion that he rarely reaches in other poems. But if the poem had ended with the first verse paragraph, Cleveland probably himself would have considered it a failure. For his task is not only to describe the contradiction between the servant's clothing and the royalty within, or even to express his sadness over this reversal of fortune; he also feels a duty to put a royalist spin on the disguise, to vindicate the king's strategy so that he does not portray Charles as the cowardly deceiver that his enemies believe him to be. In short, Cleveland needs a view of history that

4. Ruth Nevo, *The Dial of Virtue: A Study of Poems on Affairs of State in the Seventeenth Century* (Princeton: Princeton University Press, 1963), 45–47, examines, unfortunately too briefly, the poem's mixture of satire and praise of Charles. In the process, she also makes the important point that in chiding the king, Cleveland is also attacking those who put him in his difficult position. On the "*Hue* and *Cry*," see Joseph Frank, *The Beginnings of the English Newspaper, 1620–1660* (Cambridge: Harvard University Press, 1961), 99–100, and his illustration of *Mercurius Britanicus,* no. 92, July 28–August 4, 1645.

5. The 90 lines of the first verse paragraph may be compared to the 98 lines both of "The Mixed Assembly" and of "Smectymnuus, or the Club-Divines," in many ways the poems most similar to "The Kings Disguise." Cleveland was clearly comfortable with that length. It is interesting to note, though, that "The Rebell Scot" runs to 126 lines, two longer than "The Kings Disguise."

can take him beyond the obvious interpretation of the disguise in such a way that the poem compliments Charles and gives hope to his forces.

II

So Cleveland catches himself up and begins to rethink the meaning of the disguise and its implications for the future of the nation. As he puts it in the second verse paragraph, he will now offer another view of the king's strategy:

> But pardon Sir, since I presume to be
> Clarke of this Closet to Your Majestie;
> Me thinks in this your dark mysterious dresse
> I see the Gospell coucht in Parables.
> The second view my pur-blind fancy wipes,
> And shewes Religion in its dusky types.
> Such a Text Royall, so obscure a shade
> Was *Solomon* in Proverbs all array'd. (ll. 91–98)

If the king's motives in disguising himself and fleeing to the Scots were unfathomable to Cleveland before, in this second view they become overtly mysterious in a religious sense, like a parable in the gospels. Indeed, Cleveland transforms Charles into an antitype and places him on the same plain as Solomon when he arrayed himself in his proverbs, presumably a humble garb for a king more frequently noted for the splendor of his apparel. Furthermore, as Korshin reminds us, because Solomon himself is a type of Christ, his introduction here pushes praise of Charles as far as it can go.[6] This spiritualization of the king's disguise no doubt is Cleveland's attempt to salvage a happy interpretation of the disastrous circumstances of the time. For as long as Charles is wrapped in divine mystery as tightly as he is in a servant's garb, the poet can remain optimistic about the future.

But there is also another advantage to this second reading; it provides Cleveland with the opportunity to use typology to criticize those in the enemy camp who would too facilely interpret the royal text. Reading the secret meanings of Charles and his actions had by 1646 become a commonplace activity among his opponents. Two instances especially may have been on Cleveland's mind. First, pro-Parliament commentators responded to a prophecy allegedly discovered in 1643 and reputed to have survived from the time of Edward IV. This prophecy of a white

---

6. Paul J. Korshin, "The Evolution of Neoclassical Poetics: Cleveland, Denham, and Waller as Poetic Theorists," *Eighteenth-Century Studies* 2 (1968): 112–14. Korshin includes a helpful footnote on possible sources of Cleveland's understanding of typology.

king who would be king and not king received various interpretations both before and after Charles's flight to the Scots. It must have seemed particularly accurate when Charles chose to hide his royalty in a servant's clothing. Second, in the aftermath of Naseby, much to the Royalists' chagrin, the victorious army captured many of the king's secret papers, including those referring to the use of foreign troops against his own people.[7] These papers were published on July 18, 1645, with the title *The King's Cabinet Opened*. As one would expect, they created quite a stir and led to desertions among the royal supporters. Against these kinds of interpretations Cleveland feels the need to defend the king by suggesting that the opposition commentators have not been privy to the true sense of the royal secrets.

So in the penultimate verse paragraph the poet moves to the attack:

> Now all ye brats of this expounding age,
> To whom the spirit is in pupillage;
> You that damne more then ever *Sampson* slew,
> And with his engine, the same jaw-bone too:
> How is't *Charles* 'scapes your Inquisition free,
> Since bound up in the Bibles Liverie? (ll. 99–104)

The key point is that, despite the zeal with which the Puritans damn their opponents, Cleveland thinks that Charles has cleanly escaped from their charges. From the poet's perspective, the opposition writers are merely the brats of an age given to interpretation according to one's own interests. After this confident condemnation, he compares these misreaders to unsuccessful picklocks and suggests that only the keys of St. Peter may open the king's cabinet. One has to wonder whether Cleveland's strategy in this section of the poem is not stretched thin: it is not at all clear, except by an assertion of Cleveland's faith that it be so, why Charles's actions in this desperate state of his reign are in any sense less open to public scrutiny and interpretation than his earlier political messages. Nevertheless, the poet insists upon the holy mystery of the kingship in the couplet concluding the paragraph: "A Prince most seen, is least: What Scriptures call / The Revelation, is most mysticall" (ll. 113–14). He clearly wishes to assert that the divine nature of kingship puts it above human understanding, a belief that the opposition could not share.

---

7. See *The Prophecie of a White King of Brittaine* (London, 1643), and William Lilly, *A Prophecy of the White King: and Dreadfull Dead-man Explained* (London, 1644). Morris and Withington, *Poems of John Cleveland*, 87, are right to suggest that such mysterious interpretations form part of the implicit targets of Cleveland's attack on false readers. On the capture of Charles's papers, see Lois Potter, *Secret Rites and Secret Writing: Royalist Literature, 1641–1660* (Cambridge: Cambridge University Press, 1989), 57–70.

Having to his own satisfaction disposed of the disloyal opposition, in the fourth and final verse paragraph of the poem Cleveland returns to direct address to Charles, urging him on in his journey in a moment of constructed optimism: "May thy strange journey contradictions twist, / And force faire weather from a Scottish mist" (ll. 117–18). In recreating the scene of Charles's journey and arrival among the Scots, Cleveland is rightly suspicious of the latter's reliability. Forcing fair weather from a Scottish mist is no easy task even for a king. Still, the poet is ready to make positive sense out of an eclipsed Charles and hope that all may end well despite the oddity and outrage of the disguise.

But this forced and uncertain optimism cannot hold without Cleveland's expressing reservations even as he attempts a final full mystical reading of the disguise. In the last two couplets of the poem, still pursuing his strategy of sacred mystery, he first sees the flight of Charles in terms of the Exodus, with the king as Israel moving toward the Holy Land: "Thus *Israel*-like he travells with a cloud, / Both as a Conduct to him, and a shroud" (ll. 121–22). If the word "shroud" recalls the coffin image with which the poem begins, the final couplet even more completely complicates the typology: "But oh! he goes to *Gibeon*, and renewes / A league with mouldy bread, and clouted shooes" (ll. 123–24). The reference to Gibeon recalls the story in the ninth chapter of Joshua: Fearful of the coming Israelites, the Gibeonites disguised themselves as migrants from a distant country and made a pact with the invaders, promising to become slaves in return for their lives. Without seeking the guidance of Yahweh, as the text is quick to mention, the Israelites agreed to the pact. Later, when they discovered the true identity of the Gibeonites, the Israelites kept their word and enslaved the native people.[8]

Although Morris and Withington remark that the "whole story is apposite to the King's action,"[9] it seems to me that Cleveland is raising a troubling question in the typology of this final couplet, namely, who is

---

8. This passage was interpreted typologically by such commentators as Thomas Taylor, *Christ Revealed: A Facsimile Reproduction*, intro. by Raymond A. Anselment (Delmar N.Y.: Scholars' Facsimiles and Reprints, 1979), 50–51, but not in the way that Cleveland interprets it. According to Taylor, as Joshua graciously accepted the petition of the Gibeonites, so Christ accepts a contrite heart. The Gibeonites also appear in 2 Samuel 21, in a passage showing David's attempt to compensate them for the slaughter that Saul visited upon them. For the possible influence of this passage on Cleveland's poem, see M. L. Donnelly, "Caroline Royalist Panegyric and the Disintegration of a Symbolic Mode," in *"The Muses Common-Weale": Poetry and Politics in the Seventeenth Century*, ed. Claude J. Summers and Ted-Larry Pebworth (Columbia: University of Missouri Press, 1988), 173.

9. Morris and Withington, *Poems of John Cleveland*, 93.

supposed to be who? On the one hand, because in the previous couplet Charles is associated with the Israelites, it is natural to assume that he remains in that role. According to this reading, Cleveland may be suggesting that Charles is making a pact with a contingent of Scots as disguised as he himself is, that is, who pretend to want to negotiate with him, but who all along know that they will betray him. In that case, does the passage indicting the Israelites for not seeking God's guidance in this matter indict Charles as well? On the other hand, Charles is the one in disguise, like the Gibeonites in the story. Is Cleveland hinting that the king is placing himself into slavery by surrendering to the Scots? If this is the correct reading, then the criticism of Charles is patent, and also accurately prophetic. But whichever possibility Cleveland intends, the typology is not purely laudatory, for neither the Gibeonites nor the Israelites are innocent in the scriptural passage. Thus, the introduction of the Exodus and Joshua stories at poem's end unsettles the positive tone of the preceding typological reference to Solomon and so leaves the reader with a powerfully ambivalent sense of the historical moment.

If Cleveland's purpose in the second reading of the king's disguise is to counteract the obvious negative interpretations of Charles's flight, then to some degree he succeeds. By seeing the disguise in terms of a sacred mystery, he reminds his readers of the Royalist view of the divinity and inexplicability of the kingship. The king's ways, like those of God himself, are by definition mysterious. But at the same time Cleveland also reminds his readers that just as God acts in history, so too must the king, and that means that he has to deal with perfidious groups like the Scots. In light of the fact that Charles appears to be as much a Gibeonite as he is an Israelite, it is not obvious that his strategy will succeed, as Cleveland surely feared, in the event it did lead to the metaphorical enslavement of Charles. Even when he is most optimistic, then, Cleveland maintains a sense of reality that makes even the typological interpretation of history an ambiguous and painful task.

To underscore how radical a move Cleveland is making by means of his use of typology, we might briefly compare his poem to Henry Vaughan's effort on the same event, "The King Disguis'd." Like Cleveland, Vaughan too makes sense of the disguise by alluding to Biblical passages. But the differences are immediately apparent. First, the Biblical figures in Vaughan's poem occur early, whereas Cleveland introduces them only at the end, and so makes them appear to be a last-ditch effort at finding some redemptive meaning in the king's political tactic. Second, and even more importantly, Vaughan's typology is not ambiguously valued. The king in disguise is likened to the esoteric books of Esdras, to the flying roll of Zechariah 5, to Ezekiel's sighs for Israel (Ezekiel 21), and to Saul's rending of Samuel's robes (1 Samuel 15:27–28). Even when the biblical text might be construed in a complex way, for example, in the Ezekiel passage in which God promises to cut off both the righteous and the wicked, Vaughan changes the sense so that destruction only of rebels is signified by the disguise. As we have seen, Cleveland's typology is neither so clear nor so positive. On the contrary, by ending the poem with an allusion to the double-edged Gibeonite story, Cleveland anticipates the incisive use of typology in political satire to be perfected in Dryden's *Absalom and Achitophel*.[10]

"The Kings Disguise" is Cleveland's best political poem. For once he has to explain what cannot be easily explained on the basis of simple party politics. He has to confront the possibility that partly through the king's own fault, the Royalists are about to lose the war and maybe the monarchy itself. He has to deal with his own disappointment and his ambivalent attitude toward Charles, and at the same time he wishes to provide some glimmer of hope that all may yet be saved. We cannot, of course, equate Cleveland's response to the beginning of the end of his political hopes with the truly great poetry of Milton after his side had lost. Cleveland seems bent on the more modest task of justifying the dubious ways of Charles to man, and even then he achieves only partial success. Yet in its kind, "The Kings Disguise" remains one of the best poetic records of the complex emotions of the Royalists as they neared defeat; reading and then rereading history is the only way Cleveland knows to make sense of the moment in which he is living.

10. *The Works of Henry Vaughan*, ed. L. C. Martin, 2d ed. (Oxford: Clarendon Press, 1957), 625–26. Under his title "The King Disguis'd," Vaughan adds "Written about the same time that Mr. John Cleveland wrote his." On typology in Dryden, see Steven N. Zwicker, "Politics and Panegyric: The Figural Mode from Marvell to Pope," in *Literary Uses of Typology from the Late Middle Ages to the Present*, ed. Earl Miner (Princeton: Princeton University Press, 1977), 132 n.

Erna Kelly

"Small Types of Great Ones"

Richard Lovelace's Separate Peace

Many critics, Earl Miner and Raymond Anselment among them, have claimed that Lovelace's poetry, like other Cavalier poetry, responds to political turmoil with stoicism. Indeed, his poems show the influence of stoicism as they transform a prison cell into "an Hermitage" or advocate retreat from public turmoil to the more certain society of friends. In Lovelace's poetry, however, there is a tendency to take stoicism to such an extreme that it fails, becoming instead a self-imprisonment that generates anxiety and gnawing self-awareness. Bruce King and Bronwen Price also note a thread of anxiety running throughout Lovelace's poetry, and William Empson's reading of the final stanza of "To Althea, From Prison" makes even that poem's "Hermitage" suspect. While allowing for the popular interpretation, which sees a stoic mind transforming a prison into a calm retreat, Empson maintains that the poem's power derives from its suggestion of a simultaneous counterreading: walls and bars are irrelevant because the mind has already imprisoned itself.[1] Anxiety revealed by lines earlier in the poem—the poet's boast that his song is "shriller" than that of "committed

I wish to thank the Humanities Institute at the University of Wisconsin for the fellowship that made possible the portions of this essay that refer to emblem literature.

1. Miner, *The Cavalier Mode from Jonson to Cotton* (Princeton: Princeton University Press, 1971), 110, 118–19, 257–59; Anselment, *Loyalist Resolve: Patient Fortitude in the English Civil War* (Newark: University of Delaware Press, 1988), 97–126. King, "Green Ice and a Breast of Proof," *College English* 24 (1964): 511–15; reprinted in *Seventeenth Century English Poetry: Modern Essays in Criticism*, William R. Keast, rev. ed. (London: Oxford University Press, 1971), 324–32; Price, " 'Th' inwards of th' Abysse': Questions of the Subject in Lovelace's Poetry," *English: The Journal of the English Association* 43 (1994): 117–37; Empson, *Seven Types of Ambiguity* (New York: Chatto and Windus, 1956), 210.

Linnets"[2]—reinforces Empson's alternate reading. Moreover, the anxiety generated by severe withdrawal, in turn, often prompts Lovelace to indulge in the epicurean side of the Cavalier code. However, like extreme control, sensual abandon also proves an unsatisfactory response to political turmoil. When Lovelace and his comrades "steepe" their "thirsty griefe in Wine," it is only the "Healths and draughts [that] go free" ("To Althea," ll. 13–14). He and his friends remain imprisoned in their grief because *"joyes so ripe, so little keepe"* ("To Amarantha," l. 28). Despite his tendency to take the stoic and epicurean sides of the Cavalier code to extremes, Lovelace did write a number of poems that show him able to deal with political turmoil without excessive withdrawal or abandon. Among the most successful are the poems that address insects and other small creatures. Dissimilar enough from him to allow an unanxious assessment yet similar enough in the difficulties they face to evoke empathy, the subjects of these poems enlarged Lovelace's understanding of England's civil wars, enabling him to make a private or separate peace.

The Cavalier code included several interdependent ideals: loyalty to monarch and to friends, a show of courage when loyalty demanded it, and enjoyment of the pleasures life affords, e.g., the arts, wine, food, and love. A stable monarchy assisted in making life's pleasures accessible; sharing pleasures with friends increased the enjoyment. Spending rather than hoarding, that is, living fully, whether through martial prowess or simply through conviviality, figured largely in Cavalier philosophy. This prodigality was, in part, a response to the possibility of life being cut short or of the political climate becoming hostile. Although seemingly paradoxical because it implies a reining in, the stoical belief that reason and will should control the passions is also a part of the Cavalier code. Ideally, reason and will enable one to find a calm center that can protect the self from adverse external conditions, a place from which to judge when to retreat and when to act. Contemplating small creatures apparently afforded Lovelace the conditions he needed to create a calm center. From that center Lovelace could examine with some equanimity behaviors that grew out of Cavalier ideals as well as behaviors that undermined those ideals. While the poems that address small creatures retain the loyalty to monarchy found in many of Lovelace's poems, they are less strident than his other poems. In them moralizing is muted and empathy extended.

    2. "To Althea, From Prison," ll. 18, 17, in *The Poems of Richard Lovelace,* ed. C. H. Wilkinson (Oxford: Clarendon Press, 1930). All quotations from Lovelace's poetry are taken from this edition and cited by line numbers in the text.

The calm center that Lovelace evoked by writing about small creatures apparently not only expanded his political insights but also enhanced his craftsmanship. The group of poems that examine the actions of small creatures contains not only one of the undisputed examples of Cavalier achievement, "The Grasse-hopper," but also many other fine poems. The occasional lapse in meter, awkward transition, confusing image, or overly ambiguous syntax found in Lovelace's poetry as a whole are rarer here than in other groupings of his works. Perhaps resolving the conflict between stances of frozen self-control and reckless abandon allowed Lovelace to pour more of his energy into careful crafting of his lines. In terms of artistic merit these poems not only stand out within the body of Lovelace's poetry, they also stand apart in a century that A. Lytton Sells dubbed "the golden age of animal poetry." As Manfred Weidhorn notes, "Nothing in the seventeenth century—not quite Drayton's or Herrick's 'fairy-land' poems, certainly not Donne's ratiocinative seduction poem 'The Flea'—is similar."[3] Lovelace's poems are not elegies or epitaphs for pets and small wild creatures as are so many of those by his contemporaries. Nor are they, like others, translations or close imitations of classical predecessors. Nor are they, like "The Flea" and Crashaw's "Musick's Duell," primarily a display of the poet's ingenuity that leaves the world of the creature far behind. Although Lovelace does not shrink from displays of ingenuity, his witty comparisons are reinforced with realistic touches like the descriptions of a fly's leg or of a grasshopper perched upon an "Oaten Beard." Furthermore, poems like "Musick's Duell" and "The Flea" do not include empathy for their ostensible subjects; Lovelace's poems, on the other hand, not only convey empathy but do so without becoming saccharine, as elegies for pets (Cotton's "On my Pretty Martin," for example) often do.

It is tempting to say that by placing political discourse in the world of ants, flies, and snails, Lovelace points out the inhumanity of the current political situation, its power to reduce England's inhabitants to insignificant stature and mean behavior, aligning his poems with the beast fable. It is, of course, true that "The Grasse-hopper" and "The Ant" have roots in Aesop's fables. However, Lovelace's poems are also related to a wide tradition of literature addressed to, describing, and even celebrating small creatures, a tradition available to him through Greek and Latin models as well as neo-Latin and French versions of these models. Furthermore,

3. Sells, *Animal Poetry in French and English Literature and the Greek Tradition* (Bloomington: Indiana University Press, 1955), 110; Weidhorn, *Richard Lovelace* (New York: Twayne, 1970), 46.

Lovelace adapts his literary inheritance to suit his own vision, departing, as many have noted, from even the Anacreontic verses on the grasshopper. Therefore, to align his poems too heavily with the didactic beast fable tradition is to miss their subtlety.

If Lovelace's poems about small creatures resemble any of the many forms in the rich tradition of literature associated with small creatures, it is the emblem. Indeed, Lovelace wants the reader to see this connection: "The Snayl" is a "Wise Emblem of our Politick World" (l. 1) and the "Fly caught in a Cobweb" is a "Small type of great ones, that do hum, / Within this whole World's narrow Room" (ll. 1–2). As Raymond Anselment cautions in his discussion of "The Falcon" and "The Ant," to expect the consistent allegory of fable is to be disappointed.[4] Although many emblems have roots in fables and like beast fables can teach lessons (indeed, seventeenth-century emblem collections such as George Wither's heightened this aspect of the emblem), the original intent of the emblem was to provide a puzzle for the viewer or reader to solve. Emblems are more aligned with the epigram than with the fable, the terseness of emblems prompting their audience to move back and forth between picture and text, fusing the two forms and reconciling any apparent tension. The emblem tradition, like Renaissance painting, began in Italy, and like Renaissance painting, its popularity spread northward gradually. English emblem books, compiled near the end of the genre's popularity, were often intended for an audience less educated than that of their Continental counterparts, which encouraged English compilers like Wither to explain an emblem's iconology to the point of tedium. Earlier emblems, created for a more sophisticated audience, put the burden of interpretation on the viewer or reader. Lovelace, who dismissed English painting in favor of Continental art, not surprisingly aligns his poems with the form and intent of Continental emblems.

Finally, although aligning these poems with the emblem tradition may deepen our understanding of individual poems, what is more important is that the subjects of these poems enabled Lovelace to see the plight of all who were involved in the English civil wars, not just the plight of Royalists. Lovelace is able to admire the "Puritan" heron, show some sympathy for the "Puritan" ant and the turncoat fly, and perhaps even convey slight disdain for the "Cavalier" grasshopper. Taken as a whole, these poems become a prism refracting light shed on the problem of political disruption, each poem yielding a point of view that is only a

---

4. Anselment, " 'Grief Triumphant' and 'Victorious Sorrow': A Reading of Richard Lovelace's 'The Falcon,' " *Journal of English and Germanic Philology* 70 (1971): 410.

fraction of the spectrum. By enhancing both his and his readers' ability to see, if not always to agree with, more than the Cavalier party line, Lovelace may have helped create a more humane world.

Lovelace wrote eight poems that focus on small creatures. Two, "A Flye about a Glasse of Burnt Claret" and "The Toad and the Spider," are apolitical and for that reason not included in the discussion that follows. A third, "Another," which immediately follows "The Snayl" in the 1659 volume of Lovelace's poetry, is glanced at only briefly because the points it makes are subsumed in its more complex predecessor. The remaining five poems are grouped according to the protagonists' political alignment as well as the courses of actions that they choose. I begin with the Royalist grasshopper, falcon, and fly, whose courses of action all fail to some degree, move to the Puritan ant, who likewise fails, and then back again to a Royalist protagonist, the snail, a protagonist who makes successful choices.

"The Grasse-hopper," the best known of these poems, is an anomaly, differing from the others in that it focuses as much on the world of human beings as on the world of small creatures. Furthermore, it is the only political poem about a small creature in *Lucasta, 1649*. Perhaps because events did not seem as dire to Lovelace when he wrote "The Grasse-hopper" as they did when he wrote the other poems, he did not need as much distance from the world of human affairs. Unfortunately, dates of composition can be estimated for only a few of Lovelace's poems. It is possible that the poems printed in the posthumous 1659 volume were composed at the same time as those printed in the earlier volume; Lovelace may simply have chosen not to publish them. Still, many critics feel the second volume projects a darker view of the world, tentatively concluding that its poems were written later, by a more disillusioned Lovelace.

The first half of Lovelace's poem repeats the Greek Anacreonta's association of the grasshopper with royalty, aristocracy, and poets. These multiple associations suggest an emblematic rather than allegorical approach to Lovelace's poem. Another argument against a strict allegorical interpretation is that the poem contains other images of kingship besides the grasshopper, for example, the sun, gold, and flames. Finally, while the grasshopper could represent Charles I, seeing it simultaneously as a king, a Royalist, a poet, and even more simply as itself works equally well, perhaps even better. A close allegorical reading would apply both the epithet "Poore verdant foole" and the epithet "green Ice" to Charles I. Earl Miner observes that, at the time Lovelace wrote the poem, "Poore verdant foole" could apply to Charles I, but "green Ice" could not. *Lucasta* was licensed in February 1648; Charles was not executed until January 1649. Leah Marcus even questions the application of the first epithet, noting Kevin Sharpe's reminder that Charles I was not as naive as we might think: during his reign state business was dispatched "with considerable efficiency."[5] Historical accuracy aside, I find applying either epithet to Charles I too irreverent for a poet who addresses his monarch elsewhere in the following manner:

> Oh from thy glorious Starry Waine
> Dispense on me one sacred Beame
> To light me where I soone may see
> How to serve you, and you trust me.
> ("To Lucasta. From Prison," ll. 53–56)

Still, despite the multivalence of the grasshopper image as well as the abundance of reinforcing images, the poem is able to focus on a set of strategies that work for Royalists during the years of the civil wars. This poem celebrates the use of the mind to outwit the enemy by opposing it with quiet, scaled down rebellion. Its protagonists rebel by spending resources freely, seizing the day, and enjoying the pleasures of holiday mirth, all actions that run against the Puritan grain.

The poem is filled with references to motion and countermotion. In the second half of the poem, summer gives way to winter, life to death; political systems change and with them personal fortune. Here Lovelace departs from the Anacreontic ode's joyful mood, its emphasis on spring and perpetual song. Given the reality of change, what stance can one take? The grasshopper ignores change to its own peril. "Golden Eares" of grain and the sun's "guilt-plats" disappear in the dark of winter (ll. 13, 10). Only the green of the grasshopper, the color of spring and thus of hope, new life, and naiveté, is preserved as—"green Ice!" (l. 17). The poet, like winter, mocks the insect's previous mobility, yet also mourns the transience of the insect's former status: "Large and lasting, as thy Peirch of Grasse" (l. 18). The fragility of grass as well as the precariousness implied by the verb *to perch* (*perch* was used colloquially in the seventeenth century to mean "vanquish, upset, or ruin") echoes the delicate balance that the

5. Miner, *Cavalier Mode*, 289; Marcus, *The Politics of Mirth: Jonson, Herrick, Milton, Marvell, and the Defense of Old Holiday Pastimes* (Chicago: University of Chicago Press, 1986), 231, 306 n. 24; Sharpe, "The Personal Rule of Charles I," in *Before the English Civil War: Essays on Early Stuart Politics and Government*, ed. Howard Tomlinson (London: Macmillan, 1983), 53–78, 63–67.

grasshopper had momentarily achieved. What better stance can human beings take against similar turns of fortune? Aware of winter, men can oppose it with—what? Curiously enough, like the grasshopper, they can with merrymaking, but within the context of friendship. The poem is dedicated and addressed to Lovelace's friend, Charles Cotton. In this poem the weight of winter's wet gloom is counterweighted "with an o'erflowing glasse" (l. 20). Flowing freely, the fortifying liquor symbolizes a thawing of the ice that arrested the grasshopper's movement. It also refers to the Cavalier practice of drinking healths among friends in defiance of the Puritan government.[6]

The friends' defiance also takes another form. In 1644, Parliament, in an attempt to remove pagan associations from the holiday, banned traditional Christmas festivities. Cotton and Lovelace, however, ignore this ordinance and restore the "Raigne" of the winter feast paradoxically within the political "Summer" they have created (ll. 30, 22). December, who has "come weeping in," bewailing "th' usurping of his Raigne; . . . / Shall crie, he hath his Crowne againe!" as Lovelace and Cotton shower the season with "old Greeke" (ll. 29–30, 32). Although many critics interpret "old Greeke" as a reference to wine, it could refer to "talk" or to "the academic days of both men."[7] In fact, Lovelace's circle of friends included his kinsman, Thomas Stanley, who became known for translations of the Greek Anacreontic odes. Furthermore, Greek, as the language of a pre-Christian culture, helps reinforce the affront to Puritans embodied in the references to Roman religious practices in stanza 7: "Vestall Flames" and "sacred harthes." Both suggestions, wine or language, work well as interpretations of "old Greeke." December's "weeping" (l. 29), which echoes stanza 5's description of winter as a season of "Raine," is reinforced by the pun in "Raigne" (l. 30). The excessive rain or crying, which is described as "flouds" (l. 20), is destructive, not beneficial like summer's moderate, single, "Delicious teare / Dropt . . . from Heav'n" nightly to refresh the grasshopper (ll. 3–4). The flood of "an o'reflowing glasse," or Christmas rain, on the other hand, works as a cordial or restorative, warming the heart as practices inimical to the Puritans are reinstated (l. 20). Although they could be seen as frivolous, the actions of Lovelace and Cotton are more than an escape into an alcoholic haze; they are calculated

6. On the Cavalier practice of drinking healths, see Raymond Anselment, " 'Stone Walls' and 'Iron Bars': Richard Lovelace and the Conventions of Seventeenth-Century Prison Literature," *Renaissance and Reformation* 29 (1993): 23.

7. John T. Shawcross and Ronald David Emma, eds., *Seventeenth-Century English Poetry* (Philadelphia: J. B. Lippincott, 1969), 358; Shawcross and Emma suggest "talk" although they concede it may mean "wine."

to counter psychologically the forces pulling them down. Encased in ice, the grasshopper's death is an emblem of its isolation. The men, on the other hand, "Thaw" (l. 24) the political winter with the warmth of friendship, a defiant Cavalier toast, and a celebration of a banished holiday. If the practice of Cavalier values is inhibited in public, Cotton and Lovelace will practice them privately among friends.

Finally, the fullness of life displayed in the first stanza of the poem by the "well-filled Oaten Beard" and the grasshopper's actions—its drinking, its flying and hopping, its ability to make itself, men, and melancholy streams merry—can be restored by Lovelace and Cotton because they choose retreat, a strategy frequently suggested in Cavalier poetry. It is reason and will that make Lovelace's and Cotton's "rebellion" possible. Reason leads them to retreat; will enables them to rebel despite the dispiriting effect retreat might prompt. The first half of the poem, describing the fate of the grasshopper, is cast in present tense; the second half, prescribing the fate of the poet and his friend, is cast in future tense, even as it paradoxically attempts to return to the past. While the grasshopper is frozen because it does not heed the change of seasons, the grasshopper-like men control change by freezing time. Once they have recreated an acceptable season, their hearths "burne eternally" (l. 31). The verbs in the second half of the poem, however, display more than a promise of an eternal present. Lovelace uses "will" with first person and "shall" with third person, indicating not mere future tense but volition and obligation. The friends "will create / . . . Summer"; "harthes shall burne"; "the North-wind . . . / Shall . . . flye" (or flee); December "Shall crie, he hath his Crowne againe"; and candles "shall . . . whip" night away from their windows.

Cavalier stoicism is evident here in the use of will to overcome difficult situations, yet the poem contains something beyond stoical assurance and control and even beyond tipsy conviviality. The imagery associated with will in the last two stanzas of the poem is disturbing. The ninth stanza's depiction of winter and night as a "Hagge," its verbs "strip" and "sticke," and its phallic tapers suggest rape. Likewise, the "Aetna," that Lovelace and Cotton create "in each others breast" (ll. 28, 22) is capable of violent outbursts as well as warmth. While the final stanza's declaration of self-possession is congruent with a stoical retreat to a calm center, coming after the violence of the previous stanza, it is somewhat suspect. Furthermore, the expression of self-possession in negatives—"asking nothing, nothing need" as well as the poem's last phrase "poore indeed"—undermines to a degree the warmth and life of stanzas 6, 7, and 8. As Claude Summers says of Herrick's political poetry, beneath the celebratory surface in "The Grasse-hopper" are indications of despair, intentional signals, perhaps, of the poet's own doubts.[8] More successful than the grasshopper, the men nonetheless meet with only qualified success.

In contrast to "The Grasse-hopper," the poems about small creatures in the second volume do not depict human understanding as superior to that of smaller creatures. If anything, the protagonists of these poems illuminate the dark tangle of the world for human beings. Perhaps weary of the limitations that come from retreat, Lovelace examines more extreme Royalist actions: combat and defecting. The grasshopper men use their minds to uphold the Cavalier ideals of loyalty and independence, opposing the Puritan reign symbolically by creating monarchies within each others' breasts and drinking healths to their king. In "The Falcon," a third element of the Cavalier code, courage, is added while loyalty and independence take on new dimensions. The falcon's opposition to Puritan power is open and largely physical; indeed, she risks, and ultimately loses, her life for her cause.

Lovelace clearly admires open confrontation, calling the falcon "Brave Cousin-german to the Sun," and "bold Gen'ral" (ll. 10, 67). The association with the sun as well as the first line's "Fair Princesse" and the seventh line's "Bright Heir t' th' Bird Imperial" connect the falcon with royalty. However, the falcon is royalty that has forsaken its "Throne and Sphere"; she has become a "Free beauteous Slave," "an humble Pris'ner," who wears "silver Fetters" (ll. 11, 21, 12, 22). The poem's first six stanzas resemble "A Lady with a Falcon on her fist" in their praise of the bird's owner as well as of the bird itself; however, they differ by making the bird, not the woman, their primary focus. Lovelace marvels that this noble bird deigns to serve human beings, who are unable to "Advance a foot into the Sky"; it is we, who are "quarter'd below stairs," that should be her servants (ll. 6, 3). In the remainder of the poem, the falcon teaches Lovelace and his readers how to behave nobly in an adverse political climate. However, even the first six stanzas are not without political meaning. The associations with sun and eagle suggest the falcon may be a symbol for Charles I. The references to captivity would be consistent with this reading as well. Furthermore, the associations with Christ (the falcon is "humble" in that it "forsake[s]" a superior sphere, subjecting itself to human conditions as Christ did through the incarnation) also connect it with Charles. Royalist

8. Summers, "Herrick's Political Poetry: The Strategies of His Art," in *"Trust to Good Verses": Herrick Tercentenary Essays,* ed. Roger B. Rollin and J. Max Patrick (Pittsburgh: University of Pittsburgh Press, 1978), 171–83; "Herrick's Political Counterplots," *Studies in English Literature, 1500–1900* 25 (1985): 165–82.

iconography frequently depicted Charles I as a type of Christ. Anselment suggests, however, that the phrase "Heir t' th' Bird Imperial" might better be applied to Charles's son. "Like the falcon who resigned 'the Royal Woods command,' Charles II left Scotland to invade England; and the poem might commemorate his defeat at Worcester in 1651." Anselment also observes, though, that this reading breaks down at the poem's end, which describes the falcon's funeral; Charles II, of course, had not died.[9] Finally, the references to imprisonment might as easily allude to Lovelace's own interments or imprisonment of any Royalist as much as it might allude to the capture of Charles I. Rather than attempt to attach a narrow meaning to the images of royalty and captivity in the poem's opening stanzas, a more fruitful approach is simply to see the falcon as a Royalist and allow the poem to remind us of the specific instances outlined above as background for the battle that is at the heart of the poem.

Although the falcon's opposition is physical, it is not without intelligence. She is an "expert" tactician as well as brave warrior: climbing "to advantage . . . / She gets the upper Sky and Wind"; and there "lies a pol'tick Ambuscade" (ll. 53–56). Her bravery is evident as she makes the first move and "charges" with a "brigade of Talons" (ll. 64). Compared with the falcon, the heron is mundane: "Secure i' th' Moore, about to sup," a creature who tries "fortification" and later "retreat" from battle (ll. 47, 59, 66). Emblem books emphasized marsh birds' ability to disguise themselves and hide. Still, even though a less heroic bird than the falcon, Lovelace admires the Puritan heron: fortification, retreat, and disguise are, after all, legitimate martial strategies. Furthermore, the heron's martial repertoire goes beyond these strategies. When "hedg'd-in" by the falcon above and "Dogs below," the heron "makes him ready for surprize" (ll. 57–58, 60). Although "desp'rate," "he is resolv'd to fall" in order to kill his enemy, a brave or "Noble" decision (ll. 71, 73–74). The climax of the poem occurs when the heron impales the falcon with "the palizadoes of his Beak" as the falcon simultaneously bears down on him and splits open his "naked breast," managing to kill her enemy "ev'n in her expiring pangs" (ll. 78, 83, 85). The "double Funerall" procession (l. 90) includes lesser falcons, which, Anselment notes, suggest nobility. The funeral also includes two birds with Anglican clerical titles, "Doctor *Robbin*" and "Prelate Pye." Anselment is puzzled by Lovelace's linking Anglican clergy with birds that have rather negative reputations, the pie being associated with frivolous chattering and the robin having acquired his red breast by killing his father. He speculates that Lovelace may have used these birds

9. Anselment, " 'Grief Triumphant' and 'Victorious Sorrow,' " 409–10 n. 10.

for the consonance they create when paired with "Doctor" and "Prelate" and that Lovelace "may have intended an indirect criticism of the clergy's role in the civil war."[10] Both reasons are plausible. It is interesting that Lovelace also predicts their demise. The pie and robin are grouped with a common emblem for poets, the swan, who according to legend sings only when it dies. In lines 109–11 the verb "dye" applies to all three birds. Perhaps the clerical birds' deaths allude to Puritan purging of Anglican clergy. What is clear is that the falcon's "Victory [is] unhap'ly wonne" (l. 91). Abandoning oneself to the moment, no matter how nobly done, can, if done without moderation, take its toll; Lovelace is realistic enough to admit this. Rather than the defiance tinged with despair found in "The Grasse-hopper," this poem conveys admiration tinged with sadness.

"A Fly caught in a Cobweb" presents a very different reaction to a hostile political climate. While the falcon puts much of her energy into a physical response to adversity, acting out of the promptings of her heart, spurred on by loyalty and courage, the fly puts all of its energy into a mental solution that replaces the Cavalier ideals of loyalty and courage with self-interest. Although the grasshopper men also use their heads in responding to adversity, outwitting it by creating a miniature monarchy within their homes, the monarchy they create is also a product of their hearts and a display of loyalty. The source of the fly's actions, on the other hand, is solely the head; the motive, solely self-interest. Having analyzed its options, Lovelace's fly casts its lot with the Puritans: defecting might lead not only to survival but to political and economic advancement in a Puritan-controlled England. The poem's opening phrase, "Small type of great ones," indicates that Lovelace is rewriting a popular emblem, which combines an image of a fly caught in a cobweb with an epigram observing how laws trap common folk but let the wealthy and powerful escape. In Lovelace's poem the fly represents a "great one" or an aristocrat, not a commoner; "small" refers to its functioning as an emblem, not its social status. Furthermore, as the poem unfolds, the reader sees that the opening line's "small" also means petty or base as this aristocrat's actions are compared with those of aristocrats who remained loyal to their king. It is possible that Lovelace had another emblem in mind as well, the twenty-fifth emblem in Julius Zincgreff's *Emblematum Ethico-Politicorum*, which shows a fly or gnat caught in a spider web as a lion looks on. Both its motto and epigram indicate that the insect's fate is a result of its overreaching;

10. See Henry Peacham, *Minerva Britanna* (London, 1612), K3v for an emblem of a marsh bird; Anselment, " 'Grief Triumphant' and 'Victorious Sorrow,' " 413–14 n. 25.

the lion, a symbol of royalty, is glad to be rid of "The chit-chat . . . [that] rub on . . . [him] / stick and grieve the heroic one greatly."[11] Lovelace's fly, also an overreacher, has allowed greed and false pride to replace loyalty and courage. Still, the poet sympathizes to some extent with the creature, acknowledging that siding with the monarch courts danger: the "Majestick Ray" or "noble Flame" "Might sindge" the fly's "upper down attire" (ll. 16, 23, 18). Here is just one of the many places in the poem in which Lovelace complicates the tone of sympathetic understanding, in this instance with humor evoked from the wordplay of "upper down."

The fly of this poem could be a housefly, but it is as likely a moth, since in seventeenth-century usage *fly* designated any winged insect. While there are emblems of houseflies caught in cobwebs, there are also emblems of moths hovering near flames; and this poem refers to flame as well as cobweb. Furthermore, the fuzz or "upper down" on the moth's body and the gaudiness of the butterfly or moth fits well with the undue attention that Lovelace's fly gives to his attire, possibly a source of disapproval as well as amusement and hence another facet to complicate the sympathy extended to the creature. These lines not only show the complexity of tone found in this poem and many of the other poems in this group, but they also demonstrate one of the many instances in which Lovelace combines his talent for keen observation of natural phenomena with his talent for creating metaphor.

The next lines show more serious concerns that the fly may have factored into its decision to abandon its monarch. In fighting for the king, the fly could lose "an Eye, / A Wing, . . . a Thigh," all serious losses, though the unusual substitution of so specific a term as *thigh* for the more commonly used term *leg* again undercuts the serious tone somewhat (ll. 19–20). Lovelace makes sure that *thigh* is noticed not only by rhyming it with "Eye" and placing it at the end of the line but also by reminding the fly that it is a "self-trapping Thigh," the very thigh responsible for the fly's current fate. It would have been better to have lost the thigh or even its life as the falcon did and as the reference to Icarus or to Phaeton in lines 21–22 implies, than to be "Trapp'd" so "basely" (l. 24). The fly, who attempts to outwit danger and simultaneously to raise its status, becomes victim of its mental machinations; hence its demise is in a "Strange" way a "witty Death" (l. 35). Although throughout the seventeenth century *wit* most frequently refers to overall mental ability, the more specialized meaning of *wit* as the joining of opposites had begun to gain currency midcentury. The fly's death corresponds to this definition as well: attempting to use

11. Zincgreff, *Emblematum Ethico-Politicorum* (Heidelberg, 1619) (my translation).

flight to keep its freedom, it is trapped in midair; attempting to attain greater political status, it becomes a "Slave" to the spider; a creature of the air, it is eventually reduced to earth when the spider, "the spawn of Mud and Lome," devours it, thus incorporating it into himself (l. 26). Like the grasshopper and grasshopper men, the fly plays but not so innocently: its vanity is shown not only in its undue attention to attire but in its use of people's opinion to puff it up. He and others like it "Catch at people's vainer Voice, / And with spread Sails play with their breath / Whose very Hails new christen Death" (ll. 4–6). Ironically, breath, which normally symbolizes life, here is reborn (christened) as death. Instead of continuing to support and to take support from the king, the fly depends on the people beneath it to keep it aloft. Their praise, though, cannot keep the fly from the machinations of the government that they support: it is caught in "an airy net," from which its "fatal buzzes rore" until its "all-belly'd foe (round Elf) / Hath quarter'd . . . [it] within himself" (ll. 7, 12–14). Although some critics apply the epithet "round Elf" to the fly, Lynn Veach Saddler makes a good case for applying it to the spider: She sees "round" fitting well with other descriptors of the spider's body, e.g., "all-belly'd" and "swoln" (l. 28) and cites many literary references that connect spiders with elves. She also notes that the "political associations [of these lines] with Roundheads and 'quartering' " are additional reasons to apply the epithet to the spider.[12] I would add that Lovelace uses the image of a governing body being reduced to a belly to describe the Commonwealth government in another poem:

> Now *Whitehalls* in the grave
> And our *Head* is our slave,
>
> . . . .
>
> Now the *Thighs* of the Crown,
> And the *Arms* are lopp'd down,
> And the *Body* is all but a Belly.
> ("A Mock-Song," ll. 1–2, 118–20)

The fly is both prisoner and potential jailer. Its actions affect not only itself but also its kin, since the spider will digest the fly, then spin it out as a thread for yet another web, which will, in turn, snare the fly's relatives. Still, Lovelace offers the defector some slight consolation. Although critics have debated the exact meaning of certain phrases in the poem's conclusion, they agree that Lovelace's intention is to extend solace to the fly by

---

12. Saddler, "Lovelace's 'A Fly Caught in a Cobweb,' " *Literatur in Wissenschaft und Unterricht*, 6 (1972): 25.

comparing it with creatures who kill their foe even as they are being killed. Lines 43–44 compare the contest between the fly and spider to that of the rhinoceros and elephant: The horn of the rhinoceros pierces the elephant as the elephant crushes it to death, a parallel to the simultaneous death depicted in "The Falcon." The final lines of this poem compare the fly to an asp:

> As through the *Cranes* trunk Throat doth speed,
> The *Aspe* doth on his feeder feed;
> Fall yet triumphant in thy woe,
> Bound with the entrails of thy foe. (ll. 45–48)

Perhaps, in spinning out his web, the spider depletes himself, so while the fly has brought on the demise of itself and its kin, in a small way, the fly in the spider's belly now also contributes to the demise of the enemy to whom it defected.[13] Even a turncoat Royalist merits some sympathy.

It is natural that a number of these poems, written by a Royalist, should scrutinize the various courses of action open to Royalists: retreat, combat, and defection. However, as Lovelace's lines on the heron and on the spider indicate, he takes some note of enemy actions as well. Furthermore, in the case of the heron, Lovelace can admire and understand enemy action if not the ideals for which they stand; he can, as shown above, even extend sympathy to a defector. Again he is disposed to empathy, at least initially, as the enemy becomes the sole focus of his attention in "The Ant." The poem begins by gently urging the ant to rest, but as the ant continues on its path, the tone becomes increasingly severe. The opening of the second stanza begins "Cease" and the first stanza's genial appellations, "little Ant" and "great good Husband," are replaced in the fourth stanza by the epithets, *Austere* and *Cynick*." Actually, the concern shown for the difficulty of the ant's labor with words such as "spacious tent," "prodigious heat," "double load," and "Granarie" begins to evaporate even in the first stanza, when these words expose the ant's self-importance: the "spacious tent" is after all only a "Plant"; the "double load" and "Granarie," "one grain."

Royalist protagonists such as the falcon, the grasshopper, and the grasshopper men exhibit the ability to let go. More is gained than lost by spending. Even if the falcon's actions spend her very life, while she lives, she lives nobly. In contrast, the Puritan ant, who focuses on hoarding rather than spending, moves through a "lifetime," yet never "one

---

13. Anselment suggests a reading similar to this for the poem's last line (see *Loyalist Resolve*, 120–21).

poor Minute" lives (l. 23). Because accumulated wealth can be seized by another, spending energy in hoarding can be seen as a waste of time or "unthrifty": "Scattering to hord 'gainst a long Day, / Thinking to save all, we cast all away" (ll. 31, 35–36). Spending or giving away wealth, as Lovelace himself did in outfitting troops for the king's cause, is a wiser use of time because it affords the giver some voice in how his wealth is used.

The pinched nature of the ant's life is made especially clear after the creature ignores an invitation to observe a holiday:

> *Lucasta*, She that holy makes the Day,
>   And 'stills new Life in fields of Fueillemort:
> Hath back restor'd their Verdure with one Ray,
>   And with her Eye bid all to play and sport. (ll. 13–18)

These lines glance at James I's publication of the *Book of Sports* in 1618 and its reissuing by Charles I in 1633. The observance of traditional festival practices was promoted as a means to affirm royal authority, to link the monarch with his people, and to dissipate potentially disruptive tensions through the temporary suspension of the normal hierarchy. In addition to helping the Stuarts maintain power, ritual play is an expansive way of being in the world. The poem underscores the relative fullness of this behavior by enlarging its scope spatially, including not only the ant and the earth but Lucasta and the heavens as well. In this poem, Lucasta is simultaneously sun, monarch, and goddess. As goddess, she is honored by holidays; as monarch, she promotes their observation; as the sun, she demonstrates the creative power of spending energy in play. In contrast to the ant, who struggles with a single grain, Lucasta easily restores fertility to the fields with a single ray, the fields upon which the ant depends for the grain it is so determined to hoard.

The poem's scope expands in time as well as in space as the poet retrieves a historical precedent: even the moral Cato "sometimes the nak'd Florals saw" (l. 10). C. H. Wilkinson comments that "Cato did not see the 'nak'd Florals'" because, according to Valerius Maximus, "the respect in which he [Cato] was held was so great that the people forbore to demand 'ut Mimae nudarentur' till he, rather than prevent a popular custom, left the theatre." Still, Lovelace's line is accurate in spirit: Cato, although he may not have supported all aspects of the Floralia, did support the notion of festival. Marcus points out that May Day, one of the celebrations most objectionable to Puritans, was linked in their minds with the Roman Floralia, since both were spring festivals "associated with flowers, fertility, and also with sexual license." The ant ignores historical example as well as Lucasta's regal request and acts like a proper Puritan, obeying the 1647 Parliamentary ordinance that decreed "festivall dayes commonly called holy dayes be no longer observed."[14] However, by neglecting to play, the ant risks undermining its work by displeasing Lucasta, who, both as a fertility goddess and as a monarch, has the power to ensure conditions conducive to productivity. Ants were not merely symbols of industry; they frequently symbolized democracy; in fact, Sambucus's twenty-first emblem depicts ants in confusion and alarm as a warning against the dangers of democracy. Lovelace's ant also undermines its work in a more immediate way: refusing to halt its "ore charged Wain" results in "Tearing high-ways" (l. 22). Thus the ant destroys the very means that would have made its work more efficient, which, ironically, would have allowed it more time for play. An additional incentive to play is the possibility that fate can intervene at any moment, permanently deferring it. For the ant, the poet projects an ironic and ignoble death. By keeping its focus on the earth and on its deadening work, the ant fails to see the magpie and jackdaw that swoop down to devour not only its cache of grain but also the ant itself. As the birds fly off, the ant is elevated from its mundane position and concerns but to no avail. Within the dark tomb of a bird's "Crop," Lucasta's life-giving light can no longer reach it (l. 30).

The Cavaliers understood well the pertinence of the imperative carpe diem. The poem's concluding stanza moves beyond the fate of the ant to a general "we."

> Thus we unthrifty thrive within Earths Tomb
>   For some more rav'nous and ambitious Jaw:
> The *Grain* in th' *Ants,* the *Ants* in the *Pies* womb,
>   The *Pie* in th' *Hawks,* the *Hawks* in th' *Eagles* maw. (ll. 31–36)

"We" may indicate a return to empathy for the ant. It may also admonish Royalists who were compounding to save their estates, as Elizabeth Skerpan has suggested.[15] Whether the ant is a Puritan, or, as Skerpan suggests, a Royalist, Lovelace's advice is the same. If recklessness fails, or fails in part, it is still a more noble course of action than is the excessive control implied by the ant's hoarding.

---

14. *Poems of Richard Lovelace,* ed. Wilkenson, 300; Marcus, *Politics of Mirth,* 151–52; William Hughes, *An Exact Abridgment of Publick Acts and Ordinances of Parliament* (London, 1657), 271; quoted in Miner, *Cavalier Mode,* 113.

15. J. Sambucus, *Emblemata,* 1569; Marcus, *Politics of Mirth,* 306 n. 22 (Marcus mentions an unpublished manuscript by Skerpan, which I have not found in published form).

The small creatures examined up to this point fail in various ways and to varying degrees; Lovelace's snails, however, are successful in meeting the challenges confronting them. The environment in "The Snayl" is not described in great detail, yet in "Another," which is "another" poem about a snail, immediately following "The Snayl," the setting is clearly politically hostile: the snail is praised for being able to take its home with it even in exile. While it is immediately evident that "Another" is sympathetic to Royalists, at first glance "The Snayl" seems to promote Puritan principles. The snail is a "stay'd Husband," who practices "Oeconomick Virtues" (ll. 38–39). In its ability to be both parent and progeny, womb and tomb, and to draw its bounty from "rich Mines within" (l. 50), it appears to share the ant's undue emphasis on self-sufficiency:

> Thou thine own daughter, then, and Sire,
> That Son and Mother art intire
> . . . .
> And as thy House was thine own womb,
> So thine own womb, concludes thy tomb. (ll. 27–36)

The poem's second line, "Sage Snayl, within thine own self curl'd," is reminiscent of the withdrawal in the second half of "The Grasse-hopper." But self-sufficiency and withdrawal are only part of the portrait. Anticipating sunrise, the snail breaks open into a "Beauteous Noon" (l. 16). The "stay'd Husband" is not a hoarder. Prudent husbanding includes a knowledge of when and how to spend one's bounty:

> Then after a sad Dearth and Rain,
> Thou scatterest thy Silver Train;
> And when the Trees grow nak'd and old,
> Thou cloathest them with Cloth of Gold. (ll. 45–48)

Finally, the snail's end is not one of darkness and confinement within other creatures but instead the glorious explosion of a shooting star. Not only does the expansiveness of these images align the snail with the Cavaliers rather than with the Puritans, so too does the emphasis on light. Throughout the poems dedicated to small creatures, Lovelace consistently uses light to symbolize monarchy or those associated with it: the sun, flames, and gold in "The Grasse-hopper"; sun in "The Ant"; and flames in "A Fly caught in a Cobweb." As sun, star, and giver of gold, the snail is likewise aligned with the monarchy. In "The Snayl," Lovelace gives his readers an example of a creature who has learned to live, both fully and safely, within a hostile environment without resorting to the falcon's brave but somewhat reckless abandon or the ant's excessive control.

In "The Snayl," Lovelace not only balances freedom and control but also the homely and the spectacular. The juxtaposition of the first pair of qualities may be seen mainly in the description of the creature as it is found in nature, a creature an inch in diameter, brittle and soft, slow, earthbound. The contrast of the homely with the spectacular comes largely from Lovelace's imagination, feigning so convincingly that it seems to come from within the snail itself. The snail draws its power simultaneously from a lack of ordinary restrictions and from self-control. The reverence of the first stanza's "Wise Emblem," "Sage," and "Instruct me" set the tone. The snail, no ordinary creature, has achieved an impossible state because it is an anomaly. In other words, success in a world fraught with political turmoil comes only to exceptional beings.

Nature fears the snail in lines 23–25 because previous and subsequent lines indicate that the snail defies all natural law. With its trail it can create all forms and thus is perhaps essentially formless:

> A Figure now Triangulare,
> An Oval now, and now a Square;
> And then a Serpentine dost crawl,
> Now a straight Line, now crook'd, now all. (ll. 9–12)

The snail also creates its own time as it outraces the sun:

> And ere the Morn cradles the Moon,
> Th' art broke into a Beauteous Noon.
> Then when the Sun sups in the Deep
> Thy Silver Horns e're *Cinthia's* peep. (ll. 15–18)

Furthermore, it shapes its destiny as well as itself. Lines 64–65 suggest that it decides when and how it will die: "Who now with Time thy days resolve, / And in a Jelly thee dissolve." If "Time" is read as a personification, the snail consults with Time to determine when it will pass away. However, a reading more consistent with the rest of the poem sees the snail deciding to melt away after it feels sufficient time has passed; that is, after a while or "with Time," it will dissolve itself into a jelly. The verb "resolve" carries a wealth of meaning. One cluster of meanings—determine, settle, conclude, satisfy—reinforces the snail's independence. Another cluster of meanings—relax, withdraw, melt, pass away—reinforces the next line's "dissolve." Of what substance the snail is composed is a mystery. In line 19 it is seen as "liquid"; in line 60, as a solid ("Marble"); in line 64, as a

"Jelly," the essence of a shooting star according to seventeenth-century lore. Whatever its substance, it is not a product "of Seas and Earth" (l. 24), the mothers of all natural creatures. All forms and formless, not bound by the laws of time, and of unknown substance, a self-originator, self-preserver, and when it has lived a full and satisfying life, a self-destroyer, the snail is extraordinary.

Not only is it impossible to assign a form to the snail, ascertain its substance, or place it in time, it is also difficult to confine it to a single emblematic social role: compared to a king and to a monk, the snail is simultaneously the ideal public man and the ideal private man. It expands and expends, contracts and saves; it is generous to others, strict with itself, a source of opulence, but without show. Its end? Not death at the hands of an enemy like the falcon but a self-determined dissolution. The snail experiences neither the corporeal decay and return to earth of the fly, nor the frozen immobility of the grasshopper, nor the limited range of the grasshopper men. Its departure is as elusive as its birth; not created of earth or water, the snail ends its life in the air as a purifying fire, a shooting star.

Randolph Wadsworth connects the poem's final image, the shooting star or meteor, with earlier lines that compare Nature's fear of the snail with its fear of earthquakes: "Bold Nature that gives common Birth / To all products of Seas and Earth, / Of thee, as Earth-quakes, is afraid" (ll. 23–25). Both earthquakes and meteors, as Wadsworth reminds us, were in "Lovelace's time commonly feared as premonitions of God's judgment." On the basis of this association as well as a number of others, such as the fifty-eighth psalm's use of the snail as a figure of "divine retribution," he argues that the poem is "a menacing affront to the ruling faction," predicting its downfall in terms associated with the apocalypse. Although the associations he links to meteors can be found in literature of the period, so can other associations. For example, Cotton's "On my Pretty Martin" ends with the creature becoming a shooting star, and yet rather than an ominous image, it is a tribute: for the creature that gave him so much pleasure, Cotton envisions a rare, splendid ending. Likewise, alternative associations can be found for the other images and lines that Wadsworth thinks put forth a belligerent message. While Wadsworth's readings of individual lines are interesting, I think they push too far in the direction of "menacing." We are in agreement, though, when he concludes that despite a certain combativeness, the poem ultimately is "a quiet, dignified, even affecting affirmation."[16]

16. Wadsworth, "On 'The Snayl' by Richard Lovelace," *Modern Language Review* 65 (1970): 756–60.

Just as it would be a mistake to see this poem chiefly as a threatening message for the Puritans, it is also a mistake to see this poem as mainly extolling withdrawal. Anselment sees the poem as a celebration of withdrawal but of "responsible withdrawal," a "companion piece" for "The Ant," warning against the ant's "frantic energy" and exaggerated husbandry. The snail exerts energy but not frantic energy. Furthermore, as Ted-Larry Pebworth and Claude Summers point out in their discussion of Donne's verse letter, "Sir, more then kisses," the snail—although a traditional symbol of Stoic self-containment—"does not retire from the world but on the contrary 'every where doth rome' (line 49)." In Lovelace's poem much of the wisdom that the snail imparts to the poet is that movement, that is, change from form to form and from stance to stance, is compatible with self-containedness. The snail's self-containedness does not lead to the sterility of the ant's repetitive and ultimately futile attempts to control its future but instead is evidence of the steady center found in much of Jonson's poetry, a balance between freedom and control that Anthony Low notes is absent in the poetry of Thomas Carew and that I find absent in much of Lovelace's poetry.[17]

Lovelace finds paradox and mystery within his homely subject. The miracle of being able to live fully within whatever circumstances one finds oneself leads Lovelace to a tone best described as one of marvel. The body of his poetry, even the highly successful group of poems about small creatures, demonstrates how difficult he found these tasks. Unlike the Royalists of the other poems, creatures who act in order to survive in the world of political vicissitudes, creatures who defect, confront, or retreat, the snail merely is. Lovelace's search for a response to political conflict and the chaotic world it creates culminates in "The Snayl." The poem's protagonist achieves what Lovelace the lover, friend, art critic, and drinker fails to achieve. The snail does not have the wings of a fly, grasshopper, or falcon. Its feet go "slowly" but are "fast," that is, steadfast. Yet it achieves much more than the other small creatures are able to achieve with their Puritan control or even Royalist abandon, a paradox often conveyed in emblems of snails like those in Jacobus Bruck's *Emblemata Moralia*. One of his emblems shows a snail crawling up a pillar with the following commentary: "Look at the snail, how she crawls / Yet finally reaches the

---

17. Anselment, *Loyalist Resolve*, 115–16; Pebworth and Summers, " 'Thus Friends Absent Speake': The Exchange of Verse Letters between John Donne and Henry Wotton," *Modern Philology* 81 (1984), 371; Low, "Agricultural Reform and the Love Poems of Thomas Carew; with an Instance from Lovelace," in *Culture and Cultivation in Early Modern England*, ed. Michael Leslie and Timothy Raylor (Leicester: Leicester University Press, 1992), 63–80.

high point" (my translation). Another emblem in this collection depicts a snail resting on top of a globe.[18] Within the poem itself, Lovelace practices both freedom, through a free-roaming imagination that creates fantastical figures, and control, through constant reminders of the reality upon which he builds his fantastical images. The horns and rays that outrace daybreak and evening are the snail's tentacles; the silver train and cloth of gold, the snail's trail; the cloister and hood, the snail's shell. Not only are the images controlled by their attachment to the reality of a mundane snail's essence and existence; they are also set up within a carefully wrought structure. Lovelace's art in this poem mirrors the psychological and social states that he searches for in all the others.

---

18. Jacobus Bruck, *Emblemata Moralia* (1615), emblems 37 and 3, respectively.

Alan Rudrum

Resistance, Collaboration, and Silence

Henry Vaughan and Breconshire Royalism

Henry Vaughan's neighbor, Rowland Watkyns, writing of "the mournful death" of Charles I, remarked that "He went to Canaan for three Kingdoms good, / Through the red-Sea of his own sacred blood"; and "By his beheading it may well be sed, / Three Kingdoms by injustice lost their head." Charles I was king of three countries and a principality; the part played by the Scots, Irish, and Welsh was sufficiently significant to suggest that we should think of the British, rather than of the English, civil wars.[1] This observation is especially relevant when considering Henry Vaughan and his circle in Breconshire. In Vaughan's case a sense of locality clearly enters into his self-presentation, as witness his volume *Olor Iscanus,* and his adoption of the title *Silurist,* a title that linked him with an ancient tribe of his region, which also fought courageously against an enemy based in London. In focusing upon Vaughan's responses in the context of those of neighboring Royalists, I hope both to illuminate the individuality of his responses, and also to show that the literary persona projected in *Silex Scintillans* is a deliberate artistic construct, in the service of a political end.[2]

1. Rowland Watkyns, *Flamma Sine Fumo* (1662), ed. Paul C. Davies (Cardiff: University of Wales Press, 1968), 4–5. Conrad Russell wrote, "I have become convinced that it is impossible to tell the English story by itself, and this book has been slowly transformed into an attempt at genuinely British history" (*The Fall of the British Monarchies, 1637–1642* [Oxford: Clarendon Press, 1991], vii). It is worth noting that both Herbert and Vaughan wrote poems titled "The British Church."

2. Students of Vaughan, down to and including F. E. Hutchinson, tended to deplore his more obvious references to current events as detracting from his excellence; more recently, critics have come to suggest that his poetic involvement in the politics of civil war and the Interregnum was deliberate and virtually unremitting, even though sometimes veiled. See, for example, Claude J. Summers and Ted-Larry Pebworth, "Vaughan's Temple in Nature and the Context of 'Regeneration,' " *Journal of English and*

The absence of an evident sense of the social world, which has been remarked on in relation to *Silex Scintillans,* should not mislead us into thinking of Vaughan as a solitary mystic, communing only with God as manifested in the streams, waterfalls, hills, and clouds of the Brecon Beacons.[3] That view captures an important part of his literary persona, and no doubt also of his human personality, but it is not the whole view. The social poems published in his 1651 volume *Olor Iscanus* should warn us of the incompleteness of that view, as should those published long after the civil conflict that made Vaughan the poet he was, in the *Thalia Rediviva* of 1678. There is clear evidence that poems addressed to friends in that volume had been written in time for inclusion in some issue of *Silex Scintillans,* and they had been omitted not from practical discretion—Vaughan was not a timid man—but because they were at odds with the literary persona he wished to project in his major contribution to the religio-political conflict. Vaughan's social relations are sufficiently documented and sufficiently interesting to be the subject of a separate paper; here I shall confine myself to discussing the responses to Interregnum conditions of six men only, as these six indicate a range of reactions. Charles Walbeoffe was Vaughan's cousin and friend; the other five were members of the Anglican clergy, all of whom were ejected from their livings: his tutor Matthew Herbert of Llangattock; his friends Thomas Powell of Cantref and Thomas Lewis of Llanfigan, to all of whom he addressed poems; his brother Thomas Vaughan of Llansantffraed; and Rowland Watkyns of Llanfrynach. All six were Royalists; four of them were what historians have come to call "ultra-Royalists," in the sense that their opposition to the victorious regime was uncompromising, and publicly expressed. This, and the stance adopted by the two others, yields the three terms of this essay's title.

Germanic Philology 74 (1975): 351–601, reprinted in *Essential Articles for the Study of Henry Vaughan,* ed. Alan Rudrum (Hamden: Archon Books, 1987), 212–25; Claude J. Summers and Ted-Larry Pebworth, "Herbert, Vaughan, and Public Concerns in Private Modes," *George Herbert Journal* 3 (fall 1979–spring 1980): 1–21; Robert Wilcher, " 'Then keep the ancient way!': A Study of Henry Vaughan's *Silex Scintillans,*" *Durham University Journal* 76, no. 1 (1983): 11–24; Graeme J. Watson, "The Temple in 'The Night': Henry Vaughan and the Collapse of the Established Church," *Modern Philology* 84 (1987): 144–61; Claude J. Summers, "Herrick, Vaughan, and the Poetry of Anglican Survivalism," in *New Perspectives on the Seventeenth-Century English Religious Lyric,* ed. John R. Roberts (Columbia: University of Missouri Press, 1994), 46–74.

3. A. J. Smith writes of "Vaughan's self-isolation from the public life of his day after the debacle of 1648–9" and comments that "one of the idiosyncrasies of *Silex Scintillans* is that it conveys no effective sense of community with living men at all, or of a communion with [the] regenerate few" ("Appraising the World," in *The Metaphysics of Love* [Cambridge: Cambridge University Press, 1985], 290–302; reprinted in *Essential Articles,* ed. Rudrum, 309).

Vaughan was a member of a class, the Welsh gentry, which on the one hand, lived in conquered territory, and on the other, through its national affinity with the Tudor monarchy, had become comfortable in its allegiance to the conquering power, as Henry Vaughan's first name might be held to signify. What most members of that class did not want was a second conquest, by forces whose natural base was Puritan London (as Londinium had been the base of the Romans who conquered the Silures of old). This second conquest threatened to turn gentlemen into peasants, and its psychological effects were exacerbated by the class difference between the Welsh gentry and the "mechanic preachers" who came into Wales, after Anglican priests were ejected from their livings. The gentry of south Wales were sufficiently intransigent in their Royalism to warrant special attention from the victorious enemies of the king.

The aim of the conquerors, in this case, was not the extirpation but the subjugation, and religious conversion, of the conquered people. The civil wars were very unpleasant, but no leader in them foreshadowed Stalin, Hitler, or Pol Pot. For effective rule of a civilian population left in situ, conquerors need the cooperation of those with administrative skills or with natural authority within their localities—in other words, of the gentry. I believe that it helps us to understand Vaughan's literary persona better if we see him within what we know of his circle, and if we compare the major poems published during the period of Royalist defeat, in the *Silex Scintillans* of 1650 and 1651, with some of those he published outside that period.

As already mentioned, we know of Vaughan's acquaintance with four members of the Anglican clergy: Matthew Herbert, Thomas Powell, Thomas Lewis, and his brother Thomas Vaughan. All four were ejected from their livings. In three cases no substitute minister was supplied, and we may assume that the churches were closed. The evidence suggests that all four were ultra-Royalists and probably Laudian Anglicans also; none cooperated with the new regime and some were clearly active in their opposition. Matthew Herbert was displaced as early as 1646, but he preached in one of the chapelries of Llangattock until 1655; in that year he went so far as to sue some parishioners for not paying tithes. In 1656 he was jailed in Brecon for seventeen weeks and threatened with banishment. Thomas Powell and Thomas Lewis were both evicted in 1650 under the Propagation Act; both continued to try to serve their parishioners, and both organized resistance to the regime.[4] A threatening letter to Lewis

---

4. F. E. Hutchinson, *Henry Vaughan: A Life and Interpretation* (Oxford: Clarendon Press, 1947), 113, 110–11.

in connection with his opposition was passed on to Henry Vaughan's father, Thomas Vaughan the elder, who took the occasion to try to stir up trouble for the threatener, Jenkin Jones.[5] Another acquaintance, Vaughan's friend and cousin Charles Walbeoffe, who will figure in this paper a little later, was among those described in May 1652 as being "so refractory that, without some special course is taken with them, no satisfactory result will be obtained" and in consequence fined £20.[6] One could go on at some length listing friends and acquaintances of Vaughan who were unremitting in opposition to the Puritan regime; here I shall only add that Donald Dickson has recently identified, with great probability, Henry Vaughan's sister-in-law Rebecca, and if his identification is correct she also came from an intransigently Royalist family.[7] The opposition of Henry Vaughan and his brother Thomas was, as far as we know, expressed only in print after military defeat; it is worth remembering that outspoken expression in print must have taken some courage. It is not easy to find authors, publishing in their own names, who were as outspoken as Vaughan was. In summary, there is sufficient evidence, in his writings and elsewhere, that Henry Vaughan was himself both an ultra-Royalist and a member of a circle that actively opposed the new regime.

A different aspect of Breconshire royalism is apparent in considering the case of Rowland Watkyns, rector of Llanfrynach, another Anglican clergyman who was opposed to the Puritan regime, and who was ejected from his living in 1649. Watkyns has not figured largely in Vaughan scholarship. His name is missing from the index of Hutchinson's *Life*, and does not seem to have been brought to the attention of readers of Vaughan until Roland Mathias published his essay "In Search of the Silurist." He deserves attention when we are considering what Vaughan's writings, published between 1646 and 1655, meant in relation to the times. For Watkyns was not only one of the Anglican clergy, he was also a poet of whose existence, if not his poetic activity, Vaughan must have been aware, and who must have been aware of him. Llanfrynach is just across the river from Vaughan's home. Moreover, Watkyns moved in circles not merely Royalist, but overlapping Vaughan's. Roland Mathias justly remarks, of his many poems dedicated to people within Vaughan's circle, "It is as though the outline of Vaughan's effigy is being picked out with arrow-points," but "not one word does he write of Henry Vaughan, and

5. The correspondence is preserved in Bodleian Library MS Rawlinson A.11, fols. 334–35. See Hutchinson, *Life*, 117 n. 1.

6. Hutchinson, *Life*, 112.

7. I am grateful to Donald Dickson for sending me a copy of his paper, publication of which is pending.

Vaughan not a word of him."[8] Mathias might have written more accurately that not one word does Watkyns write explicitly of Vaughan. In fact, Mathias's statement consorts oddly with what he writes on the following page, to the effect that the poem "To the Reader" prefaced to *Flamma Sine Fumo* suggests that "Watkyns objected both to Vaughan's Hermetic interests (and particularly those of his brother Thomas) and his personal manner—which he regarded as high-flown."

The poem is short enough to quote in full:

> I am not Eagle ey'd to face the Sun,
> My mind is low, and so my Verse doth run.
> I do not write of Stars to make men wonder.
> Or Planets how remote they move asunder.
> My shallow River thou may'st foord with ease,
> Ways, which are fair, and plain can nere displease.

In these lines at least, Watkyns certainly seems to have had Vaughan in mind. Consider the first line, in relation to Vaughan's statement in "The Star" that "eagles eye not stars"; the third, in relation to the fact that the words "star" and "stars" occur forty-six times in *Silex Scintillans*[9] and the last, in relation to the fact that Vaughan, in the title of *Olor Iscanus*, laid claim to be the poet of a river.

If the brief poem just quoted does reflect Watkyns's hostility to Vaughan, there is nevertheless a great deal in *Flamma Sine Fumo* to suggest that, in attitude if not in poetic habit, the two had much in common. Like Vaughan, Watkyns wrote on Christ's nativity, that feast so disliked by many Puritans; and on the Virgin Mary.[10] We may be sure that Vaughan, as the brother of an ejected clergyman and the friend of three others, would have entered into the spirit of Watkyns's poem titled "The new illiterate Lay-Teachers." Watkyns writes:

8. Roland Mathias, "In Search of the Silurist," *Poetry Wales* 11 no. 2 (1975): 6–35. Reprinted in *Essential Articles*, ed. Rudrum, 189–214, 205. Watkyns's editor, Davies, also remarks that "there is no mention of Vaughan in *Flamma Sine Fumo* and no reference to his poetry" (*Flamma Sine Fumo*, xxiv).

9. See Imilda Tuttle, *Concordance to Vaughan's "Silex Scintillans,"* (University Park: Pennsylvania State University Press, 1969), 195.

10. Vaughan's "Christ's Nativity" appeared in the 1650 *Silex Scintillans;* "The Nativity" and "The True Christmas" in *Thalia Rediviva* (1678); see *Henry Vaughan: The Complete Poems*, ed. Alan Rudrum (Harmondsworth: Penguin Books, 1976), 372, 374. The last of these poems, indicating Vaughan's conception of how Christmas should be celebrated, reminds us that he was a Puritan among Anglicans. For Watkyns's "Upon Christ's Nativity," see *Flamma Sine Fumo*, 3. Vaughan's poem upon the Virgin Mary, "The Knot" (*Complete Poems*, 372), appeared in the 1650 *Silex Scintillans;* for Watkyns's "The Virgin Mary," see *Flamma Sine Fumo*, 16.

> The Tinkar being one of excellent mettle,
> Begins to sound his doctrine with his Kettle.
> And the laborious ploughman I bewail,
> Who now doth thresh the Pulpit with his flail.
> The louzy Taylor with his holy thimble
> Doth patch a sermon up most quick and nimble.
> He doth his skill, and wisdom much expresse
> When with his goose he doth the Scripture presse.

Vaughan would have entered too into the antidemocratic spirit of Watkyns's poem, even though Watkyns's manner has more in common with Butler's *Hudibras* than with anything in *Silex Scintillans*. Vaughan's dislike of lower-class preachers is evident in an interpolation in his life of Paulinus, which reads: "Certainly extraction and a virtuous descent (let popular flatterers preach what they will to the contrary,) is attended with more Divinity, and a sweeter temper, than the indiscrete Issue of the multitude." This conservative spirit is also shown in Vaughan's reference to "the crowd and populacie" in *Of Temperance and Patience*; and to "the populacy and throng" in *The World Contemned*. He asserts that "the greatest part of men, which we commonly term the populacy, are a stiffe, uncivil generation, without any sense of honour or goodnesse, and sensible of nothing but private interest, & the base waies of acquiring it."[11]

Watkyns desiderated a severity against these "new illiterate lay-teachers" that foreshadowed the persecution of nonconformists that began soon after the Restoration:

> Not disputation, but a rigid law
> Must keep these frantic sectarists in aw.

Further, the language of this poem reminds us how bitterly the Royalists of south Wales resented the zeal with which their opponents took advantage of the provisions of the Act for the Propagation of the Gospel in Wales, which ran from 1650 to 1653. Watkyns writes that "Mad men by vertue of this propagation, / Have Bedlum left, and preach't for Reformation" and that

> The ruder sort are by these teachers led,
> Who acorns eat, and might have better bread;
> If this a propagation shall be found,
> These build the house, which pull it to the ground.[12]

11. *The Works of Henry Vaughan*, ed. L. C. Martin (Oxford: Clarendon Press, 1957), 363, 270, 322, 363.
12. *Flamma Sine Fumo*, 43–44.

That Vaughan would have agreed with these sentiments we may be sure. In the last paragraph of the preface to *Flores Solitudinis,* dated April 17, 1652, he informs his readers that he writes "out of a land of darknesse, out of that unfortunate region, where the Inhabitants sit in the shadow of death: where destruction passeth for propagation" and in his *Life of Paulinus* he writes that Paulinus "preferred the indignation and hatred of the multitude to their love, he would not buy their friendship with the loss of Heaven, nor call those Saints and propagators, who were Devills and destroyers."[13] Vaughan and Watkyns shared with Milton a propensity to make use of the political catchwords of the day.

Why, given their considerable mutual acquaintance, shared Anglicanism and Royalism, and a shared habit of versification, did Vaughan and Watkyns sheer away from each other, as they apparently did? Roland Mathias suggests that it may have been because Watkyns, a Herefordshire man, simply did not like Breconshire people; and indeed in a brief autobiographical poem in Latin, one moreover in which the first line recalls Vaughan's adopted title of Silurist, Watkyns does suggest reservations about those among whom he had settled: *"Breconium quondam veteres coluere Silures, / Terra bona est, mala gens, litigiosa, sagax"* ("The ancient Silures formerly inhabited Breconshire, a good land, a bad people, litigious, crafty").[14] The Welsh were indeed notoriously litigious, and the Vaughan family lived up to the national stereotype in this respect. However, this explanation, a simple dislike of Breconshire people, is difficult to accept until research establishes that all of Vaughan's and Watkyns's mutual acquaintances were of non-Breconshire stock. It is possible that one or other of them had caught a salmon in the other's stream. A more satisfactory explanation of the silence between the two might be the fact that there is no known record of activism on Watkyns's part, beyond poems that circulated in samizdat among Royalist acquaintances in effect as begging letters. Given the financial straits of the majority of the ejected clergy, these begging letters were in all probability justified. Watkyns would almost certainly have been aware of Vaughan's constant stream of publication from 1646 to 1655, during which entire period the enemies of the king and of Anglicanism were in control. He might have resented Vaughan's courage as well as his obviously greater poetic ability. A possible point of contention between them might lie in the fact that Watkyns did not publish his poems until 1662, when it had become not merely safe but possibly advantageous to do so. Full of Royalist and Anglican sentiment

13. Hutchinson, *Life,* 115.
14. *Flamma Sine Fumo,* 118.

as Watkyns's poems are, they were virtually meaningless in relation to the ideological struggle with which Vaughan identified in publishing *Silex Scintillans*. Rowland Watkyns stands for the third option of this paper's title: He neither opposed, like Vaughan and his clerical friends, or sought to mitigate, like Walbeoffe, who will be discussed shortly. He was merely silent.

A different reaction to defeat was also possible for Breconshire royalists, namely collaboration. In considering local administration during the period of Royalist defeat, and the role of local gentry within it, there is some evidence to suggest that outspoken opposition to the regime did not automatically result in being banished from consideration as a possible collaborator. Some known Royalists, including more than one in Vaughan's circle of friends, did hold office under the Commonwealth. In Vaughan's case perhaps it is just possible that his literary work was unknown both to local Puritans and to those who came into Wales from London. That Vaughan was approached for his cooperation, and refused it, has long been considered likely. His poem "The Proffer" is our principal clue. It appears, significantly for my present argument, in the second part of *Silex Scintillans*, first published in 1655.[15] It appears early in that collection, and the poems that lead up to and away from it provide significant context, indeed a sort of commentary. The first poem is "Ascension-Day," an extraordinary evocation of a spiritualized landscape, which ends with the apocalyptic hope sanctioned by the biblical account of its occasion:

> Come then, thou faithful witness! come dear Lord
> Upon the clouds again to judge this world!

God's judgment upon "this world" is precisely what is at issue in "The Proffer."

If in "Ascension-Day" we find a spiritualized landscape, in the poem that follows, "Ascension-Hymn," we find even less evidence of the social world: the poem opposes the "dust and clay" of humanity, with its soiled brightness and spoiled garments, to the nakedness, innocence, and brightness of the prelapsarian world and to the glory that is to be revealed. This simple opposition between the mists of this life and the "world of light" for which the poet yearns is carried on through the next poem, "They are all gone into the world of light." The fourth in the sequence, "White Sunday," returns to the liturgical interest with which the volume begins, but in a new mode that clearly engages with the contemporary, with its reference

15. *Complete Poems*, ed. Rudrum, 249.

to "new lights" in the third stanza and its reminder that the times brought forth, for those in Vaughan's position, unwelcome developments in religion as well as in politics more narrowly understood.[16] Its ending provides a clear transition to the concerns of "The Proffer," if that poem is correctly understood as Vaughan's refusal to cooperate with the new authorities:

> Let not thy stars for Balaam's hire
> Dissolve into the common dross!

This conclusion clearly calls up Numbers 22:18: "And Balaam answered and said unto the servants of Balak, If Balak would give me his house full of silver and gold, I cannot go beyond the word of the Lord." Given the wider context of Balaam's story, the allusion might be seen to predict the ultimate victory of those who now seemed defeated, a technique Milton would later use in many a proleptic simile in *Paradise Lost*. In thus modulating from a liturgical occasion, with the repeated recollection and reenactment of a significant past that this implies, to a clear concern with the immediate here and now, "White Sunday" sets the scene for "The Proffer," which calls up a particular moment in time:

> Be still black parasites.
>   Flutter no more;
> Were it still winter, as it was before,
>   You'd make no flights;
> But now the dew and sun have warmed my bowers
> You fly and flock to suck the flowers.

F. E. Hutchinson suggested that there might be an allusion here to Vaughan's recovery from an illness, or, more probably, to an improvement in his fortunes, owing perhaps to inheritance after his first wife's death. There might seem to be an odd discrepancy, in this latter interpretation, between a reference to Vaughan's current prosperity and the ending of

16. In the phrase "new lights" in the ninth line of Vaughan's poem "White Sunday," there is a specific reference to those who believed that it was not only in the apostolic period that men had been directly inspired by the Holy Spirit, but that this was happening again in their own time. The dissenters that Morgan Llwyd gathered around him in Wrexham upon his return in 1647 held this belief and were referred to as "New Lights" because of their expectation of progressive illumination. See M. Wynn Thomas, *Morgan Llwyd* (Cardiff: University of Wales Press, 1985), 5. While the political nature of Vaughan's poem was clear before, recognition of this allusion yields both a more precise reading and a more local context. On the political significance of the apocalypticism that features in the sequence under discussion, see Summers, "Herrick, Vaughan."

the previous poem, with its implicit rejection of financial prosperity. While it may be both difficult and of doubtful utility to attempt to extract biographical data from such references, it is fair to say that such a discrepancy might be more apparent than real, given the tendency in those times for offices to be bought and sold.

What is clear about the poem is its quite categorical rejection of any suggestion that Vaughan should be cooperative. His position as an ultra-Royalist is firmly stated: "I'll not stuff my story / With your Commonwealth and glory." Here there is no room for doubt or second thoughts; the imagery of the poem clearly sets the matter out in black and white. The transcendent atmosphere of the preceding poems is again conjured up, in such lines as:

> That glass of souls and spirits, where well dressed
> They shine in white (like stars) and rest.

Within that atmosphere, the blackness of the "black parasites" and the "flies of hell" could scarcely be more emphatic. While a temporal occasion seems to be at issue, the terms in which it is set forth are still otherworldly: the imagery is that of heaven and hell rather than of earth. The point I want to make is precisely that the rhetoric of *Silex Scintillans* is the product of art, rather than of spontaneity. "The Proffer" ignores the moral complexities of real life in order to make a stark statement, which, in pursuit of a real-life purpose, masks Vaughan's actual awareness of the difficult choices faced by his contemporaries. He has no intention, here, in *Silex Scintillans,* of wasting verbal capital on moral analysis such as he undertakes elsewhere, as I shall show. It should be added that it is not of great importance whether "The Proffer" was written in response to an actual offer of a place in local administration, though such an offer would not seem inherently unlikely; it is equally significant as a merely imagined response to a hypothetical offer.

The imagery of "The Proffer" is that of heaven and hell rather than of earth, and there is little of the social world in the poems that precede it or in the poems that immediately follow it. "Cock-Crowing" and "The Star" are both concerned with the vertical relationship between earth and heaven, time and eternity. The setting of "The Proffer," then, like the poem itself, firmly places the temporal in its eternal context. The paradox is that this is done in pursuit of an earthly purpose, albeit one that Vaughan sincerely considered as the furthering of God's will.

The significance, suggested earlier, of "The Proffer" appearing in the 1655 *Silex,* is made clear if we consider another poem, almost certainly written before 1655, and therefore in time to have found a place in the 1655 *Silex,* had Vaughan so wished. This is the elegy with the headnote: "To the Pious Memory of C. W. Esquire who Finished His Course Here, and Made His Entrance into Immortality upon the 13 of September, in the Year of Redemption 1653," which appears in *Thalia Rediviva,* published in 1678. In this poem too the issue of a Welsh Royalist and Anglican cooperating with the new, unwelcome authorities is addressed, but in terms more explicit and less allegorical than would have been suitable within the overall atmosphere of *Silex Scintillans.*

Charles Walbeoffe, the C. W. of this poem, was Vaughan's first cousin, a neighbor, a close friend, and a staunch Royalist who, as we have already seen, was fined in 1652 for his intransigence. Vaughan's elegy for him was probably written late in 1653 or in 1654. During the Interregnum, Royalist gentry were confronted with complex problems of loyalty and duty. In his elegy for Walbeoffe, Vaughan contemplates the life of a kinsman, whom he obviously loved and respected, who chose to confront the times in a way different from that chosen by Vaughan himself. Vaughan's poem on Walbeoffe is more complex and less clearly conventional than the two elegies of *Olor Iscanus,* on Mr. R. W. and Mr. R. Hall, both slain in battle in the Royalist cause.

Whereas Vaughan took no office under the Commonwealth, and seems, on the evidence of "The Proffer," to have rejected overtures to do so, Walbeoffe became a magistrate; his signature occurs many times in the Brecon Gaol Records for 1651 and 1653. I found none for 1652, perhaps because of the activities for which he was fined in that year. He was, then, a public man, and the poem's opening refers somewhat satirically to the "public sorrow" at his death, as Vaughan contrasts the "outside mourners" to his solitary self:

> Now, that the public sorrow doth subside,
> And those slight tears which custom springs, are dried;
> While all the rich & outside mourners pass
> Home from thy dust to empty their own glass:
> I (who the throng affect not, nor their state:)
> Steal to thy grave undressed, to meditate
> On our sad loss, accompanied by none,
> An obscure mourner that would weep alone.

There is some complexity here, reinforced by the possible double entendre of the fourth line: "to empty their own glass." If Walbeoffe's death attracted public sorrow of such a quality, what kind of man was he really? The poem's opening in effect acknowledges a problem; its satire is softened as Vaughan modulates into a long, shifting simile, the terms of which are mostly drawn from the natural world, but which ends with Vaughan, the "obscure mourner that would weep alone," nevertheless claiming for himself the office of "the just recorder of thy death and worth." The encomium that follows acknowledges the moral ambiguities created by the times, which gave rise to "such mists, that none could see his way"; Walbeoffe did what other Royalists in his immediate circle refused to do, but Vaughan stresses that he yielded neither to intimidation nor to bribery. Lines 31–41 acknowledge that other Royalists might feel tempted to blame Walbeoffe for agreeing to serve as a magistrate under the Commonwealth. Vaughan argues that Walbeoffe should be seen as patient rather than agent, as suffering rather than as committing crimes: we should no more blame him than we blame the sun when it is eclipsed by the moon. Then, becoming less metaphorical and more explicit, he explains why Walbeoffe should not be blamed; just as poisons can be "corrected" and so turned into antidotes, so the magistrate Walbeoffe's "just soul did turn even hurtful things to good." (Compare the imagery of poisons in line 13 of "The Proffer.") Vaughan refers to those who throve "by fraud and blood and blasphemy" and to the "bribes" and "fees," which are "our new oppressors' best annuities." Walbeoffe, on the other hand, did not multiply his "just inheritance" by "sacrilege, nor pillage"; his hands were clean. The historical context of these assertions is well described by Geraint H. Jenkins, who writes that "one of the shrillest anti-Propagation cries was that the commissioners had feathered their own nests while religion decayed." Jenkins describes a petition to Parliament of 1652, claiming to represent the views of fifteen thousand disaffected citizens in south Wales, and charging the Propagators with "gross neglect, misappropriation of tithe revenues, and maldistribution of sequestered livings." He adds that "opponents of the regime were swift to notice that large sums of money remained unaccounted for."[17]

There may well have been more to Vaughan's assertion of Walbeoffe's financial probity than mere conventional praise. A member of Watkyns's circle, as well as one of Vaughan's, enters into this story. One of Watkyns's complimentary poems is headed "Upon the most Hospitable, and Courteous Gentleman, the Worshipful, Thomas Lewis, Esq., of Langorse."[18]

17. Geraint H. Jenkins, *The Foundations of Modern Wales, 1642–1780* (Oxford: Clarendon Press, 1987), 59.
18. I have not yet undertaken firsthand research and do not pretend to understand fully the episode for which Walbeoffe was fined £20 in 1652, the year during which he appears not to have acted as a magistrate. It has caused disagreement among historians: see *Flamma Sine Fumo*, 162. Thomas Lewis of Llangorse should not be

Lewis is presented there as an uncompromising Royalist whose "untainted heart disdains to be / A friend to Schism, or Disloyalty"; the poem ends with the statement that "his most Noble resolution stood / Firm for the Church, the King, and Countreys good." According to Paul C. Davies, "in the conflict between royalists and the Parliament [Lewis] occupies a more ambiguous position than Watkyns would suggest. His brother, Sir William Lewis, was one of eleven members of the House of Commons impeached in 1647 for frustrating the activities of the Welsh Committee for Sequestration, for protecting notorious delinquents, for restoring Colonel Herbert Price's estates to him without satisfaction to the State, and for putting his brother in the Commission of the Peace. Sir William denied these allegations and asserted of his brother, Thomas Lewis, that "he could safely say that in his fidelity to the Parliament he had suffered as much as any of double his fortune." Davies cites W. R. Williams as noting that in May 1652 the Breconshire Committee for Compounding was complaining to the Commissioners in London that some members of the "late Committee" were unwilling to account for "good sums of money" in their hands. Three of these members, one of whom is Thomas Lewis of Llangorse, are described as being "so refractory that without special course is taken no satisfactory result will be obtained." This is the same episode that Hutchinson notes, citing documentation from the Record Office, as resulting in a fine for Walbeoffe of £20. Davies cites T. Richards as disagreeing with W. R. Williams's suggestion that Lewis "was no true friend to the Parliament; if this be really so, it is difficult to understand how he could become the sequestrator of Church livings."[19] It would seem that Richards was seeing things in the black-and-white terms suggested by Vaughan's poem "The Proffer" and Watkyns's poem to Thomas Lewis, rather than in terms of the moral complexities and ambiguities realistically addressed in Vaughan's elegy for Walbeoffe. As for Walbeoffe's part in this affair, a number of questions arise. Was the charge of being unwilling to account for "good sums of money" justified? If so, did the money go into Walbeoffe's pocket and stay there, or was it used, for example, for the relief of one or more of the pauperized ejected clergy?

Vaughan's elegy for Walbeoffe, after asserting that his cousin was honest, then improves upon his claim to be the just recorder of Walbeoffe's death and worth by saying that he had the key to his heart, "man's secret

---

confused with Thomas Lewis of Llanfigan, to whom Vaughan addressed an invitation poem in *Olor Iscanus,* and who was named by Watkyns his "loveing friend . . . Thomas Lewis clericus Rector of Llanvigan" as one of two executors in his will, drawn up on October 18, 1664, very shortly before his death (*Flamma Sine Fumo,* 166).

19. *Flamma Sine Fumo,* 83, 162–63. Davies is quoting from W. R. Williams, *Old Wales* 1 (1905): 44. Hutchinson, *Life,* 112. *Flamma Sine Fumo,* 163.

region and his noblest part." The obscure mourner, we now learn, was an intimate of the public figure. The poem concludes that Vaughan will not weep, because "the great Victor" "counts every dust, that is laid up of thee." This turns the locus of the real struggle from this world to the next. At the end we see Vaughan comforting himself, for his bereavement but even more for the disordered times, with the thought that the world is nearing its end: "The next glad news (most glad unto the just!) / Will be the Trumpet's summons from the dust." That is, in this poem too he reverts to the apocalypticism of "Ascension-Day" and "Ascension-Hymn"; it is in that context that human decisions made in this life are, for him, significant.

There are elegies in *Silex Scintillans,* in the 1655 as in the 1650 issue. Why did Vaughan not publish his elegy for his cousin in the 1655 volume? It does not seem likely that he feared its explicitness might bring the authorities down upon his head; he is often explicit, and uncomplimentary toward his enemies, in *Silex.* As I indicated earlier, it may be that the comparatively straightforward way in which it is written, in clear contrast to the abstracted and allegorical manner of "The Proffer," would have seemed out of place in the 1650 *Silex.* In addition, it seems equally likely that, at a time when considerations of propaganda were still highly relevant, Vaughan would not have wanted to present himself as a moderate, who could readily condone a conscientious office-taker like his cousin. It seems fair to say that the entire range of clearly political reference in *Silex Scintillans* presents a literary persona that is uncompromisingly that of an ultra-Royalist and Laudian Anglican.

Within those limits, however, there is, within *Silex Scintillans,* what might appear to be self-division, tension, perhaps what we might want to characterize as ambivalence, in relation to political concerns. In his poems on the "Four Last Things," the negative aspect of the eschatological theme (God's judgment upon the wicked) looms less large for Vaughan than does the positive. While there are poems in which he gives way, either in the text or in the biblical reference to which the text points, to an imagination of his enemies' utter defeat, for the most part he retains a Christian concern with forgiveness, as if in recognition that his own mental equilibrium could not be sustained within an attitude of pure hostility. The desire that the fracturedness of the times might give way to unity is very strong in Vaughan, and comes out clearly in the last poem in *Silex Scintillans,* "L'Envoy," a title that refers, significantly, to the author's parting words. However, it is expressed without any compromise in Vaughan's positioning on the political spectrum.

It opens with a sustained passage, based upon Revelation, in which the diction *(light, white, bright, cloudless, transparent)* recalls that with which the

1655 volume began, but abstracted yet further from quotidian actuality.
It is a beautiful expression of the theology of participation that Vaughan
learned so well from St. Paul. This transcendent opening leads to a reprise
of Vaughan's most important themes, in a context that suggests that even
his most "religious," most apparently "other-worldly" concerns, enter
into his sense of his place within the political world. We find for example
in lines 21–24 an expression of his certainty that the meaning of Christ is
not just for humanity, but for all creatures, of the theme, that is, of "And
do they so?" with its headnote from Romans 8:19, and of "The Book,"
his most lovely poem on the Last Things, in which lyricism is wedded to
a fierce intellectual engagement with English Calvinism's contempt for
"the creatures" as expressed in many a commentary.[20]

The apparent serenity of the opening of "L'Envoy" is then followed by
an expression of religio-political partisanship, which might suggest that
for all his striving Vaughan had not yet attained quietness of mind:

> Only, let not our haters brag,
> Thy seamless coat is grown a rag,
> Or that thy truth was not here known,
> Because we forced thy judgements down.
> Dry up their arms, who vex thy spouse,
> And take the glory of thy house
> To deck their own; then give thy saints
> That faithful zeal, which neither faints
> Nor wildly burns, but meekly still
> Dares own the truth, and show the ill.
> Frustrate those cancerous, close arts
> Which cause solution in all parts,
> And strike them dumb, who for mere words
> Wound thy beloved, more than swords.

The polemicism of this passage is clear, with its implication that the
Church has been robbed for the sake of private interests, and in the way in
which Vaughan appropriates two favorite Puritan words: saints and zeal.
Here is no compromise; the truth as Vaughan saw it is forcefully stated.

The poem ends, however, on an apparently more conciliatory note:

> Dear Lord, do this! and then let grace
> Descend, and hallow all the place.
> Incline each hard heart to do good,

20. See Alan Rudrum, "Henry Vaughan, the Liberation of the Creatures, and
Seventeenth-Century English Calvinism," *The Seventeenth Century* 4 no. 1 (1989): 33–54.

And cement us with thy son's blood,
That like true sheep, all in one fold
We may be fed, and one mind hold.
For sin (like water) hourly glides
By each man's door, and quickly will
Turn in, if not obstructed still.
Therefore write in their hearts thy law,
And let these long, sharp judgements awe
Their very thoughts, that by their clear
And holy lives, mercy may here
Sit regent yet, and blessings flow
As fast, as persecutions now.
So shall we know in war and peace
Thy service to be our sole ease,
With prostrate souls adoring thee,
Who turned our sad captivity!

This conclusion does not pretend that the situation is other than it is, as the words "persecutions" and "sad captivity" make clear. Nevertheless it is in sum irenic, in the only sense of the word available to a Royalist of Vaughan's stamp.[21] The poem longs for a "hallowed" country, in which the people will have come into one fold and hold one mind. It prays for, rather than excoriates, those in power, even as persecutions are flowing fast. Vaughan's dealing in "L'Envoy" with the anger that has been held to mar some of his other work, perhaps best represents a merging of his literary persona and his personal morality. Readers inclined to dispute the epithet "irenic" might contrast Vaughan's tone here with the lines of Watkyns already quoted, in which he calls for "not disputation but a rigid law" to keep "these frantic sectarists" in awe; or with those post-Restoration sermons in which the note of "Compel them to come in" is so strongly sounded.

Can the irenic quality of this final poem be seen as falling within the expected parameters of an ultra-Royalist and Laudian Anglican? I think so, especially if we apply that metaphor from mathematics with some exactness, recalling that a parameter is a "constant whose value varies with the circumstances of its application." After the military defeat, the

21. J. R. Tanner writes that "In that age it was unthinkable that there should be more than one Church; the discussion centred on the question in whose hands the one Church should be," and he quotes Goldwin Smith to the effect that "Only on the minds of a few lonely thinkers or hunted sectaries had the idea of religious liberty yet dawned" (*English Constitutional Conflicts of the Seventeenth Century, 1603–1689* [Cambridge: University Press, 1928], 13). See also the introduction to John Spurr's *The Restoration Church of England, 1646–1689* (New Haven: Yale University Press, 1991).

motto of the ultra-Royalists might well have been "La lutta continua";
propaganda is warfare carried on by other means. The final poem in *Silex
Scintillans*, in its certainty of the righteousness of its author's cause, in its
placing of contemporary conflict against the backdrop of eternity, in its
yearning for a peace prepared for by the repentance of the enemy, has
much in common with another work clearly intended for the propaganda
wars, that is, *Eikon Basilike*.

Jay Russell Curlin

"Is There No Temperate Region . . . ?"

Coopers Hill and the
Call for Moderation

Our Sovereign and the members of this Parliament at London seem very near agreed in their general and public professions. Both are for the Protestant religion; can they draw nearer? Both are for the privileges of Parliament; can they come closer? Both are for the liberty of the subject; can they meet evener? And yet, alas! there is a great gulf and vast distance betwixt them which our sins have made, and God grant that our sorrow may seasonably make it up again.

—Thomas Fuller, *Thoughts and Contemplations*

Of the variety of themes prevailing in the literature of the English civil war, one recurring note is, expectedly, the desire for reconciliation and peace. As partisan as much of the literature is, writers of contrasting political sympathies, before, during, and after the hostilities, frequently take positions that are as irenic as they are polemical. Even Milton, an unapologetic Parliamentarian, was wearied enough by the war that by 1648 he reminded the commander-in-chief of the New Model Army that war breeds only "endless war." His assistant Andrew Marvell, himself a tutor to Fairfax's daughter but a friend, as well, of such Royalists as Lovelace, is so seemingly ambivalent in his allusions to the conflict that his own political sympathies are often far from clear. After having heard his Horatian ode to Cromwell described, William Hazlitt thought it, instead, a "tribute to King Charles," and his markedly ambiguous praise of Cromwell in that ode has been the subject of considerable recent debate. Even in his "Bermudas," recording the "holy and . . . cheerful note" of the religious exiles of the early seventeenth century, Marvell is concerned less with attacking Charles' policies or

119

praising Parliamentarian resistance, than with identifying with those who would wish to seek a paradisal haven "[s]afe from the storms, and prelates' rage."[1] Among the Royalists, even so ardent a supporter of the king as Richard Lovelace pronounces Parliament "a main prop from Heaven sent" and is willing to admit the justice of certain Parliamentarian grievances:

> A Reformation I would have,
> As for our griefs a sov'reign salve;
> That is, a cleansing of each wheel
> Of state that yet some rust doth feel;
>
> But not a Reformation so
> As to reform were to o'erthrow;
> Like watches by unskillful men
> Disjointed, and set ill again.[2]

Another poet sympathetic to the crown treats this idea at considerably greater length in a poem that manages to reprove both the excesses of Parliamentarian reform and the abuses of the royal prerogative. The general adoration of John Denham's *Coopers Hill* in the eighteenth century was based, as W. Hutchings has maintained, on its "depiction of topography," its successes as a "landscape poem," and recent studies of the work have

---

1. John Milton, "On the Lord General Fairfax at the siege of Colchester," *Milton: Complete Shorter Poems,* ed. John Carey (London: Longman, 1971), 319–21. Michael Wilding has argued that both *Paradise Lost* and Samuel Butler's *Hudibras,* the "two most famous heroic poems of the Restoration," reconsidered "the heroic epics and romances of the past in the light of the tragic experience of civil war" (*Dragons Teeth: Literature in the English Revolution* [Oxford: Clarendon, 1987], 173). Hazlitt quoted in Wilding, *Dragons Teeth,* 114. On the debate on Marvell's ode, see, for example, Blair Worden, "Andrew Marvell, Oliver Cromwell, and the Horatian Ode," *Politics of Discourse: The Literature and History of Seventeenth-Century England,* ed. Kevin Sharpe and Steven N. Zwicker (Berkeley and Los Angeles: University of California Press, 1987), 172, and Thomas Corns, *Uncloistered Virtue: English Political Literature, 1640–1660* (Oxford: Clarendon, 1992), 228. Wilding sees the poem as partisan in spirit but agrees that "[a]mbiguity, balance, detachment, judgement . . . is the reading that the poem is designed to elicit" (*Dragons Teeth,* 117). Andrew Marvell, "Bermudas," *The Complete Poems,* ed. Elizabeth Story Donno (Harmondsworth, Middlesex: Penguin, 1972), 116–17.

2. Richard Lovelace, "To Lucasta. From Prison: An Epode," in *Seventeenth-Century Prose and Poetry,* ed. Alexander M. Witherspoon and Frank J. Warnke, 2d ed. (Fort Worth: Harcourt, 1982), 947–48. Corns has dismissed Gerald Hammond's "attempt to read as 'neutralist' many of the poems of the first *Lucasta*" and the "Marvellian ambivalence" Hammond ascribes to Lovelace's political perspectives (*Uncloistered Virtue,* 244, 78). See Hammond's introduction to his edition of Lovelace's *Selected Poems* (Manchester: Carcanet, 1984). While Lovelace's allegiance to Charles is beyond doubt, even in so moderate an account of his sympathies as "To Lucasta. From Prison," the praise of Parliament and his allowance of the need for reform are equally explicit.

focused primarily on questions of genre. But its controlling theme is far more topical than topographical, its emphasis being, as Thomas Healy has noted, "to seek a middle course between extremes" leading up to and culminating in the civil war.[3]

The desire for such a course was hardly unique to either Royalists or Parliamentarians in the final months leading up to the war. John M. Wallace has noted that "almost every page of the great historical collections of the period bears witness to the universal concern with 'the publike peace, safety, and happinesses of this Realme,' or the 'Honour, Greatnesse, and Security of this Crowne and Nation.' " To this general call for reconciliation, Denham added his voice in a poem that is, as Wallace has claimed, above all "about peace." Though *Coopers Hill* was first published in August 1642, the very month in which Charles raised his standard at Nottingham, Wallace has argued convincingly that an initial draft, "Draft I" of Brendan O Hehir's critical edition in *Expans'd Hieroglyphicks*, must have been written and circulated as early as September 1641, when war might still have been averted. At one level, Denham's contribution to the debate must be perceived as "effective propaganda for the king," but the rhetorical technique of that propaganda is clearly "to raise his discourse above the fevers of political disputation, and to be topical in such an oblique way that no tempers would be aroused."[4] Indeed, so balanced is Denham's position between the two parties that Wallace has applied to his political beliefs a name that aptly effects the very fusion for which Denham longed: "parliamentary royalism," "the opinions of a growing body of thoughtful men whose principles were equally parliamentarian and royalist":

> At their center lay a patriotic regard for England, the monarchy, and the person of the king; no less formidable was the desire for peace, recently symbolized by the treaty [with Scotland], and a wish for a reformed episcopacy between the alternative extremes.[5]

Wallace is chiefly interested in the polemical purpose behind Denham's initial draft and its attempt to formulate the "manifesto" of beliefs by

---

3. W. Hutchings, " 'The Harmony of Things': Denham's *Coopers Hill* as Descriptive Poem," *Papers on Language and Literature* 19 (1983): 375–84. See also David Hill Radcliffe, "These Delights from Several Causes Move: Heterogeneity and Genre in 'Coopers Hill,' " *Papers on Language and Literature* 22 (1986). Thomas Healy, " 'Dark all without it knits': Vision and Authority in Marvell's *Upon Appleton House*," in *Literature and the English Civil War*, ed. Thomas Healy and Jonathan Sawday (Cambridge: Cambridge University Press, 1990), 179.

4. John M. Wallace, "*Coopers Hill:* The Manifesto of Parliamentary Royalism, 1641," *ELH* 41 (1974): 498–99, 525, 524, 497.

5. Ibid., 534–35.

which civil war could be averted. My own concern, however, is with the more generally known revised version of 1655 and 1668, which first appeared five years before the Restoration and which reflects the views of one whose earlier calls for peace have not been heeded. As O Hehir has maintained, the two principal texts of *Coopers Hill* "are products of two distinct periods and sets of circumstances in Denham's life, set apart by more than a decade."[6] As a consequence, what Wallace has shown of the conciliatory nature of draft 1 is largely absent in the revised version of 1655, when Denham could evoke the fresh memory of war's chaos to illustrate the dangers of immoderation, both in the earlier abuses of royal prerogative and in the subsequent zeal of political and ecclesiastical reform. In the revised draft, we find not only the early statements of the *via media* by which war might have been avoided but new passages noting the results of England's not having followed such counsel. Even after the dust of the war had long settled and the monarch for whom he had fought had found peace only in the grave, this defeated Royalist could speak of the evils of arbitrary power—and indicate how the victors had imitated the very abuses they had sought to reform.[7]

Much of the poem is as hyperbolic in its praise of the crown as any Royalist propaganda of the period, and Denham is never explicitly critical of Charles himself, who is described as "the best of Kings" (24), the "mighty Master . . . in whose face / Sate meekness, heightned with Majestick Grace" (47–48), and the "Souldier," "Saint," and "Martyr" prefigured by the selection of St. George by Edward III as England's patron saint (101–10). Moreover, Denham is so far from attacking the English crown in general as to place former monarchs on a level with the "Celestial host" and pantheon of heroes of classical mythology (59–64). Yet it is in his description of this list of stellars that Denham also shows himself to be clearly critical of past abuses of royal power. In his apostrophe to "great" Edward III, Denham immediately modifies, and deflates, that praise by reminding him of his "greater" son, the uncrowned Black Prince, who won the "lillies which his Father wore" (77–78). While Edward III

6. Brendan O Hehir, *Harmony from Discords: A Life of Sir John Denham* (Berkeley and Los Angeles: University of California Press, 1968), vii.

7. The two versions of *Coopers Hill* I have used in the following discussion are those of O Hehir's "A" text, draft 3, the first edition of the poem published in August 1642, and the "B" text, draft 4, the final revised version of 1668, which is, aside from the addition of lines 193–96, substantially the same text as that published in 1655. John Denham, *Coopers Hill, Expans'd Hieroglyphicks: A Critical Edition of Sir John Denham's "Coopers Hill,"* ed. Brendan O Hehir (Berkeley and Los Angeles: University of California Press, 1969). All references to both versions of *Coopers Hill* are to this edition and are cited parenthetically in the text.

is credited with having named among his prisoners the kings of both France and Scotland, Denham is quick to point out that Edward owed the first conquest to his son, the second to his wife. Denham appears to praise Edward's founding of the Order of the Garter, only immediately to question, in a parenthetical aside, his motives for having done so: "(whither love / Or victory thy Royal thoughts did move)" (83–84). The account grows gradually more critical with every couplet, as Denham calls into question Edward's vision and power ("Had thy great Destiny but given thee skill, / To know as well, as power to act her will"), a cupidity exceeding that power ("all that thy mighty power, / Or thy desires more mighty, did devour"), and a rapaciousness that led him to bleed not only "sister Nations" but the very ancestors of his descendants: "had happy *Edward* known / That all the bloud he spilt, had been his own" (99–100).

But such censure is mild compared to what the poet says shortly after of Henry VIII, whose pillaging of the abbeys is described unequivocally as a "monstrous dire offence" and whose motives are not only called into question but explicitly denounced as criminal acts of hypocrisy:

> What crime could any Christian King incense
> To such a rage? was't Luxury, or Lust?
> Was he so temperate, so chast, so just?
> Were these their crimes? they were his own much more:
> But wealth is Crime enough to him that's poor,
> Who having spent the Treasures of his Crown,
> Condemns their Luxury to feed his own. (118–24)

The caution with which Denham approaches his earlier critique of Edward III—the backhanded compliments, the brief parenthetical asides—is thrown to the wind in this scathing account of Henry, who is described as having all of Edward's rapaciousness with none of his glory. As the monarch who initiated England's separation from Rome, of course, Henry is a fairly safe target even among Royalists, especially among those sympathetic to the heavily Catholic sentiments of the court. Indeed, though a powerful symbol of divine-right monarchy, Henry was also so intimately associated with the Reformation that Denham's censure of him could easily be perceived as an indirect criticism of the ecclesiastical views of Parliament. Indeed, in 1655, Henry's destruction of the abbeys in the name of religious reform bore a far closer resemblance to the destruction wreaked by the New Model Army than to any abuse ever attributed to Charles. In addition to the naked greed of a king eager to fill his coffers, Denham pays special attention to the religious hypocrisy of a "Defender of the Faith" who has no compunction about destroying its institutions:

"And thus to th'ages past he makes amends, / Their Charity destroys, their Faith defends" (133–34).

Though the selection of Henry VIII for such condemnation could not but be perceived with considerable ambivalence by both sides; the combination of this portrait with that of Edward III shows Denham's royalism hardly to extend to such notions of divine-right kingship as the freedom of royal prerogative from reproach. Absolute power in the hands of former monarchs *has* resulted in abuses that Denham is perfectly willing to denounce and upon which he reflects " 'twixt anger, shame, & fear" (157). Yet these accounts of royal abuses, as with the closing allusion to the "Arbitrary power" of King John, are set as obvious foils for "the best of Kings," Charles I, the worst abuses of whose reign cannot but pale considerably before what Denham has reminded his readers of earlier monarchs. As Wallace has argued, Denham's criticisms of the former reigns "revealed his abhorrence of arbitrary government and his attachment to what he believed were the courses of moderation and agreement."[8] Yet the criticisms are also, especially in 1655, clearly to be read as equally applicable to the Parliamentarian forces that, with a hypocrisy reminiscent of Henry VIII, have ended up imitating evils they set out to reform. It is the particular genius of Denham's rhetorical position that this Royalist manages to attack the opposition through an ostensible denunciation of his own party.

The critique of the rebels is not always so indirect, of course. The opening description of St. Paul's Cathedral rising over London makes perfectly clear where Denham's political sympathies primarily lie. The cathedral is, like Windsor Castle and the former St. Anne's Chapel, a "crown" rising above a city that threatens it with "sword," "fire," and "zeal more fierce than they." In his later account of St. Anne's Chapel, Denham will show a crown that has indeed fallen prey to such elements; but he argues here that Charles's preservation of St. Paul's will secure it against even time itself. In speaking of this recent preservation, Denham so intimately associates Charles with St. Paul's that the cathedral becomes not only metonymic of his reign but a manifestation of Charles himself: "Preserv'd from ruine by the best of Kings. / Under his proud survey the City lies" (24–25). While *his* must, at one level, refer to the personified cathedral in this context, the placement of the possessive adjective so near "the best of Kings" cannot but lead the reader, if only briefly, to assume that Charles is the grammatical referent, so that the king himself appears to rise majestically above his city. His subjects, however, those who may threaten this structure with sword, fire, and the fiercer zeal, are reduced to

8. Wallace, "Manifesto," 536.

the pejorative metaphors of a surrounding mist and "darker cloud" (26, 28). When the elements of that cloud assume human attributes, Denham's critique of those who oppose the king becomes even more explicit:

> Where, with like hast, though several ways, they run
> Some to undo, and some to be undone;
> While luxury, and wealth, like war and peace,
> Are each the others ruine, and increase;
> As Rivers lost in Seas some secret vein
> Thence reconveighs, there to be lost again. (31–36)

While the image of the river will become later in the poem an emblem for a state in perfect harmony, here the controlling image is the destructive, chaotic force of a tempestuous sea, the elements of which appear no less rapacious or destructive than the later description of Henry VIII. Indeed, the picture Denham paints of an anarchic London populace is ultimately *more* destructive, for the destruction is mutual, endless, and motivated by, in addition to Henry's simple greed, the mindless desire "to undo" or be "undone."[9] No less a Parliamentarian than John Pym himself had admitted the possibility of such anarchy if the cause of liberty were not held in check. At the trial of the Earl of Strafford, Pym had confessed that

> The Law is the boundary, the measure betwixt the Kings Prerogative and the Peoples Liberty. . . . If the Prerogative of the King overwhelme the Liberty of the People, it will be turned into Tyranny; if Liberty undermine the Prerogative, it will grow into Anarchy.[10]

If Denham is fairly direct in his criticism of the Parliamentarians in his opening description of London, his technique is considerably more subtle in his later account of Henry VIII, especially in the revised version of 1655. Here he is able to denounce the abuses of absolute power in the hands of such a monarch as Henry VIII, while letting his readers see the clear

---

9. A few years later, Samuel Butler would describe the endlessly busy spirit of parliamentarian reform in similar terms: "Call fire, and sword, and desolation / A godly, thorough reformation, / Which always must be carried on / And still be doing, never done; / As if religion were intended / For nothing else but to be mended" (Samuel Butler, *Hudibras*, I.i.199–204, in *Seventeenth-Century Prose and Poetry*, ed. Witherspoon and Warnke, 910–15).

10. Quoted in Robert Cummings, "Denham's *Cooper's Hill* and *Carolus Rex et Leo Papa*," *Philological Quarterly* 64 (1985): 339. Pym's remarks are based upon contemporary notions of *concordia discors*, the controlling theme of *Coopers Hill*: "Even unopposed good, in terms of the dialectic of *concordia discors*, becomes evil through excess and thereby destroys itself, just as in the state too much power becomes tyranny, too much liberty chaos." Earl R. Wasserman, *The Subtler Language: Critical Readings of Neoclassic and Romantic Poems* (Baltimore: Johns Hopkins Press, 1959), 63.

parallels between what Henry has done to English abbeys and what the Parliamentarian forces have done to churches and cathedrals throughout England.[11] As O Hehir has noted, a number of highly specific allusions to Henry VIII in the "A" text of 1642 are replaced in the 1655 version by generalizations that can easily apply to religious hypocrisy and the abuse of power in any context. Moreover, lines 149–56, describing the general desolation that would shock any visitor to England, are entirely new and are a particularly resonant reminder of the civil war by which England had been wracked since the last edition of 1642:

> Who sees these dismal heaps, but would demand
> What barbarous Invader sackt the land?
> But when he hears, no Goth, no Turk did bring
> This desolation, but a Christian King;
> When nothing, but the Name of Zeal, appears
> 'Twixt our best actions and the worst of theirs,
> What does he think our Sacriledge would spare
> When such th'effects of our devotions are?

At one level, the lines are a logical expansion of what Denham had already described of Henry's peculiar method of "reform" through the pillaging of church property. At another, the innovation clearly points the readers of the 1650s to the much more recent desolation of the civil war, when churches were destroyed far more in the "Name of Zeal" than had been the case with the financial policies carried out during Henry VIII's reign. Moreover, the epigrammatic nature of the lines could not but be read as a general attack on the effects of such religious zeal in any context, regardless of whether such desolation had been brought about by "Christian King" or Puritan soldier.

Though ultimately royalist in spirit, then, *Coopers Hill* is far more a call for moderation on both sides, a plea to work toward the "temperate Region" about which Denham asks rhetorically in his comments on the desolation brought about by religious zeal: "Is there no temperate Region can be known, / Betwixt their Frigid, and our Torrid Zone?" (139–40). The majority of the poem is devoted to answering this question, to providing a variety of examples in both society and nature in which a happy medium can be found. As Wallace has noted, the "poem proclaims a balance, the keeping of which (while balance was still feasible) would always

11. O Hehir quotes a telling couplet from Bishop Henry King's *An Elegy Upon the most Incomparable K. Charls the I*: "Churches unbuilt by order, others burn'd; / Whilst *Pauls* and *Lincoln* are to Stables turn'd" (*Expans'd Hieroglyphics*, 148 n. 153).

require some judicious concessions by both sides."[12] In 1642, such a call for the *via media* was not particularly unique among Royalists, who could easily argue that any parliamentary attempt to reform the status quo was immoderate, that the only truly moderate course the loyal subject could take would be to obey his sovereign's behests. In 1655, however, when there could be little point to maintaining such a position, the sentiment appears far more generally addressed to all parties and to any force in society whose immoderate action could plunge the country again into the anarchy and destruction of civil war. In this respect, Denham's version of 1655 serves less to attempt to persuade his opponents of the preceding decade than to anticipate the values of the Neoclassical Period, in which both substance and style of the poem would be universally admired.

By Denham's argument, creating a society in which oppositions are balanced is not only possible but the very essence of Nature's wisdom: "Wisely she knew, the harmony of things, / As well as that of sounds, from discords springs" (203–4). In other words, as Earl Wasserman and others have noted, Denham's solution lies in the concept of *concordia discors,* a simple fact of the composition of nature that both sides of the recent conflict would do well to acknowledge. Like nature, "[s]ociety is composed of differing elements. Proper recognition and achievement of the ideals can only be gained through reconciliation."[13] Yet neither has society, especially, for Denham, in the last twenty years, very frequently mirrored nature's balanced discords. Again reminding us of his Royalist sympathies, Denham finds examples of society's *concordia discors* chiefly in an irretrievable past, in the person of Charles I and of his marriage with Henrietta Maria, the Mars and Venus by which Beauty and Strength had been united (39–40) and in whose persons the political trinity of England, Scotland, and France had been manifested (92–100). The absence of such harmony, on the other hand, Denham notes chiefly in the chaotic discords of the London populace, where we find merely the warring and mutually destructive opposites of mindless energy: "Where, with like hast, though several ways, they run / Some to undo, and some to be undone" (31–32).

In nature, however, Denham is presented with examples of successful harmonies wherever he looks, most especially in the great river that stretches below him. In deliberate contrast to Henry VIII's pillaging of

12. Wallace, "Manifesto," 537.
13. Hutchings, "Harmony of Things," 380. The most comprehensive recent discussion of the concept of *concordia discors* is to be found in O Hehir, ed., *Expans'd Hieroglyphicks*, 165–76.

the abbeys and the endless "ruine, and increase" of London's "luxury, and wealth," the Thames is a boundless supply of "less guilty wealth" (167).[14] Where Henry is rapacious and London set on "undoing" and "ruine," the Thames distributes its wealth generously ("Ore which he kindly spreads his spacious wing, / And hatches plenty for th'ensuing Spring") and teaches monarchs not to destroy the effects of such generosity ("Nor with a sudden and impetuous wave, / Like profuse Kings, resumes the wealth he gave"). In place of the desolation that Henry has effected and the ruin of London's daily mayhem, Denham offers the image of "God-like" creation and "unwearied Bounty," a power that "[f]irst loves to do, then loves the Good he does" (177–78). But rather than concerning itself only with the affairs of a single country, the Thames presents an example by which harmony can exist at an international level, for "his fair bosom is the worlds exchange" (188). In his own copy of the 1668 edition, Denham added six lines that expand this notion and show his concern for a universal harmony among nations:

> Rome only conquerd halfe the world, but trade
> One commonwealth of that and her hath made
> And though the sunn his beame extends to al
> Yet to his neighbour sheds most liberall
> Least God and Nature partiall should appeare
> Commerse makes everything grow everywhere.[15]

After offering the Thames as an example of the type of *concordia discors* by which society should live, Denham suggests that he has attempted to follow his own advice in his very verse form. In the most famous passage of the poem, which first appeared in the edition of 1655, Denham describes the perfect harmony of discords exemplified by the Thames and mirrored in the type of careful balance of parallelism and antithesis he and Waller brought to the heroic couplet:

> O could I flow like thee, and make thy stream
> My great example, as it is my theme!
> Though deep, yet clear, though gentle, yet not dull,
> Strong without rage, without ore-flowing full. (189–92)

14. O Hehir glosses this line in the "A" text with the reminder that the notion that "gold in itself is specifically guilty or evil was a Renaissance commonplace traceable to Ovid," but surely Denham's primary point here is to contrast the comparative innocence of the Thames's wealth with the tainted gold of Henry VIII and London merchants.

15. Without altering line numbers, O Hehir has bracketed this addition and inserted it between lines 188 and 189.

Though extraordinarily "full" in what the couplet asserts, the thought flows gracefully within the narrow channel of the closed pentameter line. Moreover, the antithesis so common in the heroic couplet displays how opposites can be yoked not only in a new order but in a productive synthesis in which depth remains clear, gentleness is vital, strength is controlled, and a fullness of all these elements keeps safely within its boundaries. Within a single line like "Strong without rage, without ore-flowing full," we find an initial trochee perfectly conjoined with and complemented by its iambic opposite, while contrasting half lines are united by a medial caesura in the reminder that a current whose strength is controlled can be full without threatening to overflow. In short, Denham presents, both contextually and metrically, a perfect emblem of the type of united balance capable among seemingly incompatible elements in society. And yet the couplet is merely one area of Denham's verse form that mirrors the harmony found in nature. David Hill Radcliffe has shown how the "crazy quilt" of the poem, a patchwork of georgic elements, epigrams, and meditations, becomes on a much larger level "a model of the heterogeneous state, the poem and the state in each instance organized by balance, subordination, and mixture."[16]

Like the "untrac't ways" and "aery paths" of this discursive poem, through which the reader is led from London to Runnymede, from war to stag hunts, and between present and past, nature is filled with "strange varieties" that are the foundation of harmony, not conflict. "Such was the discord, which did first disperse / Form, order, beauty through the Universe," discord that serves as the very fabric of creation and growth (205–6). But the essential criterion for such a balance is that no one element dominate, that a middle ground be found between the extremes of tyranny and liberty, between a "Frigid" faith and the "Torrid Zone" of religious zeal. In the varying discords of 1641, Denham entertained the hope that a constructive agreement could be found by which the river of society could keep within its channels. By 1655, however, he could only look back at the deluge of the 1640s, in which the extreme of "Arbitrary power" had merely changed hands,

> And popular sway, by forcing Kings to give
> More than was fit for Subjects to receive,
> Ran to the same extreams; and one excess
> Made both, by striving to be greater, less. (345–48)

16. Radcliffe, "These Delights," 370.

Elizabeth Clarke

The Garrisoned Muse

Women's Use of the
Religious Lyric in the
Civil War Period

In this essay I want to consider two critical comments on the religious lyric in the civil war period: Helen Wilcox's judgment that the devotional writing in the English Revolution is characterized by a "female aesthetic" and Nigel Smith's description of the genre as "an instrument of religious policy." Taken together, these statements would seem to have important implications for women entering into authorship in the mid-seventeenth century through the agency of the religious lyric. Far from the exclusively private mode posited by Germaine Greer and others, the religious lyric as used by women would seem in this particular historical context to offer access to the political debate being conducted in religious terms. Even inscription in manuscript, that most private of media, did not necessarily exclude women from participation in politics and culture in the civil war. This essay considers poetry that exists in manuscript as well as in print because, as Harold Love points out, the manuscript miscellany was the primary mode by which seventeenth-century verse was circulated, and as Margaret Ezell has shown, printed publication is the exception and not the norm for women writing in the early modern period.[1] In this, the medium most often adopted by seventeenth-century women, and yet most unfamiliar

1. Helen Wilcox, "Exploring the Language of Devotion in the English Revolution," in *Literature and the English Civil War*, ed. Thomas Healy and Jonathan Sawday (Cambridge: Cambridge University Press, 1990), 86; Nigel Smith, *Literature and Revolution in England, 1640–1660* (New Haven: Yale University Press, 1994), 276. Harold Love, *Scribal Publication in Seventeenth-Century England* (Oxford: Clarendon Press, 1993), 5. Margaret J. M. Ezell, *The Patriarch's Wife: Literary Evidence and the History of the Family* (Chapel Hill: University of North Carolina Press, 1988), 62.

to modern scholarship, some of the most radical literary comment on the civil war and its politics is expressed.

Germaine Greer admits that religious writing by women was "used as ammunition in a veritable propaganda war" in midcentury England but insists that it was "intended to remain private."[2] It is difficult to see how such a statement could be proved. By the 1640s the word *private* had already become part of a public discourse, associated with the religious lyric, which had achieved political instrumentality. The title "Private Ejaculations," implying a discourse directly inspired by God, had been established by George Herbert's hugely popular devotional volume and annexed as the title for more politically committed works such as Christopher Harvey's *The Synagogue: or Sacred Poems and Private Ejaculations* (1640), and Francis Quarles's son John's *Gods Love and Mans Unworthiness* (1651), which included 149 "Divine Ejaculations." The large number of poets whom Stanley Stewart has designated the "school of Herbert" exploited the function of the religious lyric as established by him for reasons both of politics and profit. Even unsophisticated women writers such as Anna Cromwell Williams show an awareness of the rhetorical and political value of "private" discourse. Her manuscript volume, entitled *A Booke of Severall devotions collected from good men by the worst of siners*, shows the word *private* inserted before "devotions" and then crossed out again, as if she were considering its rhetorical and political implications.[3] As it stands, the title stresses the derivative, masculine nature of the contents, which is an understandable defensive strategy but misleading. The anthology contains not only poetry by "good men," such as Francis Bacon and Francis Quarles, but also poems by female members of the Cromwell family and possibly by Anna herself: she is certainly the author of some of the prose pieces in the manuscript. Despite their kinship with the Lord Protector, from whom the Cromwells tried to distance themselves by changing their name to Williams in 1660, the members of the family were enthusiastically Royalist. The amateur pieces in the manuscript use the rhetoric of the professional poets who are clearly their models. One piece is entitled "Holy eiaculations"; another, "A Divine Fancy," Francis Quarles's title. Anna Cromwell Williams's manuscript demonstrates all the characteristics of Royalist "cultural rebellion" as described by Lois Potter, including poems for Christmas and Easter, and one in celebration

2. Greer, introduction to *Kissing the Rod: An Anthology of Seventeenth Century Women's Verse*, ed. Germaine Greer, Jeslyn Medoff, Melinda Sansone, and Susan Hastings (London: Virago, 1988), 13.

3. Stanley Stewart, *George Herbert* (Boston: Twayne Publishers, 1986), 128–56. British Library MS Harley 2311.

of the local Maypole feast, as well as the little hagiographic epigram beginning: "Reader take but from Charles A: L: & E / & put thereto but only I and T."[4] The answer to the anagram is as inevitable as it is hyperbolic.

The "private" discourse of the religious lyric, I suggest, becomes politically instrumental in this period because of its value in a particular symbolic economy. The history of discourse in the civil war is characterized by the number of private writing enterprises made public for political reasons. The publication of private letters is a particular obsession: the perceived spontaneity and disingenuousness of such writing allowed its use as an indicator of the spiritual state of the author, a kind of knowledge in great demand in the 1640s. The Parliamentarian annotators of *The Kings Cabinet Opened* used the correspondence between Charles and Henrietta Maria in exactly this way. At the other end of the social and political spectrum is the publication of the letters of anonymous Parliamentarian soldiers to their wives, presumably to show their faith and fortitude under pressure.[5] These pamphlets represent an absolute identification of private and political discourse: if such letters had not been written it would have been necessary for the seventeenth-century equivalent of "spin doctors" to have invented them. Other types of "private" writing could function in this way. At the funeral sermon for the Earl of Warwick in 1658, entitled *A Patterne for All*, Edmund Calamy singled out as the most important element of this universal "pattern" Warwick's exactness in "closet duties," that is, private prayer: "He hath left behind him *reall manifestations* of his personal piety, by many *religious collections,* written with his own hand."[6] Both sides exploited the political worth of private discourses in exemplary biography that set out to show that God's sympathies were firmly on the side of the holiest. Barnabas Oley and Isaac Walton used a combination of "proofs" from George Herbert's personal life and his "private ejaculations" to present him as the ideal of loyal, conformist religion. The perception of his poetry as inspired writing allowed his lyrics to be used as propaganda in different civil war contexts.

The tropes of spiritual inspiration current in the civil war play on the interaction of divine impulse and human passivity implied in the notion of "ejaculation." For the spiritual benefits induced by inactivity, even male authors embrace a state of confinement when it is forced upon

---

4. Lois Potter, *Secret Rites and Secret Writings: Royalist Literature, 1641–60* (Cambridge: Cambridge University Press, 1989), 33.

5. *An Extract of Letters from Yorke and Hull* (London, 1642).

6. Edmund Calamy, *A Patterne for all, especially for Noble and Honourable Persons, to teach them how to die Nobly and Honourably* (London, 1658), 34–35.

them. The choice of title and subtitle of Henry Vane's work *The Retired Mans Meditations: or, the Mysterie and Power of Godliness* (1655) represents a spiritual transaction, which he enlarges upon in the preface: sequestration from what he terms the "busie and boundless Spirit of Men" allows him access to a supernatural and limitless power. Confinement is of course the preferred state of women as constructed by conduct books such as Richard Brathwait's *The English Gentlewoman* of 1633. Once a strategy to silence women, sequestration becomes in the spiritual economy a qualification to speak. The midcentury perception of the symbolic value of private writing offers a potentially public voice to women simply because the closet has been their privileged domain. Hilary Hinds points out that a biblical text, Luke 12:3, lies behind women's claims to the privacy of their closet-authorship. The verse stresses the authenticity of such writing and God's intention to publish it: "that which ye have spoken in the ear in closets shall be proclaimed upon the house-tops." This kind of rationale informs the poem in praise of Jane Cavendish's poetry by her scribe, John Rolleston, at the end of her verse miscellany. It celebrates the coincidence of the battles of the civil war with the composition of her verses: "in garrison your muse durst stay / When that shee heard the drumms and cannon play."[7] Jane Cavendish spent the civil war in a literal state of confinement at Welbeck, which served as a garrison for Royalist troops until the Earl of Manchester took Welbeck in August 1644. Thereafter the Parliamentary garrison must have turned the house into a kind of prison for Jane and her sisters.[8] In a poem to her father at the end of her manuscript, she declares that the best use of her captivity is to carry on the literary tradition started by him (f. 76). John Rolleston, relieved of his post of secretary to her father, who had left England after the battle of Marston Moor, resumed his prewar task of scribal publication of the Cavendish family poetry. While men were fighting the civil war, it seemed to him, the muse actually preferred to stay in garrison, with the women.

Jane Cavendish's "booke of verses," as Rolleston called it, exists in two scribal copies, of which Bodleian MS Rawlinson poet. 16 is rather better known than Beinecke MS Osborn b. 233. The volume is closer to the standard Royalist miscellany than any of the other poetry discussed

7. Henry Vane, *The Retired Mans Meditation, or, the Mysterie and Power of Godliness* (London, 1655), A3r. Text from Luke as quoted by Hilary Hinds, *God's Englishwomen: Seventeenth-Century Radical Sectarian Writing and Feminist Criticism* (Manchester: Manchester University Press, 1996), 101. John Rolleston verse from Beinecke Library Osborn MS b. 233, f. 77: 'Upon the right honourable the Lady Jane Cavendish her booke of verses.' Further quotations are from this manuscript.
8. *The Quarrel Between Cromwell and the Earl of Manchester*, Camden Society (1875), 6.

here. Adam Littleton, in Jane Cavendish's funeral sermon, celebrated her private writing of "pious reflections," but this volume self-consciously exploits the conventions of the religious lyric to explore political success and ambition.[9] Cavendish's volume shows a strong awareness of the restrictions on women's authorship and political participation in this period. The poetry everywhere asserts its limitations in the classic rhetorical moves of religious discourse, but Cavendish is clearly aware of the benefits to be gained by an insistence on physical and rhetorical restriction in the symbolic economy of religious authorship. The "sad Garrison of rest," the garrison celebrated by Rolleston as the site of her inspiration, is a physical and emotional space in which she feels "coffin'd," a word that strengthens the confinement trope, which it paranomasically suggests with the implication that she is in some sense "dead," a thoroughly useful condition for the Protestant author whom God is going to inspire (f. 22). Throughout her volume, Cavendish makes a blasphemous equation between the Christian's traditional source of inspiration and her own, her father, the Marquess of Newcastle, beginning with the dedicatory epistle on the first folio of the Beinecke manuscript: "what I have of good, is wholly derived from you, as the soule of bounty, and this booke desires no other purchas, then a single one from your [Lordshipp] or a word of like, [which] will glorifie your creature." This passage may echo dedications in Royalist volumes such as Herrick's verse to Prince Charles, at the start of *Hesperides*. However, Cavendish sustains this identification between the Creator and her earthly father throughout the poems in the volume. She represents herself as dying with her father and being resurrected with him in "Passions [Letter] to my Lord my father." She compares the absence of God with her father's absence in "Passions Contemplation" and hopes to be "saved" by his presence. "Your comeing is a Sacrament to mee," she declares in "Hopes preparation" (ff. 3, 6, 39). In terms reminiscent of those used by women prophets about God, she expresses a sense of mere instrumentality. As his pen, she simply inscribes Newcastle's own authoritative writing (f. 76).

Two companion pieces from the volume show this play between the sacred and the profane operating at different levels. "On the 30th of June, to God" is a poem in honor of Newcastle's victory at Adwalton Moor in 1643 (f. 38). Jane Cavendish seems to have correctly judged the significance of a battle now overshadowed by Marston Moor a year later. In 1643,

9. Adam Littleton, *A Sermon at the Funeral of the Right Honourable the Lady Jane Eldest Daughter to his Grace William, Duke of Newcastle, and Wife to the Honourable Charles Cheyne, Esq. at Chelsey* (London, 1669), F3r.

Newcastle's victory appeared to have secured the north for the Royalists, although Royalist lapses in strategy later ensured that this advantage was never fully followed up.[10] It begins conventionally with reference to authorized religious discourses in which the writer promises to engage: sermons and prayers. In fact the immediate production of the author is the less pious activity of sonnet making. The decisive move towards secularity is, I think, in the complete identification of Newcastle's victory with God's "workes," in line 7:

> This day I will my thankes sure now declare
> By Sermons, Bounties of each harty prayer
> To thee great God who gave thy bounty large
> Saveing my ffather from the Enemies charge
> Not onely soe, but made him victour leade
> Chargeinge his Enemies [with] linckes of lead
> To let them now thy workes plaine see
> Sayeinge my little flock shall Conquerers bee. (ll. 1–8)

Hereafter the addressee of the poem becomes unstable. The celebration of Newcastle in line 10 distracts attention from the original subject, God: "And it was true ffairfax was then more great / But yet Newcastle made him sure retreat" (ll. 9–10). It is Newcastle's victory, then, that Cavendish covertly celebrates in the aristocratic medium of scribal publication:

> Therefore Ile keepe this thy victorys day
> If not in publique, by some private way
> In spite of Rebells, who thy Lawes deface
> And blott the footesteps of thy sonns blood trace. (ll. 11–14)

The return to uniquely sacred subjects is a surprise that underlines the implicit and blasphemous equation in this poem between her father and God. Margaret Ezell sees this volume as a significant contribution to the political project to affirm Cavalier identity.[11] The "private way" in which she is marking Newcastle's victory is of course her choice of the manuscript medium, which would allow circulation to an elite Royalist coterie; it is also a rhetorical strategy that turns the celebration of Newcastle's victory into the observation of a religious feast, a more pious and appropriate activity for a young lady.

10. Martyn Bennett, *The Civil Wars in Britain and Ireland, 1638–1651* (Oxford: Blackwell, 1997), 167.

11. Margaret J. M. Ezell, " 'To Be Your Daughter in Your Pen': The Social Functions of Literature in the Writings of Lady Elizabeth Brackley and Lady Jane Cavendish," *Huntington Library Quarterly* 51 (1988): 287.

The next poem in the volume, "The minds salvation," is an even more daring experiment with sacred tropes (f. 39). The subject of the poem is a woman writer, and it is not immediately clear that it is Cavendish herself: "This day I did in perpestive one veiw / A Lady who did looke as if 'twas you." However, as the poem progresses, the familiar eulogy of Newcastle confirms the identification between the writer in the poem and the author of the poem. The distancing implied by the siting of the subject "in perpestive," implying a view in a distorting mirror, or possibly a portrait, is perhaps a sensible strategy, as the female author described here is indulging in expressly transgressive behavior. The pious female activity at the start of the poem, the reading of Scripture, is literally a cover for her writing. She is hiding her compositions behind a very big Bible: "With Bible great upon her Table layd / Yett, with her pen & Inke expresses made" (ll. 3–4). She continues this subversive practice by using some of the central doctrines of the Christian faith as literary strategies to flatter her father. She adopts Christ's resurrection as a trope for Newcastle's political advancement, "to rise a Generall great in state" (l. 9). In a parody of biblical doctrine she requests that "by his resurrection shee might live" (l. 8). This line is less a spiritually orthodox request than a thinly veiled desire for the wealthly and powerful environment that she would enjoy as a result of Newcastle's success. The "minds salvation" of the title, a strange formulation, is clarified in another poem later in the document, which makes clear that although religious practices absolve her soul from guilt, they cannot save her mind from despair (f. 41). There is an implicit opposition set up in "The minds salvation" between the private salvation of the soul and a kind of worldly equivalent, linked both to writing activity and political success. The final couplet collapses both kinds of salvation, but it is clearly Newcastle's "meritts" by which she hopes to achieve freedom from hell and the devil:

> For then hir soule of mind is iustly saved
> By him who sure in this world had her made
> Thus by his meritts hopes of heaven that's glad
> Soe free hir selfe from Devill, Hell, that's sad. (ll. 10–14)

Traditional Christian redemption is being subordinated to this parodic and blasphemous "minds salvation."

All the rhetorical moves made by Cavendish in this manuscript—the equation of her own political cause with God's and the reference to conventional tropes of inspiration—are commonplace in civil war writing. What is extraordinary is the simultaneous and self-conscious exploitation and undermining of these discourses. Cavendish, who is not writing for publication but for a sophisticated literary and political elite, does not require the validation of the tropes of religious inspiration. The transformation of her father into a godlike original "Author" represents a deliberate overplaying of patriarchal rhetoric. She offers a parody of the rhetorical strategies demanded of all authors, and of women in particular, by a theory of religious authorship that requires that human writing take place under the direction and inspiration of a divine Author. In Cavendish's playful aristocratic poetry, the use of the tropes desirable and indeed necessary for women's authorship, particularly religious authorship, is exposed for what it is—a rhetorical strategy, operating not for God's benefit in a holy private realm, but for the reader, and therefore being in some sense "political." This ironic inversion may represent the "private way" into which she has to deflect public utterance in line 12 of "On the 30th of June, to God." As the physical activity of writing is hidden behind the "Bible great," so her political opinions and ambitions are veiled behind an apparently religious rhetoric, which Adam Littleton could term "pious reflections." An elite Royalist readership, of the kind that participated in literary culture at Welbeck before the civil war, and in particular her father, whose poems show the same kind of witty exploitation of religious rhetoric, would have detected the irony.

Women writers whose poetry appears in print depend upon a less sophisticated reading of the tropes of inspiration. An Collins uses the same formula as Henry Vane to validate her *Divine Songs and Meditacions* in 1653: "I inform you, that by divine Providence, I have been restrained from bodily employments, suting with my disposicion, which enforced me to a retired Course of life; Wherin it pleased God to give me . . . inlargednesse of mind, and activity of spirit."[12] The biblical Song of Songs is the intertext for Collins's poetry. In the poem "Another Song" (55–56), her mind is the enclosed garden, the site of inspiration, where she receives the spiritual motions that inspire her verse and produce "fruit":

> Yet as a garden is my mind enclosed fast
> Being to safety so confind from storm and blast
> Apt to produce a fruit most rare. (ll. 26–28)

She retreats to the safety of this garden from the natural world that is the opening scene of many of her poems, a physical garden often blasted

---

12. An Collins, *Divine Songs and Meditacions,* ed. Sidney Gottlieb (Tempe, Ariz.: Medieval and Renaissance Texts and Studies, 1996), 1. Subsequent quotations from Collins are from this edition; page references are cited in the text.

by storms that are themselves metaphorical representations of the "evil mocions" of error, distrust, and terror, products of "commocion" in the political world. The visionary and even prophetic insight bestowed by this privileged position is expressed in poems such as "A Song composed in time of the Civill Warr, when the wicked did much insult over the godly." In the first stanza she rejects the "Poems neat" of classical authorship in a move that seems to echo her rejection of ancient liturgy elsewhere in the volume as "frozen Forms long since compos'd" ("Another Song," 63, l. 69). She presents her poetry as a discourse of spiritual liberty, so much so that it resists literary structures:

> Such mentall mocions which are free
> Concepcions of the mind,
> Which notwithstanding will not be
> To thoughts alone confind. (ll. 5–8)

In fact, An Collins experiments with various lyric forms throughout her collection, but for this, perhaps her most overtly "political" poem, she chooses a meter echoing that of the sung Psalter, that most holy of verse forms, relatively free and therefore conducive to divine inspiration, which was often adopted in the civil war for political purposes. Her preferred model for authorship is represented in stanza 2: she is a biblical woman prophet manqué, a Deborah without a victory to celebrate. The language of millenarianism is used to attack the Cromwellian regime, a brave public enterprise so soon after the 1651 Presbyterian plot.

> That there are such auspicious dayes
> To come, we may not doubt,
> Because the Gospels splendant rayes
> Must shine the World throughout:
> By Jewes the Faith shall be embrac't
> The Man of Sin must fall,
> New Babell shall be quite defac't
> With her devices all. (ll. 89–96)

For An Collins, the civil war is primarily conducted through various discourses, as she describes it in stanzas 3, 4, 5, and 6. The "Foes of Truth" use slander against their opponents, and they make false application of biblical discourses. Moreover, they subject the conquered to binding with oaths, which must refer to the various oaths required by Parliament. Collins's own poems, represented as nonrhetorical and therefore "truthful," play an active part in the struggle, speaking out "betimes in Truths

defence" (l. 18). Nothing is known of An Collins's history and it is impossible to fix her political position from her poetry, despite the attempts of
various critics. In the introduction to his recent edition, Sidney Gottlieb
supplies a useful corrective to those who have stressed conservatism in the
poetry. He points out how much of her discourse is reminiscent of Quaker
writers. This poem, and others like it in An Collins's volume, come within
the scope of Nigel Smith's observation that poets of this period tend to
sound like their cultural opposites.[13] The recurring imagery of nature and
the seasons, the need to destroy Babel, the suggestion of a truly godly
remnant within sectarian England, and the millenarian vision of peace
on earth, is as characteristic of lyrics by the Fifth Monarchist Morgan
Llwyd as it is of Royalists like Henry Vaughan. An Collins's poem does
not contemplate further military struggle, but it does suggest an earthly
reign of Christ:

> The Sonns of strife their force must cease,
> Having fulfild their crime,
> And then the Son of wished peace
> Our Horizon will clime. (ll. 85–88)

She seems to be taking up a position between the militancy of the radical
sects and the nonmillenarianist Anglican survivalism described by Claude
Summers.[14]

Germaine Greer, in the introduction to *Kissing the Rod*, is dismissive of
the use of women's religious writing in politics because of the discourses of
female inferiority that inevitably accompany it: "the use made of women
in religious controversy has often more to do with the idea that God speaks
through the mouths of 'babes and sucklings,' and idiots and others who
would otherwise be dumb and of no account, than any conviction of the
sexlessness of souls." However, in the funeral sermon he preached for
Anne Clifford, Edward Rainbowe gives as one reason why women's lives
are often exemplary the fact that the soul is sexless. Other reasons do
conform to the pattern identified by Greer. Women are chosen by God, not
as an index of their worth, but as a humbling strategy for men: women are
"instruments" for God's use, such as when Mary bore Jesus.[15] The poet

---

13. Gottlieb, introduction to *Divine Songs and Meditacions*, xviii. Smith, *Literature and Revolution*, 268–69.
14. Claude J. Summers, "Herrick, Vaughan, and the Poetry of Anglican Survival-ism" in *New Perspectives on the Seventeenth-Century English Religious Lyric*, ed. John R. Roberts (Columbia: University of Missouri Press, 1994), 51.
15. Greer, introduction to *Kissing the Rod*, 15. Edward Rainbowe, *A Sermon preached at the funeral of the Right Honourable Anne, Countess of Pembroke, Dorset and Montgomery* (London, 1677), 7.

Eliza consciously adopts the role of the Bride of Christ for her authorial enterprises, and stresses the mere instrumentality of her role in bringing forth her poetic "babes," in a move that is intended to establish divine validation of her discourse:

> Looke on these Babes as none of mine,
> For they were but brought forth by me;
> But look on them, as they are Divine,
> Proceeding from Divinity.[16]

The impulse to publish is described by her in the same terms that An Collins uses for divine inspiration, as a "motion" that she "would faine have supprest." This clear sense of the prompting of God seems to have emboldened her to undertake daring authorial enterprises. In 1644, she sent her "babes" to Charles I with some very specific political advice:

> Do not with war my Babes affright,
> In smiling peace is their delight,
> My Prince by yeelding won the field,
> Be not too rigid, dear King yeeld. (23, ll. 7–10)

This was of course the period of one of Charles's flirtations with peace, after the disaster of Marston Moor at the beginning of July 1644. Belief in an outright victory was beginning to wane in the Royalist army and Charles was finally pressured from within his own ranks to offer Essex a deal that would bring peace to England, though not on the humble terms that Eliza's injunction to him to "yeeld" suggests.

Eliza's poem to Cromwell, in the 1652 printed edition, also shows an awareness of political issues (p. 54). The compilers of *Kissing the Rod* took their title from this poem, quoting lines 3–6 as an epigraph to the volume:

> But why do I complain of thee?
> 'Cause thou'rt the rod that scourgeth mee?
> But if a good child I will bee,
> I'le kiss the Rod, and honour thee.[17]

This reads like an archetypal text of private female devotion. In the context of an address to Cromwell, however, Eliza's poem appears as an entirely

---

16. *Eliza's Babes, or, The Virgins-Offering* (London, 1652), A1v. Further quotations are from this edition.

17. Greer et al., *Kissing the Rod*, iii.

different kind of text. The first two lines of the poem, which immediately precede the *Kissing the Rod* epigraph, make clear that the rod in question is Cromwell himself:

> The Sword of God doth ever well
> I'th hand of vertue! O Cromwel,
> But why doe I, complain of thee? (ll. 1–3)

The intention to "kiss the Rod," in this context, seems to refer to Cromwell's increasingly obvious intentions to assume the trappings of monarchy, including the scepter and the rod. However, the following lines make clear that Eliza's obedience vowed to the rod is conditional, to say the least: "And if thou'rt vertuous as 'tis sed, / Thou'lt have the glory when thou'rt dead" (ll. 7–8). The poem as a whole is a rather subtle expression of political negotiation rather than the abject surrender suggested in the extract. The posture of humble obedience described here is a safe position from which to utter the demands about legal reform in stanza 2:

> Sith Kings and Princes scourged be,
> Whip thou the Lawyer from his fee
> That is so great, when nought they doe,
> And we are put off from our due.
> But they for their excuse do say,
> 'Tis from the Law is our delay,
> By Tyrants heads those laws were made. (ll. 9–15)

In the year after the publication of Eliza's volume, the Nominated Parliament voted to abolish the Star Chamber in just this spirit, accusing the lawyers of "Delatories, Chargeablenesse and a facultie of letting Bloud the people in the purse-veine, even to their utter perishing and undoing." The law itself was also to be purged and simplified.[18] Once again Eliza shows herself very much in touch with contemporary political issues, and the final lines of her poem include an implicit accusation of tyranny, a gesture of resistance to the rod of the first stanza:

> If then from Tyrants you'l us free,
> Free us from their Laws Tyranny.
> If not! wee'l say the head is pale,
> But still the sting lives in the tail. (ll. 17–20)

18. L. D., *An Exact Relation of the Proceedings and Transactions of the Late Parliament* (London, 1654), 12, 15.

This sting in the tail of her own poem is a kind of threat, a stance far removed from the abject submission that lines 3–7 seem to indicate when quoted out of context.

Playing the submission card is one way to gain an audience, and as soon as it is consciously used as a strategy it indicates female agency rather than male exploitation. Ann Marie McEntée shows how the female petitioners of Parliament adjusted their discourse between 1649 and 1653, abandoning confident self-representations for deliberate self-abasement in an attempt to find an effective rhetoric.[19] The women who use the tropes of inspiration, which are themselves feminized in this period, are surely aware of the power of these tropes as rhetorical strategies. Eliza's poem "My intention" (19) reads like a conflation of Herbert's "Jordan" poems and Herrick's "Prayer for Absolution," writing that functions as a kind of baptismal rite for poetry:

> Go vaine invention, get you hence,
> With me share not your residence,
> Court not my Muse with fine Invention
> To praise my God tis my intention
> Lord let no line be writ by me,
> That excludes, or includes not thee.[20]

The complete submission, which involves a stated preference for silence over any hint of godlessness on the part of the poet, is the strongest version of the invocatory strategy optimistically described by Cowley in the preface to his 1656 *Poems:* "the whole work may reasonably hope to be filled with a *Divine Spirit,* when it begins with a *Prayer* to be so."[21] What this allows for is an "inlargednesse of mind" in which the poet has absolute freedom of speech, in exchange for what is finally a rhetorical gesture towards God, as Eliza's poem "The onely bound" makes clear: "My boundlesse spirits, bounded be in thee / For bounded by no other can they be" (36). As we have seen, even heads of state cannot restrict Eliza's liberty to write.

In a sense, the claims of male religious writers to weakness and silence, noted by Wilcox, have ungendered the traditionally female position of dependence: all devotional writers of this period rely on God for utterance. This sense of equality before God appears to release women into

19. Ann Marie McEntée, " 'The [Un]Civill-Sisterhood of Oranges and Lemons': Female Petitioners and Demonstrators, 1642–53," in *Pamphlet Wars: Prose in the English Revolution,* ed. James Holstun (London: Cass, 1992), 107.

20. *Eliza's Babes,* 19.

21. Abraham Cowley, *Poems* (London, 1656), 24.

published speech.[22] Moreover, the site for holy poetry has been shifted into a peculiarly female reserve: the privacy of the prayer closet. Some women fully grasp the logic of this privileged position and the opportunities it presents. Robert Quarles reacts in mock alarm to the political implications of Anne Bradstreet's religious verse in the 1650 publication of her *The Tenth Muse:*

> Arme arme, soldado's arme, Horse, Horse, speed to your Horses,
> Gentle-women make head, they vent their plot in Verses.[23]

Women's discourse is often surprisingly radical as they speak from within the temple, the closet, or the enclosed garden. For some women, this radicalism entails staying within the confines of manuscript culture, but others see the tropes and rhetorical structures that endow a midcentury discourse with holiness as sanctuary enough. Their "boundlesse spirits," as Eliza put it, are "onely bound" within the forms and conventions of the religious lyric as it is practiced in the civil wars.

22. Hinds, *God's Englishwomen*, 70.
23. Joseph R. McElrath Jr. and Allan P. Robb, eds., *The Complete Works of Anne Bradstreet* (Boston: Twayne Publishers, 1981), 529.

Hugh Jenkins

Two Letters to Lord Fairfax

Winstanley and Marvell

Renewed interest in the country-house poem of late has brought with it renewed interest in Marvell's great contribution to the genre, "Upon Appleton House." Recent readings of the poem have generally moved away from earlier studies focusing on its formal or perspective ingenuity, and have instead sought to chart the ideological strategies behind these features. Most current readers tend to agree with Christina Malcolmson, who has argued that in the poem, "Marvell expresses his own sophisticated ideology: the cultivation of the country, like the cultivation of the land, must occur under the auspices of enlightened property owners." Thus Christopher Kendrick states that " 'Upon Appleton House,' however much it may honour Fairfax's line, amounts to a surreptitious celebration of absolute property." Such arguments vitally extend the more narrow focus of earlier studies. Yet given their concentration on property rights, it would seem that they would have to address closely one of Marvell's most ingenious formal adaptations of the genre, his giving voice to "the tawny mowers" in the fields of the estate in the poem's long middle section. These mowers' work allegorically represents the turbulent politics of the post–Civil War era and ultimately recreates in the estate's meadows the "naked equal flat / Which Levellers take pattern at" (449–50). After all, through his depiction of the mowers, Marvell has graphically represented precisely that labor whose "magical extraction," as Raymond Williams has pointed out, is necessary to the ideological workings of the genre. Yet current readings tend to

I would like to thank my colleagues Ruth Stevenson, Jim McCord, Andreas Kriefall, and Paul Halliday of Union College for their help in preparing this article, as well as Claude Summers and Ted-Larry Pebworth for their editorial patience and acuity in seeing it through to publication. Union College provided funding for two research assistants, Lori Malinoski and Jonathan Yarkony, without whose efforts this article could never have been completed.

underestimate the role of the "Levellers" in the poem. While Malcolmson does acknowledge the mowers' significance, she reads the apocalyptic flood imagery accompanying their introduction not as overt political allegory, but rather as a form of agricultural improvement ("floating" the meadows). This interpretation emphasizes Fairfax's absolute command of his estate and cleanses it of its radical elements. Kendrick goes even further: he sees the mowers and their remarkable responses to the poet as "a return of Catholicism"—that is, as representing the latent threat to property embodied by the residual culture of the poem's "subtle nuns," rather than the blatant threat of the potentially emergent culture of the Civil War–era radicals.[1]

By slighting the mowers and the whole episode in the meadows, such readings tend to overlook the dominant subtext of the poem. That subtext is the *threat* to property and property rights posed by such "Levellers" and other, more radical, elements set free by the Revolution. "Upon Appleton House" was composed just after a time when, as Simon D'Ewes noted in his diary, "the rude multitude in divers counties took advantage of those civil and intestine broils to plunder and pillage the houses of the nobility, gentry, and others." If this pillaging never reached the levels of that in the French Revolution, it was widespread enough to convince the Earl of Berkshire that the soldiery of both sides "had resolved to make their fortunes out of noble estates." Such inchoate demonstrations of class hostility had increasingly been given coherent voice in the years following the Civil War, first in a limited fashion by the army "Levellers," whom Fairfax himself had finally suppressed at Burford in 1649, then most dramatically later that year by Gerrard Winstanley and his "True Levellers" digging at St. George's Hill. It is the latter, I will argue, who provide the subtext I have referred to. In "Upon Appleton House," Marvell does not simply allude to such Levellers, but rather incorporates them as a parodic and ultimately

---

1. Christina Malcolmson, "The Garden Enclosed/The Woman Enclosed: Marvell and the Cavalier Poets," in *Enclosure Acts: Sexuality, Property, and Culture in Early Modern Europe,* ed. Richard Burt and John Michael Archer (Ithaca: Cornell University Press, 1994), 262, 265; Christopher Kendrick, "Agons of the Manor: 'Upon Appleton House' and Agrarian Capitalism," in *The Production of English Renaissance Culture,* ed. David Lee Miller, Sharon O'Dair, and Harold Weber (Ithaca: Cornell University Press, 1994), 50, 52. Raymond Williams's comments on the genre come from *The Country and the City* (New York: Oxford University Press, 1973), 26–34. As I was preparing this essay for publication, John Rogers's discussion of the poem in *The Matter of Revolution: Science, Poetry, and Politics in the Age of Milton* (Ithaca: Cornell University Press, 1996) was brought to my attention. Rogers, too, notes the possible influence of Winstanley's tracts on Marvell's poem, though he emphasizes a common "rhetoric of monistic vitalism" (43) in both, rather than seeing Marvell's text as parodying Winstanley's.

destabilizing third term throughout the poem. This third term subverts the established antinomies of the country-house poem—between high and low, as established in the poem's hierarchical organization; between inside and out, as established by the poem's contrast of the celebrated estates and their ostentatious counterparts; and between positive and negative, as established in the metonymical and ethical equation of the estates and their owners. It thus provides a parodic inversion of each constitutive element of the genre. This results in part in the pronounced distancing, the shifting perspectives, of the poet and the poem. From a wider angle, however, such inversions foreshadow Marx's famous definition of ideology, in which "men and their circumstances appear upside down, as in a *camera obscura.*" In effect, the poem's inversions turn upside down the ideological bases of the genre in which Marvell writes. The poem thus does not celebrate Fairfax's "right of absolute property" on his estate. Rather, in answering the voice of the Levellers, it questions the whole idea of the estate; its larger referent, the state itself; and, as a result, the very genre in which it works. The answers the poem supplies account for the unique formal adaptations to the genre Marvell works; these together can be seen as an ideological preemptive strike, a parody of the parody. Or another way of putting it would be that when faced with the challenge of the insurgent radicals, Marvell has to destroy a genre in order to save it.[2]

Marvell signals his strategy from the very beginning. When he subtitles his poem "To My Lord Fairfax," he draws on the country-house poem's relation to the epideictic epistle, the "To . . ." formula being common to the genre. But Marvell here also alludes to the persistence of the radical ideas Fairfax had opposed, and whose defeat had seemingly justified his retirement. The subtitle recalls a series of similarly addressed epistles to Lord Fairfax from the Diggers, written in December 1649—more than six months after Burford. In their third and last letter to Lord Fairfax (itself subtitled, like Marvell's poem, "To the Lord Fairfax"), Winstanley and the Diggers make clear their view of the logical outcome of the Civil War:

2. D'Ewes is cited by Christopher Hill in "The Many-Headed Monster," in *Change and Continuity in Seventeenth-Century England* (New Haven: Yale University Press, 1991), 195; the Earl of Berkshire by Lawrence Stone in *The Crisis of the Aristocracy, 1558–1641,* abr. ed. (Oxford: Oxford University Press, 1967), 354; Marx by Raymond Williams in *Keywords,* rev. ed. (New York: Oxford University Press, 1983), 155. The extent and nature of Winstanley's radicalism, and that of the period in general, has been the subject of several revisionary studies in recent years; my concern here is only on how ideas like those contained in the letters to Lord Fairfax were read in relation to the country-house poem. The best discussions of the country-house poem itself are Williams's and that of Don Wayne in *Penshurst: The Semiotics of Place and the Poetics of History* (Madison: University of Wisconsin Press, 1984).

Now Sir, the end of our digging and ploughing upon the common land is this, that wee and al the impoverisht poore in the land may gett a comfortable livelyhood by our righteous labours thereupon; which wee conceive wee have a right unto . . . by vertue of the conquest over the King[;] . . . wee have by this victory recovered ourselves from under his Norman yoake, and the land now is to returne into the ioynt hands of those who have conquered, that is the commonours.

To Fairfax such letters must have seemed like yet another of the Hydra's heads of the "many-headed beast" he thought he had defeated the year before; to Marvell they must have seemed to threaten a complete inversion of the country-house genre and its emphasis on stability, hierarchy, and property. To answer Winstanley's demands, Marvell proposes another series of inversions—again, seeking to invert the inversion, to parody the parody. These inversions continue throughout the poem, which can be divided (in a slight simplification) into four sections: the celebration of the estate; the history of the estate (the "virgin Thwaites" episode); the episode in the meadows; and, finally, the poet's retirement into the woods and the intervention of Maria.[3]

The strategy of double inversion underlies even the most Jonsonian elements of the poem, its opening ten stanzas. The poem begins with a traditional celebration of the house itself. The opening can be read as justifying Fairfax's ideological retreat, the return to his estate a move toward naturalizing the order he and other moderate leaders of the Parliamentary side attempted to impose on the Revolution. "Upon Appleton House" thus begins with a number of typical country-house conceits. Marvell praises the house for its "naturalness," emphasized by the traditional negative comparison to its unnatural neighbors: it is built by "no foreign architect" (2); instead, it is simply a natural fit for its owner, like the "low-roofed tortoises" who "dwell / In cases fit of tortoise shell" (13–14). The house in this way reflects the virtues of its owner; its "naturalness" justifies the lord's position at the top of the poem's hierarchies. So in the fashion of a typical country-house poem, Marvell concludes the opening section by praising the marriage of the natural and social through the concept of "use": "And yet what needs there here excuse, / Where everything does answer use?" (61–62).[4]

---

3. Gerrard Winstanley, "To My Lord Generall and His Councell of Warr," in *The Works of Gerrard Winstanley,* ed. George Sabine (Ithaca: Cornell University Press, 1941), 347. All further citations of Winstanley are to this volume. On the country-house poem's relationship to the epideictic epistle, see Heather Dubrow, "The Country-House Poem: A Study in Generic Development," *Genre* 12 (1979): 153–79.

4. All citations of Marvell's poetry are to Andrew Marvell, *The Complete Poems,* ed. Elizabeth Story Donno (Harmondsworth, Middlesex: Penguin, 1972), and will hereafter be cited parenthetically by line number.

These initial metaphors provide a metonymical justification for Fairfax's mode of living, his "right" to the property. At Appleton House, "use" is manifested, in a manner typical of the country-house poem, through hospitality. Marvell's emphasis here seems to answer the questions Winstanley himself has posed. Winstanley had radically redefined the concept of "use" as the "right" of *all* to "gett a comfortable livelyhood by . . . righteous labours" upon the land. Marvell answers this "low" desire to ascend to an equal level with the "high" by inverting it: through hospitality, the high really support the low. At the same time, however, Marvell uses another country-house trope to parody this move. While he seeks to incorporate the poor directly into the house, his metaphors emphasize that it is they who sustain it as much as it sustains them: they are the estate's "stately frontispiece" without, and within, its "[d]aily new furniture" (65–68). Marvell's naturalization of the estate's social function paradoxically ends up reifying its human component. This paradox is reinforced by the house's final figuration; it is only "an inn to entertain / Its Lord a while, but not remain" (71–72). "Inn" refigures hospitality not as something permanent and natural, but rather temporary and mercantile, and it draws attention to the fact that Fairfax was in the process of building a new, and more ostentatious, home to replace the modest dwellings his family had made out of the converted nunnery they had acquired in the early sixteenth century.[5]

This deconstruction of the estate's moral and social justification prompts the first formal swerve from Jonson's model, the long disquisition on the origins of the house that constitutes the second section of the poem. Marvell emphasizes these origins not only to provide a more solid religious foundation for the estate, but also to answer more fully Winstanley's arguments on the foundations of property ownership. Winstanley had demystified the origins of ownership, observing that the right of "use" is derived directly from the right of conquest: the "Norman oppressour[s]" took the land from the "common people of England," who have now taken it back. Marvell redirects Winstanley's argument from the right of property to the right religion, grounding the history of the estate and the state not in the Norman Conquest, but rather in the Protestant Reformation.

Thus the "subtle nuns" who seduce Fairfax's ancestor, the "virgin Thwaites," are stock anti-Catholic figures, parodies of true religious devotion. They pervert their retired life into "holy leisure"; their devotion

5. On Fairfax's renovations to the estate, see William McClung, *The Country-House Poem in English Renaissance Poetry* (Berkeley and Los Angeles: University of California Press, 1977), 157–58. Kendrick also discusses the reification of the poor in this section ("Agons," 25–26).

into idolatry; their celibacy into homoeroticism (97–98; 129–32; 185–86). Their final goal is more material than erotic: they desire Thwaites, "an heir / Which might deformity make fair" for "thy 'state, / Not thee, that they would consecrate" (91–92; 221–22). The nuns' motives justify the storming of the monastery for her release by Fairfax's progenitor, who, although he "would respect / Religion," must also "not right neglect" (225–26). His actions are, in effect, an allegory of Protestant history: the storming of the monastery is a figure for England's break from Rome, a symbol of the dissolution of the monasteries, through which the Fairfax family had indeed gained control of Nun Appleton. Marvell thus redirects the country-house poem's traditional mystification of the estate's origins to an exact historical moment. Yet this moment itself serves a mystifying purpose, countering the claim that "the Lords of Mannours" hold the land because of their conquest of the "common people" after the Norman invasion. Instead, the Fairfaxes become the champions of the common Protestantism of the English people: the right of conquest becomes the right of religion. Rather than a blatant land grab, Marvell and Fairfax can claim " '[t]was no religious house till now" (280). The final "now" links the generations of the family, referring both to the date of the family's initial acquisition of the house and the early 1650s, when Marvell composed the poem.[6]

Still, Marvell's "now" also blurs the allegory of the Thwaites episode. For if the "subtle nuns" figure the Protestant struggle against Catholic vices, they also allude to other contemporary religious issues for which Lord Fairfax (who himself largely supported the Presbyterians) had fought.[7] They offer the rhetoric not only of the residual past, but also of a threatening present: their excesses duplicate those of many radical sectarians of the post-war period. They espouse a leveling kind of equality, both sexual and social: "[e]ach one a spouse, and each a queen" (118). They internalize the holy in a more than enthusiastic way, "interweav[ing]" the "face and graces of the saint . . . in their lives" (124–26). Finally, they unite with nature in a way bordering on the antinomian, infusing the divine throughout creation:

> 'For such indeed are all our arts,
> Still handling Nature's finest parts.

6. "Upon Appleton House" is difficult to date precisely. Marvell was tutor to Mary Fairfax from late 1650 to mid-1652; the poem was probably written during that time. See Donno, *Complete Poems*, 14.

7. For an excellent discussion of Fairfax's religious and political moderation—and his consequent notorious indecisiveness in these matters—see David Underdown, *Pride's Purge: Politics in the English Revolution* (Oxford: Clarendon Press, 1971), 190–93.

> Flowers dress the altars; for the clothes,
> The sea-born amber we compose. . . .' (177–80)

Fairfax's ancestor must rescue his "fate" from this tainted religious perversion; yet the threat remains a vital one, as the ending of the poem will
make clear, when another Fairfax (Maria) must rescue another too easily
seduced figure (the poet) from his own antinomian revelry in the woods.

The temporary overthrow of the nuns' antinomianism prepares the
way for a formal transition to the third section of the poem, which begins
with an exploration of the estate's well-ordered "garden" and grounds,
a common country-house trope replete with micro- and macrocosmic
associations. The neat ranks of Fairfax's garden impose a new sense of
order on an unruly nature. They also serve as a parody of Fairfax's New
Model Army:

> See how the flowers, as at parade,
> Under their colours stand displayed:
> Each regiment in order grows,
> That of tulip, pink, and rose. (309–12)

Yet this seemingly gentle parody has a clear political referent, made clear
as the poet exits the gardens and moves toward the meadows:

> The sight does from these bastions [of flowers] ply
> The invisible artillery;
> And at proud Cawood Castle seems
> To point the battery of its beams.
> As if it quarrelled in the seat
> The ambition of its prelates great. (361–66)

Just as the episode of the nuns contains a clear and current political
referent, so too here the imagery actualizes the historical situation of just
a few years before: Fairfax's role in the Civil War did indeed align him
against Cawood's prelate, the Archbishop of York John Williams, seen by
many Parliamentarians as a symbol "of episcopacy and its abuses."[8]

So in one sense, Fairfax's gardens identify him with a kind of Cavalier
retirement; in another, with an active opposition to precisely such a notion.
Marvell uses the conflicts inherent in this oscillation to compare the estate
and the state, contrasting the order of the former with the decline of the
latter:

8. Cited from Patsy Griffin, " ' 'Twas no Religious House till now': Marvell's 'Upon
Appleton House,' " *Studies in English Literature, 1500–1900* 28 no. 1 (1988): 61.

Oh thou, that dear and happy isle
The garden of the world ere while

. . . .

What luckless apple did we taste,
To make us mortal, and thee waste? (321–28)

So what began as playful comparison has now become historical and admonitory elegy. By converting prewar England into Eden, Marvell transmutes original sin into the war itself: "war all this doth overgrow; / We ordnance plant and powder sow" (343–44). The image clearly parodies Fairfax's own "New Model" gardens—once more, parodying the parody—as well as questioning his role in bringing about the "Fall." As the scenes in the meadow that conclude the section will make clear, the forces the war has unleashed leave no one, or no estate, safe.

Through the "Fall" imagery, Marvell furthers his dialogue with the genre and the radical sects. He again undoes a common country-house trope—equating the estate with the unfallen golden age—in order to answer a direct ideological challenge to the country house itself. Fundamental to the radicals' arguments was their own allegorical reading of the Eden myth, which they linked with the Norman Conquest. For Winstanley and others, overcoming the effects of the conquest could overcome the effects of the Fall, and institute a true "golden age" in England. Winstanley had written in his "Appeal to the House of Commons" (1649) that "since the fall of man . . . The Nations of the world . . . by their power of their conquests, have stil set up some to rule in tyranny over others." This tyranny is embodied in the unjust use of the land, which must "be freed from "the Norman Task-masters." If Parliament fails to do so, Winstanley threatens, "you will be the first that break covenant with Almighty God." With property refigured as original sin, and the "Norman yoke" equated with property, the issue in the Fall imagery becomes the very nature of the war itself. For Marvell, the war has brought the Fall about; for Winstanley, the war promises an end to its consequences. In the succeeding meadows section of the poem Marvell seeks to justify the war, while also countering Winstanley's justification. Not surprisingly, the leveling mowers serve as the central metaphorical vehicle of the allegory.[9]

D. C. Allen has illustrated how Marvell draws on images of harvest and flood as metaphors for civil war: in his words, under "a rural disguise

---

9. On the Winstanley and other radicals' reading of the fall, see Christopher Hill, *The World Turned Upside Down: Radical Ideas during the English Revolution* (London: Penguin, 1987), 145. The citations from "An Appeal to the House of Commons" are from Sabine, *Works of Winstanley*, 303–5.

the war against the King is fought in rime." The sides of the conflict are soon apparent. On one are the "tawney mowers . . . / [who] massacre the grass along . . ." (388–94). On the other is "the rail" (perhaps punning on "royal"), "carve[d]" by one such mower (395). The reference to Charles seems clear; and the studied ambiguity of the lines echoes Marvell's earlier depiction of Charles's execution in the "Horatian Ode." The echoing of the earlier poem continues when Marvell emphasizes more overtly the third element of the conflict: class. In the "Ode," the spectators, who in "armèd bands / Did clap their bloody hands" at Charles's beheading, contrast with the studied ambivalence of the poet ("Horatian Ode," 55–56). So too here an onlooker, "bloody Thestylis," looks on approvingly, while the baffled poet laments for the "[u]nhappy birds" (401–9). Thestylis, in fact, proves even more bloody-minded and threatening than Charles's audience; she turns directly on the speaker, challenging him for control of his own poem: " 'He called us Israelites; / But now, to make his saying true, / Rails rain for quails, for manna, dew' " (406–8).[10]

Thestylis's intrusion is stunning, in part for its formal ingenuity, yet also for the ideological significance of that ingenuity. It is a clear break with the genre Marvell is working in, not simply because the poet recognizes laborers, but also because he grants them a voice, a voice that moreover opposes his own. At the moment that the allegory represents the Civil War getting out of hand, the poet himself seems to lose control of his poem. The reversal of the speaking voice in this stanza prompts the most telling inversion of the poem, when Marvell switches the relation of the micro- and macrocosm, focusing now on the effects of the latter on the former. He now asks, "what does it boot / To build below the grass's root," for "Or sooner hatch or higher build: / The mower now commands the field . . ." (409–10, 417–18). The emphasis on lowness in these lines alludes not only to the fate of the carved "rail," but also to the opening praise of the house, which emphasized its modesty, or lowness—precisely what is now threatened. As such, the lines question Fairfax's choice of retirement, by stressing that no place is safe or neutral in times of conflict. The inversion is parodic, though now self-referentially so: it takes the ideological stance of the beginning of the poem to its logical extreme, unreifying the "poor" who support the house there and, in giving them

10. D. C. Allen, *Image and Meaning: Metaphoric Traditions in Renaissance Poetry* (Baltimore: Johns Hopkins University Press, 1960), 134–37. On the poet's loss of control over the poem, see also Jonathan Crewe's "The Garden State: Marvell's Poetics of Enclosure," in *Enclosure Acts*, ed. Burt and Archer, 270–89, especially 284. Crewe's deconstructive reading of the poem parallels my own emphasis on parody, but Crewe does not discuss Winstanley's challenge in any particular way.

their own voice, producing a new kind of lowness—one not supporting, but rather leveling.

The whole pattern of the meadows section of the poem follows the lowering pattern of the poem's opening praise of the country house. Only now, its allegorical extension becomes inverted, with signifier and signified almost indistinguishable. Through such multiple meanings the allegory almost disappears, part of the strategy Leah Marcus has called "unmetaphoring," through which "[w]ar and harvest are interchanged." Just as the harvest at Nun Appleton becomes first a figure for the war, then the war itself, so too does the figuration recede back into the harvest, becoming again the harvest, thus questioning the allegorical signification. Thus the next change of perspective returns to the harvest and its end result:

> A new and empty face of things,
> A levelled space, as smooth and plain
> As cloths for Lely stretched to stain.
>
> For to this naked equal flat,
> Which Levellers take pattern at,
> The villagers in common chase
> Their cattle, which it closer rase;
> And what below the scythe increased
> Is pinched yet nearer by the beast.
> Such, in the painted world, appeared
> D'Avenant with the universal herd. (442–56)

The stanzas set up an opposition between the "painted world," filled with Lely's portraits and the allegorical painting of the sixth day of Creation in Davenant's epic *Gondibert,* and the "naked equal flat" of the Levellers. Lely versus the Levellers; allegorical herds versus leveling cattle: in these contrasts Marvell questions the ability of figuration to control the forces that the same figuration has (allegorically) released. Just as the house itself is undone by its very lowness, so too is the poem seemingly undone by its insistence on an allegory it cannot contain.[11]

What this means is that the "golden age" topos, so central to the country-house genre and its ideological justifications of property rights, is no longer viable as a topos. It has, instead, become a political possibility, a plan of action that, like Winstanley's reading of the Fall, combines a

---

11. On "unmetaphoring" in the poem and particularly this episode, see Leah Marcus, *The Politics of Mirth: Jonson, Herrick, Milton, Marvell, and the Defense of Old Holiday Pastimes* (Chicago: University of Chicago Press, 1986), 241–50. Marvell alludes to *Gondibert* 2.6.60.

metaphorical reading of the myth with an insistence on its historical specificity (the "Norman yoke" and its equation with private property), and thus opens the possibility of its effects being overcome. The mowers cannot function simply as allegory, a representation of the affairs of those higher; they now have their own voice and their own "pattern." They even have their own forms of representation. Marvell not only alludes to the Levellers here, but also practically quotes them, as his leveling imagery recalls that of the song ending the Digger or "True Leveller" pamphlet "A Mite Cast into the Common Treasury," which foretells of the time shortly to come when "we shall see / Brave Community, / When Vallies lye levell with Mountaines." Thestylis now truly has a voice.[12]

At this point Marvell has almost exhausted the genre's constitutive tropes. Modesty and proper use, genealogical precedent, social and topographical order, and the microcosmic golden age: each has been inverted by outside pressures rather than buttressing the estate against them. Physical and parodic distance, a poetic retirement mirroring Fairfax's political retirement, are at this point seemingly the only generic options left. Marvell thus in the final section of "Upon Appleton House" moves from the model of the Jonsonian country-house poem to that of the Cavalier retirement poem, emphasizing personal retirement at the expense of broader poetic and political engagement:

> But I, retiring from the flood,
> Take sanctuary in the wood,
> And, while it lasts, myself embark
> In this yet green, yet growing ark. . . . (481–84)

Outside the grove is the apocalyptic flood, turning the world upside down so that "boats can over bridges sail" (477). Inside the grove, Marvell stands alone, a Noah in his ark.

Despite the poet's attempts at distancing, political conflict intrudes even into the grove. Just as there, in a macrocosmic allegory the "traitor-worm" (a figure for the radicals) enfeebles and eventually kills the "tallest oak" (a figure for the king), so too do the ambiguous self-representations of the poet figure the conflicts on a micropolitical level. In the quiet solitude in the woods, the poet reads alone "Nature's mystic book," and sees "how chance's better wit / Could with a mask my studies hit," transforming him with a covering of oak leaves and ivy into a "great prelate of the grove"—a confused parody of the earlier image of the Archbishop of

---

12. The poem is cited from Sabine's *Works of Winstanley*, 659.

York (584–92). This image of the poet is an odd, self-parodic mix of High Anglican, Hermetic, and even Druidic connotations. It seeks to resolve the antinomies created by the third section of the poem—the order of the garden and grounds compared to the allegorical chaos of the meadows—into a celebration of mystic authority. In the woods, the poet tries to recreate the authority of the dead monarch in his own mind, and impose it on the limited sphere he commands.[13]

Marvell's withdrawal at one point even seems to verge on the Christ-like (or Charles-like), when he asks the woods to "nail me through" (616). But like everything else in the poem, Marvell's martyrdom is parodic: it is solipsistic, not sacrificial, an attempt to save his poetic integrity rather than safeguard the property of the estate. Marvell draws on the solipsism inherent in Cavalier retirement poems to rebuild the idyll formerly contained in the estate within the security of "my mind . . . / . . . where the world no certain shot / Can make, or me it toucheth not" (602–6). Thus in the woods he parodically recreates the estate he constructed in his first ten stanzas, and which the mowers had "levelled" in the episode of the meadows. First, he rebuilds the house itself, with "Corinthean porticoes," "arching boughs," "columns of . . . temple green," and "wingèd choirs" (508–11); then the house's gardens, even down to the military metaphors: "the two woods have made a lane, / While, like a guard on either side, / The trees before their Lord divide" (618–20). By making himself "Lord" of this arboreal reconstruction, Marvell has completely internalized the estate.

So what began as a political debate with the Levellers has by now become an internal debate within the poet. Marvell has moved to self-parody at this point, parodying his own poem and his own self-representation. He seems in this final section consciously to recreate the perverse retirement from the world of the "subtle nuns" he had earlier condemned. At the same time, his own solipsism parodies the antinomian "paradise within" of the radical Protestant sects. That is, Marvell internalizes, albeit parodically, the twin threats to the estate in order to rebuild it. The contraries that the country-house poem has traditionally negated here become, through ironic inversion, the very foundations of its viability within the poet's mind. In Marvell's retreat into the woods, parody becomes reality.

It is at this point that Marvell at last proposes a form of mediation with the entrance of Maria, Fairfax's daughter and Marvell's pupil. She is the catalyst for making order out of the chaos from which the poet has fled: "See how loose Nature, in respect / To her, itself doth recollect . . ." (657–58). Her entrance, like that of the monarch in a masque, dispels the forces

13. My discussion here draws on that of Marcus in *The Politics of Mirth*, 254–59.

of anarchy and leveling and reinstitutes those of order. Maria "vitrifie[s]" nature (688), returning it to the harmony undone in the meadows section of the poem. And when Maria restores order to the landscape, she also restores order to the poem—and the poet. Marvell signals this change at Maria's entrance, when the parodic speculations and "idle utensils" of the poet give way to the more "judicious eyes" of Maria, "her age's awe" (649–56)—what Patsy Griffin has called a "transferal of the guiding vision of the poem." Her appearance marks a return to the Jonsonian model, reestablishing the link between ordered nature and humanity. Malcolmson is certainly correct in asserting that Maria answers that section's "bloody Thestylis"; she is also a poetic reconstruction of Lady Sidney in "To Penshurst," a mediating figure who allows Marvell to circumvent the troubling mowers and establish a direct connection between the estate's owner and what he owns. Lady Sidney's figuration as "fruitfull" yet "chaste" is an emblem of the merging of nature and culture at Penshurst. Maria functions in a similar way; the gift of order Maria gives to nature it returns in its bounty: "Therefore what first she on them spent, / They gratefully again present" (697–98). Here Marvell alludes to the famous self-sacrificing nature of Jonson's "To Penshurst," thereby reinstituting the genre's "magical extraction of the curse of labour." With this image, what was before parody has now become homage.[14]

Or so it seems. In a poem built (and rebuilt) out of inversions and parodies, the line between parody and homage must be a thin one, if it exists at all. How seriously are we supposed to take Maria's intervention? There is much in her presentation that also seems parodic. She enters as a diminutive version of her famous male forebears, a female Fairfax rescuing the seduced and helpless male poet (like the "virgin Thwaites" episode), a female Fairfax restoring order to a nature grown as unruly as the pre-Burford New Model Army. Even so, her greatest victories are those of the field of love, where she escapes the "ambush" of "those trains [i.e., artillery] by youth against [her] meant" (714). The question is, does this new Fairfax compensate for the retirement and displacement of her father? Can parody indeed undo parody?

Leah Marcus has proposed comparing Maria to the Lady in Milton's *Comus*. She notes that both are "severe and reforming by temperament":

14. Griffin, "' 'Twas no Religious House,' " 73; Malcolmson, "Garden Enclosed," 261. On Lady Sidney's mediating function in "To Penshurst," see Wayne, *Penshurst*, 68–72. The description of Lady Sidney can be found in l. 90 of "To Penshurst"; the self-sacrificing animals that sustain the estate in ll. 27–58. The citations are from *Ben Jonson*, ed. C. H. Herford and Percy and Evelyn Simpson, 11 vols. (Oxford: Clarendon Press, 1925–1952), vol. 8.

Maria's "moral energy even in retreat is inseparable from the pervasive militarism of the estate." She thus counteracts the Cavalier elements of the poem, those that emphasize retirement and inner content.[15] Yet Maria's intervention is certainly of a different kind from that of Milton's Lady. Rather than an active opposition to the forces threatening the estate, like the Lady's defiance of Comus, Maria's intervention is magical, akin to Sabrina's role in that masque as *dea ex machina*. In the woods she never truly confronts the forces she magically overcomes. Moreover, she overcomes just what Milton's Lady hopes for. Whereas the Lady proposed a leveling program (railing against "lewdly-pamper'd Luxury" and asking that "Nature's full blessings . . . be well-dispens't / In unsuperfluous even proportion" to "every just man"), Maria silences just such a program, reinstituting the estate's "natural" and social hierarchies.

A better comparison, I believe, would be to the changes in form both texts enact. Milton placed a full stop in the development of the masque by inverting its ideological referents, creating a "puritan masque" by reversing the categories of the court masque. Marvell, as we have seen, follows a similar strategy of inversion, parodying the forms of the country-house poem to such an extent that even Maria's intervention seems parodic. What previous country-house poems negate, carefully contain, or drive from their ideal estates, Marvell's poem not only exposes, but also gives voice to. Though manifestly an answer to the voices of Winstanley and the Levellers, the inversions of "Upon Appleton House" work in a way similar to those voices: in effect, they turn the genre, and its world, upside down. The poem concludes by moving once more away from Jonson's vision (and Maria's), towards a proposed synthesis uniquely Marvell's own:

> But now the salmon-fishers moist
> Their leathern boats begin to hoist,
> And like Antipodes in shoes,
> Have shod their heads in their canoes.
> How tortoise-like, but not so slow,
> These rational amphibii go!
> Let's in: for the dark hemisphere
> Does now like one of them appear. (769–76)

The poem ends with a final inversion, one that moves from the particular— the Antipodean salmon-fishers—to the universal—the movement of the

---

15. Marcus, *Politics of Mirth*, 261–62. The citations of *Comus* (ll. 768–73) are from *John Milton: Complete Poems and Major Prose*, ed. Merritt Y. Hughes (Indianapolis: Bobbs-Merrill, 1984).

spheres. Marvell has been unable to banish completely the "Levellers" from the poem; the world has irretrievably been turned upside down, been "[a]ll negligently overthrown" (763). Even "the lesser world" of Nun Appleton "contains the same," only "in more decent order tame" (765–66). The concluding image of the fishermen as tortoises parodies the opening image of Nun Appleton as a "tortoise shell" (14), reminding readers how these common laborers can both support and even overturn the great estate at which they work.[16]

Winstanley's Diggers, and their redaction in Marvell's leveling mowers, represent in many ways the apogee of Civil War–era political radicalism. Of course their optimism, and the poet's ambivalence, have ironic postscripts. The world that had been turned upside down would soon be righted again: within ten years, Lord Fairfax would help restore Charles II and with him the "Norman Yoke"; Marvell would be a member in the last of the Commonwealth and the first of the Restoration parliaments; and Winstanley would become, apparently, a respectable tenant and businessman in and around the very areas upon which he had established his Digger communities.[17] Country-house poems of a sort would continue to be written. But never again would such a poem be written in the dominant Jonsonian mold of the seventeenth century. Marvell's poem marks the effective end of that genre. Perhaps more so than any other major poem of the period, "Upon Appleton House," with its parodic inversions and ambiguous perspectives, captures the full impact of the radical forces so briefly liberated by the breakdown of traditional authorities during the Civil War period. That the country house of the leader of the New Model Army should be remembered today largely because of Marvell's parodic engagement with Winstanley and the Diggers shows the persistence of these ideas, and the troubling truths they continue to reveal.

16. My discussion of *Comus* draws on that of Mary Ann McGuire in *Milton's Puritan Masque* (Athens: University of Georgia Press, 1983).
17. On Winstanley's later life, see J. D. Alsop, "Gerrard Winstanley: Religion and Respectability," *Historical Journal* 28 (1985): 705–9.

Andrew Shifflett

"A Most Humane Foe"

Colonel Robert Overton's War with the Muses

I

"My discourse is on fire to commemorate the names of . . . illustrious men," exclaims John Milton in his *Second Defense of the English People* (1654). He calls out first to Cromwell and Fairfax, and then to several lesser *viri illustrii* in a series of epic vocatives. He singles out one of these men for special, personal praise:

> You, Overton, who for many years have been linked to me with a more than fraternal harmony, by reason of the likeness of our tastes and the sweetness of your disposition. At the unforgettable Battle of Marston Moor, when our left wing had been routed, the leaders, looking behind them in flight, beheld you making a stand with your infantry and repelling the attacks of the enemy amid dense slaughter on both sides. Then, in the war in Scotland, once the shores of Fife had been seized by your efforts under the leadership of Cromwell and a way laid open beyond Stirling, the Scots of the West and the North admit that you were a most humane foe, and the farthest Orkneys confess you a merciful conqueror.[1]

It is worth looking more closely at this "humane foe" and "merciful conqueror" of the English civil wars, Colonel Robert Overton of Hull, an exemplary if now little-known man who dwelt for a time upon superlatives before falling on days more evil than any Milton knew.[2] For

1. *Complete Prose Works of John Milton*, gen. ed. Don M. Wolfe, 8 vols. (New Haven: Yale University Press, 1953–1982), 4:676; hereafter cited as *CPW*.
2. Overton was born in 1609 and died sometime in the early 1670s. The standard biography remains the entry in the *Dictionary of National Biography* by C. H. Firth. See also J. F. McGregor's less favorable account in *Biographical Dictionary of British Radicals in the Seventeenth Century*, ed. Richard L. Greaves and Robert Zaller, 3 vols. (Brighton: Harvester Press, 1982–1984), 2:279–81; and "Robert Overton," by John Shawcross, in *A Milton Encyclopedia*, ed. William B. Hunter, 9 vols. (Lewisburg, Pa.: Bucknell University Press, 1978–1983), 6:43.

in Overton may be seen an unusually close and, in many ways, painful intersection of military experience, political and religious idealism, and literary imagination—major themes of this volume and, indeed, of English culture from 1642 through 1688.

Inspired in part by Milton's praise of his martial prowess in the *Second Defense*, Blair Worden has linked Overton to "the classical republicanism of the Puritan revolution" and such "literary republicans" as George Wither, Marchamont Nedham, and Milton himself. This respected soldier "proves also to have been a poet, a lover of Donne and Herbert, and a devotee of Roman history." To Andrew Marvell it must have seemed at once politically and poetically correct to mention Overton, then Governor of Hull, in his letter to Milton of June 2, 1654, on the *Second Defense*. Having praised the text as "a Trajans columne in whose winding ascent we see imboss'd the severall Monuments of your learned victoryes," Marvell adds that he has "an affectionate Curiosity to know what becomes of Colonel Overtons businesse" in London. Yet after 1654, Overton's most familiar places of study and writing were the prisons of Oliver Cromwell and King Charles II. His enemy, Sir James Turner, put the political problem succinctly: he was "a great Independent, who hath since had his share of imprisonment, both under the Usurper Oliver, and under his present Majestie; so it wold seeme he hath beene ane enemie to monarchie, whatever name it had, whether King or Protector." The most noticeable thing about Overton's literary activities after the civil wars is how poorly they exemplify either the rhetorical *negotium* that republicans like Nedham and Milton favored or the poetic *otium* that we have come to associate with those who suffered through the long Cavalier winter. No matter how much "likeness" there was between his tastes and Milton's, Overton could find in literature neither an effective political platform nor an easy retirement. His appearance in the *Second Defense* marks the beginning of a long, frustrating war with the Muses over the expression of his political aims—a war that he won only by "Overturning," in the words of David Norbrook, "the Poetic Canon."[3]

3. Blair Worden, "Classical Republicanism and the Puritan Revolution," in *History and Imagination: Essays in Honour of Hugh Trevor-Roper*, ed. Hugh Lloyd-Jones, Valerie Pearl, and Blair Worden (New York: Holmes and Meier, 1981), 191. *The Poems and Letters of Andrew Marvell*, ed. H. M. Margoliouth, rev. Pierre Legouis and E. E. Duncan-Jones, 3d ed., 2 vols. (Oxford: Clarendon Press, 1971), 2:306. Sir James Turner, *Memoirs of His Own Life and Times* (Edinburgh, 1829), 78. David Norbrook, " 'This Blushinge Tribute of a Borrowed Muse': Robert Overton and His Overturning of the Poetic Canon," in *English Manuscript Studies, 1100–1700*, ed. Peter Beal and Jeremy Griffiths (Toronto: University of Toronto Press, 1993), 220–66.

To describe Overton's postwar life in this way is to simplify events and, perhaps, to make an "enemie to monarchie" seem too much a man of letters; but it is also to remain true to what the historical record, such as we have it, is concerned to stress. Three topics stand out emblematically in the history of this "humane foe": his imprisonment during the Protectorate on account of a "copy of verses" found in his possession; his eloquent but unsuccessful appeal to Cromwell on the model of Cremutius Cordus in Tacitus's *Annals* 4.34–35; and finally his transcription and rewriting of poems by John Donne, George Herbert, and other famous poets while imprisoned after the Restoration. I shall argue that a process that begins with Colonel Overton being interpreted, so to speak, by a poem ends with him interpreting poems—and sometimes destroying them—for his own purposes.

II

"Nothing is more unsatisfactory than an attempt to unravel a plot, especially at the distance of two centuries"—or so writes Wilbur Cortez Abbott of his own impressive attempt to make sense out of the flurry of arrests, seizures, and threats recorded in John Thurloe's *State Papers* and the various Parliamentary newsbooks of late 1654 and early 1655. The Protectorate was then busy ignoring its second Christmas, concerned with the activities of levelers, fifth monarchists, royalists, republicans, and anyone else who might seem in any way disaffected. A January 1655 issue of the *Perfect Diurnal* told readers that "there have been divers arms taken, and several persons apprehended upon the plot lately discovered, so that there is cause of strengthening guards, but the particulars are not yet fit for publication" (quoted in *WSOC*, 3:556). Also in January 1655, Nedham's *Mercurius Politicus* mentions "discontents" and assures readers that Colonel Overton, one of the alleged ringleaders, "having been twice sent for . . . and not coming, is secured."[4]

Overton made a slow journey down to Leith from Aberdeen, but General George Monck wasted no time in sending him on to London. "The last night col. Overton comeing in custody to Leith"—Monck wrote Cromwell from Dalkieth on January 4, 1655—"I have this morneing sent him on board the Baseing frigott, whereof captaine Harley is commander, whom I have ordered to bring colonel Overton into the Hope. I send your highnesse heere inclosed copies of papers found with him, and

---

4. Wilbur Cortez Abbott, ed., *The Writings and Speeches of Oliver Cromwell*, 4 vols. (Cambridge: Harvard University Press, 1937–1947), 3:567; hereafter cited as *WSOC*. I silently change dates throughout this essay to reflect the beginning of the new year on January 1. [Marchamont Nedham], *Mercurius Politicus* (London, 1650–1660), 5049.

particularly of verses written with his owne hand."[5] In place of harder evidence, Overton was being accused of treason on the basis of a poem—the only poem in all of Thurloe's massive *State Papers:*

> *A copy of verses writ with colonel* Overton's *own hand, and found with him upon search.*
>
> A Protector, what's that? 'Tis a stately thing,
> That confesseth itself but the ape of a king:
> A tragicall Caesar acted by a clowne;
> Or a brass farthing stamp'd with a kind of a crown:
> A bubble, that shines; a loud cry without woole;
> Not Perillus nor Phalaris, but the bull.
> The eccho of monarchy till it come;
> The but end of a barrell in the shape of a drum:
> A counterfeit piece, that woddenly showes
> A golden effigies with a copper nose.
> The fantastick shadow of a sovereign head,
> The arms royal revers'd, and disloyal instead.
> In fine he is one, we may protector call,
> From whom the king of kings protect us all. (*SP*, 3:75–76)

This poem appears to have been received by the authorities as an entirely self-explanatory and conclusive "information" concerning Overton's activities. In a legalistic letter to a friend, written "From my imprisonment in the Tower of London, Jan. 17 1655," Overton claimed—perhaps truthfully, perhaps not—that he did not compose it:

> Objection III. But, say some, you made a company of scandalous verses upon the lord protector, whereby his highness and divers others were offended and displeased for your so doing.
>
> Reply III. I must acknowledge I copied a paper of verses, called the Character of a Protector; but I did neither compose, nor (to the best of my remembrance) shew them to any, after I had writ them forth. They were taken out of my letter case at Leith, where they had lain for a long time by me neglected and forgotten. I had them from a friend, who wished my lord well, and who told me, that his lordship had seen them, and I believe laughed at them, as (to my knowledge) heretofore he hath done at papers and pamphlets of more personal and particular import or abuse. (*SP*, 3:111)

This denial of authorship would later solve a messy problem for David Masson, the enthusiastic nineteenth-century biographer of a grandly Whiggish Milton,[6] but to Cromwell and Monck the "scandalous verses"

---

5. *A Collection of the State Papers of John Thurloe, Esq.,* 7 vols. (London, 1742), 3:76–77; hereafter cited as *SP.*

6. "It is really a relief to know that Overton . . . was not the author of [these lines], and this not because of their peculiar political import, but because of their

suggested a festering discontent in all who touched them. Along with some intercepted letters that Monck felt proved "colonell Overton had a designe to promote the Scots king's busines" (*SP*, 3:217), they were enough to keep Overton confined to the Tower and then to a castle on Jersey for the rest of Cromwell's life. He never received the justice of a trial.[7]

Ruth Nevo has remarked that a version of "The Character of a Protector" beginning with "What's a Protector?"—a version first printed in *J. Cleaveland Revived* (1660)—poses "the bitter question of a royalist." Monck and Cromwell apparently thought the same of Overton's poem. But poetry, as we keep reminding ourselves these days, is politically multivalent. As Richard Flecknoe observed in his *Enigmaticall Characters* (1658), the literary "character" is "more *Seneca* than *Cicero*, and speaks rather the language of *Oracles* than *Orators*: every line a *sentence*, and every two a *period*."[8] Such brevity can, indeed, be enigmatic. For instance, saying that the Protector's "arms" are the "arms royal revers'd, and disloyal instead," is not the same as saying that enemies of the Protectorate are necessarily loyal to the Stuarts. Moreover, "The Character of a Protector" is filled with paradoxes, and paradoxes, of course, are paradoxical; they do not "make sense" for readers in any simple, rhetorically predictable way. I think it likely that an "enemie to monarchie, whatever name it had," would, when faced with such ambiguity, allow his interpretation to be shaped by his prejudices. Overton, who was loyal only to God and England, may well have heard "The eccho of monarchy till it come" with republican pessimism rather than royalist hope—the problem being not this or that man but monarchy itself.

Worden writes that the "chief objection" of the classical republicans "to hereditary monarchy was that it was irrational," and certainly "The Character of a Protector" is a study in irrationalism.[9] Cromwell is merely an "ape" (l. 2), "a loud cry" (l. 5), a "fantastick shadow" (l. 11), and "A

---

utter vulgarity. How else could we have retained our faith in Milton's character of Overton?" (David Masson, *The Life of John Milton: Narrated in Connexion with the Political, Ecclesiastical, and Literary History of His Time*, 7 vols. [reprint, Gloucester, Mass.: Peter Smith, 1946], 5:164).

7. An informer eventually told Monck that his "person was first to have benne secured; then major generall Overton to have given out orders, and to have drawen 3000 foot, besids horse, into the field, and sone after to have marcht for England" (*SP*, 3:185). For more details, see *WSOC*, 3:556–68, and Samuel Rawson Gardiner, *History of the Commonwealth and Protectorate*, 4 vols. (1903; reprint, New York: AMS Press, 1965), 3:226–32.

8. Ruth Nevo, *The Dial of Virtue: A Study of Poems on Affairs of State in the Seventeenth Century* (Princeton: Princeton University Press, 1963), 13. Sir Richard Flecknoe, *Enigmaticall Characters* (London, 1658), 92.

9. Worden, "Classical Republicanism," 193.

tragicall Caesar acted by a clowne" (l. 3). He has neither the evil *gravitas* of Phalarus, the tyrant of Agrigentum, nor the evil wit of Phalarus's servant Perillus: he is "the bull" itself (l. 6), a tool and an animal. Jesus Christ, "the king of kings," is England's only hope in this poem, and Overton knew that all monarchs, "whether King or Protector," will depend on His final justice. Overton might have argued, with some potential for success, that "The Character of a Protector" is only a less dignified version of Milton's warning to Cromwell in the *Second Defense* that he must not "attack that liberty which he himself has defended," an act that would be "dangerous and well-nigh fatal not only to liberty itself but also to the cause of all virtue and piety" (*CPW*, 4:673).

But if Overton read the poem like a Milton, a Wither, or a Nedham—and even if he had been able to make that reading quite clear to his accusers—it did not and could not have helped him. Republicanism was unworkable as politics after 1653 and it was also, in Overton's case, unworkable as literature. This must have seemed strange and cruel to a man who had allowed his own prisoners the freedom to read and write privately in the 1640s. Sir James Turner, Overton's prisoner at Hull for fourteen months in 1648–1649, writes in his *Memoirs of His Own Life and Times* that the colonel was "Civill and discreet," that he "had been at ane Inns of Court, was a schollar, bot a litle pedantick," and even that he "was the most curteous Independent I ever met with" (78–79, 86). Overton paid Turner several courtesies, the most memorable of which was the use of books, pens, and paper:

> Among other favours I received from Colonell Overton, Governour of Hull, this was not the least, that he permitted me the use of all the bookes the stationers of the place could afford, for which I payd them money weeklie; and, which I valued more, he allowed me the use of pen, paper and inke; which were two very comfortable and profitable divertisements to me in that affliction. Heere it was where I wrote some collections of the state of Europe, from the year 1618, that the dreadfull comet appeared, till the year 1638, that the Scots Covenant appeared in the world, which produced as sad and lamentable effects as that comet did. Here I wrote also some essays and discourses, and that with so much confidence and freedome, as if I had beene at my full libertie, that I am sure if Overton had perusd them, he had found so much spoke to the disadvantage of his masters of the new Commonwealth, that he wold have given a stop to my releasment. Bot he sufferd me to cary all my papers with me untouchd and unseene by himselfe or any other. (*Memoirs*, 87–88)

Turner recalls this imprisonment as a calm amid a storm. Overton is depicted as a good man whose virtue is demonstrated by his respect for the literary possibilities of his captive's forced retirement. In spite of their profound political differences, the two men identified with each other as readers and writers, as members of a literary elite whose right it was to respond to political "affliction" in "essays and discourses" composed with "confidence and freedome."

Such courtesies were not to be expected from Cromwell and Monck in the 1650s. Overton's letter case was no longer his alone: it belonged also to Monck, Cromwell, and the entire rhetorical culture that the Protectorate had spawned. Against the private circulation and private interpretation of such poems as "The Character of a Protector" stood the continual public "informations" of *Mercurius Politicus* and the *Perfect Diurnal*. Even such *viri illustrii* as Overton came to be scrutinized under the "reformation of manners" fostered by the Protector and the Saints, men determined to "reform" what Worden has termed the "classicism of the household."[10]

III

While Monck was reading Overton's poem, Overton was reading history. He may have thought of several relevant loci. Surely this "devotee of Roman history" was familiar with Suetonius's *De Vita Caesarum* 1.73, in which Julius Caesar forgives Catullus instantly, in spite of the poet's satirical verses on a crony, which had left a *perpetua stigmata* on Caesar himself. But that example did not apply in 1655. Neither Monck nor the Protector, a "tragicall Caesar acted by a clowne," would dismiss "scandalous verses" so readily—not even if the Protector had "laughed at them" and at other "papers and pamphlets of more personal and particular import or abuse" in the past. Rather than finding hope in Suetonius, Overton fixed instead on a famous example of republican martyrdom. In an anguished letter to the Protector, perhaps written while he was waiting to be shipped off on Captain Harley's frigate, Overton records histories both personal and ancient. He and Cromwell, Overton recalls, had both "fought" for "freedome" in the civil wars. Acutely aware that in his present circumstances he is quite unfree—indeed, that he has been betrayed by his own past—he appeals finally to an episode in Tacitus's *Annals:*

> If any expressions have through the freedome, which wee fought for, fallen from me, I shall desire no more ingenuity in my adversaries constructions, than what my 14 yeares faithfull services will warrant me to clayme.
>
> But sutch, my lord, is my misfortune, that I am yet kept hoodwinkt as to the cause of my attendance; and all that I can grope out of this darknesse is, that my condition resembles that of Cremutius in Tacitus, *verba mea arguunter, adeo factorum sum innocens.*

10. Ibid., 188. For Cromwell's "own thoughts about the reformation of manners," see his 1656 speech to Parliament in *WSOC*, 4:273.

> But I am yet bold to beleeve, I am happier in my judge, than hee was; and woulde your highnes vouchsafe to ad a litle expedition to your wonted condissention, I shoulde quickly putt a period to all the trouble, that you might further in this respect receive from
> Your highness's humble and obedient servant. (*SP*, 3:67)

The Protector responded with silence. But Overton was not speaking gnomically here. If Edmund Waller's report is true—if in fact Cromwell "was well-versed in the Greek and Roman historians, and made observations on them with uncommon penetration and taste"—it is likely that the Protector understood the meaning of a modern Cremutius Cordus.[11]

In *Annals* 4.34–35 Tacitus tells the story of a historian accused of the novel crime of praising Brutus and Cassius. Not the Latinist Overton was, I shall quote Tacitus from Richard Grenewey's seventeenth-century translation:

> *Cornelius Cossus, Assinius Agrippa* being Consuls, *Cremutius Cordus* was accused of a new crime never before heard of, that in certaine Annales by him published he had praised *M. Brutus,* and said that *C. Cassius* was the last of the Romans. . . . *Caesar* with a sterne looke hear[ed] his purgation, which *Cremutius* being assured to lose his life, began in this manner. "I am accused for words (Lords of the Senate) because in deedes I am innocent [*verba mea arguunter, adeo factorum sum innocens*]. . . . I am saide to have commended *Brutus* and *Cassius,* whose acts manie have written, and all in honorable termes. . . . Do not they . . . as they are knowen by their images which the Conqueror himselfe hath not pulled downe, so retaine some remembrance of them by writings? Posteritie doth render unto every man the commendation he hath deserved. Neither will there want some if I be condemned which will make mention, not only of *Cassius* and *Brutus,* but of mee also." Having thus said, he went out of the Senate & ended his life by abstinence. Order was given by the Senatours that the Ædiles should burne his bookes, which notwithstanding were still extant, some secretly, some publickely: which maketh me the willinglier to laugh at the witlesse uncircumspection of such as thinke with the power and authority they have in their own time, they can also extinguish the memory of future times. But it falleth out contrary, that when the good wits are punished their credit groweth greater: neither have forren Kings, or such as have used the like cruelty, purchased any other thing then discredit to themselves, and to such wits, glorie.[12]

Ben Jonson had lifted the whole passage for use in *Sejanus* (1605), and by the 1650s it had become something of a touchstone in the "vocabulary"— as Annabel Patterson would say—of the Good Old Cause. Cromwell probably knew the story, and he may have concluded that if Overton

11. Elijah Fenton, "Life of Waller," in *The Poetical Works of Edmund Waller,* 2 vols. (Edinburgh, 1784), 1:xxxi. My thanks to David Armitage for this reference.
12. *The Annales of Cornelius Tacitus,* trans. Richard Grenewey, 4th ed. (London, 1612), 100–101.

resembled Cremutius *he* must resemble the wicked Tiberius. Overton's strategy is hard to figure. Did he really expect to be released by a modern Tiberius, or that name-calling would help his cause? Perhaps he hoped that Cromwell would see Tiberius, not in himself, but in General Monck. Thus Monck would resemble Tiberius and Cromwell would resemble Tacitus—the wise voice of history which sees through the stupidity of "such as have used the like cruelty" to punish "the good wits." Tacitus was held in high repute by most English republicans as a critic of monarchy, so to quote him against either Monck or Cromwell in the mid-1650s was in fact to do what Nigel Smith has said classical republicans were "never forced" to do until after Cromwell's death: "use literature . . . to fight a cause."[13] Overton's cause failed: "the *forum fori*" was, as he says in a letter to John Desborough, "shutt againste" him (*SP*, 3:68).

IV

I have suggested two possible interpretations of Overton's intentions in quoting Tacitus, but there is no evidence that the Protector was interested in his intentions. Indeed, there is a sad quality of pointlessness to Overton's humane literacy in the 1650s. "One of the aspects of tyranny," writes Arnaldo Momigliano, "is to impose a difficult choice between adulation and empty protest. . . . Such a situation, in which even the free word is only seldom appropriate, is the indication that something is radically wrong with human nature."[14] He is thinking of Tacitus's Roman Empire, but a similar tension may be sensed between Overton's "humble and obedient" obsequiousness on the one hand and his political and intellectual arrogance on the other—between his plea that "your highnes vouchsafe to ad a litle expedition to your wonted condissention" and his brave Tacitean protest, *"verba mea arguunter, adeo factorum sum innocens."*

Overton's understanding of his actions and difficulties as being continuous with those of the republicans of the ancient past was itself the product, as he says in the letter quoted above, of a sort of "darknesse"—a "darknesse" that did not brighten with time. Literacy for such men as Overton usually meant knowing the most eloquent ways of expressing imprisonment, not freedom. Having finally been freed by Richard Cromwell's Parliament in early 1659 and then restored to his commands by the restored Long Parliament, he observed in his *Humble and Healing*

13. See Annabel Patterson, *Reading between the Lines* (Madison: University of Wisconsin Press, 1993), 210–75. Nigel Smith, *Literature and Revolution in England, 1640–1660* (New Haven: Yale University Press, 1994), 178.

14. Arnaldo Momigliano, *The Classical Foundations of Modern Historiography* (Berkeley and Los Angeles: University of California Press, 1990), 118.

Advice (1659) that "darknesse is so intermixed with our light, and self is so interwoven with all our publique assaies and attempts, that Babel-like, our buildings are accompanied with nothing but confusion and contempt."[15] It may have seemed that the best way out of such "darknesse" was to plunge further into it, for as he says, perhaps punning on his own name, "the Lord . . . hath been overturning and overturning, and will overturn, till he come whose Right it is" (*HHA*, 2). Soon enough, however, Overton was overturned by the return of King Charles II. Sent back to the Tower in December 1660 and back to Jersey in 1664, his "experience of defeat" bridged Protectorate and Restoration.

Overton had ample opportunity to test the paradoxical proposition that, "when the good wits are punished, their credit groweth greater" during his final years on Jersey. The surprising result—nothing we know of his background can quite prepare us for it—was his *Gospell Observations,* a lengthy manuscript volume of letters, devotions, and poems in which he pays tribute to the memory of his wife, Ann Gardiner Overton, and expresses directly and indirectly their shared political and religious ideals.[16] That this "lover of Donne and Herbert" was as much a *user* as a *lover* of their poems has been amply demonstrated in regard to Herbert by Sidney Gottlieb and in regard to Donne (and George Wither, Francis Quarles, and Katherine Philips) by David Norbrook. Overton, writes Gottlieb, "repeatedly describes his poetic practice using the term 'applied,' assuming a malleable base text that he freely copies, absorbs, personalizes, and modifies."[17] But it is not simply that Overton changes poems to suit his circumstances. What has not been emphasized enough by these scholars— and what cannot be gathered from Overton's own fascinating justification of "applicatory Poetry" in his preface "To the Reder, &c" (*GO*, 151)— is that his "applicatory" method sometimes "absorbs, personalizes, and modifies" a poem so much that it destroys that poem and its memory, making a mockery of any notion of therapeutic dialogue between himself

15. Robert Overton, *The Humble and Healing Advice of Collonel Robert Overton Governour of Hull* (London, 1659), 1; hereafter cited as *HHA*.

16. Quotations from *Gospell Observations* (hereafter cited as *GO*) appear by permission of the Manuscripts Division, Department of Rare Books and Special Collections, Princeton University Library. It was probably compiled sometime after January 12, 1665[6?], the date of Ann Gardiner Overton's death as indicated in *GO*, 214. For a detailed description of the manuscript, see Norbrook, " 'This Blushinge Tribute,' " 246–63.

17. See Sidney Gottlieb, "George Herbert and Robert Overton," in *George Herbert in the Nineties: Reflections and Reassessments,* ed. Jonathan F. S. Post and Sidney Gottlieb (Fairfield, Conn.: *George Herbert Journal* Special Monographs and Studies, 1995), 185– 200; and Norbrook, " 'This Blushinge Tribute,' " 233–45. Gottlieb, "George Herbert and Robert Overton," 189.

and literary tradition. Overton raids poetry for scraps of syntax and metaphorical language and makes out of those scraps a poetry whose ultimate subject is, I think, the confusion and violence that he had come to see as being "interwoven . . . Babel-like" with language itself.

This occasional destructiveness is, to my mind, so far from being a mark against Overton that I am inclined to take it as a kind of moral or artistic victory that perhaps only a writer with his memories of violence and cruel misprisions, linguistic and physical, could appreciate. A particularly complex example is "The Dissolution," a poem that takes its title from a poem by Donne, mimics at length the poem immediately preceding that poem in Overton's edition of Donne's *Poems,* and concludes by alluding to the poem immediately following it.[18] Two twenty-four-line poems and one twelve-line poem are dissolved into one sonnet, and Donne's poetry becomes both agent and victim of Overton's "Dissolution" of literary and political languages:

> When I am deade, Docter^s suruey each Part, =
> yo'ule finde her picture in my heart:
> I thinck then, w^t a sad damp of Loue =
>   will thurrough all their Sence^s moue,
> workeinge on them, a^s me, & soe prefer
>   her Murder, to the name of Massacre.
> poore victorie^s! had C & M been braue,
>   they coulde noe comforte, in her conques^t haue.
>   Her virtue triumph^t ouer men ==
>   None but a Monster kild her then.
> w^t though he weares the Star, and Garter?
> his mallise made, her virtue, his Martyr.
> Greate Sainted Soule, thy Glory thi^s shall be =
> He Broke his faith wth God, & Man, eare he Broke the.
>   *(GO,* 166)

Like Donne's "Dissolution," Overton's "Dissolution" expresses grief for the death of a loved one and elaborates some sort of triumph over death and grief. This hero who stood his ground, as Milton wrote, "repelling the attacks of the enemy amid dense slaughter on both sides" must have noticed that the final, triumphal image of Donne's "Dissolution" is drawn from musketry: virtuous souls rise to heaven "As bullets flowen"— and fly faster with their "powder being more" (ll. 23–24).[19] Moreover,

18. Overton appears to have "used either the 1635 edition [of Donne's *Poems*] or a subsequent one prior to 1669" (Norbrook, " 'This Blushinge Tribute,' " 265 n. 25).

19. When quoting Donne I use *Poems, by J. D. with Elegies on the Authors Death* (London, 1635).

given that there is a "possible pun" in Overton's title, as Norbrook notes, "on the dissolutions of republican Parliaments," it would seem that this "application" of Donne's "Dissolution" is at once emotionally fitting and politically clever—an "elegy for a lost love" that "becomes also an elegy for a lost political cause whose values of mutuality and godly solidarity the marriage epitomized."[20]

But if Overton's title suggests one kind of imitative dialogue, the body of his poem suggests other dialogues, other arguments. For, as any avid reader of Donne has already surmised, Overton's "Dissolution" is less an "application" of Donne's "Dissolution" than of Donne's "The Dampe," a poem that does not itself offer any admirable moral, spiritual, or political lessons at all. It is pleasant to think that Overton was drawn to the *Songs and Sonets* because, as Norbrook says, "they offer images of a particularly intense and reciprocal love," but "The Dampe" is not an example of such love. "It is," as Theodore Redpath observes, "essentially a poem of seduction which works by accumulation of subtle detail to achieve its aim by cajoling the woman avid of conquest into deciding on the *kind* of conquest most welcome to her lover."[21]

The moral gulf between source text and applied text is so wide that it is hard to accord even the loosest dialogical coherence to Overton's "Dissolution." One is reduced, for the most part, to enumerating differences. On the one hand, Overton makes the reader his friend with "yo'ule finde" (l. 2), substituting readers for Donne's third-party "friends" whose "curiositie" is said to lead to his strange autopsy (ll. 2–3); on the other hand, Overton's lover is not a *you* (as in Donne's "your Picture in my heart" [l. 4]) but a *she* (as in "her picture in my heart" [l. 2]). The ironic intimacy of address established in Donne's poem is transformed by Overton to an intimacy of reading—an intimacy perhaps equally ironic because it is expressed in a text whose very possibility was predicated on privacy. But then, having condensed four lines into two lines accentuating Donne's striking image, Overton again modifies a crucial pronoun. Donne's "You thinke a sodaine dampe of love / Will through all their senses move" (ll. 5–6) becomes "I thinck, then, w^t a sad damp of Loue = / will thurrough all their Sence^s moue" (ll. 3–4). Overton's "I" governs "prefer" (i.e., "elevate") in line 5 as well, and so a ludicrous sentiment that Donne puts in the mind of his vain lady becomes a direct statement by Overton of his own opinions about his wife and the world. *I think*—he is saying to himself, to "you," to anyone

20. Norbrook, " 'This Blushinge Tribute,' " 237.
21. Ibid., 236. Theodore Redpath, ed., *The Songs and Sonets of John Donne,* 2d ed. (New York: St. Martin's Press, 1983), 154.

who can read him—*that everyone will be as heartbroken by my wife's death as I have been, and so I feel that the murder of my wife will in turn become a massacre of many other persons!*

These poems, already so far apart in tone and purpose, diverge even further as we contrast Overton's increasingly obscure lines to Donne's second and third stanzas. In "The Dampe" the "Poore victories" (l. 9), the "conquest" (l. 10), and the acts of violence against "th'enormous Gyant, your *Disdaine*" and "the enchantresse *Honor*" (ll. 11–12) are practiced or should be practiced by the lady; and they all lead, finally, to one of Donne's favorite sexual puns: "kill me" (l. 16). Overton ignores Donne's pun, preserves his imagery of violence, and makes Ann the victim, not the agent, of violence. Identifying "C & M" (l. 7) for certain is not easy. Norbrook argues that Overton "censure[s] the malignant activities of 'C & M' (Cromwell and Monck) and blame[s] them for [his wife's] death." This, of course, makes a good deal of sense in the contexts that I have discussed above: Overton had been imprisoned by Cromwell and Monck in the 1650s, and he may have blamed them for any hardships that befell Ann during that time—including, possibly, stays that she may have voluntarily made with him in the Tower.[22] But whomever "C & M" actually names, they are not actually blamed for anyone's death: in Overton's opinion, they had *not* been "brave" and they did *not* make any kind of "conquest" of his wife (ll. 7–8). The most likely subjects for these contrary-to-fact subjunctives are, in fact, King Charles I and Queen Henrietta-Maria, a famous pair whose names were sometimes similarly abbreviated by Royalist poets in the 1640s. The cause of this royal "C & M" had expired in 1649, but surely Overton had not forgotten them and the fact that they stood in the way of the "freedome" that he had once "fought for" (*SP*, 3:67). As he had successfully "repell[ed] the attacks of the enemy amid dense slaughter on both sides," so his wife had "triumph^t ouer men" spiritually in the 1640s.

But the times had changed and all had been thrown into "darknesse." The rise of the "Monster" in line 10 records a change from what Overton perceived to be the morality of open warfare to the immorality of Interregnum and Restoration politics. The "Monster" who "weares the Star, and Garter" may be Charles II and it may also be Monck, now Duke of Albemarle and Companion of the Order of the Garter, but perhaps it is best understood more generally in the language of the Good Old Cause as

22. Norbrook, " 'This Blushinge Tribute,' " 237. Masson writes: "On the 3rd of July, 1656, I find, his wife, 'Mrs Anne Overton,' had liberty from the Council, 'to abide with her husband in the Tower, if she shall so think fit' " (*Life of John Milton*, 5:165).

a "character" of tyranny masquerading as godly political authority. Ann's special "Glory" (l. 13) is that she exposed the violent underpinnings of that authority by means of a "passive valour" fully redeemed, of course, from the supine eroticism that Donne advises in "The Dampe" (ll. 22–24). She forced the tyrannical "Monster" to break "his faith wth God, & Man" (l. 14) and to make from her "virtue" a "Martyr" for all to see (l. 12)—a victory denied even to Cornelia, the famous republican heroine of Overton's admired Katherine Philips, in *Pompey* (1663).[23] Yet even in this pious and dramatic conclusion Overton is playing tricks with Donne and with us. His final line revises not *Pompey*, "The Dampe," or "The Dissolution" but "A Jeat Ring sent," the next poem in his edition of Donne's *Poems*. "She that, Oh, broke her faith, would soon breake thee" (l. 12), exclaims the jealous lover, and by "thee" Donne means not a woman, of course, but a ring.

With concrete references to at least three different poems by John Donne, with a dead king and queen, with a tyrannical "He" for a "She" and a dead wife for a ring; with a tortured counterbalancing of virtues and vices that has less to do with Donne than the heroic drama of Katherine Philips; and with a title taken from a poem that concludes with souls "flowen" like musket balls to God, Overton's sonnet strains even the most generous limits of literary coherence. Indeed, I do not expect that it will ever be a coherent piece of poetry or even rhetoric for many readers. Claims for its coherence can be made only after the idea of coherence has been distributed from the one to the many, from poetic wholeness conceived as monologue to wholeness conceived as dialogue. The problem, however, is that not even dialogue is a model adequate to such "applications" as this strange "Dissolution" of the first Stuart Restoration. They register without apology the truth of Abraham Cowley's apologetic advice that "a warlike, various, and a tragical age is best to *write of*, but worst to *write in*."[24] When Colonel Overton undermines several famous poems to build one obscure poem, when he refers simultaneously to political "characters" and darkly personal histories of love and war, he repels our sophisticated interpretive forays and escapes our best attempts

---

23. Monck was made a Companion of the Order on May 26, 1660, one of the first official acts of the new regime. See Sir Nicholas Harris Nicolas, *History of the Orders of Knighthood of the British Empire* (London: William Pickering, 1842), 247. No cruel stroke of fortune, says Cornelia to Caesar, "can make me blush, but that I live, / And have not follow'd *Pompey* when he dy'd" (*Pompey* 3.4.15, in *The Collected Works of Katherine Philips*, ed. Patrick Thomas, G. Greer, and R. Little, 3 vols. [Essex: Stump Cross Books, 1990–1993], 3:51). On Overton's use of Philips's *Poems* (1667) and his "explorations of a female rhetoric," see Norbrook, " 'This Blushinge Tribute,' " 237–45.

24. Abraham Cowley, *Poems* (London, 1656), A2v.

to confine his projects within the generic walls of "applicatory Poetry" and the commonplace book. The most fitting hermeneutic and formal metaphors for such writing are the free democracy of "Publique spirits" of which he dreamed, the prisons in which he spent so much of his later life, and the bloody, chaotic battles by which his God thought it necessary "to rend and teare us in pieces" (*HHA*, 5–6).

Robert C. Evans

Paradox in Poetry and Politics

Katherine Philips in the Interregnum

Katherine Fowler Philips was a poet of contradictions who lived and wrote in highly contradictory times. One of her earliest poems, written when she was probably fourteen or fifteen and while her country was embroiled in civil war, already expresses the royalism she embraced until she died. Yet Philips herself had been born into a family with strong Puritan and Parliamentary connections.[1] Although she vows in that early poem to marry only a man who is "Ready to serve his friend his country & his king," by the age of sixteen she was wedded to James Philips, a fifty-four-year old Welshman who loyally served the Commonwealth and Cromwell.[2] Yet while James often helped

1. For the text of this poem and for other biographical data, see Claudia Limbert, "Two Poems and a Prose Receipt: The Unpublished Juvenalia of Katherine Philips," *English Literary Renaissance* 16 (1986): 383–90, especially 389–90. Good brief overviews of Philips's life and writings are provided by Patrick Thomas, *Katherine Philips ("Orinda")* (Cardiff: University of Wales Press, 1988), and by Elizabeth Hageman, "Katherine Philips," in *Dictionary of Literary Biography*, vol. 131 (Detroit: Gale, 1993), 202–14. See also Hageman, "Katherine Philips: The Matchless Orinda," in *Women Writers of the Renaissance and Reformation*, ed. Katharina M. Wilson (Athens: University of Georgia Press, 1987), 566–608.
2. The details of James Philips's political and religious allegiances need much further exploration; currently available accounts are sketchy and often contradictory. For the basic facts, see Basil Duke Henning, *The History of Parliament: The House of Commons, 1660–1690*, 3 vols. (London: Secker and Warburg, 1983), 3:239–40. See also, for example, Geraint H. Jenkins, *The Foundations of Early Modern Wales, 1642–1780* (Cardiff: University of Wales Press, 1971); and Austin Woolrych, *Commonwealth to Protectorate* (Oxford: Clarendon Press, 1982). Woolrych claims that Philips was at first a Royalist and asserts that his later involvement with the puritanical Commission for the Propagation of the Gospel in Wales shows "that that body did not consist exclusively of sectarian enthusiasts" (183). If these assertions are true, they would greatly help to explain the marriage of James and Katherine. On the other hand, other

suppress Royalist dissent, Katherine enjoyed many links with Royalist writers and intellectuals.[3] How she managed to be both the faithful wife of a Commonwealth official and the devoted friend of so many Royalists is, however, just one of many intriguing puzzles posed by her brief but fascinating life.

By the time Katherine Philips died at age thirty-two, she was the most widely respected woman poet of her day. Her influence on later women writers was enormous, and she is still seen as a significant transitional figure in the history of English literature. Although, by the nineteenth century, she was largely neglected and unknown, she provides a crucial link between the eras of Donne and Dryden and was an important innovator both in subject and in form. Her poems, however, have received surprisingly little attention *as* poems, and even scholars who have helped preserve her memory have often damned her with faint (or sexist) praise. Poems extolled in her own day have more recently been condemned—as much, apparently, for political as for aesthetic reasons. Ironically, although Philips is recognized as an important woman writer, she also has been neglected or patronized even by many feminists, and when feminists *have* championed her, they have sometimes done so for reasons she would probably have rejected.[4] Even in death, then, her career

---

sources assert that James was himself a Fifth Monarchist radical; see, for example, Jenkins, *Foundations,* 70. If this were true, the marriage (or at least its success) would be much harder to understand.

On the general political situation in Wales from 1640 to 1660, see also, for example, W. S. K. Thomas, *Stuart Wales, 1603–1714* (Llandysul: Gomer Press, 1988); Gareth Elwyn Jones, *Modern Wales: A Concise History, c. 1485–1979* (Cambridge: Cambridge University Press, 1984); and A. M. Johnson, "Wales during the Commonwealth and Protectorate," in *Puritans and Revolutionaries: Essays in Seventeenth-Century History Presented to Christopher Hill,* ed. Donald Pennington and Keith Thomas (Oxford: Clarendon Press, 1978), 233–56. On the political and religious background of Katherine Philips, the best source is still probably Philip Webster Souers, *The Matchless Orinda* (Cambridge: Harvard University Press, 1931), especially 3–38.

3. See, for example, Claudia A. Limbert, "'The Unison of Well-Tun'd Hearts': Katherine Philips' Friendships with Male Writers," *English Language Notes* 29 (1991): 25–37.

4. On Philips's reputation, see especially Marilyn L. Williamson, *Raising Their Voices: British Women Writers, 1650–1750* (Detroit: Wayne State University Press, 1990). See also Paula Loscocco, "'Manly Sweetness': Katherine Philips among the Neoclassicals," *Huntington Library Quarterly* 56 (1993): 259–79, and the studies cited therein. The most obvious example of faint praise is Souers in his groundbreaking biography, *Matchless Orinda;* see, for example, 5, 104, 108, 145, 204, 252, 263, 269–70, and 277. On poems condemned by recent critics, see, for example, B. G. MacCarthy, *Women Writers: Their Contribution to the English Novel, 1621–1744* (Oxford: Blackwell, 1946), 29–31. On the championship of poems for the wrong reasons, see, for example, Ellen Moody, "Orinda, Rosania, Lucasia, *et aliae:* Towards a New Edition of the Works of

brims with contradictions: she is both noted and neglected, and her poems, though known to many, are rarely closely read.

This essay, then, has several purposes. One is to examine how Philips's pre-Restoration poems complexly respond to one of the most complex periods in English history. Another goal is to argue that this historical complexity can contribute to the poems' artistic richness, and that the poems often deserve to be read with far more attention and appreciation than they tend to receive. Finally, I also hope to suggest that the difficulties and dilemmas posed by Philips's career should help discourage simplistic responses to the Interregnum as a whole. Trying to make sense of Katherine Philips is one way of realizing how difficult it can be to generalize, at least with any confidence, about the larger period in which she lived, thought, and wrote.

I

Philips, of course, is most famous for her many poems celebrating friendship between women. Lilian Faderman sees her as one of the first English poets to articulate ideals of "female bonding," and her poems to other women have been praised for undermining stereotypes by exploiting them.[5] Yet the poems have also been seen as abstract, artificial, idealistic, and highly mannered—as both "precious" and "Platonic" in the least attractive senses of those words.

The poems on friendship, however, seem more complex when seen within the context of civil war. Rather than merely rejecting the public world, they respond to it in oblique and complicated ways. Certainly this is true of a poem dated "Feb: 25. 1650" and entitled "Philoclea's parting. M[rs] M. Stedman" (#41).[6] Apparently addressed to a sister-in-law,

---

Katherine Philips," *Philological Quarterly* 66 (1987): 325–54, especially 336. See also Claudia A. Limbert, "Katherine Philips: Controlling a Life and Reputation," *South Atlantic Review* 56 (1991): 27–42, especially 34–36. For a different view, see Arlene Stiebel, "Subversive Sexuality: Masking the Erotic in Poems by Katherine Philips and Aphra Behn," in *Renaissance Discourses of Desire*, ed. Claude J. Summers and Ted-Larry Pebworth (Columbia: University of Missouri Press, 1993), 223–36.

5. See Lillian Faderman, *Surpassing the Love of Men: Romantic Love and Friendship between Women from the Renaissance to the Present* (New York: William Morrow, 1981), 68–71. See also the selection from Elaine Hobby, *Virtue of Necessity: English Women's Writing, 1649–86* (Ann Arbor: University of Michigan Press, 1989), reprinted in *Literature Criticism from 1400 to 1800*, ed. Jennifer Allison Brostrom (Detroit: Gale, 1996), 30:287.

6. Texts of cited poems are from the first volume of *The Collected Works of Katherine Philips: The Matchless Orinda* (Stump Cross, Essex: Stump Cross Books, 1990). Two later volumes focus on the plays and letters. The volume of poems is edited by Patrick Thomas, whose commentary provides much useful information, especially

the poem describes how Steadman's presence comforted Philips when "Rosania" (another friend) had not been heard from. Philips notes how "by Rosania's silence I had been / The wretched'st martyr any age hath seen" (4–5)—surprising language from a Royalist poet writing shortly after the shocking martyrdom of Charles I. The poem, in fact, brims with references to "Traytors" and their "Tormentors," and such political overtones are emphasized again in the final couplet, where Philips fancifully claims of herself that "none ever dy'd before / Upon a sadder or a nobler score" (11–12). However one interprets this language (crudely hyperbolic? deliberately shocking?), the poem certainly becomes more intriguing when we see it partly in the context of recent political events. Indeed, the title's explicit dating makes that context flagrant. The date inevitably raises questions about the poem's tone that could easily have been otherwise ignored.

Similar complexity results from the political language in her poem, "To Mrs M. Karne . . ." (#23). Here, Philips compares Karne to "some great Conquerour" who, "hunting honour in a thousand wounds," is not satisfied until she slays "Some royall Captive," and yet who, having obtained that goal, treats her other defeated enemies with "mercy" because she "doth abhorre a bloody Victory" (1–2, 6, 10, 12). Such phrasing, penned not long after the final Royalist defeat in the second civil war, is hard to dismiss as merely clever. Surely Philips's first readers, most of them Royalists, would have heard her darker undertones, and the poem's subsequent pleas for Karne's "mercy" (16), "clemency" (18), and "peace" (27), as well as its warning against pursuing a "rigour" that would "blot" the "Triumph" of Karne's victory (17, 25), add to the work's complexity. Indeed, the poem can even be read as an implicit call for mercy and moderation toward political enemies, and clemency is in fact a keynote of the openly political poems Philips composed both before and after the Restoration. The poem to Karne, however, becomes all the more fascinating when Philips warns Karne to "Take heed least in the Story [posterity] peruse / A murder which no language can excuse" (31–32). On one level such phrasing seems merely whimsical, but on another level

---

about identities and datings. In discussing datings I have also relied on the previously cited article by Ellen Moody. The numbers used by Thomas are also used by Moody.

On textual matters relevant to Philips's verse, see, for example, Moody, "Orinda, Rosania, Lucasia," and also the following: Patricia M. Sant and James N. Brown, "Two Unpublished Poems by Katherine Philips," *English Literary Renaissance* 24 (1994): 211–28; Peter Beal, *Index of English Literary Manuscripts,* vol. 2, part 2 (London: Mansell, 1993): 125–40; and Claudia A. Limbert, "The Poetry of Katherine Philips: Holographs, Manuscripts, and Early Printed Texts," *Philological Quarterly* 70 (1991): 181–98.

readers (especially Royalists) could not help hearing an allusion to the stunning and unprecedented execution of Charles I.

Many of Philips's poems on friendship radiate extra energy when their immediate political contexts are borne in mind. Examples include the references to "triumph(s)," "conquerours," "captives," "conquests," "Victory," and "plots" in a poem (ca. 1650–1651) to "Mrs: Anne Owen" (#26: 1–2, 6, 10, 13); or the reference, in "A Dialogue between Lucasia and Orinda" (ca. 1653), to the "Uselesse . . . Crownes" of "captive Kings" and to the ways in which religion can be "by niceties [i.e., over-subtle disputations] destroied" (#19: 16, 20); or the very blatant and powerfully sarcastic accusation, in a poem "For Regina" (ca. 1653–1654), that this woman, in her treatment of a suitor, is "lately Roundhead growne," since "whom you vanquish you insult upon" (#39: 19–20). Here as elsewhere, political language helps complicate the friendship poems; and, to the extent that such complexity seems under Philips's control, it typifies her artistry.

II

The poems on feminine friendship, however, provide only one example of Philips's generic innovation. She was also one of the first English poets to compose verse essays,[7] and these poems, too, often gain in resonance when read in historical context. Their political language makes them seem less abstract, less ethereal, giving them an immediate relevance to Philips's first readers but also linking them, more broadly, to the general complications of "real life." "L'amitié" (#150), subtitled "To Mrs. M. Awbrey" and helpfully dated "6ᵗ Aprill 1651," provides a nice example of a friendship poem evolving into a verse essay. Yet the poem gains interest when we recall that at the time of its composition, Royalists and Parliamentarians alike were anticipating Charles II's imminent invasion of England at the head of a Scottish army. It is in this context that Philips counsels Awbrey to

> Let the dull world alone to talk and fight,
> And with their vast ambitions nature fright;
> Let them despise so inocent a flame [as friendship],
> While Envy, pride and faction play their game:
> But we by Love sublim'd so high shall rise,
> To pitty Kings, and Conquerors despise,
> Since we that sacred union have engrost,
> Which they and all the sullen world have lost. (15–22)

7. On this point, see, for example, Sayre Greenfield, "Philips, Katherine," in *British Women Writers: A Critical Reference Guide* (New York: Ungar, 1989), 537–38, especially 538.

Especially intriguing here is the subtle distinction Philips draws between "Kings" and "Conquerours"; she can "pitty" the first but only "despise" the second (20). Does this line imply sympathy for Charles but disdain for Cromwell? Or does it, even more complexly, suggest that Charles as rightful king deserves some sympathy but that Charles as potential conqueror, leading an invading foreign force and shedding English blood, merits some contempt?[8] The line, which at first seems so neatly pointed and so simply balanced, seems on reflection more darkly ambiguous.

Political language also colors and complicates some more obvious verse essays. "L'accord du bien" (#65), for instance, not only celebrates concord in general but also insinuates the specific need for political and religious harmony. Apparently Philips rejected puritanism partly because it violated her sense of the "happy meane," which "would let us see / Knowledge and meekness may agree; / And find, when each thing hath its name, / Passion and Zeale are not the same" (65–68). She contends that "It will with the most learned suit / More to enquire then to dispute" (81–82), and she endorses an ideal reconciliation of "Obedience" and "Liberty" (92). She links puritanism with pride, yet her own political language seems modestly balanced when she argues that "Rightly to rule one's self must be / The hardest, largest monarchy: / Whose passions are his masters grown, / Will be a captive in a Throne" (97–100). Here as so often, Philips, hardly a naive Royalist, suggests that the specific features of the political constitution are less important than the moral constitution of a society and its leaders; she champions kingship less than virtuous rule, especially personal self-control. Her poem expresses nicely balanced skepticism, not only about the king's opponents but also about any Pollyannaish view of kings.

A similarly moralistic view of politics can be glimpsed in another important verse essay, "La Grandeur d'esprit" (#60), probably written in 1653. In a wonderfully evocative phrase, Philips here argues that "Death is a Leveller" (23) and contends that "Kingdoms have their fates as well as men" (28). Such words not only discourage readers from distancing themselves from the fallen king or from seeing his fall as the result of merely personal failings; they also imply a warning to his successors, the new rulers, who are reminded that "The world no longer flatters with the

8. On events preceding and following Charles's invasion from the north, see Samuel Rawson Gardiner, *History of the Commonwealth and Protectorate*, 4 vols. (1903; reprint, New York: AMS Press, 1965), 2:1–48, especially 47–48. For similar comment on reaction to the Scots, see Richard Ollard, *This War Without an Enemy: A History of the English Civil Wars* (New York: Atheneum, 1976), 198.

great" (34). The world is now "weary of deceit" (33)—a phrase that can be read not only as a specific glance at the notoriously unreliable Charles I but also as an admonition to those who have succeeded him. The verse essays, like the poems to friends, seem far richer when read closely and in the context of contemporary political disputes.

III

Given the frequently complex political implications of Philips's verse essays and poems on friendship, it is not surprising that her most obviously political poems are also among her most intriguing. This is true even of the post-Restoration panegyrics, although those works have often suffered from a contempt sometimes rooted in prejudice or neglect. Here, though, I will focus on two fascinating, effective, but relatively neglected poems from the Interregnum.

The first, placed literally first in most editions, is entitled "Upon the double murther of K. Charles, in answer to a libellous rime made by V. P." "V. P." was Vavasor Powell, "a Puritan preacher with strong Fifth Monarchist sympathies,"[9] who was both a colleague and a rival of Philips's husband. In this poem, as in others, Philips disclaims any interest in politics per se, adopting the more generally moralistic stance that was also, paradoxically, one of her most potent political weapons. By claiming to speak not on behalf of a particular party or ideology but in defense of basic ethics, Philips could, ironically, make her own political arguments all the more effective. Because she was a woman, adopting this moral stance gave her greater license to speak politically, as a mouthpiece for ungendered virtue. Indeed, she begins here by denying that she is "concern'd" with the "great Helme" of the "state"; instead, she defends Charles in the same way "as that sonne whose father's danger nigh / Did force his native dumbnesse, and untye / The fettred organs" (1–5). By comparing herself to a male, a son, she not only further objectifies her response, making it seem rooted in a powerful human instinct, but also gains greater license, as a woman, to speak out. As she puts it, "here is a cause / That will excuse the breach of nature's lawes" (5–6). Ironically, Philips breaks "nature's lawes" that silence women so that she can protest acts even more obviously unnatural, including not only the murder of a king but also the act of "libel[ing]" him after his death. By offering her poem as an "answer" to a "libel," she not only justifies its vehement tone but also makes her strong emotion the sort that any person (man or woman) might feel. Thus, when she abruptly asserts that "Silence were now a Sin" (7), her brevity

9. Thomas, *Katherine Philips*, 1:321.

and effective alliteration exemplify a reasonable passion ostensibly rooted in a fundamental human nature. "Wise men [the noun is significant] themselves" would "allow" such "passion": that is, they would both approve of it in others and permit themselves to feel it. Philips's effective exploitation of apolitical ethics to advance her specific political argument is especially clear when she asks, "Hath Charles so broke God's lawes, but he must not have / A quiet crown, nor yet a quiet grave?" (11–12). Although one can imagine "yes" as an answer to the first half of line 12, such an answer to the second half would make the libeller seem by far the greater breaker of "God's lawes." Similarly effective is her ensuing claim that "Had any heathen been this prince's foe, / He would have wept to see him injur'd soe" (17–18). This couplet is doubly powerful: it not only appeals once again to common human reactions (reactions that transcend distinctions between genders or religious differences even greater than those between Anglicans and Puritans), but it also plays with our expectations. Thus, while we might have expected Philips to finish the couplet by claiming that even a heathen would have treated Charles better than have his supposedly Christian enemies, she also further implies that a heathen would even have grieved to see him treated so badly by others, including other Christians.

Indeed, Philips ironically plays with the double connotations of "reason" in lines 19–20, where she claims that Charles's enemies had "reason good / To quarrell at the right they had withstood." Here "reason" is not an abstract, objective principle of conduct but a synonym for highly personal, self-interested motives. Whereas Philips claims to speak from disinterested motives, she suggests that her (and Charles's) opponents had and have selfish motives for wanting the king first murdered and then maligned. Yet her attack on Charles's attackers is all the more potent because she does not dispute their charges against him; instead, she trumps them. For example, at first she seems merely to echo their standard claim: "He broke God's lawes, and therefore he must dye" (21). But then the next line undercuts the pride inherent in this claim: "And what shall then become of thee and I?" (22). This indictment of the accusers' arrogance is all the more effective because Philips includes herself (and all her readers, not simply Vavasor Powell) in the indictment. Yet this very ability to engage in self-criticism, and thus to link herself as a fellow flawed human to Charles's enemies, also subtly distinguishes her from them: this is the kind of self-indictment (she implies) in which they would never engage. The attack on the pride exhibited by herself and others thus becomes a way of demonstrating her own humility and moral stature.

Philips's diction, however, is rooted not only in general ethics or in moral psychology. She also demonstrates an effective ability to use words loaded with political significance. Thus she notes that the rebels, having already "seiz'd upon all our defence," now try to "sequester our common sense" (25–26). The first half of this couplet can suggest not only the literal military defeat and disarmament of the Royalists but also the physical capture of Charles I, while the verb "sequester" alludes to the appropriation of an enemy's estates. This practice, designed to help finance the war effort, was often associated with greedy corruption, thus lending even further ironic punch to the adjective "common" in "common sense."

Philips's poetic skill is apparent again when she begins line 29 by claiming that "Christ will be King." In one respect this is a swipe at Powell's views as a Fifth Monarchist, since that sect expected the Lord's imminent return and earthly reign. In another sense, however, the phrase simply states a point all Christians accepted: Christ would indeed someday be king and would someday sit as judge. Philips's phrasing can thus be read simultaneously as sarcastic mimickry, as a concession, and as a subtle threat, especially in view of her ensuing statement that "I ne're understood, / His subjects built his kingdom up with blood, / (Except their owne) or that he would dispence / With his commands, though for his owne defence" (29–32). How would Christ, Philip implicitly asks, someday judge those who, in his name, had violated his commandments, especially his prohibition of murder, especially by murdering a king?

By attempting to "dispence / With [God's] commands," the rebels show themselves as enemies both of their earthly and of their heavenly king; their arrogance, Philips suggests, goes far beyond their opposition to Charles. Similarly, she implies that her own allegiance is not simply to a mortal but to an eternal monarch. Her final couplet, moreover, is an expression of both intense passion and cool reason, and in general her language contrasts the chaotic instability of her opponents with her own rhetorical and mental balance.

Philips's poem on Charles's death is both rhetorically and politically effective. In another poem (inspired by the dead king's son), however, Philips displays equally sure command of a tone less hortatory than meditative, less propagandistic than richly reflective. This poem, "On the 3rd September 1651" (#11), is political in a way that keeps mere politics at a thoughtful distance. Reading this work after reading the poem on the murder of Charles I further enhances one's appreciation of Philips's range as a political poet.

In this work, Philips responds to the devastating Royalist defeat at Worcester, where the young king just barely escaped. Later, disguised, he made his way to France, not returning until the Restoration. There were even rumors, after the battle, that he had been killed,[10] and it would be interesting to know precisely when Philips's poem was composed and whether she may have been influenced by these reports. Certainly she does not allude to Charles's survival or escape, and in general she depicts the lost battle as a royal eclipse. The poem opens by describing the setting sun as a "Glorious Magazine of Light" (1)—thus already implying a potential not only for explosive devastation but also for self-destruction.

One aspect of this poem's success, indeed, is the way Philips revivifies the hoary analogy linking king and sun. The real sun, after all, will rise again, but Philips's analogy ironically highlights the potentially different and final fate of the royal sun. Similar irony is also implicit in Philips's reference in line 14 to the sun "pull[ing] down others" with it, since "others" can refer not only to the king's enemies but also to his supporters, both on and off the battlefield. The poem hints at the potential self-destructiveness of Royalist allegiance, and it even hints that Charles may have been partly motivated by all-too-human vindictiveness and ambition. To write that the sun "now spake more / Of Terrour then in many months before" (15–16) not only reinforces these dark connotations but also, through the word "spake," can imply hollow self-assertion.

The long, suspenseful opening analogy ends with an abrupt conclusion. After all the preparation describing the awesome, glorious spectacle of the declining royal sun, Philips quickly concludes that Charles "Yet but enjoy'd the miserable fate / Of setting Majesty, to dy in State" (19–20). Suddenly, in a couplet, all the glory dies: the final three words abruptly undo all the power earlier implied. Once again, moreover, Philips's diction is rich: "State," ironically, could suggest the crisis or acme of a disease or sickness, in addition to suggesting high rank, pomp, dignity, and power, especially when attended by a great train of followers. Indeed, the simple phrase "to dy in State" effectively sums up the essential tension and paradox at the heart of this poem, which describes a glorious (but possibly tainted) end to glory. Here as throughout this poem, Philips's royalism is not without some dark and even critical undercurrents. The powerfully simple and nicely balanced phrase describing fallen kings reminds us of the wider losses involved when a leader falls.

Searching for analogies, Philips first compares Charles, aptly, to Pompey (23)—himself an exiled loser in a famous civil war, and himself an

10. Gardiner, *History*, 2:49.

ambiguous figure (an ambitious defender of a lost cause).[11] Even more intriguing is her reference to "Captive Samson," who "could not life conclude, / Unless attended with a multitude" (25–26). In pulling down the pillars on himself and the Philistines, the apparently defeated Samson, like Christ, enjoyed a final triumph. When read with such common connotations in mind, the lines imply both an ominous eventual fate for Charles's opponents and a satisfying eventual reward for his surviving supporters. Perhaps Philips implies that Charles, like the sun and Son, would inevitably rise again. More immediately obvious, though, is her stress on the "multitude" who accompany both Samson and Charles in their destruction. Ironically, the analogy seems to work to Charles's disadvantage, since Samson destroyed only a "multitude" of evil opponents; he took no loyal followers with him. Once again Philips exploits the ironic potential of "attended" (with all its associations of royal power) subtly to press her point.

Similar resonance is crammed into the simple verb "trust" when Philips next asks, "Who'd trust to Greatness now, whose food is ayre, / Whose ruine sudden, and whose end despaire?" (27–28). Does she ask who, born royal, would now trust greatness? Or does she instead ask who, not born royal, would now depend on the greatness of royalty? Either reading seems to fit. As the stanza proceeds, the poem can seem simultaneously to offer both orthodox moral commentary and specific reflection on Charles, and once again the meaning of "who" is open to question: "Who would presume upon [that is, rely on, take for granted] his Glorious Birth, / Or quarrell for a spacious share of earth, / That sees such diadems become thus cheap, / and Heroes tumble in the common heap?" (29–32). Philips seems to have been a Royalist capable of seeing even a king as a flawed, fallible man. Both Charles and his father felt that they were fighting in God's cause, and Philips probably concurred. Yet she can also see a king as someone willing to "quarrell" merely "for a spacious share of earth."

In the opening words of her final couplet, Philips manages to reconcile an impassioned emotional outburst with a sense of logic and reason. Faced with the possibility of the king's defeat and perhaps even with his death, and faced, too, with a vivid object lesson in the unreliability of earthly power, Philips reaffirms her allegiance to the abstract principle of personal "vertue," which "summs up all, / And firmely stands when Crowns and Scepters fall" (33–34). Even in its final lines the poem achieves a deliberate,

11. After the Restoration, of course, Philips herself translated Corneille's drama on Pompey. For a brief comment on its relevance to her own political stance, see, for example, Thomas, *Katherine Philips*, 40.

richly crafted balance, an equilibrium characteristic not only of Philips's poetic skill but also of her nuanced political insight.

Philips's poetry in general merits closer reading than it has tended to receive, either from historians or from literary critics. Her works have much to tell us about the psychological impact of the English civil wars on a thoughtful, complicated mind. Her personal circumstances symbolize many of the contradictions and divisions implicit in the larger era, and many of her poems merit further scrutiny as crafted and compelling (if never wholly autonomous) works of art.

Jonathan Rogers

"We Saw a New Created Day"

Restoration Revisions of Civil War Apocalypse

In his *Discourse by way of a Vision, Concerning the Government of Oliver Cromwell* (1661), Abraham Cowley describes an apocalyptic vision of sorts, occasioned by the death of Oliver Cromwell. Retiring to his chamber after the Protector's funeral, he "began to reflect upon the whole life of this prodigious man," and, rocked to sleep by his contradictory thoughts on Cromwell's career, he falls into a dream. He finds himself transported to his own personal Patmos, atop the highest hill on the Isle of Man, from which he can see all three kingdoms of Britain. Reminded of "all the Sins, and all the Miseries that had overwhelmed them these twenty years," he breaks forth into a jeremiad for England, that "happy Isle" now "chang'd and curst."[1]

He is soon interrupted, however, by the appearance of a "strange and terrible Apparition, . . . the figure of a man taller than a Gyant, or indeed than the shadow of a Gyant in the evening." He is naked and painted head to toe with "the representation of the late battels in our civil Warrs." The apparition identifies himself as the "Northwest Principality," the angel to whom God had entrusted the government of Britain in the 1640s and 1650s. He is a parody of an apocalyptic angel: his eyes like burning brass and the three crowns on his head recall the description of the martial, victorious Christ of the Apocalypse. In his right hand he holds a bloody sword emblazoned with the motto, *Pax quaeritur bello* (one of the Cromwell family mottoes), and in his left he holds "a thick Book, upon the back of which was written in Letters of Gold, Acts, Ordinances, Protestations,

---

1. *The Works of Abraham Cowley* (1681), Lll2v–3. All subsequent quotations from Cowley will come from this, the seventh edition, and will be cited parenthetically in the text by signatures.

Covenants, Engagements, Declarations, Remonstrances, &c."—an unmistakably Parliamentarian version of the book "written within and on the back side" that God holds in his right hand, the book of Revelation (Lll3v–4).

The Northwest Principality is a Parliament man through and through; in a lengthy and vigorous debate with the Royalist narrator, he ardently defends Cromwell and the Puritan cause. He voices familiar arguments in the Protector's favor—mostly variations on the theme that, because Providence directs history, Cromwell's success is its own legitimation— and is rebutted at every point by his opponent. By the end of the debate the angel's arguments have shaded into outright Machiavellianism. The narrator interrupts him in the middle of a versified history of power and violence (all the poems in this work, like so much of Cowley's opus, break off in the middle) and identifies him as a devil in disguise: "I understand now perfectly (which I guessed at long before) what kind of Angel and Protector you are; and though your stile in verse be very much mended since you were wont to deliver Oracles, yet your Doctrine is much worse than ever you formerly (that I heard of) had face to publish." Enraged, the fiend nearly has the poor poet in his talons when a friendlier angel intervenes and overcomes the devil without a fight:

> Lo, e're the last words were fully spoke,
> From a fair cloud which rather op'd than broke,
> A flash of Light rather than Light'ning came,
> So swift, and yet so gentle was the Flame.
> Upon it rode, and in his full Career,
> Seem'd to my Eyes no sooner There than Here,
> The comeliest Youth of all th' Angelique Race;
> Lovely his shape, ineffable his Face.
> The Frowns with which he strook the trembling Fiend,
> All smiles of Humane Beauty did transcend,
> His Beams of Locks fell part dishevel'd down,
> Part upward curl'd, and form'd a nat'ral Crown,
> Such as the Brittish Monarch used to wear;
> If Gold might be compar'd with Angels Hair. (Ooo3–3v).

If England had a tutelary angel in the 1640s and 1650s, it was surely, as Cowley suggests, an angel of violence and destruction. The Puritans had believed the civil wars to be meaningful violence—violence that chastises the wicked and purifies the righteous, preparing the world stage for the final revelation of Christ. They believed themselves to be the very arm of God—or at least the sword of God—acting out the events described in God's "book written within and on the backside." But Cowley offers another way of mythologizing the violence and disorder of the civil wars and the Interregnum. The spirit that appeared to be an angel of apocalypse is actually a fiend from hell. The violence prompted by this spirit does not fulfill the divine will but rather opposes it. When the angel of God intervenes in human affairs in Cowley's poem, he does not, as in so many apocalyptic configurations, crash through the clouds in a thunderbolt. The clouds open peaceably, and the angel beams down in a ray of light, illuminating rather than fulminating. Not surprisingly, this agent of Providence and divine peace reminds the Royalist poet of a British Monarch. Cowley's *Discourse* presents monarchy as a direct answer to Puritan apocalypse. On the Puritan/Cromwellian side of the ledger Cowley places not only acts of mayhem, but the apocalyptic mythology that justifies them. Divine peace, divine order, and divine-right monarchy chase away the devils of apocalyptic violence.

Cowley's parodic vision illustrates the combination of ridicule and moral repugnance that characterizes Royalist treatments of radical apocalypse, both before and after the Restoration. In the Royalist poetry of the 1660s we see a conscious attempt to establish a new historical mythology to replace the radical vision of apocalyptic history that had prevailed in the previous decades. As J. G. A. Pocock has argued, Royalist efforts to reorder the cultural chaos of the Interregnum required that the chaotic language of enthusiasm be controlled. Pocock identifies a decreasing tendency after 1660 to speak of English politics in "the vocabulary of Godly Rule and the Elect Nation." Indeed, the iconoclastic nature of the Puritans' apocalyptic rhetoric made it impossible to sustain through the Interregnum, when the Puritans, now the establishment, became the target of apocalyptic rhetoric from the more radical of the radicals.[2] While the failure of the Puritan project had reduced the appeal of prophecy and apocalypse after the Restoration, the success of the Puritan project, insofar as it did succeed, had done just as much to make the apocalyptic mode unattractive to moderate Englishmen—including moderate Puritans. Nevertheless, we should be careful not to think of the declining status of apocalyptic rhetoric after 1660 as somehow inevitable; the assiduity with which Royalist myth-makers sought to discredit the Puritan apocalypse in the 1660s suggests that they did not expect it to die on its own. The Royalists who laid the foundations for English Augustanism—both political and literary—had first to clear away the rubble of radical apocalypse.

---

2. Pocock, *The Machiavellian Moment: Florentine Political Thought and the Atlantic Republican Tradition* (Princeton: Princeton University Press, 1975), 403. See B. S. Capp, "The Political Dimension of Apocalyptic Thought," in *The Apocalypse in English Renaissance Thought and Literature,* ed. C. A. Patrides and Joseph Wittreich (Ithaca: Cornell University Press, 1984), 114–17.

After the Restoration, England clearly needed new metaphors. As Steven Zwicker has argued, the Royalists' first imperative was to avoid the further fracture of the social order; they embraced the rhetoric of Augustanism as an alternative to the absolute claims of biblical prophecy. Whereas the Puritans had spoken of themselves as latter-day Israelites, God's peculiar people marching by God's grace toward the New Jerusalem, the Royalists spoke of themselves as latter-day Romans, establishing an empire to be compared with that of Augustus. But, as a number of scholars have pointed out, that Augustan empire was itself figured as a kind of millennial paradise. In this essay I will examine the complicated relationship between two rhetorical modes—the Augustan and the apocalyptic—during the 1660s. The Royalist poets of the Restoration quite literally demonized apocalyptic rhetoric as the language of radical politics, social unrest, intestine violence, and cultural iconoclasm. And yet, aware of its power—perhaps acknowledging that "the apocalyptic dimension was . . . too integrally a part of the age's thinking to be merely canceled and annulled"—the Royalists appropriated certain aspects of that very rhetoric. As Paul Korshin has argued, millennial speculation never really declined in the century after the Restoration. The forms of that speculation changed radically, however.[3] Royalists in the 1660s turned the radicals' own language against them by portraying Restoration England as a type of the New Jerusalem—by portraying Charles's return as the apocalyptic deliverance they had longed for during the tribulation that was the English civil wars and the Puritan ascendancy.

The very flexible language of the Book of Revelation had never belonged exclusively to the Puritans, even during the civil wars and Interregnum. Claude Summers has shown that the poetry of "Anglican survivalism" in the 1650s was surprisingly apocalyptic, expressing the persecuted Royalists' deepest longings for divine intervention in a world

3. Steven N. Zwicker, "Israel, England, and the Triumph of Roman Virtue," in *Millenarianism and Messianism in English Literature and Thought, 1650–1800*, ed. Richard H. Popkin (Leiden: Brill, 1988), 39–40. On the Augustan empire, see Capp, "Political Dimension," 117; Michael McKeon, *Politics and Poetry in Restoration England: The Case of "Astraea Redux"* (Cambridge: Harvard University Press, 1984), chapter 8; Alberto Caciedo, "Seeing the King: Biblical and Classical Texts in 'Astraea Redux,'" *Studies in English Literature* 32 (1992): 407–27; Jonathan Sawday, "Rewriting a Revolution: History, Symbol, and Text in the Restoration," *The Seventeenth Century* 7 (1992): 171–99; and Nicholas Jose, *Ideas of the Restoration in English Literature, 1660–1671* (Cambridge: Harvard University Press, 1984), 60. Pocock, *Machiavellian Moment*, 403. Korshin, "Queuing and Waiting: The Apocalypse in England, 1660–1750," in *Apocalypse*, ed. Patrides and Wittreich, 260.

"drawne low, and in the dreggs"—for the settling of accounts at the end of time. The Anglican vision of the end avoids much of the violent language of radical apocalypse as well as the specific application of prophecy to contemporary events, focusing rather on such mystical themes as the Marriage Supper of the Lamb and the Last Judgment. This eschatological hope—this waiting posture—was an answer to the prevailing Puritan eschatology of the 1640s and 1650s, which was not so much consolatory as hortatory, calling the saints to action. In the Puritan scheme, history is conflict. The godly manifest the will of God on earth through their actions opposing "Antichristian interest"; earthly peace, therefore, is not a legitimate goal. The duty of God's historical agents is to wreak havoc in the world and so to make the will of God "open and visible to all." Thus Matthew Newcomen exhorts the members of Parliament to labor to make peace with God, to labor to make peace within the Church, but not to labor to make peace with their enemies: "And then we need take no thought of . . . peace with our enemies: God will either subdue them under us, or make the desire of peace with them: only let neither the desire of peace with them, nor of peace among ourselves, bribe us to tolerate any thing in the Church of God that might make him to be at war with us."[4] God can and finally will cause peace to reign on earth; but the saints' first duty is to fight.

In a 1649 sermon before Parliament, John Owen preached on "The shaking and translating of heaven and earth." In the shocks and tumults of contemporary history, Owen saw the work of God's spirit, crumbling "the splendour and strength of the Nations of earth" so that he might establish his own, unshakable kingdom.[5] In Hebrews 12:27, Owen's sermon text, the

---

4. Claude Summers, "Herrick, Vaughan, and the Poetry of Anglican Survivalism," in *New Perspectives on the Seventeenth-Century English Religious Lyric*, ed. John R. Roberts (Columbia: University of Missouri Press, 1994), 46–74; see also Noel Kennedy Thomas, *Henry Vaughan, Poet of Revelation* (Worthing, West Sussex: Churchman, 1986), especially 134–96; Barbara Lewalski, *Protestant Poetics and the Seventeenth-Century Lyric* (Princeton: Princeton University Press, 1979), 324–26; John N. Wall, *Transformations of the Word: Spenser, Herbert, Vaughan* (Athens: University of Georgia Press, 1988); and Jonathan F. S. Post, *Henry Vaughan: The Unfolding Vision* (Princeton: Princeton University Press, 1982), 186–211. John Owen, *Ouranon Ourania, the shaking and translating of heaven and earth* (1649), F2v. Matthew Newcomen, *Jerusalem's Watchmen* (1643). William Allen's *Faithful Memorial* (1648), describes a prayer meeting in which the officers of the army, with bitter mourning, repent of the sin of making peace with Charles I: "And in this path the Lord led us not only to see our sin, but also our duty; and this so unanimously sat with weight upon each heart that none was able hardly to speak a word to each other for bitter weeping, partly in the sense and shame of our iniquities of unbelief, base fear of men, and carnal consultations (as the fruit thereof), with our own wisdoms, and not with the Word of the Lord. . . ."

5. Owen, *Ouranon Ourania*, C2v.

voice of God "shook the earth." This shaking, Owen carefully argues, is not only a spiritual, but also a "civil shaking," the destruction of governments and human institutions. Owen does not bother to explain this civil shaking to an audience who had just lived through the 1640s, for "truly the accomplishment hereof is in all Nations so under our eyes that I need not speak one word thereunto" (C2v). In the battles of the civil wars, God spells out his purposes in "letters of blood"; the works of God are "vocall speaking workes; the minde of God is in them. They may be herd, read, and understood; *the Rod may be heard, and who hath appointed it*" (E2v).

In these last days no human institution can stand; the corrupt must give way to the incorruptible. "All the present States of the world, are cemented together by Antichristian lime," preached Owen: "unless they be so shaken to have every cranny searched and brushed, they will be no quiet habitation for the Lord Christ, and his people" (C3v). Puritan iconoclasm—in all its manifestations—grows out of an apocalyptic view of history and revelation that requires the destruction of earthly things so that the eternal may be established on earth. "All flesh is grass," according to the prophet Isaiah, "and all the goodliness thereof is as the flower of the field. The grass withereth, the flower fadeth because the spirit of the Lord bloweth upon it: surely the people is grass. The grass withereth, the flower fadeth, but the world of our God shall stand forever" (Isaiah 41:6–7). For a seventeenth-century radical, Isaiah's remarks are not only a philosophical reflection on the contrast between the eternal and the human; they encapsulate a view of providential history: when the spirit of God blows, human endeavor *must* wither and fade to give place to the eternal word. And thus the conservative urge to conquer mutability by achieving a man-made (and typically backward-looking) stasis is not only futile but sacrilegious. The providential design requires the crumbling of all human institutions, the frustration of all human efforts to arrest temporal change, the smashing of all monuments to human achievement.[6]

6. See David Loewenstein, " 'Casting Down Imaginations': Iconoclasm as History," in *Milton and the Drama of History: Historical Vision, Iconoclasm, and the Literary Imagination* (Cambridge: Cambridge University Press, 1990); Achsah Guibbory, "Charles's Prayers, Idolatrous Images, and True Creation in Milton's *Eikonoklastes*," in *Of Poetry and Politics: New Essays on Milton and His World*, ed. P. G. Stanwood (Binghamton: Medieval and Renaissance Texts and Studies, 1995); Sharon Achinstein, *Milton and the Revolutionary Reader* (Princeton: Princeton University Press, 1994); Margaret Aston, *England's Iconoclasts*, vol. 1 (Oxford: Oxford University Press, 1988); and Lana Cable, "Milton's Iconoclastic Truth," in *Politics, Poetics, and Hermeneutics in Milton's Prose*, ed. David Loewenstein and James Grantham Turner (Cambridge: Cambridge University Press, 1990), 1–16.

In their own eyes and in the eyes of the Royalists (though not in the eyes of the more extreme radicals), Cromwell and his party had made considerable headway in their campaign "to ruin the great work of time." The Puritans' prophetic language seemed to validate itself in the overturning of English culture. The Restoration, therefore, in its suddenness and in its bloodlessness, seemed all the more miraculous. The combination of exultation and wonderment that prevails in the celebratory poems of the 1660s arises from the fact that the apparently irreversible course of doom has been reversed, and the apparently irredeemable state of chaos has been replaced by divine order and peace. The return of Charles II, according to Cowley and many of his fellow Royalists, brought an end to the apocalyptic fears occasioned by the chaos of the 1640s and 1650s. According to Cowley's "Ode Upon His Majesties Restauration and Return" (1660), the English had heard the approaching hoofbeats of three of the four Horsemen of the Apocalypse:

> We fear'd (and almost toucht the black degree
>   Of instant Expectation)
> That the three dreadful Angels we
> Of Famine, Sword, and Plague should here establisht see.
>   (Ggg1v)

Cowley admits that even he had begun to think during the Commonwealth that the Puritan's predictions of universal destruction were coming true. The Restoration revealed, however, that the chaos and destruction predicted by the Puritans were chaos and destruction of their own making, not God's:

> Already was the shaken Nation
> Into a wild and deform'd Chaos brought
>   And it was hasting on (we thought)
> Even to the last of Ills, Annihilation.
> When in the midst of this confused Night,
> Lo, the blest Spirit mov'd, and there was Light.
> For in the glorious General's previous Ray,
>   We saw a new created Day.
> We by it saw, though yet in Mists it shone,
> The beauteous Work of Order moving on. (Ggg2)

The Restoration, Cowley insists, was apocalypse averted. He had feared utter destruction, but he saw instead a second Creation: Stuart order out of the chaos of the Interregnum.[7] As the Puritans had predicted, God

---

7. Jose discusses the Royalists' portrayal of the Commonwealth as "The State Chaos" and the Restoration as Creation in the second chapter of *Ideas of the Restoration*.

has visited England. But he comes bearing a golden scepter, not a rod of iron; God has come to England not to annihilate but to re-create out of chaos—to establish again his Work of Order upon the earth. The shaken nation, brought "into a wild and deform'd chaos," seemed to be hasting "Even to the last of Ills, Annihilation." The intervention of God (or, more immediately, Charles II) halted what had seemed to be an inexorable movement toward entropy. The "hurly-burlies" of the civil wars and Commonwealth were not, as it turns out, England's death throes, but a fever now broken.

Throughout the Royalist political poetry of the 1660s, the fires of judgment give place to the bonfires celebrating the beginning of a new Golden Age. According to John Crouch, the prophets' predictions that London should go up in flames have come true—not because God has rained down fires of judgment, but because Charles's subjects have lit the sky with the celebratory bonfires that the Puritans had banned.

> Such flames in to the aire proud Bonfires sent,
> Threatned to change the Cognate Element.
> Event, by truth, false Prophets do beguile,
> London was (and yet stands) one burning pile:
> Now sooty Pyramids of smoak aspire,
> The whole city on Elemental fire.[8]

William Pestell offers a very similar treatment of Charles's bonfires:

> The Bonefires gild each Hill, to whose bright shine,
> The Moon grew pale and did her beames resign.
> Quakers grew lunatick, to see such Fire,
> And thought the World should now in flames expire.[9]

The language of apocalypse had quite literally been made a joke by the Royalists in the Restoration.[10] England's radicals, always on the lookout for portents of doom, were themselves portrayed as a kind of portent—a gross aberration of the natural order. The Rump Parliament, declares one poet, is a monstrous creature surely portending some evil:

8. John Crouch, *A mixt poem partly historical, partly panegyricall* (1660), C1.
9. William Pestell, *A Congratulation to His Sacred Majestie* (1661), A3.
10. We do not, of course, have to wait for the Restoration to see the Royalists poking fun at the Puritans' apocalyptic tendencies. *The Rump*, a 1661 collection of Royalist ballads and songs written during the civil wars and Commonwealth, contains a number of pieces mocking the Puritans in the language of apocalypse, including "The Mad Zealot," Q7; "A New-Years Gift for the Rump," Bb6; and "Saint George and the Dragon," Mm8.

> Come well-vers'd Augurs and Astrologers,
> That by Beasts Entrails and the rolling Spheares
> Do seek for new Portents, run here and see
> A strange, fatall, and monstrous prodigie:
> For now 'gainst Nature, O sad Destiny,
> All is hurled most preposterously;
> The World is turned upside down, the Head now
> Is become Tail, the Tail to Head doth grow.[11]

But portents, as Royalist poets were well aware, are usually short-lived. A comet or meteor (or, for that matter, a two-headed calf) may point toward some future event, but seldom does it survive to see its own legitimation or discredit. The Restoration, according to the Royalists, restored natural order, vanquishing not only the prodigies of the Interregnum, but also the fears they had occasioned. "But now those Meteors which we feared and felt / Are by a Northern Star to vapours melt."[12] The doomsday stars that had lowered over England in the 1640s and 1650s cannot remain in the same sky with Charles's steadfast star.

Rarely did the Royalist poets of the Restoration forgo an opportunity to ridicule those who had fought to establish the rule of the saints in England. Claiming to be the scourges and ministers of God, the agents of Providence, the Puritans were hardly to be refuted so long as they enjoyed military success and civil authority. Their rhetoric, while they maintained power, was self-ratifying. But the return of Charles, the final collapse of the Puritan hegemony, and the world's stubborn refusal to come to an end seemed to be an undeniable rebuttal of the Puritans' version of apocalyptic mythology. Abraham Cowley challenges his Puritan opponents to explain the failure of their apocalyptic schemes:

> Where are those men who bragg'd that God did bless,
>   And with the marks of good success
> Signe his allowance of their wickedness?
> Vaine men! Who thought the Divine Power to find
> In the fierce Thunder and the violent Wind
>
> . . . .
> The cruel business of Destruction,
> May by the Claws of the great Fiend be done.
> Here, here we see th' Almighty's hand indeed,
> Both by the Beauty of the Work, we see't, and by the Speed.
>   ("Restoration Ode," Ggg2)

11. J. G. B., "On the Tribe of Fortune, the Rump of the Long Parliament," in *Royall Poems Presented to His Sacred Majesty Charles the II* (1660), A4.

12. Anon., *Vox Populi* (1660), B2v.

The Royalists are as eager as the Puritans had been to show that God reveals his will in the events of human history. But God's work in history, Cowley insists, is not to destroy; that is the role of the Fiend. God's work is to establish peace and order out of warfare and chaos. It is also to bring low the haughty, as he has done in the overthrow of the Puritans.

Throughout the Restoration odes of the 1660s, the poets turn the Puritans' own rhetoric against them. The king's radical enemies, suggests John Crouch, know very little of reason or good sense. But they do claim to know a great deal about Providence, and God by his Providence has displayed his favor toward Charles:

> O ye Phanaticks! Whose hot brimstone zeal
> Produced Confusion for a Common-weal;
> [Be] Convinc'd, if not by Reason, Sight, nor Sence,
> Yet by your great Diana Providence.[13]

Edmund Elys taunts the King's enemies who had claimed to read the will of God in the overthrow of the monarchy. The Restoration has set things aright, and God has at last shown his hand: "See, Rebels, see the Hand of God." Elys continues,

> O, that They, who did Boast their Cause to be
> Most Just, because 'twas Prosperous, would See
> What God has Wrought for Him, whom They'd Withstand.[14]

To those who had boasted that their cause was just because it was prosperous, the Royalist poets respond with their own not altogether satisfying boast that *their* cause is just because it has proven prosperous: "Thus straight when God will Have't, the Thing is Done."[15] In the end, the Royalist poets are no more circumspect than the Puritan propagandists of the

13. John Crouch, *To his Sacred Majesty*, (1660), B2v. Crouch suggests that Providence, like Diana of the Ephesians, is the object of mob worship; see Acts 19:28. In *Eikonoklastes* Milton speaks of Charles I's "old Ephesian goddess, called the Church of England," in *John Milton: Complete Poems and Major Prose*, ed. Merritt Y. Hughes (New York: Odyssey Press, 1957), 801.

14. Edmund Elys, *Anglia Rediviva* (1660), A3v–4. On the subject of Royalist configurations of Providence in the latter half of the seventeenth century, see McKeon, *Politics and Poetry*, 161; Jose, *Ideas of the Restoration*, 60–67; Derek Hughes, "Providential Justice and English Comedy, 1660–1700: A Review of the External Evidence," *Modern Language Review* 81 (1986): 273–92; Gerard Reedy, "Mystical Politics," in *Studies in Change and Revolution*, ed. Paul J. Korshin (Menston: Scolar Press, 1972); and Harold Weaver, *Paper Bullets* (Lexington: University Press of Kentucky, 1996), 30–32.

15. Elys, *Anglia Rediviva*, A4v.

civil wars and Interregnum in claiming to be the darlings of Providence—though, of course, they appeal to a gentler manifestation of Providence. John Crouch speaks apparently without irony when he remarks that the reappearance of Charles's meridian star, portending a new age of peace and prosperity, "needs no Interpreter!"[16] If the events of 1642–1660 teach anything about Providence, it would seem, they teach that no historical event, no portent, possesses self-evident meaning. Nothing "needs no Interpreter."

When the anonymous poet of *England's Ioy for London's Loyalty* (1664) looks forward to a long Golden Age for London, he defines that future as the absence of apocalyptic fear:

> Still may she grow more Good, more Wise, more Great,
> More Rich, more Strong, till every way compleat:
> Still may she bide secure, by Heavens Defence,
> From Sword, from Famine, and from Pestilence.
> No fire consume her buildings, nor (what's worse)
> Rebellion, Schism, Faction, prove her Curse.[17]

By heaven's defense, hopes the poet, London will remain secure from the apocalyptic destruction that had loomed before 1660: from fire and from the same three Horsemen that had caused Cowley such alarm in his "Ode Upon His Majesties Restauration and Return"—Sword, Famine, and Pestilence. But even more threatening than this destruction are the schism, faction, and rebellion that had brought it on. After the fanaticism and turmoil of the 1640s and 1650s, the poet prays for tranquillity:

> But as she grows more Populous, may Peace
> And Concord, still within her Walls increase:
> Her Citizens here bless'd, till shall remove
> To New Jerusalem, and dwell Above.[18]

The positing of the New Jerusalem "above" is rhetorically significant. In seeking to establish the New Jerusalem *below,* seventeenth-century rebels and schismatics had threatened England's very existence. The author of *England's Ioy* places the New Jerusalem not ahead in time, but above, outside of time. Good Londoners "remove" to New Jerusalem as a reward

16. John Crouch, *To His Sacred Majesty* (1660), B2v.
17. Anon., *England's Ioy for London's Loyalty* (1664), broadside.
18. Ibid.

for living peaceably—as a reward for not fighting to bring the New Jerusalem to earth.

In John Dryden's poetry, as in *England's Ioy*, God's Englishmen need not bother marching to Zion—not because they cannot attain it, but because, as of 1660, they have already arrived. Too shrewd to dismiss the power of apocalyptic language, Dryden appropriated the radicals' favorite rhetorical mode, declaring Restoration England to be the fulfillment of their millenarian prophecies. The most complete and the most famous refiguration of the fires of judgment is *Annus Mirabilis* (1667), in which Dryden discusses the dire calamities of 1666: the costly war with the Dutch, the Great Fire of London, and (in passing, at least) an outbreak of the plague. Edward N. Hooker explores the rhetorical context of Dryden's poem and argues convincingly that *Annus Mirabilis* responds directly to the numerous apocalyptic pamphlets that had interpreted the catastrophes of this wondrous year as the judgment of God upon a wicked monarchy. Because it contained the number of the Beast, the year 1666 had long been the focus of eschatological speculation and anxiety. It is not surprising, then, that radicals seized on the disasters of that year as evidence of God's wrath against the people of Restoration England. In 1667 Thomas Dolittle, for example, speaks of the Plague and the Great Fire of London as manifestations of "God's Burning Anger": "God hath (after your long and great Prosperity) of late begun his Controversie with you, partly in spiritual Judgements, partly in Temporall, among these, eminently in the Judgement of the Plague, whereby he brought the top of your houses into your lowest Cellars, and turned them into ashes."[19]

Dryden engages the apocalyptic-prophetic enthusiasts in their own arena, not downplaying but emphasizing the magnitude of London's calamities. But he offers a new way of understanding these catastrophes, which have clearly not destroyed London. In the dedication of *Annus Mirabilis*, Dryden assures the people of London that these disasters are not punishments, but trials—"occasions for the manifesting of your Christian and Civil virtues."[20] The Royalist poet's response to the king's political

---

19. Edward N. Hooker, "The Purpose of Dryden's *Annus Mirabilis*," in *Essential Articles for the Study of John Dryden*, ed. H. T. Swedenberg (Hamden, Conn.: Archon Books, 1966), 281–99; see also McKeon, *Politics and Poetry*. Thomas Dolittle, *Rebukes for Sin By God's Burning Anger by the Burning of London by the Burning of the Wicked in Hell Fire* (1667), A4 (quoted in Laura Lunger Knoppers, *Historicizing Milton: Spectacle, Power, and Poetry in Restoration England*, [Athens: University of Georgia Press, 1994], 142).

20. "To the Metropolis of Great Britain," letter dedicatory to *Annus Mirabilis*, in *The Works of John Dryden*, ed. Edward Niles Hooker and H. T. Swedenberg Jr., 20 vols. (Berkeley and Los Angeles: University of California Press, 1956), 1:48.

enemies is a refutation of their whole mythology. The fires that destroyed much of London are not the annihilating fires of an angry God, he suggests; they are the renewing, purifying fires from which the Phoenix springs.

Dryden, like so many of his political opponents, styles himself a prophet, but he prophesies of new beginnings, not universal endings. War, "a consuming pestilence," and fires of destruction do not betoken an approaching end in Dryden's prefatory letter; they mark a new start:

> You who were a wonder of all Years and Ages, and who have built your selves an immortal Monument on your own ruines. You are now a Phoenix in her ashes. . . . I am therefore to conclude, that your sufferings are at an end, and that one part of my poem has not been more an history of your destruction, then the other a Prophecy of your restoration. (1:49)

Calamities, though dire, are never final. Dryden's poem reminds us that even apocalyptic destruction is not final. Rather, it clears the way for a new Heaven and a new Earth. The world "at the death of time / Must fall and rise a nobler frame by fire" (ll. 847–48); and so must London. By the end of *Annus Mirabilis,* London has become a type of the New Jerusalem:

> Methinks already from this Chymick flame,
> I see a City of more precious mold . . .
>
> . . . .
> More great than Humane now, and more August,
> New deifi'd she from her fires does rise:
> Her widening streets on new foundations trust,
> And, opening, into larger parts she flies.
> (ll. 1169–70, 1177–80)

Dryden's poetry moves the New Jerusalem from heaven to earth, and from a time beyond time to the present. Whereas the Puritans had emphasized the imminence of judgment, Dryden emphasizes the rest of the apocalyptic story, the promise of the Millennium, placing his England on the other side of cataclysm.

In *Astraea Redux* (1660), Dryden had portrayed England as having survived another cataclysm—Puritan rule—and emerging refined, a vision of millennial peace and prosperity. Charles II, who "was forced to suffer for himself and us" (l. 50), becomes a type of Christ in this poem; the return of the monarch, like the return of Christ, redeems a disintegrating world and ushers in a type of the New Jerusalem. Dryden's rhetoric is not merely blasphemous flattery (though it is certainly that) but an integral part of a whole millenarian mythology that is argued with some care. The creation, according to the apostle Paul, waits in eager expectation for Christ's return, when it will no longer be subject to the futility and corruption of its temporal existence: "For the earnest expectation of the creature waiteth for the manifestation of the sons of God. For the creature was made subject to vanity, not willingly, but by reason of him who hath subjected the same in hope. For we know that the whole creation groaneth and travaileth in pain together until now" (Romans 8:19–22). Likewise, in the absence of its sovereign, England groaned under the weight of its subjection to vanity and corruption. Under the rule of radicals and enthusiasts, England longed for the monarch's second coming. "For his long absence Church and State did groan; / Madness the pulpit, faction seized the Throne" (ll. 21–22). The corruption and the cataclysm the Puritans had warned of turn out, ironically, to have been Puritan rule. But England has survived and now enjoys the blessings of those who overcome.

> And now Time's whiter series has begun,
> Which in soft Centuries shall smoothly run;
>
> . . . .
>
> Oh Happy Age! O times like those alone,
> By Fate reserv'd for great Augustus throne!
> When the joint growth of Arms and Arts foreshew
> The World a Monarch, and that Monarch You.
> (ll. 291–92, 320–23)

Dryden's millennial vision is distinctly classical; the millennium that the triumphant Charles-Christ establishes is a recapitulation of Rome's Augustan age. Dryden presents a classical politics of reason and balance as an answer to the politics of enthusiasm. Legitimate monarchical power disciplines and reorders the chaotic excesses of a failed republic. No longer torn apart by faction, the nation grows into an empire, nurturing both arms and arts.

As Steven Zwicker writes, "under the pressure of civil war, defeat, and exile, the most urgent business for aesthetics as well as for political theory and philosophy was the restoration of the state."[21] For the Royalists, the political Restoration was also a literary and artistic restoration. The Stuarts had always considered art to be vital to the maintenance of power; art was once again marshaled in the Stuart cause after the Restoration. The return of civil order under the monarchy made possible the return of court culture and its affiliated arts, which the Puritans had discouraged or outlawed. The Puritans' rhetoric in the middle decades of the century valued action—warfare against the Dragon—not books and poetry and all

21. Steven Zwicker, *Lines of Authority: Politics and English Literary Culture, 1649–1689* (Ithaca: Cornell University Press, 1993), 25.

the other "inglorious arts of peace." In the war-torn world of the "Horatian Ode," Marvell's "forward youth"

> Must now forsake his Muses dear,
> Nor in the shadows sing,
> His numbers languishing:
> 'Tis time to leave the books in dust,
> And oil th' unused armor's rust,
> Removing from the wall
> The corslet from the hall. (ll. 2–8)

But the return of monarchy makes possible the rebirth of English letters. The return of the banished muses became a favorite trope in the celebratory poetry of the 1660s: "No more shall hapless learning lye, / The Arts and Muses shall be raised high."[22] In William Fairbrother's poem "To the Right Honorable to the Lord General Monck," the general simultaneously saves both religion and the arts from Puritan fanatics:

> But timely you stept in; Religion sav'd;
> And countenanc'd Arts, which we in vain had crav'd.
> Sword and Pen kindly meet: Thou'st giv'n thy Troth,
> That Pallas now's again Goddess to both.[23]

With the resurrection of the "Caroline circle of peace," the pen enjoys equal status with the sword. Wisdom now rules them both.

In his *Essay of Dramatic Poesy*, John Dryden also makes explicit the connection between the Restoration of the monarchy and the restoration of the muses: "And though the fury of a civil war, and power for twenty years together abandoned to a barbarous race of men, enemies of all good learning, had buried the muses under the ruins of monarchy; yet, with the resurrection of our happiness, we see revived poesy lifting up its head, and already shaking off the rubbish which lay so heavy on it." Dryden's remarks suggest why the Restoration was England's first great age of literary criticism. The cultural disintegration of the Interregnum had left English letters a shambles; to rescue "revived poesy," to put it back in order, would be an act of patriotism. The Royalists' aesthetic commitment to neoclassical principles of order, balance, and discipline was bound up with their project of disciplining and reordering a chaotic social and political order under the restored monarchy. In the *Essay*, Dryden's Crites

22. Samuel Holland, *A Panegyrick on the Coronation of His Most Sacred Majesty Charles II* (1660), A3.

23. In William Fairbrother, *Essay of a Loyal Brest* (1660), A4.

remarks facetiously "that it concern'd the peace and quiet of all honest people, that ill poets should be as well silenc'd as seditious Preachers."[24] Indeed, the rhetoric of a nascent Augustanism required that all inspired frenzy, in both religion and poetry, submit itself to the dictates of reason and proportion for the sake of civil order. The reformation of the arts was not peripheral to the project of repairing the ruins left by the political and social iconoclasm of the 1640s and 1650s. The critical treatises of the later seventeenth century hammered out a neoclassical poetics that ultimately encompassed all of British culture, not merely the plays and poems to which they were often attached as prefaces. The cool reason and strict order of neoclassicism serve as an answer to the chaotic rhetoric of a world turned upside down.

Writing at the end of the seventeenth century, Dryden reflects on the state of the English stage. He suggests that English drama, having been restored and redefined in the 1660s, has survived an apocalypse of sorts. Restoration dramatists are separated from their rough-and-ready forebears by an event no less cataclysmic than Noah's flood:

> Well, then, the promis'd hour is come at last;
> The present age of wit obscures the past.
> Strong were our sires, and as they fought the writ,
> Conq'ring with force of arms and dint of wit;
> Theirs was the Giant race before the Flood;
> And thus, when Charles returned, our Empire stood.
> Like Janus, he the stubborn soil manur'd,
> With rules of Husbandry the Rankness cur'd:
> Tam'd us to Manners, when the Stage was rude,
> And boistrous English Wit with Art indu'd.[25]

Dryden's optimism places him and his contemporaries in a new and better age—a golden age of literary refinement after the almost apocalyptic disintegration that marked the 1640s and 1650s. The stage, and all of English culture, was rough, rude, and boisterous before the Restoration, but the reestablishment of the monarchy made real civility possible in "the present age of wit." The return of the old rules—the rule of the Stuarts, the rules of neoclassicism—is both a corrective to the radicals' version of apocalypse and the very basis of a new millennial vision of British culture.

---

24. In *Works of Dryden,* ed. Hooker and Swedenberg, 17:63, 10.
25. "To My Dear Friend, Mr. Congreve," in ibid., 4:432.

M. L. Donnelly

"Ostentation Vain of Fleshly Arm"

Milton's Revaluation of
the Heroic Celebration
of Military Virtue

Though a quarrel in the streets is a thing to be hated, the energies displayed in it are fine; the commonest Man shows a grace in his quarrel—By a superior being our reasoning[s] may take the same tone—though erroneous they may be fine—This is the very thing in which consists poetry; and if so it is not so fine a thing as philosophy—For the same reason that an eagle is not so fine a thing as a truth—

—John Keats, *Letter No. 159*

Some modern critics, like Michael Wilding, E. R. Gregory, and James A. Freeman, have found in Milton's greatest works not merely criticism of certain kinds of epic-heroic posturing and romantic idealization of chivalry, but a bitter and thoroughgoing pacifism. Robert Fallon has suggested that such readings are less historically likely or inevitably entailed by Milton's words than they are the result of the pervasive hatred of most twentieth-century intellectuals for warfare and martial display of any sort. Fallon's arguments in *Captain or Colonel* convincingly call a pacificist Milton into question. But Fallon goes far in the opposite direction to imply Milton's unqualifiedly enthusiastic endorsement of the New Model Army and Cromwell's imperial designs.[1] Such a position seems equally difficult to square, not only with particular passages, but with the general tendency of the later works. It is,

1. See Michael Wilding, *Milton's "Paradise Lost"* (Sydney: Sydney University Press, 1969) and "The Last of the Epics: The Rejection of the Heroic in *Paradise Lost* and *Hudibras*," in *Restoration Literature: Critical Approaches*, ed. Harold Love (London: Methuen, 1972), 91–120; E. R. Gregory, " 'Lift not thy spear against the Muses bowre': Essay in Historical Explication," *Milton Quarterly* 11 (December 1977): 112–13; James A.

after all, difficult to read certain famous passages in *Paradise Lost, Paradise Regained,* and *Samson Agonistes* without readily seeing how the idea of a pacifist Milton *could* arise. Stella Revard's anatomy of Milton's exposure of "Satan as Epic Hero" and her representation of the true definition of "The Son of God and the Strife of Glory" in *The War in Heaven* convincingly rebut the conception of a militarist Milton.[2] While Fallon's refutation of a pacificist bard seems largely persuasive, Revard has nevertheless shown how Milton's tropes of traditional military glory merely figure values that transcend their tropological vehicles, and even ultimately deconstruct them. To sort out this hotly contested issue, it may prove useful to examine the chronology of Milton's expressed attitudes toward military virtue.

Such a survey suggests that Milton jettisoned a youthful enthusiasm for the epic tradition's glorification of the heroic man-at-arms at a particular historical moment. The timing of that revaluation strongly argues that it came as a result of his reflections on the course of events in his country during and immediately after the first civil war. The optimism and enthusiasm of Hebraic and Virgilian national aspiration that had glowed white-hot in *Areopagitica* had already cooled by 1648 as he reflected upon his country's early history of energetic battles and failed counsels.

Freeman, *Milton and the Martial Muse: "Paradise Lost" and European Traditions of War* (Princeton: Princeton University Press, 1980); and Robert Fallon, *Captain or Colonel: The Soldier in Milton's Life and Art* (Columbia: University of Missouri Press, 1984). On Fallon's side of the argument, see also the earlier article by Jackie Di Salvo, " 'The Lord's Battels': *Samson Agonistes* and the Puritan Revolution," in *Milton Studies IV,* ed. James D. Simmonds (Pittsburgh: University of Pittsburgh Press, 1972), 39–62, which presents Milton's Samson as both modeled on and intended as inspiration for the soldiers of the New Model Army. Neither Di Salvo nor Fallon, however, goes so far in depicting a hawkish Milton as G. Wilson Knight, who, in *Chariot of Wrath* (London: Faber and Faber, 1942), refers to "Milton's habitual fascination with the military and the mechanical" in speaking of the "Chariot of paternal deity" in book 6 as "at once a super-tank and a super-bomber" (158)!

2. For the oft-quoted rejections of purely military solutions, see *Paradise Lost* 6.695–96, 9.27–43; *Paradise Regained* 3.387–402; and the whole episode of Harapha in *Samson,* presenting in the Philistine giant a parodic deprecation of conventional epic military swagger and chivalric codes (see especially ll. 1065–256 and the Chorus's celebration of the righteous hero who "all thir Ammunition / And feats of War defeats / With plain Heroic magnitude of mind / And celestial vigour arm'd," ll. 1268–69). (All quotations from Milton's poems are by book, where appropriate, and line numbers, and will be taken from Merritt Y. Hughes, ed., *John Milton: Complete Poems and Major Prose* [New York: Odyssey Press, 1957], unless otherwise stated.) For a thorough and convincing survey of the tradition and interpretation of the central episode of the war in heaven, see chapters 6 and 7 of Revard, *The War in Heaven: "Paradise Lost" and the Tradition of Satan's Rebellion* (Ithaca: Cornell University Press, 1980), especially Revard's demonstration that to read the Son's triumphal return to the Father (262) as merely replicating a Roman triumph is to read it with Satanic limitation of vision.

Milton at forty was a considerably chastened man compared to the eager idealist of thirty or thirty-five. By the end of his fourth decade he could no longer embrace an epic celebration of the calling of a particular nation, bringing reformation and Christian liberty to the world in the role of God's Chosen People. Nevertheless, in the following years his wholehearted involvement in the Protectorate government prevented his lapsing into the ivory-tower luxury of pacifism. However remote he may have been from actual participation in the formulation of policy, he saw that in a fallen world, force must sometimes be answered with force, and military arts and readiness are necessary tools of policy. But he also arrived at a firm conviction that tools must always be assessed in terms of the ends they serve, and higher virtues than military prudence, discipline, and courage must direct them. Knowing well the danger of their perversion in the service of a glamorous and self-glorifying *kleos* or *kudos*, the mature poet coldly evaluates the military arts and the soldier's virtues as mere instrumentalities.

There is a natural human fascination with violence. Passersby will stop to watch a dogfight, and there are large profits to be made from "action flicks" and professional football. That fascination in its various levels is gloriously embodied and fed by the epic tradition in Western literature. In Homer, Virgil, Lucan, and Statius, the subject sung is "arms and the man"; in sagas like the *Song of Roland* and *Beowulf,* the spearman/swordsman is no less than Achilles a hero of *biou*, of force. In the romance transformations of the classic tradition, though perhaps somewhat softened and elevated by the refinements of the chivalric code in Boiardo, Ariosto, Tasso, and Spenser, the central roles designed to "fashion a gentleman or noble person in vertuous and gentle discipline"[3] are still occupied by the man-at-arms:

> For as the image of each action stirreth and instructeth the mind, so the lofty image of such worthies most inflameth the mind with desire to be worthy, and informs with counsel how to be worthy. Only let Aeneas be worn in the tablet of your memory . . . and I think, in a mind not prejudiced with a prejudicating humour, he will be found in excellency fruitful, yea, even as Horace saith, *melius Chrysippo et Crantore.*[4]

The youthful Milton seems eager to follow in the well-worn path. Even in the Nativity Ode, the babe in the manger is also a "dreaded Infant"

---

3. Edmund Spenser, *A Letter of the Authors expounding his whole intention in the course of this worke [The Faerie Queene] . . . To the Right noble, and Valorous, Sir Walter Raleigh knight . . .* , in *The Poetical Works of Edmund Spenser*, ed. J. C. Smith and E. de Selincourt (London: Oxford University Press, 1912, 1963), 407.

4. Sir Philip Sidney, *An Apology for Poetry*, ed. Geoffrey Shepherd (London: Thomas Nelson and Sons, 1965), 119–20.

who Hercules-like can "in his swaddling bands control the damned crew." Louis Martz has suggested that the 1645 volume in which that poem first appears was self-consciously constructed as a traditional pastoral opening move in a Virgilian poetic career.[5] Nevertheless, numerous poems both Latin and English intruding upon the pastoral and pacific tenor of the 1645 *Poems* bear witness in their language and imagery how attractive were the traditional subjects of the heroic poem to the aspiring young poet. Adopting in a light-hearted way in a letter to Diodati the classical opposition between the "high" heroic poet of wars, who celebrates the doings of gods and great men, and the soft elegiac poet of love and pleasure, Milton strongly hints at his personal identification with the former role. He practices mobilizing the military trappings of the traditional heroic poem with obvious excitement; he enthusiastically anticipates incorporating as well the stage props of later chivalric romance. In both *L'Allegro* and *Il Penseroso* he affectionately evokes the subjects and embellishments of romantic, heroic chivalry. In *Ad Patrem*, he alludes to the distinguished early history of courtly song ("*Carmina regales epulas ornare solebant, | . . . | Heroumque actus imitandaque gesta canebat,*" ll. 41–46), but more directly, in *Manso* and *Epitaphium Damonis*, he declares quite explicitly his ambition of someday singing heroic lays on legendary British subjects like those of "our sage and serious Spenser."[6]

However, both his direct avowals and his representations of military displays and warfare in his major poems make it clear that by the time, "long choosing and beginning late," he finally came to the selection of his actual subjects and to the composition of his epics and tragic dramatic poem, he had changed his mind, conceiving his ideal hero as very different from Achilles, or Odysseus, or Aeneas. Indeed, he at last conceived his heroic poem as virtually an anti-epic. The shift is too radical to be traceable

5. Martz, "The Rising Poet, 1645," in *The Lyric and Dramatic Milton: Selected Papers from the English Institute,* ed. Joseph H. Summers (New York: Columbia University Press, 1965), 3–33; elaborated in Martz, *Milton, Poet of Exile* (New Haven: Yale University Press, 1980), chapter 2.

6. Although the subject of *In Quintum Novembris* does not afford the youthful poet the opportunity to deploy armies in the open field, his language appropriates the stirring and violent language of military display and combat at every opportunity. In *Elegia Quarta* he goes out of his way to mobilize frightening and resonant images of warfare from the epic thesaurus in alluding to the German wars that threaten Thomas Young in Hamburg. In his *Elegia Sexta* he also seemingly alludes guardedly to his "*dona . . . Christi natalibus*" as an earnest of production on the order of the higher kind he contrasts to "*Elegia levis.*" See *Elegia Sexta,* especially ll. 49–90. For chivalric embellishments, see, for example, *L'Allegro,* ll. 117–30; and *Il Penseroso,* ll. 109–20. On the noble history of courtly song, see *Ad Patrem,* ll. 41–46; on the aspiration to sing a British heroic subject, *Manso,* ll. 78–84; and *Epitaphium Damonis,* ll. 162–78.

to a single, simple cause. But a fundamental reassessment of the place and value of military virtues and the profession of arms must have been a major factor in determining the nature of the crowning works of Milton's poetic career, and that revaluation can be localized between 1644 and 1648.

In the extraordinary covenantings with the "intelligent and equal auditor" or "elegant & learned reader" of *The Reason of Church Government* (probably finished by January 1, 1642), Milton was still meditating the traditional matter of inspired and inspirational heroic song. He had now certainly determined upon the glorification of a British subject, and was only irresolute still "what king or knight, before the conquest, might be chosen in whom to lay the pattern of a Christian hero." In his defence of himself in *An Apology for Smectymnuus* (1642), he recounts with self-approbation the ethical instruction he delightedly received in his youth from "those lofty Fables and Romances, which recount in solemne canto's the deeds of Knighthood founded by our victorious Kings; & from hence had in renowne over all Christendome."[7]

On the face of it, in undertaking a heroic poem, a bourgeois poet embraces an alien class tradition, putting himself in a line of descent from chivalric warrior aristocracies, or at least from their client-celebrators. In Milton's contemplation of a chivalric and heroic subject, it was about this time, in the early spring of 1642, that he begins to realize that the ethos he was embracing could not be entirely his without adjustment. But he does not yet discard; he adapts. In the *Apology* he qualifies his earlier uncritical admiration of the code of a feudal military aristocracy by modifying it in a meritocratic direction, explicitly opening the characteristic chivalric virtues to all who aspire and rightly endeavor: "Only this my minde gave me that every free and gentle spirit without that oath ought to be borne a Knight, nor needed to expect the guilt spurre, or the laying of a sword upon his shoulder to stirre him up both by his counsell, and his arme to secure and protect the weaknesse of any attempted chastity" (*CPW*, 1:891). Perhaps he had already reflected on the tendency of the church and court party to denigrate their opponents as uneducated tradesmen and lowborn churls, without generosity, intelligence, or social graces—precisely the sort of character from which he attempted to distance himself throughout his career.

In his treatise "Of Education," published about June 4 or 5, 1644, Milton incorporates a more sober but still positive valuation of the military

---

7. *Complete Prose Works of John Milton*, gen. ed. Don M. Wolfe, 8 vols. (New Haven: Yale University Press, 1953–1982), 1:807, 813–14 (hereafter cited in text as *CPW*); *CPW*, 1:890–91.

function, including in his program for producing future citizen-leaders the usual English civic humanist attention to military science and exercises (*CPW,* 2:377–81, 392–93, 407–14). But in anticipating what sort of commanders his proposed course of education would produce, Milton engages in invidious comparisons that are clearly pointed at the recent failures of leadership on both sides in the civil war. His students, he avers, would "come forth renowned and perfect Commanders in the service of their country."

> They would not then, if they were trusted with fair and hopefull armies, suffer them for want of just and wise discipline to shed away from about them like sick feathers, though they be never so oft suppli'd: they would not suffer their empty & unrecrutible Colonells of twenty men in a company, to quaffe out, or convay into secret hoards, the wages of a delusive list, and a miserable remnant: yet in the mean while to be overmaster'd with a score or two of drunkards, the only souldiery left about them, or else to comply with all rapines and violences. No certainly, if they knew ought of that knowledge that belongs to good men or good governours, they would not suffer these things. (*CPW,* 2:412)

S. R. Gardiner long ago pointed out the patent allusions here to the generalship of the Parliament's Essex, in particular: "The constant diminution of his army through 1643 from sickness and desertion was a constant subject of complaint, and there was information given to Parliament in the end of that year of companies with only twenty men in them near London amongst those serving under Essex" (cited in *CPW,* 2:412 n. 28).

Before 1644, then, Milton's conception and representation of heroic virtue had seemed in most respects an idealizing, classical, and civic humanist conception readily amenable to modification in the direction of Arthurian-Spenserian chivalry: an image that romanticizes martial prowess and virtuous warfare. But already in the wake of the year and more of fighting on English ground that had taken place by June 1644, another, quite different, and thoroughly discreditable image of the military leader has begun to take shape in Milton's mind.

Aside from the insignificant military actions of the *"sitzkrieg"* that was the Bishops' War, the first civil war (1642–1645) was Englishmen's first domestic experience of warfare in generations, and their first close-up view of modern war. It must have been a profoundly unsettling initiation. What Milton would have read and heard of contemporary events and what he might have gleaned from putative conversation with acquaintances who served with the trained bands during the first civil war would scarcely square with his idealized humanist image of armed heroic virtue, or the representations of "solemn cantos [of] the deeds of knighthood." Large numbers of men on both sides in the civil war were impressed into service, and so distinctly unenthusiastic in their cause that desertion—that "shedding away like sick feathers" scornfully observed by Milton—and even the threat of mutiny was a constant problem for most commanders. Cromwell commented that the Essex men impressed into his army were "so mutinous, that I may justly fear they would cut my throat." Similarly, Captain Robert Clarke reported on July 14, 1644, that "Prince Rupert marches up and down . . . but can raise noe force. . . . The Countrey people tell him that he shall rather cutt theire throates at home than carry them abroad to be slaine, as their Countrey men have beene. . . ."[8] In October 1643, Newcastle's Royalist army of the North was "filled with impressed conscripts" and so lacking in discipline and morale that "perhaps as much as half" deserted to return home, so that Newcastle had to abandon the siege of Hull.[9] Clarendon describes "Wentworth's wretched [Royalist] horse, whom 'only their friends feared, and their enemies laughed at; being only terrible in plunder and resolute in running away.'" The Cornish trained bands who were supposed to serve beside them deserted to their homes in order to protect their own hearths and dear ones from their supposed allies.[10]

Meanwhile, the populace groaned under the imposition of taxation exacted especially severely by Parliament in areas under their control— war taxes more burdensome and extralegal than the ship money and other royal expedients that had helped precipitate the war. There was widespread public feeling (in which Milton himself participated) that much of the money thus raised disappeared into the private pockets of corrupt officials and grafting suppliers; certainly little enough found its way to the armies. Speaking of "Sequestrators and Subcommittees abroad," Milton calls them "Men for the most part of insatiable hands, and noted Disloyalty" and refers to friend and foe alike being subject to "the Ravening Seizure of innumerable Thieves in Office," so that "after infinite Sums received, and all the Wealth of the Church not better imploy'd, but

8. On Milton's possible acquaintances and contacts among the London Trained Bands or the Honorable Artillery Company, see Fallon, *Captain or Colonel*, 55–57. Cromwell's remarks cited in Clive Holmes, *The Eastern Association in the English Civil War* (Cambridge: Cambridge University Press, 1974), 170; Capt. Robert Clarke in *Transactions of the Royal Historical Society* 12 (1898): 76–79. For a modern treatment, see J. S. Morrill, "Mutiny and Discontent in English Provincial Armies, 1645–1647," *Past and Present* 56 (August 1972): 49–74.

9. Philip J. Haythornthwaite, *The English Civil War, 1642–1651* (Poole, Dorset: Blandford Press, 1983), 74.

10. Edward Hyde, Earl of Clarendon, *The History of the Rebellion and Civil Wars in England* (Oxford: University Press, 1849) 4:142; book 9, p. 135 of original edition, cited in Haythornthwaite, *English Civil War*, 112.

swallowed up into a private *Gulph*," nevertheless "that Faith which ought to have been kept as Sacred and Inviolable as any thing holy, *The Public Faith*, . . . was not ere long ashamed to confess Bankrupt" (*CPW*, 5:444). In areas of military activity, or where local or regional troops were gathered, the costs of billetting and free quarter were an added burden to civilians. J. S. Morrill thinks that on the basis of the example of Buckinghamshire, "over the county as a whole, the cost of quarter would exceed the amount levied in taxation."[11] Such fiscal, logistic, and organizational realities associated with raising and maintaining even a seventeenth-century army are rarely contemplated in Plutarchan or romantic literary treatments of armed contests, but they would be impossible for an intelligent man with financial interests, like Milton, to ignore. Money and organization were essential but notably unglamorous elements of contemporary military experience.

Once assembled by exactions from the citizenry and promises of payment, the ill-disciplined, resentful, and unpaid soldiery typically added to the sufferings of civilians among whom they passed by engaging in "the systematic looting and desertion endemic to seventeenth-century warfare and widespread throughout the early years of the war," according to Morrill. Pillage was nearly universal, because payment owed the troops, sometimes "up to or more than half the total owing to them since their enlistment," was always in arrears on both sides. Haythornthwaite notes that Waller's men were among the most notoriously abandoned to looting and pillage.[12] In a list that he cautions is "not exhaustive," Morrill summarizes the widespread prevalence of "organized patterns of unrest":

> There is evidence of systematic plundering for thirty counties, of refusal to obey orders until grievances had been redressed for eighteen counties, threats of mass disbandment for ten, and the seizure of officials or officers for fourteen.

11. Morrill, "Mutiny and Discontent," 52. See Milton's further comments in the manuscript "Digression" from the *History of Britain*, and its published version, *Mr John Miltons Character of the Long Parliament and Assembly of Divines In MDCXLI*, in *CPW*, 5:442–51. And compare sentiments voiced in *The Remonstrance of the Commons of England, To the House of Commons Assembled in Parliament. Preferred to them by the hands of the Speaker*. Printed Anno Dom. 1643, Item 37 in Bodleian Godwin Pamphlets 1115. Royalist propaganda was quick to capitalize upon such resentments; see, for example, *Ad Populum, or, A Lecture to the People*. Printed in the Yeare 1644, ibid., item 45.

12. Morrill, "Mutiny and Discontent," 53, 50; Haythornthwaite, *English Civil War*, 103. See also John Eric Adair, *Roundhead General: A Military Biography of Sir William Waller* (London: Macdonald, 1969). "An Order from both Houses of Parliament for regulating of the Army," attached to *Mr. Grimston his Learned Speech . . . concerning Troubles abroad, and Grievances at home* (London, 1642), is an official recognition of the problems, blaming them mostly on lack of discipline and control by the officers.

Thirty-six of the forty English counties were involved, and for twenty-eight of them there is evidence of two or more of these forms of protest. The whole of north-east and parts of south Wales were also affected.[13]

Worse, there were notable instances of atrocities on both sides, which were played up breathlessly in contemporary pamphlets. Pamphlet representations of distinctly unchivalrous actions by knights and cavaliers and men at arms on both sides and accounts of soldiers as helpless victims of outrages performed by their enemies would have been equally corrosive of the glamorous literary ideas of chivalry and military glory the poet had accumulated in his wide course of reading before the war. Milton would surely have been moved by reports reaching London of the disaster that befell Essex's Parliamentary army of six thousand men after their capture at Lostwithiel, September 2, 1644. The defeated and disarmed Parliamentary troops were set upon by the locals as they marched to sanctuary at Portsmouth or Southampton, and Clarendon claimed that not a third reached safety.[14]

Problems from desertion and pillage to outrages and atrocities are often simply reflections of a lack of discipline appalling to modern judgment. Such unit cohesion as there was operated as often as not as an obstacle to larger strategic deployment. Despite the popular modern conception of an ideological war of Puritan against Cavalier, many troops in the war, especially near the beginning and before the New Modelling of the Parliamentary army, felt little or no commitment to war aims (usually ill-defined, anyway) or a cause and operated only on a basis of local interests or personal loyalty to their officers. To cite but one instance, in February 1645, Waller's foot, previously under Essex's command, refused to cooperate with their new commander's orders when he tried to employ them to re-take Weymouth, and only agreed to march when Cromwell joined them.[15]

Uncertain discipline, jealousies among leaders, and tentativeness in command led to repeated failures on both sides. A typical pattern is that

13. Morrill, "Mutiny and Discontent," 63.
14. Haythornthwaite, *English Civil War*, 95–96. Two notable examples of atrocities, both of which involve that model cavalier, Prince Rupert, are *A True and Perfect Relation Of the Barbarous and Cruell Passages of the Kings Army, At Old Brainceford* . . . (London, 1642); and *An exact relation of the bloody and barbarous Massacre at Bolton in the Moors in Lancashire, May 28, by Prince Rupert: being penned by an eyewitness* . . . (London, August 22, 1644). London presses under the control of Parliament were not, of course, quick to advertise atrocities committed by Parliamentary forces, though royalist propagandists made up the lack, and modern historians provide an evenhanded accounting of wretched instances on both sides. The disaster of Essex's army provides the climactic instance in Barbara Donagan's "Codes and Conduct in the English Civil War," *Past and Present* 118 (February 1988): 65–95.
15. Haythornthwaite, *English Civil War*, 105.

of a brilliant strategic victory (or astonishing piece of luck) that is not followed up through a lack of self-control, discipline, or commitment in the troops or their officers. According to Haythornthwaite, Essex was not able to follow up his victory at First Newbury because the members of his London regiments, the central bulwark of his army, "returned to their shops and businesses," so that, though he had won the field, he was unable even to prevent the capture of Reading in the fall of 1643. Similarly, after Hopton and the Earl of Forth's Royalist horse had been disastrously chewed up trying to deploy piecemeal down a narrow lane commanded by Waller's Parliamentary forces at Cheriton (March 28–29, 1644), "Waller was unable to press home the advantage as he might have wished as the London brigade, having completed the task they had agreed to undertake, went home." Yet another failure to follow up for Parliament occurred at the Second Battle of Newbury (October 27, 1644). Both sides thought themselves beaten after the engagement was broken off, but the king's forces succeeded in slipping away to Oxford, and the Parliamentary army was so disorganized and its command so fragmented that it was unable even to take Donnington Castle, let alone prevent the king's escape. "Combined with the disaster of Lostwithiel, this battle proved that Parliament needed a totally reorganized army and, perhaps, more determined leaders," says Haythornthwaite.[16] On the other side, Prince Rupert's troops displayed again and again a Hotspur-like hell-bent enthusiasm that threw aside all restraint and judgment, fighting as individuals rather than members of a unit. At Marston Moor, this kind of lack of discipline turned Lord Goring's rout of the Parliamentary right into a crushing Royalist defeat, when Goring's hot pursuit deprived the beleaguered Royalist center and right wing of crucial cavalry support.

Rumors and reports from the front detailing these kinds of incidents were quickly circulated in pamphlets and newsletters, and their sensationalized facts, claims, and blames would have been readily available to Milton in London. As a Londoner and a sympathizer with the Independents, he would also have followed in the same media with keen interest and concern the political maneuverings between the Rump and the army, as the Presbyterians in London and Parliament tried by demobilization, reassignment to Ireland, and the breakup and reorganization of units to defuse the threat they saw from restive and unpaid soldiers in general, but particularly from Independency in the New Model.[17]

16. Ibid., 73, 77, 97.
17. On reports Milton would have seen, see, in addition to publications cited in this article, Donagan's notes to her article on "Codes and Conduct" for an extensive

On the strictly military side, the lost victories and advantages not followed up doubtless bothered Milton more than the reports of inadequacies and "criminous behavior" of the common soldiery in the wars. He was frustrated by the lack of vigor shown by Parliament's commanders in prosecuting to its logical conclusion an uncompromising and relentless policy (Manchester's famous quote comes quickly to mind: "If we beat the King ninety and nine times, yet he is king still, and so will his posterity be after him; but if the King beat us once we shall all be hanged, and our posterity made slaves").[18] Factional interference with timely and adequate support of the Parliament's armies showed that military success could never be wholly divorced from politics and statesmanship.

These disquieting evidences from the public world were paralleled by unpleasant developments in Milton's private affairs at this time. He experienced firsthand the graft, corruption, and abuse of bureaucratic power by Parliamentary sequestrators and commissions when he intervened in the activities of the committees on sequestrations on behalf of his in-laws and his own loans. Meanwhile, he was receiving unexpected and unwelcome attention from censorious bureaucrats in his own right as a purveyor of scandalous and socially subversive ideas in his divorce tracts.[19] The same leaders who were mismanaging the war were also attempting to stifle his intellectual campaigns on behalf of Christian liberty.

The combination of experiences, as William Riley Parker asserts in his biography of the poet, must have been profoundly disillusioning for him. Even in his most idealistic youth, he had never really hoped for that much from hoi polloi. It was the failures of nerve, the backslidings, and the narrow self-interest and corruption of the elite few, his country's representatives and leaders, that deeply disturbed him. Parker, in introducing his chapter on the period 1645–1648, observes that although controversies over issues to which he had been committed continued to rage, and nothing was settled, "the man who had printed eleven separate tracts within the feverish space of four years sat back now as a spectator."

---

sampling of representative titles. On the uneasy peace following the first civil war, consult Mark A. Kishlansky, *The Rise of the New Model Army* (Cambridge: Cambridge University Press, 1979).

18. "Criminous behavior" is a favorite phrase of J. R. Hale's for the typical conduct of troopers in early modern armies in *War and Society in Renaissance Europe, 1450–1620* (Leicester: Leicester University Press and Fontana Paperbacks, 1985). Manchester's statement reported by Sir Arthur Hazelrig, quoted in S. R. Gardiner, *History of the Great Civil War, 1642–1649*, 4 vols., (1893; reprint, New York: AMS Press, 1965), 2:59.

19. On his efforts on behalf of the Powells, see William Riley Parker, *Milton: A Biography*, 2 vols. (Oxford: Clarendon Press, 1967), chapter 9, especially 1:307ff. (on Milton's troubles with the authorities over his writings, see 1:259ff).

Parker characterizes this withdrawal from public effort as a reaction to "an ungrateful country": "he had tried being a good citizen and, thoroughly disillusioned by his several attempts at reform, he returned to the contemplative life."[20] If the brief remarks in the second strophe of the "Ode to Rouse" might seem formal or perfunctory,[21] the sentiments in the letter of April 20, 1647, to Carlo Dati are unmistakably heartfelt in their rueful characterization of the "evils" he experiences in "the extremely turbulent state of our Britain." "Do you think there can be any safe retreat for literary leisure among so many civil battles, so much slaughter, flight, and pillaging of goods?" (*CPW*, 2:764).

As the famous "Digression" from *The History of Britain* particularly reveals, by 1648, informed by the sobering reflections induced by his nation's *recent* history, Milton read his country's past with a more critical eye. Parker, calling Milton's view of the national character at this point "cynical and disillusioned," asserts that it was "unquestionably influenced by the confusion of his own times and the general atmosphere of pessimism in 1648."[22] One prominent aspect of that disillusionment for Milton was an increasingly settled conviction that military skills and heroic qualities of courage and enterprise were inferior gifts that could not by themselves secure any great and permanent good for mankind. This conviction crops up again and again incidentally in Milton's later writings and correspondence. In the *History of Britain*, the fervent if ambivalent patriotism intensified by his experience in Italy still colors his recognition of "the native and the naked *British valour*" and "down right manhood" of his ancestors (*CPW*, 5.i.66); but he severely qualifies his praise of their courage, love of freedom, and manliness with stern condemnations of their inability to live and exercise rule with justice and prudence (*CPW*, 5.i.131, 441–51). That is, Milton acknowledges valor and manhood, soldierly virtues, as meriting praise in themselves, but ruefully notes their ineffectiveness in achieving lasting good. This judgment provides a leitmotiv scattered throughout the *History*, and is not limited to the Digression. Later, on September 21, 1656, he was to write warning his former pupil Richard Jones, future third viscount and first earl of Ranelagh,

20. Parker, *Milton: A Biography*, 1:290.
21. "*Modo quis deus, aut editus deo . . . Tollat nefandos civium tumultus, | Almaque revocet studia sanctus | Et relegatas sine sede Musas | Iam paene totis finibus Angligenum*"—"What god or what god-begotten man . . . will sweep away these accursed tumults among the citizens? What deity will summon our fostering studies home and recall the Muses who have been left with hardly a retreat anywhere in all the confines of England" (ll. 25, 29–32). But *nefandos* is a very strong word applied to civil tumults.
22. Parker, *Milton: A Biography*, 1:327.

The victories of princes, which you praise, and similar matters in which force prevails I would not have you admire too much, now that you are listening to Philosophers. For what is so remarkable if strong horns spring forth in the land of mutton-heads [usually translated "wethers"] which can powerfully butt down cities and towns? Learn now, from early youth, to consider and recognize great examples, not on the basis of force and strength, but of justice and moderation. (*CPW*, 7:493)[23]

To Mylius, apologizing for delays and misunderstandings over the Oldenburg safeguard, Milton dismissed the abilities of most members of the Council of State: "They were mechanics, *soldiers*, servants, strong and keen enough, but entirely ignorant of public political matters." And "Among the forty persons who were the Council of State, there were not over three or four who had been outside England, but among them were plenty of the sons of Mercury and of Mars."[24] It is interesting that Milton now links the sons of Mars, wasters of blood, with the sons of Mercury, husbanders of money, coupling soldiers with those shopkeepers he seems to have come to despise as much as Yeats did. To Milton's way of thinking, soldiers and shopkeepers are alike in that neither knows the true value of anything.

Most tellingly, the three sonnets written in the 1650s imitating Tasso's *sonetti eroici* all carefully qualify their praise of martial virtue with explicit notices of its scope and limitations. Two of these sonnets are addressed to the Parliamentary generals Fairfax and Cromwell, and the third to Sir Henry Vane the younger, a member of the Council of State who was actively interested in naval affairs. Each poem either recognizes explicitly the higher utility and glory of achievements in the arts of peace, or directs a successful warrior to crown his achievements now with *civic* bays. Most interesting in this respect is the sonnet to Vane, which eschews evocation of martial glory altogether, and extolls instead that other half of the Homeric heroic ethos, counsel: Vane's "sage counsell" makes him a better senator than any who "held / The helme of *Rome*, when gownes *not armes* repelld / The fierce *Epeirot* and the *African* bold." Milton's final, highest praise of Vane is that he knows the boundaries of both spiritual and civil power:

> what each meanes
> And severs each thou'hast learnt, which few have don.
> The bounds of either sword to thee wee ow.
> Therfore on thy firme hand religion leanes
> In peace, and reck'ns thee her eldest son.

23. See also *The Life Records of John Milton*, ed. Joseph Milton French, 5 vols. (New Brunswick, N.J.: Rutgers University Press, 1949–58), 4:114–15.

24. Mylius reporting an interview with Milton, February 9, 1652; *Life Records*, ed. French, 3:162–63, translation 164, emphasis mine.

Finally, in the rousing and passionate sonnet "On the Late Massacre in Piemont," despite a tide of emotion that carries through the fourteen lines in one great climactic rush, the vengeance called for is not presented as being the military retaliation we might expect, but rather, enlightenment, and a flight from popish error to truth.[25]

Milton's experiences of modern warfare and the political maneuverings that accompany the pursuit of policy by other means were secondhand in the English civil wars, mediated by the broadsides, pamphlets, and newsletters that proliferated at the time. However, these experiences came at a time in his life when he was in various ways brought up against harsh realities challenging his long-cherished idealism. It is a measure of his capabilities for growth as a man that he did not simply retreat as a result of these experiences, but used them to redefine positively his deepest aspirations and, indeed, his own sense of who he was and what he valued. Part of this adjustment was the recognition of his distance from the military and chivalric values that were the badges of the outmoded aristocracy— recognition, indeed, of how anachronistic those values were for his time, place, and countrymen in anything like the traditional forms that had celebrated them and handed them on. His often bitter or frustrating enlightenment made the uncomplicated appropriation of conventional chivalric/heroic postures for poetry nearly beyond imagining, despite the pride he still evinces in his *Defensio secunda* in having once worn a sword at his side, with which he had been in constant practice in order to be ready to defend his honor (*CPW*, 4.i.583).

Besides the inappropriateness of chivalric glorification of personal, individualized exploits, knightly *gentilesse,* honor, and achievements of arms in the face of the kind of early modern warfare being waged in the mid-seventeenth century, there was the fact that what was foregrounded in Milton's lived experience in the 1640s was *civil* strife, in which he had friends and relatives on both sides. Both these factors correspond to elements noted by Michael Murrin as contributing in the later sixteenth century to the development in Europe generally outside the Iberian peninsula of an "epic without war."[26] But most important, the war on English ground that Milton experienced through the newsletters, pamphlets, and broadsides that narrated its every incident to an anxious public was a war in which he was passionately committed to an extreme and minority posi-

25. E. A. J. Honigmann, ed., *Milton's Sonnets* (London: Macmillan, 1966), sonnets 15–18; notes pp. 138–68.

26. Michael Murrin, *History and Warfare in Renaissance Epic* (Chicago: University of Chicago Press, 1994), especially 231–45.

tion, whose ultimate triumph was effectively blocked by factional power plays, intellectual weakness, moral cowardice, indecision, selfishness, and greed, even when physical courage and firmness had amazingly won the field of battle.

At least in part, our ideas are a function not merely of our intellect but of our *lived* experience. Just as the ideas that we make our own can be clarified and confirmed for us in experience, so the myths that we come to see through can more forcefully be unmasked through personal and public histories that we live, than through reading other people's books. Milton's rejection of the heroic celebration of warfare was not the result of his private meditation on the ambivalences embedded in the representations of earlier epic verse. He did not come from lonely reflection to an enlightened realization of what scripture and his Christian faith implied about the weight and significance of worldly power and fleshly arms, though it might seem that, despite the weight of literary and cultural tradition, that should have been obvious to him all along, had he thought it through. But neither did he reject the epic tradition of military glory *merely* because gunpowder and the massed tactics of early modern warfare were unsuitable for commemoration in the traditional heroic tropes: other poets in the century or two before Milton wrote made the attempt to adapt the heroic poem to the realities of modern war, and even to colonial, guerrilla combat.[27] If it might seem that the enemy's co-optation of the chivalric values that had once inspired him cut that ground from beneath his feet, it has recently been shown that the supposed Royalist monopoly of chivalric trappings and values was anything but complete and uncontested.[28] From every point of view in evaluating his attitudes toward military heroism and chivalry, Milton had a range of choice, which he exercised free of any kind of cultural or partisan determinism. He still had available as a heroic subject the marvelously successful New Model Army, which had never lost a battle, and combined the finest and most up-to-date military discipline and organization with unimpeachable credentials of Protestant Independency. But Milton did not choose to overgo Lucan in a historical epic of contemporary intestine struggle.[29] At the time of the first civil war,

27. See Murrin, *History and Warfare.*
28. See J. S. A. Adamson, "Chivalry and Political Culture in Caroline England," in *Culture and Politics in Early Stuart England,* ed. Kevin Sharpe and Peter Lake (London: Macmillan, 1994), 161–97, and especially 185–93 on Parliamentarian attempts to appropriate the imagery of Elizabethan chivalry for the earl of Essex and Sir Thomas Fairfax in 1642–1646.
29. That is, Milton did not choose to rival Lucan as his model in any of the obvious ways: he chose for his central action a legendary plot remote in time, not a recent, historical one; his narrative does not *overtly* insist on the primacy of a *political* moral;

1642–1645, and in the uneasy hiatus that followed, he had witnessed the mismanagement, the moral and intellectual blunders, and the self-serving maneuvers of the chief factions of the victorious side—what he would at first have thought *his* side—nearly turn victory on the field into defeat. It was a chastening experience that changed his thinking in radical ways. His complicity in Cromwell's rule and his rationalization of the dominance of the army can only be justified by some rueful compromises of principles he had idealistically championed earlier. To Milton in the 1650s, preventing the return of the ancien régime of hereditary monarchical tyranny and meddling episcopal oppression while assuring liberty of conscience seemed ends that demanded the sacrifice, at least temporarily, of means he had fervently espoused before—republicanism and the individual's own absolute freedom and responsibility in moral choice. Surely altering his conception of "that which justly gives heroic name / To person or to poem" (*Paradise Lost* 9.40–41) would have been a less wrenching adjustment than that ultimately fruitless sacrifice to political realities had been.

The process of revisionary response to the matter of heroic poetry was completed by his employment after March 13, 1649, as spokesman for public men who viewed modern warfare as an instrument of state policy. Milton was, then, schooled first in the inability of raw courage and military virtue, guided by no higher discernment, to achieve anything of lasting value, and later by the example of the intelligent *Realpolitik* of the Protectorate, an attitude no less corrosive to chivalric idealism than the previous sorry spectacle of human weaknesses had been. When finally he was able to return to his long-deferred ambition of leaving something to posterity that it would not willingly let die, his experience of his country's recent history had moved him decisively beyond the possibility of constructing his heroic poem on anything like the ground plan of his predecessors' epics or romances. Conviction of the priority of inward, spiritual discipline, of wisdom and goodness, and the recognition of the ultimate inefficacy of force also made impossible for him the kind of historically grounded adaptation of the heroic mode that marked an interesting early modern development, particularly among Spanish writers in the New World.[30] In the end, instead of moving the epic tradition toward the historically

---

and his style through most of his poem is closer to the Virgilian artful grandiloquence than to Lucan's strange mixture of flat reportage and grotesquely shocking rhetorical effects. However, recent studies have for various reasons attempted to highlight Milton's affinities for Lucan: two instances are Charles Martindale, in *John Milton and the Transformation of Ancient Epic* (London: Croom Helm, 1986); and David Quint, *Epic and Empire: Politics and Generic Form from Virgil to Milton* (Princeton: Princeton University Press, 1993), chapters 6 and 7.

30. See Michael Murrin, *History and Warfare*, especially parts 3 and 4.

grounded as a result of his witness of *res gestae* in the civil wars, Milton moved to ground his poetry in, for lack of a better word, philosophy—a higher moral truth.

In the realm of history, what superior martial virtue had won on the field of battle was thrown away in 1660 under the direction of Monck's army, and without a fight; but those earlier armed victories had already been devalued in Milton's eyes by the moral and intellectual failures of the mass of his countrymen, who in the interim had shown how little they understood how to use what soldierly virtue had won. To borrow our terms from the letter of John Keats used as an epigraph to this essay, what his lived experience in the civil wars had taught Milton led him away from the poetic glorification of the fine but erroneous energies expressed in the self-assertion of a quarrel, and toward the finer truth appreciated by the superior being. The eagles of erring poetic energy soar primarily in the musterings and flourishes of Satan's legions in *Paradise Lost*, in passages like book 1, lines 522–612, that suggest a shooting script for Leni Riefenstahl's *Triumph des Willens*—"the ostentation of the damned," as Douglas Bush used to say. The loyal angels, like their predecessors in the "Nativity Ode" nearly forty years before, serve in military harness, ranks, and hierarchies, but while they are given opportunity to display their *pietas* and *firmitas*, the poet sternly limits Achillean displays of a personal, traditionally heroic *aristeia* on their part. When Abdiel bests Satan in single combat in *Paradise Lost* 6.99–202, for example, he explicitly reasons with himself as he sallies forth that it is only

> just,
> That he who in debate of Truth hath won,
> Should win in Arms, in both disputes alike
> Victor; though brutish that contest and foul,
> When Reason hath to deal with force, yet so
> Most reason is that Reason overcome. (6.121–26)

But Abdiel's victory in the single combat effects no final solution to the "perverse Commotion" (6.706) that roils Heaven; the conclusive conquest is God's work alone. Milton judges the acts and attitudes of military heroes severely in the poem, both implicitly, in the ways they are placed poetically, and explicitly, as in the catechizing Adam receives from Michael in the last books. Nevertheless, so great is the glamor of the old heroic role, the attraction of those energies of the quarrel in the streets, that many readers, and not just Romantics, have been seduced by the meretricious appeal of drums and trumpets to entertain the idea of Satan as hero of the poem.

Milton's final judgment as a result of his considered reflection on his countrymen's wars is more perfectly and chastely realized, more "finely" drawn, in the demanding pair of poems that were the last major works he published. The demilitarized heroism of the Son in *Paradise Regained,* achieved by rejecting the arms of Parthia and the glamorous power and grandeur of Rome, displays an "exercise" purely mental and moral in his duel in the wilderness. In *Samson Agonistes,* Milton deliberately sets up the possibility of a ludicrous parody of chivalric combat with the Philistine *miles gloriosus,* Harapha, only to deny his hero the satisfaction. Instead, he grants his Hebrew strongman as his greatest victory an unorthodox, unmilitary heroism, the moral reintegration of will and commitment based on unflinching self-knowledge that is anatomized in the dialogue and action of the play. This moral and psychological action lays the necessary foundation validating that violent triumph over his enemies that takes place, almost an anticlimax, off-stage. It is only the mental and moral *agon* that is directly presented to the reader/audience for contemplation in the dialogue and "action" of the play. In these strong, uncompromising works of the end of his career, Milton demonstrates more perfectly even than in his great epic his hard-won revaluation of instrumentalities and ends, and his difficult achievement of that severe discipline and exigent judgment in matters military and heroic that sees and approves that "an eagle"—or even a phoenix—"is not so fine a thing as a truth."

I **Diane Purkiss**

Dismembering and Remembering

The English Civil War
and Male Identity

I The battle of Edgehill, the first major battle of the English civil war, was fought in the bitter cold of October 1642. By the Christmas season of that year, this first battle was being remembered and reenacted in a new and strange manner. The London diary of John Greene reports that "there are now divers reports of strange sights seen, and strange noyses heard at Edgehill where our last battle was fought; in the place wher the Kings army stood terrible outcries; wher the Parliaments [stood] music and singing."[1] A pamphlet recorded that

> portentious apparitions of two jarring and contrary armies where the battell was strucken, were seen at Edge Hill, where are still many unburied karkassess, at between twelve and one of the clock in the morning. . . . These infernal souldiers appeared on Christmas night, and again on two Saturdays after, bearing the kings and Parliaments colours. Pell mell to it they went, where the corporeall armies had shed so much blood, the clathering of armes, noyse of cannons, cries of souldiers, sounds of petronels, and the alarum was struck up, creating great terrour and amazement.[2]

A ghost comes to avenge a wrong, to point out a miscarriage of justice, to make demands for itself. The pamphlet explains the phenomenon in

---

1. "The Diary of John Greene, 1635–59," ed. E. M. Symonds, *English Historical Review* 43 (1928): 391.
2. Cited in *Memoirs of the Verney Family During the Civil War,* ed. Frances Verney, 2 vols. (London: Longmans, 1892), 2:124. Other sources for this story and for other battlefield ghosts of the civil war include C. H. Cooper, *Annals of Cambridge* (Cambridge: Warwick, 1904), 2:303; *A great wonder in heaven showing the late apparitions and prodigious noyses of war and battels* (London, 1643); *Signes from heaven* (London: T. Forest, 1646), cxxxviii. Ghosts are briefly discussed in Christopher Durston, "Signs and Wonders and the English Civil War," *History Today* 37 (1987): 22–28. For the First World War parallel, Angels at Mons, see Paul Fussell, *The Great War and Modern Memory* (Oxford: Oxford University Press, 1975), 115–16.

relation to the still-unburied corpses of Edgehill. Ghosts signify the dead who have been denied, ignored, slighted; a ghost is the advocate of the silent corpses, buried without rites, not given their due. The civil war dead were often disfigured, unrecognizable, and therefore buried hastily, in unmarked graves, without the rites of communal mourning.[3] Even the higher gentry and nobility were tumbled into hasty graves, or could not be found at all; at Edgehill, Sir Edmund Verney, the king's standard-bearer, vanished, though his death was presumed when a party came across the royal standard, the staff still held in his severed hand. The Edgehill ghosts are also literary; they connect the English civil war with classical texts in which ghosts haunt the battlefield, from the ghost of Patroclus at Troy and Caesar at Philippi, to Lucan's *Pharsalia*, where the battlefield is ravaged by scavenging hags intent on carrying off body parts, a trope repeated when warring armies appeared again after Naseby.[4]

What does the appearance of these ghosts tell us about the way early modern society saw battle and mutilation and death? These dead remain powerful, haunting locale and memory, insisting on the continuing presence of the fallen, just as the cries of the wounded and consciousness of the unseen dead dominated the thoughts of both armies on the night after Edgehill. These thoughts would not be banished any more than the ghosts. The aftermath of this first major battle of the war confronted both armies not with the spectacle of their prowess, but with their helplessness, a characteristic experience in early modern warfare. The exhausted armies sat silently about the field, listening to the groans of wounded and dying comrades, unable to help or find friends in the darkness. Edmund Ludlow, a Parliamentarian, described the unnaturalness of that night:

> The night after the battle our army quartered on the same ground that the enemy fought on the day before. Nor men nor horse got any meat that night, and I had touched none since the Saturday before, neither could I find my servant who had my cloak, so that having nothing to keep me warm but a suit of iron, I was obliged to walk about all night, which proved very cold by reason of a sharp frost . . . when I got meat I could scarcely eat it my jaws for want of use having almost lost their natural faculty.[5]

Ludlow cannot eat; he cannot sleep; he cannot keep warm; he cannot separate himself from the enemy. This loss of the domestic comforts and quotidian abilities represent not just hardship, against which Ludlow can

---

3. On the usual processes of mourning, see Clare Gittings, *Death, Burial, and the Individual in Early Modern England* (London: Routledge, 1988).

4. On the *Pharsalia* and the civil war, see Nigel Smith, *Literature and Revolution in England, 1640–1660* (New Haven: Yale University Press, 1994), 204–7.

5. Edmund Ludlow, *Memoirs* (Oxford: Clarendon, 1894), 31.

and does steel himself as a proper soldier should, but also a frightening breakdown of order and knowledge. For the wounded, the experience was even more unsettling. William Harvey told John Aubrey the story of Sir Adrian Scrope, "dangerously wounded and left for dead amongst the dead men, stripped, which happened to be the saving of his life. It was cold, clear weather, and a frost that night, which staunched his bleeding, and about midnight, or some hours after his hurt, he awaked, and was fain to draw a dead body upon him for warmth's sake."[6] Scrope's condition precludes his reaching the safety of his friends. In order to survive, he denies the social and cultural boundaries rigidly separating the living and the dead. Ignoring the carefully prescribed rules for how a dead body may be seen, touched, moved, he treats it as a cloak, an inanimate possession. For Harvey, this is resourceful, but also shocking; what sanctions the act is that Scrope himself seems to be outside society at that moment. His act is forced upon him by the loss of living social supports: he had to succor himself with the dead because the living neglect both him and the adjacent corpse.

In this context, it is not surprising that the wounded themselves were prominent among the apparitions: "about Edge-hill and Keinton, there are men seene walking with one legge, and but one arme, and the like, passing to and fro in the night."[7] These ghosts signify those neglected, abandoned on the frosty field by the exhausted armies. The one-legged apparitions also signify the absence of the spectacle of the wounded from accounts of the battle. For although accounts of civil war battles mention the dead by name, frequently accompanied by short eulogies, most are far less outspoken about the wounded, the mutilated, and the spectacle of dead bodies. What these battle ghosts signify is that aspect of battle itself that is and must be repressed and silenced in traditional, sanctioned, authoritative accounts. Without memorial *as* the wounded, the battle ghosts invent their own memorials, or rather the newsbooks

6. John Aubrey, cited in John Adair, *By the Sword Divided: Eyewitnesses of the English Civil War* (London: Century Hutchinson, 1983), 55.

7. *Speciall Passages And Certain Informations* 24 (January 17–24, 1643). Amputations were common in the civil war: see John Woodall's *The Surgeons Mate, or military and domestique surgery* (reprinted by R. Young for Nicholas Bourne in 1639); and John Steer's 1643 translation of *Fabricius Hildamus his Experiments in Chyrurgerie concerning Combustion or Burnings, made with Gunpowder*. See also H. A. L. Howell, "The Story of the Army Surgeon and the Care of the Sick and Wounded in the Great Civil War," *Journal of the Royal Army Medical Corps* 3 (1904): 430; W. B. Richardson, "Richard Wiseman and the Surgery of the Commonwealth" *The Asclepiad* 3 (1889): 231–55. I am grateful to David Harley for discussing these points with me. Early modern culture believed that those who had died by violence were especially likely to be ghosts.

do it for them. Mutilation is also loss of self, loss of image and propriety, and loss of ownership and control over appearance and the body. The ghosts of the maimed dead collectively signify the dislocation of the laboriously established social, military, and gender identity at the very moment when it is called upon to display itself. All battlefields, and all textual accounts of them, are haunted by the chaos, dissolution of boundaries, filth, loss of sight, loss of control, and loss of self, which the soldier must always strive to repel both physically and psychically. These aspects of war constantly return, like the Edgehill ghosts, to haunt the military identities from which they are banished, and it is the purpose of this essay to summon up the maimed dead and the shaken survivors from their graves, graves unmarked by eager reenactments and other "heritage industry" re-presentations.

And yet the "realistic" narratives that I have just been citing are more ontologically problematic than they themselves wish to admit, and more like the ghosts of Edgehill than historians would like to admit. One can call spirits from the vasty deep, but what if only a textual shred replies? Accounts of battles are generally taken from soldiers' letters, or from the memoirs of soldiers (often written in retrospect), or from newsbooks purporting to be reports from the front to those at home. All three genres have in common a will to conjure up a series of events and persons absent from the destination of the narrative, whether that destination is imagined as posterity or as the civilian families and friends of the soldiers involved. These are attempts to reanimate lost scenes. As such they call attention to the way in which those scenes cannot in absence be grasped unmediated by discourse, by cliché, by the blurring hands of time and ideology. In this sense, our usual apprehension that the past is beyond our grasp because its pastness has reduced it to a series of textual traces is a lament early modern people might also have voiced about the very same texts. As textualized pieces of the past, they too reanimate the dead, giving spectral life to those whose voices have long been silenced. And just as Charles's observers scanned the Edgehill apparitions for familiar faces, so readers of letters, newsbooks, and memoirs hunted through the names and places for those that were familiar, loved, and temporarily or permanently lost. In this sense, the ghost story is one of the master narratives of war, and we should not be surprised to see it haunting other wars, other narratives.[8]

8. For instance, in Abel Gance's film *J'Accuse* (1919), the problem of the war can only be solved by the appearance of the ghosts of the dead; ironically, this sequence was shot by Gance using real soldiers, most of whom died in the 1918 campaigns, so that they were truly the ghosts of the dead by the time the film was released. On

Discourses of war share in the ambiguities of the Edgehill ghosts, so that narratives that most seek truth and objectivity are most unable to deliver it.

War creates a number of anxieties about gender and masculinity. Drill, training, and above all the corporate imperative to stand firm, not to give way or retreat because the greatest slaughter happens in a rout, genders the correctly military and male body as closed, hard, tight, and, paradoxically, at one with the similarly disposed bodies of other men.[9] Yet war also arouses the desire to escape the self, to avoid literal death by the figurative death of flight. The tension between these two powerful impulses shakes assumptions that the masculine self is natural and inevitable, unseating notions of the naturalness of the hard male body. To put this in psychoanalytic terms, war unleashes the death drive in a series of aggressive and repetitious acts that menace the identity of the perpetrator, who can always envisage himself as victim. The death drive, in Freud, is the desire not to be, to dissolve, to disappear, but it is also the desire to thwart the desire. The ego responds to the phenomena of fragmentation and destruction by assuring itself that life can be preserved.[10] Death is always implicated in attempts at pleasure. Whenever the subject constructs a fantasy of wholeness and security gained by an appropriation of the beloved, modeled along the lines of the infant-mother dyad, he also risks a return to a prebirth stasis or inanition, a loss of self—that is, a form of death. The masculinity of the warrior is not a simple or visible construct, but precarious, discontinuous, partaking of the dual aspects of the death drive itself, where the effort to stay alive involves and implicates the subject in fantasies of dissolution. The male identity of the soldier is haunted by what it strives to banish, just as Edgehill is haunted by the mangled dead neglected by the survivors.

The fissures in the ideal of masculinity at war are obvious even to those most eager to see war as a space where masculinity reaches its apotheosis. Among those was John Milton, here as elsewhere a victim of the discontinuity between his sharp psychic longings and his even sharper intelligence. Like the battlefield of Edgehill, Milton's representation of

---

Gance, see Jay Winter, *Sites of Memory, Sites of Mourning: The Great War in European Cultural History* (Cambridge: Cambridge University Press, 1996), 15–18.

9. One of the striking things about the civil war is the different ideologies of masculinity developed around the role of cavalry (a mobile strike force) and infantry (intended to stand firm). These differences are also heavily inflected by class. However, what is being said here applies to both.

10. Sigmund Freud, *Beyond the Pleasure Principle* (1920), in *The Pelican Freud Library*, vol. 11, *On Metapsychology and the Theory of Psychoanalysis*, trans. James Strachey (Harmondsworth: Penguin, 1984): 269–337.

war in *Paradise Lost* and elsewhere is haunted by the specters of the war, by what ideology could not suppress as well as by what it could. Just as the ghosts of Edgehill are not as evidently saturated with ideological investment as the angels of Mons of World War I, so Milton's reinvention of the civil war is not an obvious attempt simply to memorialize it, nor to memorialize it simply. Instead, both the acceptable and the unacceptable faces of battle are on display: the war in heaven struggles to confront the aspects of war usually relegated to the subtext, in part because Milton had the perspicacity to see that those irruptions of violence, anality, atrocity, and irony are intrinsically connected to what the epic tradition usually valorizes. That perspicacity in part derived from careful readings of Homer and Lucan alongside civil war newspapers, but in part it constitutes a response to pressures from within Milton's own masculine identity and its fractures and fragmentations. I want to use certain aspects of the civil war, some of which are transhistorical, less as sources for the war in heaven than as a kind of structural parable to explain the way war and masculinity intersect with but also trouble each other.

Complex discursive currents mingled in defining war as the ultimate site on which masculinity could be asserted and fulfilled. Those who, like Milton, approached war through a humanist education were used to seeing war as a metaphor for various characteristically masculine virtues, not least the virtues pertaining to good citizenship and statesmanship. This notion was expressed most clearly in Machiavelli's notorious dislike of mercenaries (or professional soldiers) as signs of tyranny, and his consequent valorization of the citizen-soldier as the acme of *virtù*: "for of whom should the commonwealth require greater faith than of him who must promise to die for her? In whom should there be more love of peace than in him who may be attacked only in war? In whom should there be more fear of God than in him who, having to submit himself to infinite dangers, has greatest need of him?"[11] Humanist writings also constantly used the metaphor of war to signify political acumen and firmness; the fondness of humanist writers and patrons for hunting manuals kept such metaphors in circulation thanks to Xenophon's equation of hunting with war.[12] Lodovick Lloyd wrote that "hunting is a military exercise,

---

11. *L'Arte della guerra, Opere*, 49; cited by J. G. A. Pocock, *The Machiavellian Moment: Florentine Political Thought and the Atlantic Republican Tradition* (Princeton: Princeton University Press, 1975), 201. See also Hanna F. Pitkin, *Fortune Is a Woman: Gender and Politics in the Thought of Niccolo Machiavelli* (Berkeley and Los Angeles: University of California Press, 1984), 80–100.

12. See Lorna Hutson, *The Usurer's Daughter: Male Friendship and Fictions of Women in Sixteenth-Century England* (London: Routledge, 1994), chapter 3.

which made Sartorius to use hunting, and to travaile the hard rocks of Africa: and that he and his soldiers thereby might better induce labour and payne against the Romanes, hee acquainted them so much with hunting, that they were able to sustain any hardnesse."[13] Even the writers of romances routinely complained of the softness and effeminacy of the court in relation to the hardness and virtue of war: Barnaby Rich, for instance, himself a sword for hire, wrote that "I see now . . . nothying so daungerous to be wounded with the lurying looke of our beloved Mistres: as with the crewell shotte of our hatefull enemie, the one possesst of a pitifull harte, to helpe where she hath hurte: the other with a deadly hate, to kill where thei might save."[14] Rich's rhetoric represents the soldier as masculine, in opposition to the lover, who is wounded by and involved with woman.

Combining with these notions was the godly metaphorization of spiritual struggle as military struggle. John Hale points to the particular role of godly ministers in inverting this metaphor by justifying actual war as spiritual war, a theme prominent in late-sixteenth- and early-seventeenth-century literature influenced by the Leicester faction.[15] Such rhetoric, like Rich's, depended on a conflation of virtue with hardness, aggression, and readiness, and hence with masculinity, and thus also depended on an often covert degradation of the feminine by comparison. And yet these ideologies were always in conflict with the fear that war was not a space of control, but a terrible sign of its loss. Alongside incitements to war from the pulpit came anxious sermons against the terrors of civil unrest; humanists noted the disorders and inversion of the social structure brought about by war. Similarly, a battle was the site of the supreme order of marching ranks, orders obeyed, and armored bodies, but it was also the site where all this order might be violated and turned to disorder. Both the praise of the hardened warrior and the disruption of that identity are apparent in Oliver Cromwell's letter to his brother-in-law on the death of his son:

> Sir, God has taken away your eldest son by a cannon-shot. It brake his leg. We were necessitate to have it cut off, whereof he died.
> Sir, you know my trials this way, but the Lord supported me with this, That the Lord took him into the happiness we all pant after and live for. There is your precious child full of glory, to know not sin or sorrow anymore. He was a gallant young man, exceedingly gracious. God give you His comfort. Before

13. Lodovick Lloyd, *The Practice of Policy* (London: S. Stafford, 1604), 32–33.
14. Barnaby Rich, *A Farewell to Militarie Profession* (London, 1581), ed. Thomas Cranfill (Austin: University of Texas Press, 1959), 3–4.
15. J. R. Hale, "Incitements to Violence? English Divines on the Theme of War, 1578 to 1631," in *Renaissance War Studies* (London: Hambledon, 1983), 487–518.

his death he was as full of comfort that to Frank Russel and myself he could not express it, it was so great above his pain. This he said to us. Indeed, it was admirable.

A little while after he said one thing lay upon his spirit. I asked him what that was? he told me that it was that God had not suffered him to be no more the executioner of His enemies. At his fall, his horse being killed with the bullet . . . I am told he bid them open to the right and left, that he might see the rogues run. Truly he was exceedingly beloved in the army, of all that knew him.[16]

The jerky inarticulacy of this letter is reminiscent of Waller's remark that Cromwell "was cautious of his own words, not putting forth too many lest they should betray his thoughts."[17] Yet its taciturnity is also a sign, of being lost for words, yes, but also of Cromwell's own hardness, his ability to withstand the assault of the spectacle of mutilation and death. Most importantly, this same hardness is attributed to the broken and mutilated body of the dead man; though his leg has been removed, and though he is dying, his one desire is to continue to act as a soldier, to continue to turn his violence outwards toward the enemy. The dichotomy between this desire and the broken body no longer capable of acting on it is intended to be both tragic and affirmatory; the man's violent desires, at least, transcend his flesh, signifying his immortality and acting as his last monument. And yet the desire to go on fighting beyond death is what constitutes— perhaps even what motivates—the uncanny dead of Edgehill. The ghosts are a reproach; they do not confirm the living. Like the one-legged ghost of Edgehill, Cromwell's dead soldier represents both the ideal of military masculinity and its dissolution.

The same ghostliness haunts the apparently prosaic text of Elton's *The Compleat Body of the Art Military*, a drill manual and training handbook published after the civil war. This shows the soldier's body likewise overwhelmed by the tireless will. The body is here utterly subject to the demands placed upon it by orders. Imperative verbs work on the body, rendering it hard, able to withstand attack even as it is utterly possessed by the single longing to be capable of such resistance. The body is utterly dominated by a force outside itself, the force of the order, becoming closed, ruthless.[18] And yet in the preface Elton constantly compares the book itself to the vulnerable body of a baby boy: already called a body, the book is not

16. *The Letters and Speeches of Oliver Cromwell*, with elucidations by Thomas Carlyle, ed. S. C. Lomas with an introduction by C. H. Firth, 3 vols. (London: Methuen, 1904), 1:176–77.

17. Adair, *By the Sword Divided*, 162.

18. See Klaus Theweleit, *Male Fantasies*, vol. 2, *Male Bodies: Psychoanalysing the White Terror*, trans. Chris Turner and Erica Carter (Cambridge: Polity, 1989), 143–52. My thinking throughout is influenced by Theweleit's *Male Fantasies*, vol. 1, *Women, Bodies,*

a soldier's body, but the undisciplined, unhearing body of a baby. Elton calls it his "eldest son and first-born," who has "broken from the wombe of my seven years endeavours," and he urges the dedicatee Fairfax to keep it alive "if your Excellencies goodnesse shall vouchsafe to foster it, and must not die, except your displeasure please to wound it."[19] The last sentence shows how military masculinity and its vulnerability had come to permeate every part of the ideology of masculinity, so that even the old familiar book-as-son trope becomes a sign of the desperate vulnerability always detectable by any musket ball under the hard facade of discipline.

What exacerbated all these tensions in the civil war was the use of cannon, muskets, and gunpowder. Milton was by no means alone in thinking that gunpowder was the product of the devil.[20] As Langer notes, the process of discovering and excavating gunpowder involves a perpetual figuration of a return to and violation of mother earth; as William Clarke writes: "the manner of the generation of minerals, vegetables and animals are as obscure, and hid, as the dark subterraneous mines, the impervious earthly vegetable, and female animal matrix, being the places of their formation. No less obscure is nitre in its birth."[21] Clarke's observations irresistibly recall the mining angels of *Paradise Lost*, who likewise invade the bowels of the earth, tearing open her organs of generation and excretion, in order to disclose the secrets of nature. As both Evelyn Fox Keller and Jonathan Sawday have recently shown, this metaphor was always central to evolving proto-Enlightenment science.[22] The gunpowder plot, too, which preoccupied the young Milton, gave gunpowder magical, diabolical, and popish connotations, as well as connotations of secrecy and darkness. It became associated not just with the secrets of nature,

---

Floods, History, trans. Stephen Conway with Erica Carter and Chris Turner (Cambridge: Polity, 1987).

19. Richard Elton, *The Compleat Body of the Art Military,* 2d ed. (London, 1650), dedicatory epistle to the Lord General Fairfax.

20. François Rabelais, *Pantagruel,* chapter 8. See J. R. Hale, "Gunpowder and the Renaissance: An Essay in the History of Ideas," *Renaissance War Studies* (London: Hambledon, 1983), 389–420.

21. Ullrich Langer, "Gunpowder as Transgressive Invention in Ronsard," in *Literary Theory/Renaissance Texts,* ed. Patricia Parker and David Quint (Baltimore: Johns Hopkins University Press, 1986), 96–114; William Clarke, *The Natural History of Nitre* (London: E. Okes for Nathaniel Brook, 1670), 28.

22. Evelyn Fox Keller, "Baconian Science: A Hermaphroditic Birth," *Philosophical Forum* 11 (1980): 299–308; "Making Gender Visible in the Pursuit of Nature's Secrets," in *Feminist Studies/Critical Studies,* ed. Teresa de Lauretis (London: Macmillan, 1986), 67–77; and *Reflections on Gender and Science* (New Haven: Yale University Press, 1985). Jonathan Sawday, *The Body Emblazoned: Dissection and the Human Body in Renaissance Culture* (London: Routledge, 1995).

but with disorder in the state and hence with supernatural disorder and evil. During the war, it threatened masculinity and its power of self-determination by representing an often quasi-comical and frequently violent loss of control. Literally, gunpowder was still new, and both armies were short of experts. Richard Atkyns's account of an accidental explosion in a powder wagon illustrates its transformative and diabolical energy:

> the Prisoners taken, some of which, were carried upon a Cart wherein was our Ammunition; and (as I heard,) had Match to light their Tobacco. . . . [T]he Ammunition was blown up, and the Prisoners in the cart with it. . . . It made a very great noise, and darkened the Air for a time, and the Hurt men made lamentable Screeches. . . . Thomas Cheldon, from as long a head of flaxen hair as ever I saw, in the twinckling of an eye, his head was like a Black-moor.[23]

The phrase "twinkling of an eye" emphasizes the legerdemain and unexpectedness, and hence the unpreparedness of the troops. Cheldon, who died of his injuries, is quite literally disfigured by the explosion, turned from gentleman-cavalier into blackamoor, hence savage; the explosion strips him of his chosen, manicured identity, replacing it with its antithesis.

Cannon fire and musket balls did dreadful damage to houses and apparently impregnable defences, but also to bodies. The experience we associate with the American Civil War and with World War I, the experience of seeing dismembered bodies torn apart and thrown about by gunfire, was shared by English civil war troops, including the London trained bands who fought at Newbury. The account of Sergeant Henry Foster, a member of the bands, illustrates that gunpowder had in action the power to replicate its origins; masculine order is destroyed and replaced with the dismemberment and chaos that gave birth to niter. Yet Foster also stresses the men's resistance to the spectacle of dismemberment, their steadfastness and hardness in the face of the ordeal:

> The enemie's cannon did play most against the red regiment of trained bands, they did some execution amongst us at the first, and were somewhat dreadful when men's bowels and brains flew in our faces: But blessed bee God that gave us courage, so that we kept our ground, and after a while feared them not; our ordinance did very good execution upon them: for we stood at so near a distance upon a plain field, that we could not lightly misse one another.[24]

The reason Foster's men had to stand close was the cannon smoke, the cannonade and musketeer's initial blow against identity. Arthur Trevor

---

23. Richard Atkyns, *The Vindication of Richard Atkyns esquire* (1669), 33–34. For another explosion, see Henry Foster, *A true and exact relation of the marchings of the two regiments of the trained bands of the city of London* (1643), reprinted in *Bibliotheca Gloucesterinsis*, ed. James Washbourne (Gloucester, 1828), 1:253–71, 270.

24. Foster, *A true and exact relation*, 1:267.

described the disconcerting aspects of this at Marston Moor: "In the fire, smoke and confusion of that day I knew not for my soul whither to incline. . . . The runaways on both sides were so many, so breathless, so speechless, and so full of fears, that I should not have taken them for men." Richard Atkyns wrote that "the Air was so darkned by the smoak of the Powder, that for a quarter of an Hour together (I dare say) there was no light seen, but what the fire of the Volleys of shot gave, and 'twas the greatest storm that ever I saw, in which though I knew not whether to go, nor what to do."[25] Unlike Foster under fire, both Trevor and Atkyns equate being under fire with confusion, and hence with disorder; they are unable to decide which way to go, unable to find their way. This loss of direction is also a loss of identity, for identity involves not only a resolute hardness, a subordination of the body to the will, but also an ability to relate oneself to surroundings. Both men are threatened with dissolving into their chaotic surroundings, as in Trevor's description others have already done.

The stress of maintaining masculine identity in war produced what later generations would call shell shock or war neurosis, and still later ones post-traumatic stress disorder or depression.[26] Thomas Mince, for example, was a shoemaker who had served in Colonel Whaley's regiment and who shot himself suddenly after a trifling dispute about a small sum of money with his mother. His suicide note says nothing about the war, but is full of the theologically saturated imagery of purity and order versus defilement and disorder, applied to the theater of religion rather than the theater of war: "there is not any thing to be found fault with in man, all that is good, but sin and wilfulness; religion is pure and undefiled, and this is my answer, that so I may justify my Lord of glory."[27] Despair among armies was sometimes recognized by contemporary medicine. The Spanish army in the Thirty Years' War suffered from a malady called *el mal de corazon*, a kind of early version of the Great War's appellation, "soldier's heart." The heart malady implied a body that refused to function, its outer hardness betrayed from within. The Spanish understood the malady in interestingly militaristic terms; they also called it *estar roto*, "to be broken."

25. "Arthur Trevor on Marston Moor," in Thomas Carte, *The Ormonde Papers* (Oxford, 1851), 55–58. Atkyns, *The Vindication of Richard Atkyns*, 32.
26. On shell shock, see Eric Leed, *No Man's Land: Combat and Identity in World War I* (Cambridge: Cambridge University Press, 1979), 163–92.
27. *The Troubled Spirited Mans Departing: Or, a wonderful relation of the wilful Murder committed by Thomas Mince, Late of Colonell Whaleys regiment, upon his own person* (London: J. Clowes, 1653).

To be broken is to fail to stand firm, to be made weak by an attacking Other. Paradoxically, the name of this misery reflects the ideology that may have led to it. Later, in the eighteenth century, physicians identified a soldiers' malady called nostalgia, a deep longing for one's own home, one's own country or town, which could affect immigrant civilians too.[28] A craving to return to circumstances known and controlled may have been a response to the intolerable strangeness of war; nostalgia reached epidemic proportions among Napoleon's much-tried army on the retreat from Moscow. If one could no longer stand firm, one had to respond to the threat of dissolution otherwise, by inventing an alternative identity in which matters were more firmly in hand, and the identity of the self at home provided this reassurance.

It was precisely these threats—of dismemberment, dissolution, and hence loss of firmness, resolution, and control—which resulted in violence. The feared Other could only be expelled from the self by a violent rite. This rite could simply be battle, or it could on occasion involve atrocity. Donald Pennington correctly notes the unreliability of atrocity reports; the Belgian-kitten-on-church-door syndrome, or the fabrication of war atrocities for propaganda value, is well known, but sometimes, then as now, the wolf was real. As Pennington reasonably concludes, at least such stories show what constitutes an atrocity.[29] The early modern moral economy of violence saw the execution and punishment of criminals and the punishment of the guilty as entirely legitimate. Beatings in the family, too, were supposed to be responses to specific events, not outbursts of uncontrolled rage. The wish to disguise atrocities as just punishment can be seen in the number of civil war stories of mock hangings to extract information.[30] Both sides made every effort to persuade the world that they too were merely rounding up the usual suspects.[31] Partly as a result,

28. George Rosen, "Nostalgia: A 'Forgotten' Psychological Disorder" *Psychological Medicine* 5 (1975): 340–54.

29. Don Pennington, "The War and the People" in *Reactions to the English Civil War*, ed. John Morrill (London: Macmillan, 1982), 115–36; for general comments on the reluctance of civil war historians to acknowledge the war's atrocities, see Ian Roy, "England Turned Germany: The Aftermath of the Civil War in its European Context," *Transactions of the Royal Historical Society* 28 (1978): 127–44, especially 129.

30. See, for example, *Mercurius Rusticus, or the Countries Complaints of the barbarous out-rages committed by the Sectaries* ([Oxford]: 1646), 97; David Underdown, *Somerset in the Civil War and Interregnum* (Newton Abbot: David and Charles, 1973), 90.

31. On violence, see Susan Amussen, " 'Being Stirred to Much Unquietness': Violence and Domestic Violence in Early Modern England," *Journal of Women's History* 6 (1994): 70–89, and "The Part of a Christian Man: The Cultural Politics of Manhood in Early Modern England," in *Political Culture and Cultural Politics*, ed. Susan Amussen and Mark Kishlansky (Manchester: Manchester University Press, 1995), 213–33. See

atrocity stories multiplied in order to justify the war. They also represented the war's dark underside. Atrocities such as those of the Thirty Years' War and the Ulster Rebellion were presented as civility collapsing into chaos. Woodcuts printed in pamphlets describing the events of the Thirty Years' War display the mutilated bodies of the victims as signifiers of barbarity, but also pander to quasi-scientific curiosity about the body and its inside. The woodcuts graphically illustrate the violent castration imagery and investment in the unclean that characterizes these stories. These events in Germany and Ireland came to act as templates for understanding and reporting civil war atrocities, thus doubly estranging the atrocious by connecting it with the foreign Other.[32] Atrocities were not seen as sadistically exciting, but as a threatening lapse into originary animality, a loss of civility and hence of masculine identity, a loss of manners in savagery, like the transformation of cavalier into "Black-moor." Violence only reinforced male identity when it could be seen as controlled, or as just punishment. Outside those parameters, it was not masculine, but paradoxically a failure of masculinity. So it is too with the rebel angels, as we shall see.

Abstract figures of death dealing and violent soldiers described in many early pamphlets were tinged with class anxiety, and hence with the rhetoric of carnival, the world upside down, the fable of the belly. This was particularly true where the soldiers were recruited from the dregs of society, or were supposed to have been: it was said that local communities had rid themselves of undesirables by making them soldiers.[33] What was horrifying about these figures was the unleashing of their unjust appetites: the allegorical figure of the Plundering Soldier was in any case almost all belly. "The Plunderer" fed on the entrails of the kingdom; the "English-Irish soldier" "had rather eate than fight," and was composed of all the goods he had plundered, a figure from someone without an identity who

---

also William Palmer, "Gender, Violence, and Rebellion in Tudor and early Stuart England," *Sixteenth-Century Journal* 23 (1992): 699–712, and J. A. Sharpe, "The History of Violence in England: Some Observations," *Past and Present* 101 (1983): 206–15. I am very grateful to Susan Amussen for drawing my attention to her excellent articles. On the relations between war and violence, see John R. Hale, *War and Society in Renaissance Europe* (London: Collins, 1985).

32. Barbara Donagan points to the prevalence of Thirty Years' War atrocity stories before the civil war in "Codes and Conduct in the English Civil War," *Past and Present* 118 (1988): 65–95, especially 67–69. See also her "Atrocity, War Crime, and Treason in the English Civil War," *American Historical Review* 99 (1994): 1137–66, especially 1145, 1147. The figure of the Thirty Years' War is used to represent the civil war's likely course of atrocities by, for example, Henry Parker, *The Manifold Miseries of Civil War and Discord in a Kingdome* (1642).

33. Donagan, "Codes and Conduct," 71–72.

had deprived others of theirs in order to manufacture a specious one of his own.[34] Violence is often figured as going with drunkenness and lust, bad manners, insulting behavior, and "hot blood" (in itself a kind of medical signifier for masculinity). Contrasting with the well-mannered or well-regulated body of the soldier, the body of a murderer might be seen as awash with uncontrolled forces. So as well as fearing the feminine, the rhetoric of atrocity exacerbated fear of more masculine disorders, or rather both fears turned on anxieties about the loss of the clean, hard, visible surface of masculine identity.

One possible response was to return obsessively to the spectacle of what had previously terrified. It was routine to establish masculine identity in war in relation to a displaced femininity. Poems on abandoning wives and mistresses for the battlefield proliferated, and (forged) letters from London women who had found Cavaliers to comfort their loneliness in the absence of their partners sought to persuade the London trained bands to give up the struggle for Parliament.[35] The finding of a love-object is always a finding of the lost maternal body. Hence another connection between the death drive and femininity emerges: the return to a prior state involves the maternal body as the real material body lost at birth, the fictional phallic mother whose body represents a lost unity, as a figure of the dust to which the human being must return; hence a female figure alone offers ways of representing and also appearing—at least in fantasy—to manage the death drive and to control and satisfy it.[36] Paradoxically, then, the lost mother is actually the model for the tight, hard body assumed to be the acme of masculinity in discourses of war. Yet that same maternal body can also be understood as engulfing and formless, and hence threatening, when it seems to be on the point of swallowing up the ego, now itself understood as the locus of tight integrity. Consequently, it is not surprising that murdering and dismembering a woman, or reading and writing about

34. *The Grand Plunderer, a subject never before written* (London, 1643); *The English-Irish Soldier* ([London?], 1642).

35. Richard Lovelace's "To Lucasta" is the best-known example of the opposition between love and war, but see also the ballads "The cavalier's farewell to his Mistress" and "The soldier's delight" in Hyder Rollins, *Cavalier and Puritan: Ballads and Broadsides Illustrating the Period of the Great Rebellion, 1640–1660* (New York: New York University Press, 1923), 86, 280. Forged letters from women who had supposedly found comfort with cavaliers because their husbands were away with the bands, or from women begging their husbands to come home, were circulated and published (for example, in *Mercurius Aulicus,* September 9, 1642, signed Susan Owen).

36. For an analysis of the negotiation of the death drive via a female figure, see Elisabeth Bronfen, *Over Her Dead Body: Death, Femininity, and the Aesthetic* (Manchester: Manchester University Press, 1992).

such acts, were possible fantasy resolutions of the intolerable pressures placed on the death drive by the war.

In its complex relation to the body of the mother and hence to femininity, the workings of the death drive recall Kristeva's notion of abjection. Kristeva understands abjection as a response to the constant threat of the mother's return and reabsorption of the ego, a return represented through chaos, pollution, dirt, and disorder.[37] War is a prolific producer of all, and in particular the spectacle of dismembered and disordered bodies, living and dead, creates acute anxieties, and not only because the corpse represents death. In representing the end of life, it must also represent the beginning, the mother. Most of all, however, the very disruptive effects of war itself on the life of the individual and the nation impact on the ego to generate fears of further engulfment and chaos, setting abjection in motion. Both aggressive actions and violent repudiations are produced by these psychic pressures.[38] Thus the rhetorical display of dismembered, dead femininity figured as both motivation for and Other of men-at-arms. A contemporary newspaper expressed this dual function as follows:

> the divided pieces of a woman abused to death, needed not the Eloquence or voyce of an orator; they spake themselves, and they spake so loud, that they were heard by a whole Nation, and drew forth this Answer; there was no such deed done nor seen, from the day that the children of Israel came out of Aegypt. Neither did they fetch only an answer of words, but of deeds.[39]

Such rhetoric was reassuring because it assigned passivity, disorder, and dismemberment to the feminine corpse, releasing the male identity of the soldier for military action on her behalf and reassuring him that his own being was different. An atrocity story from the 1641 uprising in Ulster repeats these ideas while uncannily duplicating the image both of the feared maternal body and the dissected and known anatomical specimen. Both arousing and neutralizing tensions in male identities, this female figure also replicates the logic of violation of the mother, which helped to make gunpowder appear diabolical:

> they [Irish rebels] being blood-thirsty salvages . . . not deserving the title of humanity without any more words beate out his braines, then they layd hold on his wife being big with child, & ravisht her, then ript open her wombe, and like so many Neros undantedly viewed natures bed of conception, afterward

---

37. Julia Kristeva, *Powers of Horror: An Essay on Abjection*, trans. Leon S. Roudiez (New York: Columbia University Press, 1982).

38. My thinking on this question has been influenced by work on more recent wars: see in particular Joanna Bourke, *Dismembering the Male: Men's Bodies, Britain, and the Great War* (London: Reaktion, 1996).

39. *A True and Perfect Relation of the Barbarous and Cruell Passages of the Kings Army, at Old Brainceford* (London: E. Husbands and J. Frank, 1642), B2r.

tooke her and her Infant and sacrifiz'd in fire their wounded bodies to appease their Immaculate Soules, which being done, they pillaged the house, taking what they thought good, and when they had done, they set the house on fire.[40]

Here the soldiers' violence lays bare the mysterious site of generation. The account stresses the quasi-scientific result of their violence; they view "natures bed of conception," just as the miners for the minerals of gunpowder do. As such, they assert masculinity, but in a manner that calls such scientific investigation into question. For the spectacle of the exposed and opened womb is also apotropaic; it requires that the eye flee, rather than linger and observe, because it also signifies the mutilating punishment that awaits those who look upon the mother's body. This ambiguity is repeated in the English civil war stories that also focus on the violation and destruction of the mother: at Lostwithiel, a woman three days out of childbed was stripped to her smock, seized by the hair, and thrown in the river to die within hours; another pamphlet reported that troops had "killed Ewes great with lambe, and one Ewe that was great with two lambes."[41] These rites of gore paradoxically offer to recreate the hardness lost or threatened with loss in the war by their very apotropaic nature. The rigidity imparted by the spectacle of castrating wounds reassures because the viewer is able to respond with reassuring rigidity, keeping a set face when confronted with the spectacle of the opened body. In this way, civil war newsbooks—and in some cases, civil war soldiers—were able to turn their deepest nightmares into a kind of homeopathic remedy for those nightmares, feeding on the very spectacle that threatened them.

Milton responded to and consciously or unconsciously reproduced these entangled aspects of war in his portrayal of the war in heaven in *Paradise Lost*. The war in heaven has disturbed critics profoundly; at times, Miltonists have seemed almost aggrieved that Milton has not presented a seamlessly idealistic and reassuring picture of war in order to cheer them.[42] I do not want to deal at length with critical responses to this aspect

40. *A Bloody Battell: or the Rebels Overthrow and Protestants victorie* (London, 1641), n.p.

41. Donagan, "Codes of Conduct," 90; *A True Relation of Two Merchants of London, who were taken prisoners by the Cavaliers* (London: Humphrey Watson, 1642). Many of these cases might be dismissed as formulaic, as Donagan suggests, yet the trouble with dismissing the formulaic is that one can forget to ask just why this formula seemed to need constant reiteration, or why atrocity stories assumed this particular configuration.

42. In an article of this length, I cannot fairly survey all critical responses, but I am thinking of A. J. A. Waldock, *Paradise Lost and Its Critics* (Cambridge: Cambridge

of *Paradise Lost* here, but I am of course offering an interpretation of one of the cruxes to which critics have returned again and again: Why is the tone of the war narrative so variable? Why is there so much grotesque humor?[43] The answer, I am suggesting, lies in the way the civil war disturbed the assumption that wars had a single tone, deriving from the soldier's inalienable identity. As we have seen, the process of fighting undermined the unitary hard masculinity that soldiers struggled to build, with the result that the experience of war consisted of the regular irruption of the dark, filthy, disorderly underside of combat into areas of body, personality, and narrative from which it had been laboriously banished. Responses to this varied, but one response was to reshape this dark, submerged material into an apotropaic fantasy figure who could be confronted and seen, reassuringly exposed, and symbolically penetrated. We have seen two instances of this process: the figuration of gunpowder as the secret inside a feminine nature, and the figuration of the murdered, opened body of the mother. In the war in heaven, I shall argue, Milton both portrays those moments of disruption and re-presents them as fantasies that reassure. A hint occurs right at the beginning of book 6, when the loyal angels are departing for battle; "clouds began / To darken all the hill, and smoke to roll / In dusky wreaths, reluctant flames, the sign / Of wrath awaked" (56–60). What is striking here is the apparently unthinking reuse of a civil war trope. As we have seen, civil war battlefields were dominated and rendered opaque by smoke and fire, and memoirs likened them to a storm. Yet that smoke was caused by the burning of crops and houses, by musket- and cannon-fire, or sometimes by the enemy's attempt to force opposing troops out of a particular position. Here none of these causes are present, yet the smoke, fire, and opacity are retained as pure, detached signifiers of war. This suggests that powerful psychic pressures are keeping these signs of disunity in play. Yet Milton is eager to couple these signs of disorder with the military masculine ideal. When the loyal angels set off, his emphasis on their hardness and invulnerability recalls both Elton's drill manual and the London trained bands:

University Press, 1947), and John Peter, *A Critique of Paradise Lost* (London: Scribner, 1967), among others.

43. All analyses of the war in heaven are dependent on the germinal work of Stella Revard, *The War in Heaven: "Paradise Lost" and the Tradition of Satan's Rebellion* (Ithaca: Cornell University Press, 1980), and Robert Fallon, *Captain or Colonel: The Soldier in Milton's Life and Art* (Columbia: University of Missouri Press, 1984). The issues I tackle here have been addressed recently by John Wooten, "The Poet's War: Violence and Virtue in *Paradise Lost*," *Studies in English Literature* 30 (1990): 133–50, though with little attention to gender or sexuality; and by D. M. Rosenberg, "Epic Warfare in Cowley and Milton," *Clio: A Journal of Literature and History* 22 (1992): 67–80.

> At which command the powers militant
> That stood for heaven, in mighty quadrate joined,
> Of union irresistible, moved on
> In silence their bright legions,
>
> . . . .
>   On they move
> Indissolulably firm; nor obvious hill
> Nor straitening vale, nor wood, nor stream divides
> Their perfect ranks. (6.61–71)

Here Milton presents a drilled ideal; the angels are united, utterly obedient to orders, and this is signified by the perfect order of their marching. Milton knows that this order is not available to men; the angels can fly, which is why hills and valleys do not break their ranks; man has to work much harder for the same desirable result. At the same time, he presents it *as* desirable, an instance of the angels' capacity to outdo man at what he also attempts, an instance of their superior masculinity.

That superior masculinity is equated with virtue because the first to suffer the disruptive effects of war are the rebels, and the first among the rebels is Satan. Satan's wounding, during his battle with Michael, is of course primarily Homeric, but it is Homer read through a context of civil war narratives and atrocity stories. Satan is not merely beaten; he is made to suffer and is disgraced:

>   then Satan first knew pain
> And writhed him to and fro convulsed; so sore
> The griding sword with discontinuous wound
> Passed through him, but the ethereal substance closed
> Not long divisible, and from the gash
> A stream of nectarous humour issuing flowed
> Sanguine, such as celestial spirits may bleed,
> And all his armour stained ere while so bright. (6.327–34)

Satan does not only feel pain; the pain causes him to lose control of himself, writhing convulsed, his body beyond the control of his will. This loss of control to pain, this loss of the self in pain, is of course presented as a punishment, as atrocities were, but Milton is honest enough to present it as atrocious. Milton emphasizes that the wound is discontinuous, that what makes Satan suffer pain is the loss of (phallic) wholeness, control, hardness, armor. As if to emphasize this, Milton stresses the ragged edge of the sword; it is "griding," or scraping, not only cutting but damaging the flesh by contact. What people are apt to find funny now is the temporariness of all these effects; Satan's body almost instantly recovers its wholeness, and in that sense he cannot be mutilated. Yet, as if acknowledging the desire for a more permanent sign of dismemberment, Milton portrays the spilling of angelic blood onto Satan's armor, showing his transition from a signifier of invulnerability to one of woundedness, discontinuity. Satan almost literally loses himself in this war. This is funny, in the sense that it is grotesque and undignified; Milton is aware that such indignities are the very stuff of warfare.

Satan's recovery also allows Milton to point to the dismembered bodies of human conflict again, and thus at the disorder that underlies bright armor and marching regiments drilled into perfect formations:

> Yet soon he healed, for spirits that live throughout
> Vital in every part, not as frail man
> In entrails, heart or head, liver or reins
> Cannot but by annihilating die. (6.344–47)

There is something almost angry, almost guilty, about Milton's need to mention the vulnerable human body here, even though the thrust of the poem is to subsume its frailty in angelic invulnerability. It is as if he cannot or must not forget the civil war dead; they haunt the poem in their mutilated, divided state like the ghostly amputees of Edgehill. To avoid neglecting them, Milton must bring them in, but he must also find an imaginative solution to the disorder they represent. Here, man's anatomy, and the always already known discontinuity of his internal organs, turns out to constitute his vulnerability; by contrast, the holism of the angels' substance, despite its apparently unmasculine fluidity, guarantees their ability to survive being disunited by recreating, instantly, their unmarred surface.

That fantasy of wholeness and reuniting is visible in civil war texts not at the moment when an individual man is killed but at the moment when a regiment or troops is attacked. Milton is describing individual angels as if they were entire regiments. At the same time, from the point of view of the good angels, this capacity to reunite might be experienced as frustrating or even frightening rather than heartening. Of course, I am not suggesting that Milton attributes such feelings to the good angels—they would be inappropriate to angels—but rather that he asks *us* to experience imaginatively what it might be like to fight a foe who, as it were, regroups after every encounter, as the Royalist regiments did after Parliamentarian assaults. This capacity of the foe to *keep coming* is itself one of the most frightening and problematically unsettling aspects of war, for how is it possible to go on being hard, day after day? Characteristically, Milton reverts to the model of equating masculine hardness with masculine virtue in use in the civil war when he presents the rout of the rebel angels and the steadfastness of the loyal angels. The rebels break, and the terms in which this is described are extremely suggestive: "deformed rout" and "foul disorder" equate retreat respectively with dismemberment and loss of identity, and with filth, dirt, and decay (386–87). By contrast, the loyal angels are figured in terms of male military wholeness and discipline: "in cubic phalanx firm advanced entire / Invulnerable, impenetrably armed" (339–400). Assigning all the disorderly side of war to the enemy is what produces atrocity stories like those of the 1641 uprising and the civil war itself. In succumbing to the temptation to consign the cosmic enemy to moral darkness and to loss of male control, Milton is purchasing psychic resolution with what he knows to be tainted money.

It is from this point—this point at which the rebels themselves have been, in every sense, both broken and penetrated—that they themselves begin probing and penetrating the mother earth. Now, this is in one sense realistic; troops did respond to sexualized humiliation by acting out a violation of a feminized Other that they could control. Milton is being honest—brutally honest—about war. But he is also assigning—or consigning—those impulses to the rebel angels only, and thus distancing himself and other Christian soldier-males from any imputation of structural difficulty. That is, Milton seems in danger of abandoning his careful and impartial analysis of the difficulties war generates for masculine identity in favor of straightforward Othering, where those aspects of war that cannot be tolerated by the masculine identity are abjected into or onto the enemy. That the rebels are carrying out precisely the sort of procedure described by William Clarke, and in a different way performing an atrocity analogous to the mother-murder of Ulster, is clear from Satan's rhetoric:

> These in their dark nativity the deep
>   Shall yield us pregnant with infernal flame,
> Which into hollow engines long and round
> Thick-rammed, at the other bore with touch of fire. (481–84)

The initial image is of despoiling a pregnant womb of its offspring, precisely the image used to characterize the Ulster rebels as barbarous, but also the image whose apotropaic power restores masculine identity. Exactly the same image recurs when the rebels eventually get down to the task of digging, "and saw beneath / The originals of nature in their crude / Conception" (510–12). In Satan's speech, however, the focus switches to the cannon, which becomes both a phallic image and an image of the penetrated orifice. None of this makes literal "sense," or even straightforward ideological sense; there is no simple subordination of the feminine or voiding of the sodomitical. Rather, what is figured is precisely "the perverse"; a tangle of gender images, which by its very complexity signifies the unsettling of gender itself. The images of phallus and orifice also recur when the cannon is presented to the startled loyal angels, and it has the expected effects. It reduces those who "standing else as rocks" to a tumbling mass of infantile, even laughable disorder.

All this dark and comic underside of war, this grotesquerie, is assigned unhesitatingly to the rebel angels alone, even when the loyal angels are caught up in its effects. What saves the poem from being another lying piece of recruiting posterese about affirming masculinity with reference to the chaos of the enemy is the very sequence most critics have complained of: the mountain-throwing episode. This allows the loyal angels to partake of and even to create chaos, though a simpler kind of chaos with no dark gender disorder. However, the effects are strongly reminiscent of the darkness of the civil war battlefield. Even the syntax of the narration becomes chaotic and exhausted by what it must describe:

> So hills amid the air encountered hills
> Hurled to and fro with jaculation dire,
> That under ground they fought in dismal shade;
> Infernal noise; war seemed a civil game
> To this uproar; horrid confusion heaped
> Upon confusion rose and now all heaven
> Had gone to wrack, with ruin overspread. . . . (6.664–70)

This is no longer even war because by now everyone has lost the hard, ordered masculine identity that they must collectively and individually assume to count as warriors. The fragility of such identities is comically deflated by their literal burial under thrown hills, and yet the confusion—which extends to the reader, his or her own expectations shattered by events—is serious, serious enough to provoke the Son's entirely serious intervention. What happens is that first the mountains and then crucially the Son obliterate those very hard military identities that seemed so crucial just a few hundred lines earlier. The Son's masculinity is of another order, transcending the order of war in an apotheosis that makes it irrelevant. Wiped clean, masculinity is free to re-present itself along new lines; through the family, through talk and eloquence, through resistance to temptation rather than the foe. This is not pacifism, but Milton's intelligent recognition that the masculinity of militarism is too complex, too contradictory, and too prone to excess to form a useful metaphor for Christian heroism, or to assuage the potent terrors that such militarism itself arouses.

Catherine Gimelli Martin

The Phoenix and the Crocodile

Milton's Natural Law
Debate with Hobbes
Retried in the Tragic Forum
of *Samson Agonistes*

There is no power but of God, saith *Paul, Rom.* 13. as much as to say, God put it into mans heart to find out that way at first for common peace and preservation, . . . els it contradicts *Peter* who calls the same autority an Ordinance of man. It must be also understood of lawfull and just power, els we read of great power in the affaires and kingdoms of the world permitted to the Devil. . . . If such onely [just power] be mentioned here as powers to be obeyd, and our submission to them only requir'd, then doubtless those powers that doe the contrary, are no powers ordain'd of God, and by consequence no obligation laid upon us to obey or not to resist them.

—John Milton, *The Tenure of Kings and Magistrates*

He who marries, intends as little to conspire to his own ruine, as he that swears Allegiance: and as a whole people is in proportion to an ill Government, so is one man to an ill mariage. If they against any authority, Covnant, or Statute, may by the soveraign edict of charity, save not only their lives, but honest liberties from unworthy bondage, as well may he against any private Covnant, which hee never enter'd to his mischief, redeem himself from unsupportable disturbances . . .

— John Milton, *The Doctrine and Discipline of Divorce*

> I was no private but a person rais'd
> With strength sufficient and command from Heav'n
> To free my Country; if their servile minds
> Me their Deliver sent would not receive,
> But to thir Masters gave me up for nought,
> Th' unworthier they; whence to this day they serve.
> —John Milton, *Samson Agonistes*

These lengthy epigraphs are meant to remind the reader that the legal issues involved in Samson's defense of his cause bear an obvious if often overlooked relevance to the public trial in which Milton found himself engaged throughout the revolutionary period.[1] Ironically, we tend to overlook these legal issues precisely because he was ultimately so successful in establishing what we now take for granted as inalienable human rights—including, especially, the right of private persons to resist legally constituted yet clearly "unjust" powers. For as Milton and the Independents who executed Charles I believed (and as most modern readers would agree), the systematic abrogation of such rights effectively establishes an illegal form of tyranny not sanctioned by man, God, or "natural" laws. While the universal validity of this unwritten social contract remains debatable, the necessity of having some higher court of appeal decide such cases is not. Yet in Milton's day, the only such court was the figurative forum of public opinion and the literal if often delayed judgment of history, both of which seemed to have decided against his cause. This essay proposes that his final literary work, *Samson Agonistes*, imaginatively completes the task that his *Second Defence* identifies as the cumulative aim of his revolutionary treatises: maintaining the eternal laws of "ecclesiastical liberty, personal or domestic liberty, and civil liberty" (*CPW*, 4.1:624).

Yet the poem also registers the magnified difficulty of even imaginatively maintaining these natural liberties against the consensus of religious and political authority after the Restoration. Even earlier, although Calvin considers it part of God's "wonderful goodness, and power, and providence . . . [that] sometimes he raises up open avengers among his servants, and arms them with his command to punish the wicked government and deliver his people, oppressed in unjust ways, from miserable calamity," the following chapter of his *Institutes* cautions that private persons "have received no other command than to obey and suffer."[2] The weight of this opinion eventually split the more conservative Calvinist or Presbyterian revolutionary faction from its more liberal or Independent allies, who, like Milton, read the injunction to civil obedience in Romans 13

---

1. *Complete Prose Works of John Milton*, ed. Merritt Y. Hughes (New Haven: Yale University Press, 1962) (hereafter cited as *CPW*), 3:209–10; 2:229. As Hughes points out in his note (3:209), during England's revolutionary controversies, "I Peter 2 was constantly bracketed with Romans 13:1–2,—as it was, typically, in Sir Robert Filmer's *Patriarcha* (chapter 23; ed. Laslett, 101)—to enjoin unquestioning obedience to 'every Ordinance of man, for the Lords sake, whether it be to the King as supreme, or unto Governours.' " Merritt Y. Hughes, ed., *John Milton: Complete Poems and Major Prose* (New York: Odyssey Press, 1957) (hereby cited in all poetic references to Milton, with abbreviations referring to *Paradise Lost* [*PL*] and *Samson Agonistes* [*SA*]), *SA* 1211–16.

2. Calvin, *Institutes of the Christian Religion*, vol. 2, ed. John T. McNeill (Philadelphia: Westminster Press, 1960) book 4:1517.

with the latitude of Adam's "spirit within thee free" (*PL* 8.440); that is, as a "natural" extension of the gospel law of grace. As a result, the chief impediment to justifying their cause by appealing to ultimate "laws of nature" was not actually religious but political, which is to say, not Calvin but Hobbes. Co-opting the natural-law argument for his own ends, this ultracontracturalist Royalist had argued that the only fully demonstrable law of nature is that of self-preservation, one that logically dictates that individual rights be *relinquished* in the interest of ending the reign of terror he identified as mankind's true natural state.

The task of establishing that a fundamentally different kind of natural law lay behind the social contract would thus have been *materia prima* to Milton, not only in his international role as designated apologist for the Commonwealth, but in every aspect of his life as a man of letters. With the monarchy restored—and along with it the pragmatic ethos that Hobbes had extolled as both socially and morally preferable to the dangerous religious "enthusiasm" he deplored in men like Milton—the urgency of making this case became even more critical. Yet as their common European audience was well aware, Hobbes, like Milton, was an eminent classicist and ardent polemicist who claimed to recover the ancient rules of Greek wisdom to a "barbarous Age," although unlike him, he hardly sought them in the liberty of heroic verse (the stated aim of Milton's *Paradise Lost*), or in liberty at all. Rather, Hobbes sought to derive the fundamental rules for human conduct from the protoscientific methods of Euclid and Thucydides, the latter of whom supplied an antidemagogic analysis of the failures of the Athenian experiment apparently confirmed by those of the Commonwealth. By combining his pragmatic view of politics with the rigors of a linguistic "geometry," Hobbes not only claimed to have developed the first "authentic" works of political science but also to have freed human language from the misleading *"ignes fatui"* of mere metaphor. Of these dangerous metaphors he regards conscience and free will as among the worst, especially since he insists that only in its original, objective, and plainly "unmetaphorical" sense of *consciousness* could one claim that being forced to act against conscience was evil (*Leviathan* 1.5.113; 1.7.132).[3] In avoiding the "contention, and sedition, or contempt" (*Leviathan* 1.5.116–17) inevitably produced by these rhetorical "illusions," his Galilean synthesis of observation and deduction would

3. Thus, as Robert Stillman concludes, Hobbes's project is that of converting "a debased metaphorical conscience captive to private opinion, into real public conscience, witness to sovereign authority." See Stillman, "Hobbes's *Leviathan*: Monsters, Metaphors, and Magic," *ELH* 62 (1995): 803; for a related discussion of Hobbes on conscience, see the same essay, 801–2.

therefore establish the proper functioning of the political animal that he liked to think of as Behemoth or Leviathan, the "double-mailed crocodile" of the absolutist sovereign state.[4]

While also an admirer of both Greek and Galilean science, Milton regarded them as supporting, not undermining, the neo-Roman or classical republican form of liberty whose defense had cost him his sight. Given his blind Samson's overt associations with libertarian principles that now seem more universally established than ever, it thus seems deeply ironic that his hero has begun to undergo the same political exile he himself suffered at the hands of the Hobbesian "crocodile" then in ascendancy, the monolithic sovereign state. Yet as suggested above, his Samson also seems to have fallen victim to his own success: the notion of inalienable human rights has become so well established that they now unquestioningly extend to everyone, including inimical "others" like the Philistines. Thus recent revisionist criticism of the drama would distinguish Milton from Samson as a tribal avenger representing the worst excesses of the "old" or Mosaic law, in his view an *un*natural law no longer in force (*CPW*, 6:522–23).[5] This additional departure from Calvin (who at least retains the decalogue) is stressed both in his *Christian Doctrine* and in *Paradise Lost*, where Moses is somewhat pointedly depicted as a visionary leader of faith, not as a lawgiver bearing eternal stone tablets. Yet in point of fact, Milton's legal iconoclasm ultimately weakens rather than strengthens the revisionist case, for throughout the tragedy, Samson acts not as a lawgiver but as a lawbreaker. In also pointedly eliminating the revenge motive emphasized in Judges, where Samson called "unto the LORD, and said, O Lord GOD,

---

4. For a discussion of this leviathan as a crocodile image (taken along with that of the behemoth, or hippopotamus from Job) and Hobbes's fascination with it as symbol of the "unlimited power" of "the omnipotent state," see George Shelton, *Morality and Sovereignty in the Philosophy of Thomas Hobbes* (New York: St. Martin's Press, 1992) 46–47.

5. For some interesting examples of contemporary identifications of Milton with his Samson, see *"Paradise Regain'd"* . . . *"Samson Agonistes,"* 2d ed., ed. Thomas Newton (London: W. Streahan, 1785) 1:269, cited also in Joseph Wittreich, *Interpreting "Samson Agonistes"* (Princeton: Princeton University Press, 1986), 5. The main exponents of the revisionist reading of Milton's Samson as both personally and primitively revengeful include Irene Samuel, "Samson Agonistes as Tragedy," in *Calm of Mind: Tercentenary Essays on "Paradise Regained" and "Samson Agonistes,"* ed. Joseph Wittreich (Cleveland: Press of Case Western Reserve University, 1971); Stanley Fish, "Spectacle and Evidence in *Samson Agonistes*," *Critical Inquiry* 15 (1989): 556–86; and Wittreich, who presents a book-length defense of it in *Interpreting "Samson Agonistes."* However, lengthy as it is, this work can hardly be called comprehensive, since it fails to refer to any of the specific texts cited in my epigraphs (or to *The Tenure of Kings and Magistrates* at all). Wittreich's selective treatment of evidence is ably critiqued by Philip J. Gallagher in "On Reading Joseph Wittreich: A Review Essay," *Milton Quarterly* 21 (Oct. 1987): 108–13.

remember me, I pray thee, and strengthen me, . . . that I may be at once avenged of the Philistines for my two eyes" (Judges 16:28), Milton converts the narrative climax into a legal challenge to witness "such other trial / . . . of my strength, yet greater; / As with amaze shall strike all who behold" (1643–45). Since this reworking of the legend focuses almost entirely on his ethical and juridical rather than physical strength, his "trial" must be understood as a legal test case against his fellow tribesmen, the people of the Old Law, as well as the Philistines, the upholders of an essentially Hobbesian social contract. The explicitly Sophoclean setting of Milton's tragedy further encourages this symbolic reading, for unlike Thucydides, Sophocles used his dramatic forum to critique and imaginatively *amend*, not lament the conditions that could lead a free people to abandon the universal laws or "ends," as Samson calls them, that alone make "our country . . . a name so dear" (893–94). As he insists to Dalila, if this aspect of the social contract is not fulfilled, then much as Milton had argued in *The Tenure of Kings and Magistrates* above, there is no longer any "obligation laid upon us to obey or not to resist" specific unjust authorities, whose rightful powers are to be understood not in *"concrete* but *abstract"* terms.

Both biblically and philosophically, Hobbes understands this obliga-tion in an absolutely contrary *and* concrete sense. No matter how such authority is "abstractly" constituted, it not only rightfully puts an end to the savage state of nature, but gives "life and motion to the whole body," thereby making sedition sickness, and "Civill war, Death." Moreover, under "sedition," Hobbes includes nearly every form of civic or religious dissent (public and private) to the established monarch and his church. Globally speaking, this fundamentally different interpretation of natural law stems from the fact that unlike Milton, Hobbes does not regard the sovereign state as empowered *by* the people but as empowering *them;* the *"Salus Populi* (the *peoples safety*) [is] its *Businesse."* On their side, the Puritan faction redefined the people's safety as their *salvation,* a moral emphasis effected through a Latin pun on *salus* originally made in a famous speech by Stephen Marshall and carried to its logical conclusion in Milton's *Doctrine and Discipline of Divorce,* which similarly presupposes the natural right to oppose "any authority, Covnant, or Statute, . . . by the soveraign edict of charity, [in order to] save not only their lives, but honest liberties from unworthy bondage." Here Milton is far closer to modern natural-law theory than Hobbes, who instead stresses the immutably binding *"Pacts* and *Covenants,* by which the parts of th[e] Body Politique were first made, set together, and united," and through which it guarantees only physical forms of safety.[6] To their contemporaries, this utter contrast in political temperament was so obvious that early biographers of Milton like John Aubrey merely sum it up in passing: "His widow assures me that Mr. Hobbs was not one of his acquaintance, that her husband did not like him at all, but he would acknowledge him to be a man of great parts, and a learned man. Their interests and tenets were diametrically opposite—vide Mr. Hobbes *Behemoth*."[7]

Nevertheless, Hobbesian political science was to triumph not merely during the short run of the Restoration but also in the long run of modern constitutional democracy. Although the modern state is hardly the monolith much less the monarchy that Hobbes envisioned, his stringent separation of religious from political thought proved so pragmatically and even ethically viable that, in fact, it also seems to provide an important factor in the revisionist defense of Samson's religious opponents. For as Bruno Latour has shown, although Hobbes did not advocate the separation of church and state but rather the reverse, the actual effect of his "modern constitution" is to confine the public expression of private belief to abstract and/or authoritarian forms of worship. Later, via Locke, as Christopher Hill remarks, the secular state comes into its own by synthesizing "Hobbes and Milton, science and religion; . . . leaving out everything that had made religion exciting, much that had made science politically dangerous." Yet this secularization process was already implicit in the twin Hobbesian projects of linguistic nominalism and ecclesiastical consensualism, which claim that common words, *like* common worship, only "have their signification by agreement, and constitution of men" (*Leviathan* 2.31.405). Since in case of conflict this "agreement" is irrevocably decided by sovereign authority, dissenting opinions are effectively exiled to the private sphere

6. These and subsequent quotations taken from Hobbes's *Leviathan* are from C. B. MacPherson's edition (Harmondsworth: Penguin Books, 1968), cited here in Hobbes's introduction, 81–82, and hereafter by part, chapter, and page. All quotations from Milton cited above are repeated from the epigraphs to this essay. On Stephen Marshall's speech, *Meroz Cursed*, see Michael Fixler, *Milton and the Kingdoms of God* (London: Faber; Evanston: Northwestern University Press, 1964), 87–88. In general the view of *salus* as chiefly signifying the people's *salvation* was common to Calvinists, who typically regard power as coming "from God to the people as a birthright" and thus merely "borrowed" by rulers; see John T. McNeill, *The History and Character of Calvinism* (New York: Oxford University Press, 1954), 412.

7. See John Aubrey's early life of Milton in the appendix to Hughes, ed., *John Milton: Complete Poems and Major Prose*, 1023. On his part, Hobbes was known to have treated the reasoning of Milton's *First Defence* even more "cavalierly." On the primary sources of their conflict as well as on his probable acquaintance with Hobbes's *De Cive* at the time of writing the *Tenure*, see Hughes's introduction to the text(s) in *CPW*, 3:55–73.

except in the relatively "objective" discourses of science and secular education, political "investments" that would further disinvest personal spirituality from public discourse.[8] While the wisdom or even the ultimate practicality of such a separation clearly lies beyond the scope of this essay, it is worth noting that those who respect it in theory often feel justified in violating it in fact—particularly in civil liberationist movements where something like a more truly Miltonic synthesis has prevailed.

Unlike Hobbes, but like most of his contemporaries, Milton could not conceive of a just government completely divorced from the moral guidance of those spiritually "elect above the rest" (*PL* 3.184). His Samson clearly continues to represent this type (*SA* 678), although *not* in either a Calvinistically predestinatory or a Hebraically avenging sense. Rather, he *becomes* ethically and therefore also legally superior in the same way as the other deliverers of mankind, who, like their prime exemplar, the Son of God, are Miltonically validated "by Merit more than Birthright" (*PL* 3.309). As the companion poem on the temptations of Christ (*Paradise Regained*) also suggests, this merit is attained through a strenuous exercise of "right reason," which is guided by spirit and conscience; Hobbes would rigorously police the former and exile the latter. Thus as we might expect, the foundational premise of Hobbes's *Leviathan*—that "life is but a motion of Limbs"—appears only parodically in *Samson Agonistes*, where Samson's misguided chorus mistakenly insists that their hero resign himself to the immobility "inevitably" accompanying his loss of physical sight, for "inward light, alas, / Puts forth no visual beam" (163). The magnitude of this error is revealed by the overthrow of the Philistines' Leviathan-like temple through these invisible, phoenixlike "beams," whose powerful energies cannot be confined to the private sphere. For through these mysterious "rousing motions" (1382), his chorus too experiences metaphoric visions of emergent order, of natural laws governed not by the monolithic state but by the winged force of liberty—here imagined as the combined forces of the dragon, the eagle, and finally the phoenix, "That self-begott'n bird / . . . That no second knows nor third" (1699–1701).[9]

In contrast, Hobbesian natural law, like his right reason, is *only* logical thinking: not the "'Right Reason' of the Cambridge Platonists, or

8. See Bruno Latour's important discussion of Hobbes's role in designing the "modern constitution" in *We Have Never Been Modern*, trans. Catherine Porter (Cambridge: Harvard University Press, 1993), 18–35. Christopher Hill, *Puritanism and Revolution: Studies in Interpretation of the English Revolution of the Seventeenth Century* (New York: Schocken Books, 1958), 298.

9. Mythologically, the phoenix is also the bird of the sun, and Samson's Hebrew name means "sun fire."

of Puritan thinkers such as Milton . . . not an inward illumination, 'the candle of the Lord,' an intuitive apprehension of external reality." This empirical extremism is highly conducive to Hobbes's view of natural law, since among other things, it allows him to "deduce" (by means of a blatantly false etymology) that rational "de-liberation" mercifully puts an end to liberty itself (*Leviathan* 1.6.127). Of course, as this word-mongering also suggests, despite his disclaimers, Hobbes himself *does* employ metaphors, of which the best known is leviathan itself.[10] But while Milton also employs this biblical image, he generally associates it with the satanic energies of Pharaoh the "river-dragon" (*PL* 12.191), Dagon the Philistine "Sea Monster" or fishy "Idol" (*PL* 1.462, *SA* 13), or even with Satan himself (*PL* 1.192–210). Nevertheless, there is also considerable warrant for interpreting leviathan not as a mythical *opponent* of divine power but as an exemplum of human weakness and a "vehicle" for its correction, as it is in Job 41:1–4: "Canst thou draw out leviathan with an hook? . . . Will he make a covenant with thee?" where it points to a form of sovereign power far superior to that of mere mortals like Job.[11] Yet as outlined above, the more fundamental philosophical differences between Milton and Hobbes concern their uses of the neo-Roman rather than the biblical tradition, not only in regard to the principles of "right reason"

10. On the first point, see Samuel I. Mintz, *The Hunting of Leviathan* (Cambridge: Cambridge University Press, 1962), 25. As Mintz also points out, while Hobbesian pragmatism was decried by critics who suspected him of atheism, the Restoration (and particularly its clerics) tacitly practiced what he openly preached. On the patently false etymology Hobbes employs in deriving *liberty* from *de-libare*, see Shelton, *Morality and Sovereignty*, 8; and on his sense of contract, 32–33. On Milton's quite different use of Latin roots, see John Carey and Alastair Fowler, *The Poems of Milton* (London: Longmans, Green, 1968), 337. On Hobbes's use of metaphors, see Quentin Skinner's excellent discussion of how and why Hobbes came to adopt this rhetorical strategy in *Reason and Rhetoric in the Philosophy of Hobbes* (Cambridge: Cambridge University Press, 1996). However, in an important sense, Hobbes's abandonment of the rhetorical tradition was quite real, since he continued to reject the older republican ideal of the *vir civilis*, since he felt that the arts most *practically* able to benefit society were those of *otium* rather than *negotium*, the arts of peaceful, private, and scientific contemplation encouraged by the social compact or compromise. See especially 67–88, 292–342.

11. However, Hobbes's famous title page to *Leviathan* refers to Job 46. In *Paradise Lost*, Milton's equally famous leviathan/satan simile seems to allude to Isaiah's prophecy that the Lord shall punish "Leviathan, that crooked serpent . . . the dragon that is in the sea" (27:1), as Hughes notes. Yet sea powers are generally sinister throughout the bible, no doubt due both to the influence of the Canaanite myth of Tiamat and to the actual threat posed by such powers, such as the "satanic" kings of Tyre and Tarshish, the latter of which (as *Tarsus, PL* 1.200) Milton also directly links to leviathan. Although the associations of Dagon (probably an agricultural corn deity) with the Semitic word for *fish* are conventional, Milton's exploitation of its monstrous connotations may point to the "monster of Malmesbury," Hobbes himself.

(itself a Ciceronian coinage), but also the broader understanding of natural justice it implies. Milton follows the mainline tradition set forth by both Cicero and Plutarch in objecting to tyranny as an "idolatrous" perversion of natural reason, while Hobbes instead follows Cicero's condemnation of the state of nature (as his famous "translation" puts it) "solitary, poore, nasty, brutish and short" (*Leviathan* 1.13.18).[12] According to Jean Hampton, he takes his precedent from Cicero's *For Publius Sextus:*

> Who of you is ignorant that the nature of things has been such, that at one time men, before there was any natural or civil law fully laid down, wandered in a straggling and disorderly manner over the country, and had just that property which they could either seize or keep by their personal strength and vigour, by means of wounds and bloodshed. And there is no point in which there is so much difference between this manner of life, polished by civilization, and that savage one, as the fact of law being the ruling principle of the one, and violence of the other. (Cicero, *For Publius Sextius*)[13]

This side of Cicero was generally neglected by European revolutionaries, who in common with Milton and Rousseau, envisioned the original state of nature as essentially similar to that of the early Roman republic, where humankind experienced self-sufficient forms of pastoral peace through self-government.

Hobbes was notoriously critical not only of this view, but also of the Parliamentarians' selective reading of classical history, a charge of which he was of course equally guilty. As a result, the literal existence of his original state of nature as a continual "war of all upon all" has been commonly acknowledged as no more and perhaps even less probable than that envisioned by Milton or Rousseau. Yet despite his much darker view of human nature, Hobbes's demonstration that a widely recognized, binding legal constitution is needed to foster the people's freedom and ability to conduct secular business has been taken as a kind of natural law in most subsequent political theory, since the cessation of violent competition is

12. On Milton's place in this tradition, see Zera S. Fink, *The Classical Republicans: An Essay in the Recovery of a Pattern of Thought in Seventeenth-Century England* (Evanston: Northwestern University Press, 1945); William Haller, *Liberty and Reformation in the Puritan Revolution* (New York: Columbia University Press, 1955); and Ernest Sirluck's introduction to *CPW*, 2:1–145, especially 35. On the anti-imperial context of the Bible itself, see George E. Mendenhall, *The Tenth Generation: The Origins of the Biblical Tradition* (Baltimore: John Hopkins Press, 1973). However, like Filmer and most of the Royalists generally, Hobbes justified monarchy both by reason of mankind's postlapsarian condition and through the precedent of Adam's "kingship" over the earth, a point vigorously refuted by Milton's Adam himself (*PL* 12.64–71).

13. Cited by Jean Hampton as a primary source for Hobbes's state of nature in *Hobbes and the Social Contract Tradition* (Cambridge: Cambridge University Press, 1986), 58.

clearly needed to attain the benefits of "commodious living" achieved by Reason, which "suggesteth convenient Articles of Peace" (*Leviathan* 1.13.188). On this essentially mercantile basis, Hobbes also argues that the traditional conceptions of commutative and deliberative justice have been misguided in guaranteeing: (1) that things contracted for be of equal value, and (2) that any distribution of advantages should provide "equall benefit, to men of equal merit" (*Leviathan* 1.15.208), since the goal of "commodious living" can be accomplished only by allowing the marketplace to determine all human or material values according to the laws of supply and demand. Further, the benefits of this system—which encourages advances in technical, scientific, and artistic modes of production—seem to him so compelling that he regards the social contract as both morally and/or prudentially binding (especially since he does not ultimately distinguish between morality and self-interest) even when rooted in coercion.[14]

From this standpoint alone it seems highly significant that the dragon, eagle, and phoenix symbols of Milton's drama arrive with the "cloudless thunder bolted" (1696) against the temple worshippers of Dagon/Leviathan as an overdetermined symbol of *retributive* justice—the same power that quells the rebels against divinely instituted laws in *Paradise Lost* (1.44–45, 6.858). For the issue that most clearly separates Samson's justice from that of the Philistines is also what separates Milton's reading of Cicero from Hobbes's. In the passage cited above, Cicero's reference to "natural *or* civil law" (emphasis added) alludes to a distinction between the two that was commonly recognized not only by Roman law itself but by all subsequent natural law theory. Although the terms were often ambiguous and overlapping, natural law or *lex* was usually associated with the primary and therefore universal dictates of divinely instituted right reason, while *ius* (best translated in this case as "legal privilege" or "right") was associated with more conventional and contingent notions of justice associated with local and at times obviously arbitrary customary laws. Thus in cases of conflict (local or international), this secondary domain of civil or positive law *(ius)* had to yield to the universal ideals of *lex*. For as Cicero elsewhere concludes, "the origin of justice [*iuris*] is to be found in law [*lex*], for law is a natural force[,] . . . the standard by which Justice and Injustice are measured." In the limited but important cases where local laws or authorities seemed to contradict this force of natural reason, he therefore

14. See C. B. MacPherson's *The Political Theory of Possessive Individualism: Hobbes to Locke* (Oxford: Oxford University Press, 1962), especially 63–64, where he discusses these traditional notions of legal equity, also summarized by Hill in *Puritanism and Revolution*, 282–83. On the Hobbesian thesis that even covenants undertaken in fear are obligatory, see Shelton, *Morality and Sovereignty*, 53.

urges that contradictory commands "no more deserve to be called laws than the rules a band of robbers might pass in their assembly"—a passage that Milton's Samson quotes virtually verbatim (891–95).[15]

Hobbes, on the other hand, radically departs from this tradition by placing all human law on the same positive basis as the legislation governing marriage or other civic arrangements—to which he believes even children and slaves tacitly "agree" (*Leviathan* 2.20.251–61). Further, since these laws can only be enforced by abandoning the state of nature, a "covenantal" obligation to comply with the positive laws of the sovereign authority (whether originally instituted by means of force or voluntary agreement) is essential to the maintenance of the body politic. Effectively eliminating the higher sphere of *lex* altogether, this system thus collapses all law into *ius*, for in Hobbes's "deconstruction" of Cicero, *"That men performe their Covenants made. . .* [is] the Fountain and Originall of JUSTICE" (*Leviathan* 1.15.201–2). This interpretation also implies that he *would* recognize the laws laid down by a band of robbers provided they were powerful enough to maintain them, especially since he regards "Power Irresistible" as the ultimate source of both human and divine authority. Whether it belongs to his God or his sovereign, "Omnipotence" should be worshipped on the basis of its sheer force rather than its justice, creativity, or "graciousness." This concept of godhead would of course have been anathema both to Milton and the Cambridge Platonists, whose deity sets up just and rational laws that his own infinite goodness constrains him to obey.[16] But perhaps even worse from this perspective, Hobbes's ultravoluntarist, ultranominalist theology produces a correspondingly vitiated sense of covenant.

While in this period the word *covenant* commonly means something closer to our sense of social contract—a sense in which both Hobbes and Milton use it—the Hobbesian usage effectively restricts it to the quasi-atomistic sense of "drawing together" or "materially condensing" rather than "negotiating or agreeing." To Hobbes, this eradication of the concept's spiritual *and* Ciceronian connotations would seem fully warranted by the fact that human existence is "either for gain, or for glory; that is, not so much for love of our fellows, as for the love of ourselves" (*de Cive* 1.2.24).[17] However, since like a business contract the covenant remains

---

15. Keyes trans., *de Legibus* 2:5. For a fuller discussion of these points, see Shelton's chapter on "The State of Nature and Natural Law," in *Morality and Sovereignty*, 18–41.

16. On this point, see Stephen M. Fallon, " 'To Act or Not': Milton's Conception of Divine Freedom," *Journal of the History of Ideas* 49 (1988): 425–49.

17. See the English translation of *de Cive* in *Philosophical Rudiments Concerning Government and Society*, ed. S. P. Lamprecht (New York: n.p., 1955).

nonnegotiable except by agreement of both parties (which in popular disputes with bishops and kings is unlikely, to say the least), it cancels rights widely recognized in both Roman and modern law. But, as usual, Hobbes is willing to accept this corollary of his postulates, including the collapse of religious into political authority on the premise that

> The End of Worship amongst men, is Power. For where a man seeth another worshipped, he supposeth him powerfull, and is the readier to obey him; which makes his Power greater. But God has no Ends: the worship we do him proceeds from our duty, and is directed according to our capacity, by those rules of Honour, that Reason dictateth to be done by the weak to the more potent men, in hope of benefit, for fear of dammage, or in thankfulness for good already received from them. . . . But seeing a Common-wealth is but one Person, it ought also to exhibite to God but one Worship . . . and this is Publique Worship; the property whereof, is to be *Uniforme.* . . . And therefore, where many sorts of Worship be allowed, . . . it cannot be said there is any Publique worship, nor that the Commonwealth is of any Religion at all. (*Leviathan* 2.31, 401, 405–6)

Hobbes's uncanny ability to spell out the hidden political implications of Calvin's theological voluntarism may constitute one of Milton's many reasons for moving toward Arminian or "free will" theology, motives that would also have been intensified after the Restoration, when the Anglican clergy adopted an essentially Hobbesian position (which they justified on the basis of Luke 14:16–23) concerning the necessity of a uniform and compulsory state religion.[18] These views obviously run completely contrary to Milton's belief that freedom of conscience *and* worship is the only basis of all true religion, itself the product of *non*unilateral human/divine covenants whose "conditions . . . have to be fulfilled not by one party but by both" (*CPW*, 6:506). The dual nature of these "accords" is dramatically illustrated throughout *Samson Agonistes,* which also consistently rejects the chief prop of unilateral voluntarism, the *predestined* perseverance of the elect. For as he remarks in his *Christian Doctrine,* "those who persevere, not those who are elect, are said to attain salvation" (*CPW*, 6:509); "Prov. xxiv. 16: *for the just man falls seven times, but gets up again, but the wicked fall headlong into evil*" (*CPW*, 6:513). Then, in striking contrast to Hobbes's savagely lapsarian view of the natural state, his following chapter describes natural law as continuous with Adam's prelapsarian existence: "The unwritten law is the law of nature given to the first man. A kind of gleam or glimmering of it still remains in the hearts of all mankind. In the regenerate this is daily brought nearer to a renewal of its original

---

18. On this point, see Sharon Achinstein, "*Samson Agonistes* and the Drama of Dissent," *Milton Studies* 33, ed. Albert C. Labriola (Pittsburgh: University of Pittsburgh Press, 1997), 140–41.

perfection by the operation of the Holy Spirit" (*CPW*, 6:516). As in his political treatises, God's ongoing covenant with natural man is based not on laws given by Moses but *to* Adam, who received a personal covenant of grace issuing from God's *graciousness* rather than from his testament or will. On this account Milton insists that the root sense of *covenant* is closer to the Latin *pactum* or "sign of peace" than to the Greek words usually associated with it, *diatheka* and *suntheka,* which translate into English as "God's will or testament" (*CPW*, 6:522).

Like Hobbes, Milton obviously has a polemical stake in this game, although his analysis is less logic-chopping and more consistent with the biblical account of the first "official" biblical covenant, the Noatic sign of peace given with the rainbow. Yet its political implications cannot be gainsaid: if the divine covenant has been progressively renegotiated and refined until it approximates that given to Adam, then "by the operation of the Holy Spirit" it must also reflect the *eternal lex* ever more clearly "read" in the human conscience, mind, and heart (see *PL* 12.523–24). These premises provide the basis of Milton's revolutionary faith in a holistic form of Christian liberty that, as Arthur Barker remarks, finally "ceased to be an exclusive spiritual principle possessed before God, and became a liberty to be used *not only before men but in spite of human authority, ecclesiastical or civil.*"[19] This radical covenant of grace also dictates that Christians have no right either to impose their own consciences or *to be imposed upon* by others, for as Milton understands Paul, "I Cor. ix. 19: *although I am free from all men I have made myself a slave to all*—I was not made a slave by anyone else; *free from all men*—and therefore, of course, from the magistrate, at any rate in matters of this kind" (*CPW*, 6:541; see also *Of Civil Power*). This rule of conscience would thus dismiss any law, human or (Mosaically) divine, that "disturbs believers and makes them waver" (*CPW*, 6:529), since the natural laws of charity and liberty principally apply to individual, not communal, bodies of faith (see *Colasterion,* in *CPW*, 2:750).

Milton's *Tenure of Kings and Magistrates* is again relevant here, since it not only makes compliance with the Pauline precedent of Romans 13 conditional upon the civil authority's adherence to its covenant with the people, but it also invalidates the precedent of David's forbearance against his kingly oppressor, Saul. Not only could no contemporary king claim David or Saul's divine anointing, but the precedent itself is inapplicable because "the matter between them was not tyranny, but privat enmity, and *David as a privat person had bin his own revenger,* not the peoples"

---

19. Arthur Barker, *Milton and the Puritan Dilemma* (Toronto: University of Toronto Press, 1942), 101–2 (emphasis mine).

(*CPW*, 3:216; emphasis mine).[20] As this statement clearly implies, resistance by private persons *is* legally justified when the issues at stake involve tyranny, which effectively abolishes the primary purpose of civil power: to uphold the natural laws of "ecclesiastical liberty, personal or domestic liberty, and civil liberty." These are also the principles successively defended by his Samson in his encounters—with his father and the Danite elders; Dalila, his wife; and Harapha, the "champion" of Philistine or Hobbesian power—as he establishes the divinely *defended* right (via the decree handed down through the destruction of Dagon's temple) of an *apparently* "private person" to resist unrighteous civil authority based only upon "strength sufficient and command from Heav'n" (*SA* 1212).

At this point the natural law debate between Milton and Hobbes can be summarized as roughly equivalent to the modern disagreement between upholders of merely "negative" liberty—freedom *from* lawless or criminal restraint—and Miltonic or "positive" liberty—freedom *to* conscientious, and thus "naturally" lawful, self-determination.[21] Given the completely different understandings of nature, law, and covenant inherent in both positions, in his own eyes, Samson is an ardent if failed defender of positive liberty, while to the Philistines, he is merely an inveterate offender in a legally established state properly maintained by negative force. For while both Hobbes and Milton's Samson claim that "the Law of Nations, and the Law of Nature, is the same thing" (*Leviathan* 2.30.394; *SA* 890), Hobbes would use this identity as an argument *against* the possibility of appealing to a higher court of law, the very right Samson tries to persuade Dalila she ought to have exercised in deciding her differing responsibilities to her husband and her people. Yet without it, according to both Samson and Cicero, her nation has become "No more thy country, but an impious crew / Of men conspiring to uphold thir state / By worse than hostile deeds, violating the ends / For which our country is a name so dear; / Not therefore to be obey'd" (891–95).[22]

20. As Hughes notes, Milton is directly responding to a treatise by a group of Presbyterian divines, *A Serious and Faithfull Representation of the judgements of Ministers of the Gospel within the Province of London* (January 18, 1649); for an extended overview, see *CPW*, 3:39–100, quoted 73.

21. This conflict still continues among legal scholars and political historians; generally speaking, Isaiah Berlin has supported the concept of negative liberty and Quentin Skinner, that of positive liberty. See Berlin, *Four Essays on Liberty* (New York: Oxford University Press, 1969), and Skinner, *Liberty before Liberalism* (Cambridge: Cambridge University Press, 1998). Here Skinner usefully points out that "neo-Roman" thinkers like Milton object to negative liberty as actually a form of political servitude.

22. This close paraphrase of Cicero's *de Legibus* has been (so far as I have been able to ascertain) unfortunately ignored by both critics and editors, even though Milton

However, the situation is complicated by the Danite chorus, who, unlike Samson himself, see in him a sad victim of their essentially Calvinist God's voluntarist will, which not only strictly enforces their bondage to Mosaic law, but also inscrutably predestines the fall of his presumed saints. Their view of the covenantal unilateralism of this a-rational deity "Who made our Laws to bind us, not himself" (309) is thus correspondingly flawed, even though, unlike Dalila, they are willing to stumble along with the fallen Samson's conscientious reflection upon the rights and wrongs rationally deducible from his situation. What they then (re)discover is that while the Hobbesian Philistines would equate the lack of civil power with the absence of spiritual, personal, and domestic rights, even when Samson's God is most silent or seemingly unhearing, neither he nor his worshippers are truly impotent, not even when the Philistines count the faithful as having no "Religion at all." Thus if Samson has all but given up on "delivering" himself and his contemporaries from his double yoke (40–43) of internal and external affliction, even in his most despairing moment he conscientiously refuses any easy self-absolution or any of "the sayings of the wise" among his own party, particularly their quietistic celebration of "Patience" *without* "heroic martyrdom" "as the truest fortitude" (652, 654; see *PL* 8.31–32). Instead, he vigorously reexamines his own role in his symbolically "seven" falls, which remain mysterious only insofar as they cannot be traced to mere sensuality or even simony, although like his biblical prototype, he has indeed sold "God's holy secret" for domestic peace. His hard-won peripeteia must then proceed from his most difficult and fundamental dramatic recognition: that he had fallen into the misguided voluntarism of the elect who trust in the inevitable "perseverance of the saints" without exercising their wisdom, self-restraint, or self-correction.

Thus even at his lowest ebb, Samson models a more painful but also more powerful form of liberty that is not, as he thinks, lower than that of a "bondslave" (38). Although cast into public servitude, he retains a synthetically private and public "talent": his self-reflexive ability to confront not only his literal and symbolic blindness but its relation to the unkept covenants now obliquely reflected in his self-tarnished *imago dei*. If these covenants are to be renewed, he must also be willing to correct that image by subjecting it to a profound personal, domestic, and ecclesiastical critique. But if he should instead succumb to the Philistines' "accords," he would indeed become the irredeemably failed champion of God that his revisionist critics, like his own chorus, literalistically "see":

---

ranks Cicero first among the "Philosophers and gravest Writers" authoritatively cited in his preface as upholding the moral tenor of tragic poetry.

> The Dungeon of thyself; thy Soul
> (Which Men enjoying sight oft without cause complain)
> Imprison'd now indeed,
> In real darkness of the body dwells,
> Shut up from outward light
> To incorporate with gloomy night;
> For inward light, alas
> Puts forth no visual beam. (156–63)

This visual beam is of course the inner light of Milton's "Umpire *Conscience*" (*PL* 3.195), which Hobbes would outlaw as chief among "the *Diseases* of a Common-wealth," along with "supernaturall Inspiration, or Infusion" (*Leviathan* 2.29.365–66), the force behind Samson's "rousing motions."

Yet from this perspective, to render conscience null and void is not merely to deny private inspiration, but also to confirm the chorus's gloomy identification of mind with body and soul with sight, which in the civic sphere depressingly identifies temporal power with eternal justice. The tendency of the legalistic "saints" similarly to confuse the two is represented by the Danites' confusion of their hero's godly glory with his military victory, as on the day with "what trivial weapon came to hand" he "A thousand foreskins fell, the flower of *Palestine*" (142, 144). Given that Samson *does* retain a far from "trivial weapon" to hand, his unfettered mind, their lamentation of the contrast between this triumph and his present state is actually one of the bondages that he must break: an enslavement to the past and to custom, icons that ironically conceal the actual presence of their "deliverer." Both for Milton and for the deuteronomist, the idols of custom and consensus are so many unclean "foreskins" obscuring God's hidden ways (Deuteronomy 10:16) from the spiritually uncircumcised. Should he or they succumb to their allures, the most they can expect is the merely material deliverance Samson himself rejects: a mistaken "ransom sacrifice" to a droning life of living death, only to become a "Vain monument of strength; till length of years / And sedentary numbness craze my limbs / To a contemptible old age obscure" (570–72).

The special pleadings of Manoa and Dalila at once repeat and heighten the temptation to settle for this form of deliverance as Samson wavers between the strangely congruent premises of legalistic dualism, Danite or Philistine, and the vague glimmerings of the "spirit-filled" monism that ultimately "infuses" his synthetically spiritual and material regeneration. Without exactly sharing Harapha's superstitious suspicion of the contract of "spells / And black enchantments" lying behind the Nazarite sign that had literally "hung" in his hair (1133), the Samson who first appears on stage is still far from understanding that his "Consecrated gift / Of strength" (1354–55) is only *sealed* by his hair as the mere outward manifestation of a mutual, voluntary, and inward holy vow, covenant, or "seal," which for Milton acts more like a negotiable "trope or figure of speech" than a testament sealed in stone (*CPW*, 6:555–56). Later, this higher, *because* more ambiguous, understanding of signs informs Samson's sudden apprehension of the continuity between *ius* and *lex*, which, like his "strength sufficient and command from Heav'n," is physically "diffus'd / . . . through all my sinews, joints and bones" by regaining the spiritual "pledge of my unviolated vow" (1141–42, 1144). This new sense of God's law as something *transactionally* inscribed on head and heart then allows him to re-fuse outward signs with inner apprehensions, as his uncertain self-interrogation obliquely anticipates:

> Since light so necessary is to life,
> And almost life itself, if it be true
> That light is in the Soul,
> She all in every part; why was the sight
> To such a tender ball as th' eye confined?
> And not as feeling through all parts diffus'd,
> That she might look at will through every pore?
> Then had I not been thus exil'd from light;
> As in the land of darkness yet in light,
> To live a life half dead, a living death,
> And buried; but O yet more miserable! (91–101)

Here we should again recall that Hobbes had attempted to reduce not just optics but the entire operation of the human will and understanding to the purely material motions that formed the psychological basis of his political "Arithmetique and Geommetry" (*Leviathan* 2.20.261). In confronting the higher reality of his vitally synthetic "motions," Samson gradually comes to realize that only his own mechanistic misapprehensions *truly* confine him to the moral, physical, and ocular prison of himself. Since light is not limited to mere physical vision any more than conscience to mere consciousness, his refusal to capitulate to a "land of darkness" gradually provides an insight looking "through every pore." Besieged by partially valid accusations on the part of himself and his father, friends, former wife, and overt enemies alike (960–66, 1236), a solitary and confused Samson who could never before claim mental agility as his greatest strength then begins to triumph over their pragmatic "arithmetique" by strenuously separating the higher and more negotiable covenants or "constraints" (1372) of divine law from its narrower and more local "commands" or civic contracts. This painful struggle is rewarded with a newly synthetic apprehension, but not without first awakening the anger that for Milton is the primary effect of the old law—and also the primary impetus for abrogating it (*CPW*, 6:523, Romans 4:15). At this stage Samson is aided by his basic perception that if the Philistines' civil commands are clearly unjust—as they are in forcing a faithful servant of God to perform public acts that he regards as "Idol-Worship" (1365)—then they are also "unnatural" or even unreal in the sense that they can only artificially or externally constrain his inner liberty. Moreover, because "Where the heart joins not, outward acts defile not" (1368), even the deity's *own* narrower or more local proscriptions (which in these circumstances include Samson's Nazarite vows) can be set aside in the service of his higher natural laws.

Samson signals his final apprehension of this natural legal order in advising the chorus that God can "dispense with me or thee / Present in Temples at Idolatrous Rites / For some important cause" (1377–79). In essence, this new "dispensation" is based upon the fundamental Miltonic doctrine that only the *uncoerced* consent of conscientious, rational individuals can authentically decide whether their acts stem from the "fear of Man" and "Set God behind" (1374–75) or adhere to the higher "categorical imperative" implicit in natural or universal law. In this sense, it provides the inspired basis of *both* the old and the new law as Milton understands them: "Heb.viii.10, etc: *this is the covenant. . . . I will put my law into their mind . . . and I will be a God to them and they will be my people. . . .* Joel ii.28: *your sons and daughters will prophesy; your old men will dream dreams and your young men see visions.* Compare Acts ii.16–18. And indeed all true believers either prophesy or have within them the Holy Spirit, which is as good" (*CPW*, 6:523–24).

Yet the gifts of this spirit are hardly uncomplicated or irresponsible, as Samson's final and essentially Kantian apprehension reveals. Since mere fear of or desire for benefit from any concrete or particular man or group of men—in preference to a higher fear of universal wrong—"Shall never, unrepented find forgiveness" (1376), the improper use of conscience threatens to reduce the very self who thereby "contracts" itself into a lower state of existence, as Samson has already learned to his sorrow. Such responsibility is of course "aweful" in both negative and positive senses, which make it the appropriate subject of the Aristotelian or cathartic tragedy that Milton's preface claims he has written. In this case, the cathartic "calm of mind" (1758) with which the chorus departs must be won by purging the fear attendant upon Samson's apparently irredeemable, hopelessly pitiable state, which is maintained by the Danites' *and* Philistines' false claims of "reason and obedience." Appropriately, this enslavement is broken by the ambiguous linguistic power of Samson's "striking" puns, which later literally burst his shackles and "amaze" his enemies amidst the literal maze of their seemingly all-powerful temple. Prophesying that "Now of my own accord such other trial / I mean to show you of my strength, yet greater; / As with amaze shall strike all who behold" (1041, 1043–45), Samson redefines the meaning of the new "accord" his public "trial" will "strike" in most un-Hobbesian riddles. These a-maze the unmetaphorical Philistines in ways that not only revive and reempower their iconoclastic opponent, but also make their punishment fit their Babelish crime.

Samson's contest thus finally "proves" that no simple arithmetic or geometry can calculate the truth of his self-impelled motions any more than it can sequester the literal from the metaphoric or the public from the private senses of his trial. Yet his transformation is not "magical" in the sense that Harapha had decried, since it proceeds naturally enough from Samson's inalienable conviction that personal, political, and spiritual servitude are ultimately the same thing:

> But what more oft in Nations grown corrupt,
> And by thir vices brought to servitude,
> Than to love Bondage more than Liberty,
> Bondage with ease than strenuous liberty;
> And to despite, or envy, or suspect
> Whom God hath of his special favor rais'd
> As thir Deliverer . . . ? (268–74)

This declaration equates his people's suspicion of God's "special favor" with their fearful neglect of his covenant in favor of a Philistine social contract that can never "deliver" its subjects into anything but deeper servitude, an opportunistic de-liberation that in fact unilaterally ends their liberty.[23] In terms of this self-disempowering "neglect," the quietistic chorus and the voluntaristic Philistines may be understood as opposing versions of essentially the same thing: the bondage of unintrospective religious literalism (the "blind spots" of the Danite/Puritan faction) and of legalistic political pragmatism (the "bonds" of the Hobbesian/Philistine

---

23. In *Paradise Lost*, Michael informs Adam of the historical dialectic here outlined by Samson; see 11.797–804. Also evident here is the fact that "The words *deliverer* and *deliverance* sound throughout the play in two senses: delivered from or liberated, and delivered up or enslaved." Thus he himself realizes (ll. 460–71), "God may not act through Samson, but God will act." See Mary Ann Radzinowicz, *Toward Samson Agonistes: The Growth of Milton's Mind* (Princeton: Princeton University Press, 1978), 93, 96, 108.

faction). The Danites doubt the wandering ways of divine grace and prophetic redemption, since it so frequently appears that "Just or unjust, alike seem miserable, / For oft alike, both come to evil end" (703–4). Rather than a universal lawgiver, their God is thus an inscrutable Calvinist predestinator or, worse, an arbitrary king. In trusting only in outward appearances, the Philistines too regard Samson's God as a neglectful tribal deity no longer willing *or* able to defend servants who cannot pay him his proper tribute.

In the context of the civil war controversies, Milton had pointed out the same ironic continuity between supposedly opposing parties: the "Philistine" Royalists and the "Danite" Presbyterians, both of whom relied on the letter of the law and distrusted its spirit, whose guidance the Independents of the Westminster Assembly strenuously sought.[24] In fact, this distrust ultimately led not only to the Presbyterians' "pledge of respect for the king's person in the Covenant" on the Calvinist grounds that "only magistrates [are] scripturally authorized to resist 'higher powers,' " but also to their condemnation of their former allies both for "religious toleration and . . . presuming upon God's approval of a momentarily victorious cause; the sin of abusing the law of nature under pretense of political necessity" (*CPW*, 3:107–8). The resulting schism not only doomed the Puritan revolution but led to what, on the very eve of the Restoration, Milton was to call England's return to its Egyptian captivity (*CPW*, 7:387). In re-presenting their cynical view of political "necessity" in its unchanging aspect, Samson's final answer to Harapha and his lords (much like Abdiel's answer to Satan in the epic War in Heaven) thus poetically "unriddles" *whose* "nature bids the same" as *whose* God (*PL* 6:176): the literalist God of the Presbyterians and their Philistine friends, or the ambiguously riddling yet ever *open* God of the "true" Israel's covenanting people.

If from an earthly perspective these riddles must remain relatively opaque, Milton not only challenges his audience to reexamine their own providential covenants, but also provides a broader context for the question that his party was forced to ask in the wake of seemingly hopeless defeat: "God of our Fathers, what is man!" (667). With Cromwell, Ireton, and Bradshaw exhumed and hanged; Vane condemned to death and Lambert to prison; and the blind Milton himself barely escaping the block after a Samsonian exile in his own land, the mournful choral inquiry

24. On the revolutionary uses of the idea of emergent revelation and, by implication, of the idea of an emergently free creativity in events and in nature, see Fixler's discussion of the position of the Dissenting Brethren (with whom Milton was aligned) in the Westminster Assembly in *Milton and the Kingdoms of God*, 119–21.

into why God not "only dost degrade" his champions "or remit / To life obscur'd, which were a fair dismission, / But throw'st them lower than thou didst exalt them high" (687–99), has an inescapably partisan edge. So too does Samson's response, which his father receives as prophecy (473), that "thus provok'd" God

> . . . will arise and his great name assert:
> *Dagon* must stoop, and shall ere long receive
> Such a discomfit, as shall quite despoil him
> Of all these boasted Trophies won on me,
> And with confusion blank his Worshippers. (466–71)

Yet this prophecy involves a subtle play upon words that also reinflates the issues at stake to more abstractly classical proportions. Although Samson's just God does indeed "with confusion blank" all the worshippers of Dagon or Leviathan, he does not deal with them as they would with his people, including, historically, the Danites themselves. Instead of blanking or blotting out the Philistines—which, in this version, are significantly limited to the "Lords, Ladies, Captains, Counsellors, . . . [and] Priests" (1653) inside the temple proper—Milton allows the "throng" (1609) to become "Authors to themselves" (*PL* 3.122) in a peculiarly literal sense. Although they receive the same "confusion" as the worshippers of Babel, which linguistically confirms the actual incoherence of the nominalist attempt to reduce words to things, the "blank" that defaces their trophies and contracts destroys neither their symbolic nor their actual source of power: the Hobbesian claim that words like laws and forms of worship only "have their signification by agreement, and constitution of men."[25]

This claim cannot and will not be historically laid to rest, as the drama's revisionist critics remind us. Yet the enduring relevance of Samson's sacrifice is also strongly signaled by the inspired choral ode immediately preceding his departure to the temple:

> Oh how comely it is and how reviving
> To the Spirits of just men long opprest!
> When God into the hands of thir deliverer
> Puts invincible might
> To quell the might of the Earth, th' oppressor,
> The brute and boist'rous force of violent men

---

25. In this respect Samson's many echoes of Shakespeare's *Richard II* and his "blank charters" seem significant, since during the Restoration his self-destructive might-makes-right doctrine was often compared with that of Hobbes; on the latter point, see Mintz (quoting Bishop Parker), *Hunting of Leviathan,* 135.

> Hardy and industrious to support
> Tyrannic power, but raging to pursue
> The righteous and all such as honor Truth;
> Hee all thir Ammunition
> And feats of war defeats
> With plain Heroic magnitude of mind
> And celestial vigor arm'd,
> Thir Armories and Magazines contemns,
> Tenders them useless, while
> With winged expedition
> Swift as the lightning glance he executes
> His errand on the wicked, who surpris'd
> Lose thir defense, distracted and amaze'd. (1268–86)

This choral outburst not only rehearses Calvin's comments on public avengers *without* his qualifications, but also ironically corrects their own parting injunction that Samson accept the crown of patience as the inevitable price of blindness. Yet if their words are subject to error—as all living and "negotiable" language must be—they also prophetically anticipate God's covenantal response to his witnesses against seemingly impossible odds.

The dramatic peripeteia surrounding Samson's unlikely return to his desired role as Israel's active champion is further foreshadowed by his prior encounter with the bullying Harapha, for in refusing to test either his strength or his faith against his tragically crippled enemy, Harapha smugly advises him to

> Presume not on thy God, whate'er he be,
> Thee he regards not, owns not, hath cut off
> Quite from his people, and delivered up
> Into thy Enemies' hand, permitted them
> To put out both thine eyes, and fetter'd send thee
> Into the common Prison, there to grind
> Among the Slaves and Asses thy comrades,
> As good for nothing else, no better service. (1157–64)

A firm believer in positive law understood as natural law, the Philistine "giant" equates deliverance with material advantage, merit with status or market value, and appearances with names or things—in short, behaves like a perfect Hobbesian "possessive individual." As such, he cannot begin to comprehend Samson's reply: that despite appearances, his faith precludes despair "of his final pardon / Whose ear is ever open; and his eye / Gracious to re-admit the suppliant" (1171–74). This courageous refusal to separate his private hope for pardon from his political faith in the universal deity's "natural" or higher justice not only displays his utter contrast with the merely local Dagon, but also parallels the contrast between legal contracts and covenants. Like Hobbes, the worshippers of Dagon regard legal rights as unilaterally constituted by the power of superior authorities once the state of nature has ceased, *not* as universal principles derived from rational and therefore *conditional* consent ("Reason also is choice," *PL* 3.108, *CPW*, 2:527). From the latter perspective, Harapha's might-makes-right doctrine is indeed barbaric, the last resort of "Idolists and Atheists" (453), its legitimacy as fragile as his refusal to "taste" (1091) the righteous though blind might of Samson. Coming from a hypocrite unable or unwilling to "judge or discern" (as the Latin root of "taste," *sapere* implies) the superior value of a voluntary contract to engage in individual combat unconstrained by sovereign authority, Harapha's assertions collapse much like the temple into which Samson is then led, no true temple but a mere den of thieves. This collapse may also have a more particular historical thrust, given that his flight parallels the actual course of the notoriously timid Hobbes, the first of his party to flee revolutionary England for the safer precincts of the "Papist" French court.

Dalila's hypocrisy is more subtle, which not only allows her initially to seem (as she claims) to be the more injured party, but makes her debate with Samson more challenging as well as more pivotal. Even so, her test of Samson's faith is best understood in relation to the standard patterns of Greek tragedy, where the central agon typically features two *almost* but not quite equally worthy opponents, a criterion that excludes Harapha but not Dalila. Nevertheless, her final exit triggers the relatively predictable anagnorisis in which their respective worth is finally revealed: where Dalila's recognition of the speciousness of her own self-defense causes her to flaunt her less-than-magnanimous motives and deceits (*apate*) as a parting revenge against Samson. In contrast, his mental and physical sufferings have led him to reflect upon and repair his own form of *apate*, his tendency to confuse carnal desire with connubial love and both with the divine will. Yet his unflinching re-vision of these failings also uncovers the self-serving nature of Dalila's affections, teaching him that "had thy love, still odiously pretended, / Been, as it ought, sincere, it would have taught thee / Far other reasonings, brought forth other deeds" than her literally crippling care (873–75). This insight leads to his further recognition of her more than merely feminine weakness (her chief defense), thus combining the three forms of anagnorisis that Aristotle praises as the best: recognition through reasoning, through recognition of faulty premises, and through the natural outworking of events.[26] Yet his *Poetics* reserves its highest praise for recognition scenes turning upon a natural but unexpected reversal of dramatic action, which is precisely what occurs in Dalila's sudden turn from feigned sympathy to cruel taunting at her exit. Dramatically, this separation is also portrayed as actually a divorce proceeding on the grounds of spiritual incompatibility, grounds that Milton had previously insisted should justify it on the basis of right reason if not custom, whose other "face" is that of Error herself (*CPW*, 2:223).

From this perspective, much of the recent critical defense of Dalila seems to stem from a misguidedly sentimental reading of *Samson Agonistes* as a fully mimetic (hence relatively opaque) domestic tragedy rather than as a cathartic Greek agon hinging upon a crucial (and only partially mimetic) anagnorisis. In light of Milton's preface, this anachronism can only be excused (if at all) by the fact that Dryden seems to have "borrowed" Dalila's self-representation in his highly sentimentalized retelling of the Cleopatra legend, *All for Love*. But read in the more philosophical Greek sense Milton explicitly recommends, Dalila's early and ongoing preference for the relatively narrow contracts and customs of personal and national glory is only too obvious—as it was to a great narrative artist like Goethe. Further, since her exit neatly coincides with Samson's summons to Dagon's temple (with Harapha's brief visit supplying the intervening time it would take for her to report his refusal to return with her), her parting fury may stem from her failure to summon him herself, not from other kinds of wounded feelings. Yet even had she not intended to lead a newly reenchanted Samson to the Philistines' new "sport," the coincidence of Dalila's and Harapha's exits with the arrival of the state authority makes them at least symbolically complicit in Samson's final and (no doubt also for them) fatal appearance. For in the classic space of such significant "coincidences," Greek tragedy regularly teaches us to await the double-edged recoil of destiny or fate, which in this case includes the inevitable reaction of divine law in defense of its covenants and their "witnesses."

If this highly individualistic model of authority is also elitist in the sense that those who are morally and spiritually "elect above the rest" like

---

26. See *Aristotle's Poetics*, trans. James Hutton (New York: W. W. Norton, 1982), 62. In this case, Dalila's failure to establish her repentance and love also rests on both classical and Christian ground: Samson's charges against her are founded both in Cicero (*On Friendship*, xxvii, 100) as well as St. Paul (1 Corinthians 13:1–8).

Samson are ethically obligated to provide civic and religious leadership despite enormous personal cost, it is also radically voluntarist in the nonunilateral sense of vocation, the concept Milton used to justify his own role as Puritan poet and public minister to the nation. Here Samson's election is also biblically validated not merely by his humble parentage but by the human failings he must overcome, which Milton intensifies by showing his father's persistent misunderstanding of both his vocation and his need for regeneration. In none of these details is it at all difficult to trace the sympathies of a much-maligned scrivener's son "church-outed" by the clergy his father had hoped he would join. Yet this vocational ideal also fosters a more contemporary "equal opportunity" model insofar as such "callings" are limited neither by gender, class, nor by the state itself. Dalila herself reminds us of this model in falsely comparing herself to Jael (989–90), the obscure Hebrew woman who smote the mighty enemy Sisera in her humble tent. Because Jael is closely associated with Deborah, the female judge and psalmist, here only the faulty premises of the comparison, not the role model, is invalidated; Jael attacked an arrogant enemy besieging her country, not a husband she had consented to cherish (Judges 4:14–24).

In light of her neglect of this universal "accord," the glory with which Dalila dreams her nation will reward her must vanish along with her relativistic faith that "double-mouthed" fame "with contrary blast proclaims most deeds; / On both his wings, one black, the other white, / Bears greatest names in his wild aery flight" (971–74). For Milton, this social constructivist logic is invalidated by the natural law tradition in which the good exists not because God (or man) *commands* it, but because God (or history) can uphold it only because it is good. As we have seen, Hobbes takes the opposite position, granting his deity like his sovereign the arbitrary or "transcendently" voluntarist power of the Calvinist and/or Presbyterian God. As George Shelton notes, these contrary theologies logically tend to produce two opposing models of government: "One alternative is to say that God created a world governed by certain laws and that once these were in effect even God was bound by them. On the other hand, if God were genuinely all-powerful, there was nothing to stop him from changing his own laws if he so wished. The first possibility made God resemble a constitutional monarch; the second led him to look more like a Hobbesian sovereign."[27] On this basis alone, the legal and

---

27. Shelton, *Morality and Sovereignty*, 45. In his survey of *Natural Law and Moral Philosophy: From Grotius to the Scottish Enlightenment* (Cambridge: Cambridge University Press, 1996), Knud Haakonssen associates the two main branches of natural law

marital contest between Samson and Dalila is synthetically political *and* theological: Samson worships a constitutional monarch, Dalila an absolute sovereign who in Miltonic terms is a mere tyrant, the slave of the "wild aery flight" of arbitrary opinion and hence ultimately of his own slaves as well. For as Milton had classically observed in his *Second Defence*, the tyrant is actually even less free than his subjects who "serve only their own vices; he is forced, even against his will, to be a slave, not only to his own crimes, but also to the most grievous crimes of his servants and attendants, and he must yield a certain share of his despotism to all his most abandoned followers. Tyrants then are the meanest of slaves; they are slaves even to their own slaves" (*CPW*, 4.1:563).

Thus if we remain uncomfortable with Samson's complete rejection both of Dalila and her well-"grounded maxim," "So rife and celebrated in the mouths / Of wisest men, that to the public good / Private respects must yield" (865–68), we should again recall that her ultra-Hobbesian version of natural law is here being contrasted with fundamental goods that even Hobbes affirmed as irrevocable in either civil society or the state of nature. Those are the universal laws of individual, mutual, and marital self-preservation, which decree that "if aught against my life / Thy country sought of thee, it sought unjustly, / Against the law of nature, law of nations, / No more thy country, but an impious crew / . . . Not therefore to be obey'd" (888–91, 894). Since Dalila has broken this higher covenant—which to this day is upheld in the legal principle that frees a wife from being forced to testify against her husband—Samson wisely refuses her temptation to succumb to the living death she offers: the impotence reserved for the inactive possessive individual, retired at "home in leisure and domestic ease / Exempt from many a care and chance to which / Eyesight exposes daily men abroad" (917–19). This rejection not only settles his domestic account with Dalila's house or "Gaol" as he now sees it (949), but also complements his prior settling of his spiritual account with his father's house, the dronelike existence he refuses in similar terms. What then remains to settle is his civil account with the Philistines, which Harapha's inability or unwillingness to risk his "gianthood" prevents in any personal terms.

Hence Samson's proposed test of strength *must* be deferred to the public arena, which, along with his other legal disputes, will openly try his unan-

---

tradition ("intellectualist" and "voluntarist") with Scholastic and Reformed theology respectively. However, via differing interpretations of Grotius, Milton's intellectualist position is again ironically rooted in the same Reformed source as Hobbes's voluntarist version of social contract theory.

swered challenge to Harapha: "By combat to decide whose god is God, / Thine or whom I with *Israel's* Sons adore" (1176–77). Because neither Harapha nor his people recognize the spiritual authority, the civil rights, or even the human existence of this "covenant breaker" except as "a Murderer, a Revolter, and a Robber" (1181) fit only to grind at the "Mill with slaves" (41)—that is, as a nonperson according to their social contract—this question challenges the justice of Philistine law in the broadest possible terms. The enduring nature of these issues is invoked by the "Areopagan" setting of the climax, which occurs not in the temple itself but in "a spacious Theater / Half round on two main Pillars vaulted high, / With seats where all the Lords and each degree / Of sort, might sit in order to behold" (1605–8). While in one sense the self-destructive act of liberation that follows is clearly meant to counter the "irreducibly theatrical phenomenon" created by Hobbes's *Leviathan*, it does so not by symbolically terrifying its spectators into submission, but by liberating "irreducibly" positive chaotic effects.[28] For in Milton's view, both human and divine creation emerges from destruction like a great "divorcing command out of Chaos" (*CPW*, 2:273), "The Womb of nature and perhaps her Grave" (*PL* 2.911). Similarly, Samson's memorial is no tomb in his well-meaning but mistaken "Father's house," but an empty and open "womb," "A Monument, . . . plant[ed] round with shade / Of Laurel ever green, and branching Palm, / With all his Trophies hung, and Acts enroll'd / In copious Legend, or sweet Lyric Song" (1734–37). Like Lycidas, Samson has "sunk low, but mounted high" (172), beyond the concrete victories of earthly fame, "that last infirmity of Noble mind," leaving behind a similarly empty monument that allows him to become the Christlike "Genius of the shore" (*Lycidas* 71, 183). Far more than any momentary victory over Philistine idolatry and "imperial" pomp, more even than any revitalization of Samson's sympathizers, his achievement establishes the individual's right to seal an enduring covenant with the eternal house of universal law, whose very silences are more fertilely ambiguous than Dalila's fleeting fame, which apparently dies with her on the very day she asserts it.

Yet as Milton well knew, the chaotic rhythms of history cannot be counted on to exonerate any individual faith except, perhaps, in the personal space of literary time—itself an analogue (as he claims in *Areopagitica*) of the phoenixlike bird of classical liberty. Due to the instabilities

---

28. See Christopher Pye, "The Sovereign, the Theater, and the Kingdome of Darknesse: Hobbes and the Spectacle of Power," *Representations* 8 (1984): 85–106; cited, 86. Hence it should also go without saying that I reject Michael Lieb's account of this destruction as an inscrutable act of holy terror; see, however, " 'Our Living Dread': The God of *Samson Agonistes*," *Milton Studies* 33, 3–26.

of its unpredictable cycles, Samson must compensate for the Milton who can only "stand and wait" during the Restoration, his ability to champion his cause deferred onto a kingdom whose fulfillment is not yet, bearing witness to a providential dispensation that must at times be understood more from the standpoint of failure than of success. Thus ironically much like the young poet whose self-described "ministry" was to write not for the passing politics of the moment but for posterity, his task remains that of composing works "doctrinal and exemplary to a Nation" that future generations "should not willingly let . . . die" (*The Reason of Church Government*, in *CPW*, 1:815, 810). Later, on the eve of and after the Restoration, this task leads him to defend the higher law of nature that *The Readie and Easie Way* calls

> the only law of laws truly and properly to all mankinde fundamental; the beginning and the end of all Government; to which no Parliament or people that will thoroughly reforme, but may and must have recourse; as they had, and must yet have, in church reformation . . . to evangelic rules; not to ecclesiastical canons, though never so ancient, so ratifi'd and established in the land by Statutes, which for the most part are meer positive laws, neither natural nor moral, & so by any Parliament, for just and serious considerations, without scruple to be at any time repeal'd. (*CPW*, 7:412–13)

As Milton consistently understands it, Christian liberty supersedes canon law much as Samson's "rousing motions" supplant both the old law of his countrymen and the positive law of the Philistines, now *replanted* in the open monument of grace. There "strenuous liberty," like the phoenix itself, though "giv'n for lost / Deprest, and overthrown, . . . Revives, reflourishes, then vigorous most / When most inactive deem'd, / And though her body die, her fame survives, / A secular bird ages of lives" (1697–98, 1704–7). While ultimately divine, this riddling, phoenix-like law of nature is also classical and secular, civic and domestic, and thus not exclusively identifiable with Christian states or princes any more than with Greek democracy or any other "historical particular."[29] Springing from the peculiarly "self-begotten" virtue (1699) of freedom of conscience that Milton had earlier likened to "the golden beames of Law and Right" shining in Samson's "puissant hair" (*CPW*, 1:859), this tragic

---

29. As Mary Ann Radzinowicz observes of *The Readie and Easie Way*, this political treatise most nearly contemporary with the publication of *Samson Agonistes* consistently refuses to let its readers "identify the public welfare with their own private moral well-being," but like *Paradise Lost* supplies a strongly "individualistic, voluntarist, and meritocratic basis" of the political education and action. See "The Politics of *Paradise Lost*," in *Politics of Discourse: The Literature and History of Seventeenth-Century England*, ed. Kevin Sharpe and Stephen Zwicker (Berkeley and Los Angeles: University of California Press, 1987), 207–14.

liberty remains a historical universal that irregularly but inevitably arises from its own ruins to overthrow absolutism—whether with the jawbone of an ass, between the pillars of Dagon's temple, or from within the very jaws of the Hobbesian crocodile.

Notes on the Contributors

Tom Cain is Head of the Department of English Literary and Linguistic Studies at the University of Newcastle upon Tyne. His publications include studies of Herrick, Donne, and Jonson, as well as an anthology of seventeenth-century poetry and an edition of Jonson's *Poetaster.*

Elizabeth Clarke is a Research Lecturer at Nottingham Trent University, where she is director of the Perdita Project for Early Modern Women's Manuscript Compilations. She is the author of *Theology and Theory in George Herbert's Poetry: "Divinitie, and Poesie, Met."*

Jay Russell Curlin has recently accepted a position as Assistant Professor of English at his alma mater, Ouachita Baptist University. He holds a Ph.D. from the University of Michigan, where he studied with John Knott and Michael Schoenfeldt. He has published articles on Milton and on Vikram Seth.

M. L. Donnelly is Associate Professor of English at Kansas State University. He has contributed to *The Milton Encyclopedia* and *The Spenser Encyclopedia,* and he has published articles on Bacon, Donne, Milton, Caroline panegyric, Cavalier amatory lyrics, and Marvell's poetry and prose. He is currently working on a book on classical models for literary self-representation in the patronage culture of the English Renaissance.

Robert C. Evans is University Alumni Professor at Auburn University at Montgomery. He has published essays on various Renaissance topics as well as books on Ben Jonson, Martha Moulsworth, Frank O'Connor, and short fiction. He is an editor of the *Ben Jonson Journal* and *Comparative Drama* and general editor of the forthcoming *Ben Jonson Encyclopedia.*

M. Thomas Hester, Alumni Distinguished Professor of English at North Carolina State University, is the founding editor of the *John Donne Journal.*

He is the author or editor of numerous books and articles on English Renaissance literature.

Daniel Jaeckle is Professor of English at the University of Houston–Victoria. He has published articles on Donne, Marvell, Cleveland, and Traherne. Currently, he is working on a Bakhtinian analysis of Marvell.

Hugh Jenkins is Associate Professor of English at Union College. He has recently completed a book on the country-house poem and is currently working on a study of Milton and radicalism.

Erna Kelly is Professor of English at the University of Wisconsin–Eau Claire. She has published articles on emblem literature, seventeenth-century women writers, Walt Whitman, and technical writing. Her essay on seventeenth-century autobiography and portraiture will appear in MLA's *Teaching Tudor and Stuart Women Writers.*

Catherine Gimelli Martin is Associate Professor of English at the University of Memphis, where she heads the English Honors Program. She has published widely on seventeenth-century poetry and philosophy and on literary theory. Her recent book, *The Ruins of Allegory: "Paradise Lost" and the Metamorphosis of Epic Convention,* represents a fusion of these interests. She is currently working on a companion essay to the one published here: a structural analysis of *Samson Agonistes.*

Ted-Larry Pebworth is William E. Stirton Professor in the Humanities and Professor of English at the University of Michigan–Dearborn. He is author of *Owen Felltham;* coauthor of *Ben Jonson* (soon to be reissued in a revised edition); coeditor of *The Poems of Owen Felltham* and *Selected Poems of Ben Jonson;* and coeditor of collections of essays on a variety of Renaissance and seventeenth-century figures and topics. A senior textual editor and member of the advisory board of *The Variorum Edition of the Poetry of John Donne,* he has served as president of the John Donne Society.

Diane Purkiss is Professor of English at the University of Exeter. She has published widely on women's writing in the early modern period, most recently an edition of *Three Tragedies by Renaissance Women* for Penguin. Her most recent book is *The Witch in History,* and she has completed *Broken Men: Masculinity and the Irrational in the English Civil War.*

Graham Roebuck is Professor of English Emeritus at McMaster University, where over the past thirty years he has taught humanities and English literature and occasionally history and, most recently, an undergraduate course in early modern technology, science, and mathematics. His current project is a study of the rise of mathematical navigation in Tudor and Stuart England.

Jonathan Rogers received his Ph.D. from Vanderbilt University in 1996. He lives in Nashville with his wife and three sons.

Alan Rudrum is Professor Emeritus of English at Simon Fraser University. His publications include critical commentaries on Milton and Vaughan, as well as editions of the *Complete Poems of Henry Vaughan, The Works of Thomas Vaughan,* and *Essential Articles: Henry Vaughan.*

Andrew Shifflett, Assistant Professor of English at the University of South Carolina, has published articles on Montaigne and Derrida and on Donne and Calvin. His book on *Stoicism, Politics, and Literature in the Age of Milton: War and Peace Reconciled* has recently been published by Cambridge University Press. His current project is a book on the politics of forgiveness in seventeenth-century England.

Claude J. Summers, William E. Stirton Professor in the Humanities and Professor of English at the University of Michigan–Dearborn, has published widely on seventeenth- and twentieth-century literature. Coeditor of collections of essays on a wide variety of Renaissance and seventeenth-century topics and figures and author of book-length studies of Marlowe, Jonson, Isherwood, Forster, and twentieth-century English and American gay fiction, he has recently published an edition of the *Selected Poems of Ben Jonson* and the Lambda Award–winning *The Gay and Lesbian Literary Heritage.* He is a past president of the John Donne Society.

Index of Works Cited

This index includes only primary works. Lengthy titles are abbreviated, and anonymous works are alphabetized by title.